The Catholic Tradition

REV. CHARLES J. DOLLEN
DR. JAMES K. McGOWAN
DR. JAMES J. MEGIVERN
EDITORS

The Catholic Tradition

Social Thought
Volume 2

A Consortium Book

Library of Congress Card Catalog Number: 79-1977
ISBN: 0-8434-0731-X
ISBN: 0-8434-0725-5 series

The publisher gratefully acknowledges permission to quote from the
following copyrighted sources. In cases where those properties contain
scholarly apparatus such as footnotes, such footnotes have been omitted
in the interest of the general reader.

AMERICA PRESS, INC.

Chapters 5–8 from *Interracial Justice* by John LaFarge, S.J., copyright 1937. Reprinted by permission of America Press, Inc.

ANDREWS AND McMEEL, INC.

Selection from *We Hold These Truths* by John Courtney Murray, S.J.
Copyright © 1960 Sheed & Ward, Inc. Reprinted by permission of
Andrews and McMeel, Inc.

BENZIGER BROTHERS

Quadragesimo Anno by Pope Pius XI, copyright 1943. Reprinted by
permission of Benziger, a division of Glencoe Publishing Co., Inc.

GEORGES BORCHARDT, INC.

Selection from *The Theology of Work* by M. D. Chenu. Translation
© M. H. Gill and Son Ltd. 1963. Reprinted by permission of Georges
Borchardt, Inc.

DOUBLEDAY & COMPANY, INC.

Selection from "Truth & Violence: An Interesting Era" from *Conjectures of a Guilty Bystander*, by Thomas Merton. Copyright © 1965,
1966 by The Abbey of Gethsemani. Reprinted by permission of Doubleday & Company, Inc.

DUQUESNE UNIVERSITY PRESS

Chapter 9 reprinted from *Faith and the World* by Albert Dondeyne
by permission of Duquesne University Press. Copyright © 1963 by
Duquesne University.

Table of Contents

THE CATHOLIC TRADITION: Social Thought

John Augustine Ryan
1869-1945

John A. Ryan ranks as one of the great advocates of social justice in twentieth century America. Long before it was popular to do so, he was writing and lecturing in behalf of strong legislation to help the working classes. Many of the proposals he developed concerning minimum wage, health benefits, unemployment and retirement significantly influenced the national laws that were established in these areas.

Ryan was born in Minnesota in 1869, the eldest of eleven children. His parents were Irish immigrants. After completing secondary school, he entered the seminary and, in 1898, was ordained a priest. He earned the licentiate in moral theology from The Catholic University of America in 1900 and the doctorate in 1906. His doctoral dissertation, A Living Wage: Its Ethical and Economic Aspects *gained international attention.*

The talents of Father Ryan were quickly recognized and respected. Eventually he became professor of political science and moral theology at The Catholic University, and dean of its School of Sacred Theology. But his activities took him far beyond the academic setting. He became involved with the National Consumers League, the Social Action Department of the National Catholic Welfare Council, the Catholic Association for International Peace, and the American Civil Liberties Union. Ryan's economic and social justice theories brought him into contact with national politics. He was an enthusiastic supporter of Franklin D. Roosevelt, who chose Ryan to give the benedictions at two of his inaugurations. In 1934 Ryan joined the Industrial Appeals Board of the National Recovery Administration.

Ryan's contribution to the development of social justice in America is obviously an important one. His service to Catholics was equally invaluable, for he helped bring the Catholic world into the mainstream of American thinking. He prepared the way for the education of generations of Catholics in contemporary economic and social theory.

Among the writings of John Ryan, Distributive Justice (1916) is of particular importance. It is a systematic discussion of the justice of the processes by which the product of industry is distributed. Ryan studies the four classes that make up the modern industrial society, viz., the landowner, the capitalist, the business man and the laborer, with the intention of clarifying the rights and responsibilities of each class. Accepting the existing economic system as at least not inherently unjust, yet recognizing the many injustices of the system as it operates, the book seeks to propose reforms that would remove principal defects and increase the measure of justice within the system.

Distributive Justice has four major sections which treat the morality of private landownership and rent, the morality of private capital and interest, the moral aspects of profits, and the moral aspects of wages. We have selected as our reading Ryan's discussion of the living wage to which the laborer has a right as the minimum of justice.

It is unfortunate that the ground on which he established his arguments, the intrinsic sacredness and moral independence of the human individual as person, seems to have been ignored in the economics of recent decades. Ryan's insights and principles are most relevant to America's present situation.

DISTRIBUTIVE JUSTICE

A lthough the principle of needs is somewhat prominent among the theories of wage justice, it received only incidental mention in the last chapter. Considered as a comprehensive rule, this principle has been defended with less energy and definiteness than most of the other canons. Considered as a partial rule, it is sound and fundamental, and therefore could not have been classed among theories that are unacceptable.

The Principle of Needs

Many of the early French Socialists of the Utopian school advanced this formula of distribution: "From each according to his powers; to each according to his needs." It was also put forward by the German Socialists in the Gotha Program in 1875. While they have not given to this standard formal recognition in their more recent platforms, Socialists generally regard it as the ideal rule for the distant future. The difficulties confronting it are so great and so obvious that they would defer the introduction of it to a time when the operation of their system will, they hope, have eradicated the historical human qualities of laziness and selfishness. To adopt needs as the sole rule of distribution would mean, of course, that each person should be rewarded in proportion to his wants and desires, regardless of his efforts or of the amount that he had produced. The mere statement of the proposal is sufficient to refute it as regards the men and women of whom we have any knowledge. In addition to this objection, there is the insuperable difficulty of measuring fairly or accurately the relative needs of any group composed of men, women, and children. Were the members' own estimates of their needs accepted by the distributing authority, the social product would no doubt fall far short of supplying all. If the measurement were made by some official person or persons, "the prospect of jobbery and tyranny opened up must give the most fanatical pause." Indeed, the standard of needs should be regarded as a canon of Communism rather than of Socialism; for it implies a large measure of common life as well as of common ownership, and paternalistic supervision of consumption as well as collectivist management of production.

While the formula of needs must be flatly rejected as complete rule of distributive justice, or of wage justice, it is valid and indispensable as a partial standard. It is a partial measure of justice in two senses: first, inasmuch as it is consistent with the admission and operation of other principles, such as productivity and sacrifice; second, inasmuch as it can be restricted to certain fundamental requisites of life, instead of being applied to all possible human needs. It can be made to safeguard the minimum demands of reasonable life, and therefore to function as a minimum standard of wage justice.

Human needs constitute the primary title or claim to material goods. None of the other recognised titles, such as productivity, effort, sacrifice, purchase, gift, inheritance, or first occupancy, is a fundamental reason or justification of either rewards or possessions. They all assume the existence of needs as a prerequisite to their validity. If men did not need goods they could not reasonably lay claim to them by any of the specific titles just enumerated. First comes the general claim or fact of needs; then the particular title or method by which the needs may be conveniently supplied. While these statements may seem elementary and platitudinous, their practical value will be quite evident when we come to consider the conflicting claims that sometimes arise out of the clash between needs and some of the other titles. We shall see that needs are not merely a physical reason or impulse toward acquisition and possession, but a moral title which rationalises the claim to a certain amount of goods.

Three Fundamental Principles

The validity of needs as a partial rule of wage justice rests ultimately upon three fundamental principles regarding man's position in the universe. The first is that God created the earth for the sustenance of *all* His children; therefore, that all persons are equal in their inherent claims upon the bounty of nature. As it is impossible to demonstrate that any class of persons is less important than another in the eyes of God, it is logically impossible for any believer in Divine Providence to reject this proposition. The man who denies God or Providence can refuse assent to the second part of the proposition only by refusing to acknowledge the personal dignity of the human individual, and the equal dignity of all persons. Inasmuch as the human person is intrinsically sacred and morally independent, he is endowed with those inherent prerogatives, immunities, and claims that we call rights. Every person is an end in himself; none is a mere instrument to the convenience or welfare of any other human being. The worth of a person is something intrinsic, derived from within, not determined or measurable by reference to any earthly object or purpose without. In this respect the human being differs infinitely from, is infinitely superior to, a stone, a rose, or a horse. While these statments help to illustrate what is meant by the dignity of personality, by the intrinsic worth, importance, sacredness of the human being, they do not prove the existence of this inherent juridical quality. Proof in the strict sense is irrelevant and impossible. If the intrinsic and equal moral worth of all persons be not self evident to a man, it will not approve itself to him through any process of argumentation. Whosoever denies it can also logically deny men's equal claims of access to the bounty of the earth; but he cannot escape the alternative conclusion that brute force, exercised either by the State or by individuals, is the only proper determinant of possessions and of property. Against this monstrous contention it is not worth while to offer a formal argument.

The second fundamental principle is that the inherent right of access to the earth is conditioned upon, and becomes actually valid through, the expenditure of useful labour. Generally speaking the fruits and potentialities of the earth do not become available to men without previous exertion. "In the sweat of thy brow thou shalt eat thy bread," is a physical no less than a moral commandment. There are, indeed, exceptions: the very young, the infirm, and the possessors of a sufficient amount of property. The two former classes have claims to a livelihood through piety and charity, while the third group has at least a presumptive claim of justice to rent and interest, and a certain claim of justice to the money value of their goods. Nevertheless, the general condition is that men must work in order to live. "If a man will not work neither shall he eat." For those who refuse to comply with this condition the inherent right of access to the earth remains only hypothetical and suspended.

The two foregoing principles involve as a corollary a third principle; the men who are in present control of the opportunities of the earth are obliged to permit reasonable access to these opportunities by persons who are willing to work. In other words, possessors must so administer the common bounty of nature that non-owners will not find it unreasonably difficult to get a livelihood. To put it still in other terms, the right to subsist from the earth implies the right to access thereto on reasonable terms. When any man who is willing to work is denied the exercise of this right, he is no longer treated as the moral and juridical equal of his fellows. He is regarded as inherently inferior to them, as a mere instrument to their convenience; and those who exclude him are virtually taking the position that their rights to the common gifts of the Creator are inherently superior to his birthright. Obviously this position cannot be defended on grounds of reason. Possessors are no more justified in excluding a man from reasonable access to the goods of the earth than they would be in depriving him of the liberty to move from place to place. The community that should arbitrarily shut a man up in prison would not violate his rights more fundamentally than the community or the proprietors who should shut him out from the opportunity of getting a livelihood from the bounty of the earth. In both cases the man demands and has a right to a common gift of God. His moral claim is as valid to the one good as to the other, and it is as valid to both goods as is the claim of any of his fellows.

The Right to a Decent Livelihood

Every man who is willing to work has, therefore, an inborn right to sustenance from the earth on reasonable terms or conditions. This cannot mean that all persons have a right to equal amounts of sustenance or income; for we have seen on a preceding page that men's needs, the primary title to property, are not equal, and that other canons and factors of distribution have to be allowed some weight in determining the division of goods and opportunities. Nevertheless, there is a certain minimum of goods to which every worker is entitled by reason of his inherent right of access to the earth. He has a right to at least a *decent* livelihood. That is; he has a right to so much of the requisites of sustenance as will enable him to live in a manner worthy of a human being. The elements of a decent livelihood may be summarily described as: food, clothing, and housing sufficient in quantity and quality to maintain the worker in normal health, in elementary comfort, and in an environment suitable to the protection of morality and religion; sufficient provision for the future to bring elementary contentment, and security against sickness, accident, and invalidity; and sufficient opportunities of recreation, social intercourse, education, and church-membership to conserve health and strength, and to render possible in some degree the exercise of the higher faculties.

On what ground is it contended that a worker has a right to a decent livelihood, as thus defined, rather than to a bare subsistence? On the same ground that validates his right to life, marriage, or any of the other fundamental goods of human existence. On the dignity of personality. Why is it wrong and unjust to kill or maim an innocent man? Because human life and the human person possess intrinsic worth; because personality is sacred. But the intrinsic worth and sacredness of personality imply something more than security of life and limb, and the material means of bare existence. The man who is not provided with the requisites of normal health, efficiency, and contentment lives a maimed life, not a reasonable life. His physical condition is not worthy of a human being. Furthermore, man's personal dignity demands not merely the conditions of reasonable physical existence, but the opportunity of pursuing self perfection through the harmonious development of all his faculties. Unlike the brutes, he is endowed with a rational soul, and the capacity of indefinite self improvement. A due regard to these endowments requires that man shall have the opportunity of becoming not only physically stronger, but intellectually wiser, morally better, and spiritually nearer to God. If he is deprived of these opportunities he cannot realise the potentialities of his nature nor attain the divinely appointed end of his nature. He remains on the plane of the lower animals. His personality is violated quite as fundamentally as when his body is injured or his life destroyed.

While it is impossible to define with mathematical precision the degree of personal development that is necessary to satisfy the claims of personal dignity, it is entirely practicable to state with sufficient definiteness the minimum conditions of such development. They are that quantity of goods and opportunities which fair-minded men would regard as indispensable to humane, efficient, and reasonable life. The summary description of a decent livelihood at the end of the second last paragraph, would probably be accepted by all men who really believe in the intrinsic worth of personality.

The Claim to a Decent Livelihood from a Present Occupation

The claim of a worker to a decent livelihood from the goods of the earth does not always imply a strict right to a livelihood from one's present occupation. To demand this would in some circumstances be to demand a livelihood not on reasonable but on unreasonable terms; for the persons in control of the sources could not reasonably be required to provide a decent livelihood. Their failure to do so would not constitute an unreasonable hindrance to the worker's access to the earth in such circumstances. In chapter xvi we saw that not all business men have a strict right to that minimum of profits which is required to yield them a decent livelihood: first, because the direction of industry is not generally the business man's only means of getting a living; second, because the community, the consumers, do not regard the presence and activity of all existing business men as indispensable. Of course, the community is morally bound to pay such prices for goods as will enable all the necessary business men, whether manufacturers or traders, to obtain a decent livelihood in return for their directive functions; but it is not obliged to provide a livelihood for those business men whose presence is not required, who could vanish from the field of industrial direction without affecting either the supply or the price of goods, and whose superfluous character is proved by the fact that they cannot make a livelihood at the prevailing prices. They are in the position of persons whom the community does not desire to employ as business men. In refusing to pay prices sufficiently high to provide these inefficient business men with a decent livelihood, the community is not unreasonably hindering their access to the common goods of the earth. Such men are really demanding a livelihood on unreasonable terms.

The Labourer's Right to a Living Wage

On the other hand, the wage earner's claim to a decent livelihood is valid, generally speaking, in his present occupation. In other words, his right to a decent livelihood in the abstract means in the concrete a right to a living wage. To present the matter in its simplest terms, let us consider first the adult male labourer of average physical and mental ability who is charged with the support of no one but himself, and let us assume that the industrial resources are adequate to such a wage for all the members of his class. Those who are in control of the resources of the community are morally bound to give such a labourer a living wage. If they fail to do so they are unreasonably hindering his access to a livelihood on reasonable terms; and his right to a livelihood on reasonable terms is violated. The central consideration here is evidently the *reasonableness* of the process. Unlike the business man, the rent receiver, and the interest receiver, the labourer has ordinarily no other means of livelihood than his wages. If these do not furnish him with a decent subsistence he is deprived of a decent subsistence. When he has performed an average day's work, he has done all that is within his power to make good his claim to a decent livelihood. On the other hand, the community is the beneficiary of his labour, and desires his services. If, indeed, the community would rather do without the services of an individual labourer than pay him a living wage, it is morally free to choose the former alternative, precisely as it is justified in refusing to pay a price for groceries that will enable an inefficient grocer to obtain living profits. Whatever concrete form the right of such persons to a decent livelihood may take, it is not the right to living wages or living profits from the occupations in question. Here, however, we are discussing the labourer to whom the community would rather pay a living wage than not employ him at all. To refuse such a one a living wage merely because he can be constrained by economic pressure to work for less, is to treat him unreasonably, is to deprive him of access to a livelihood on reasonable terms. Such treatment regards the labourer as inferior to his fellows in personal worth, as a mere instrument to their convenience. It is an unreasonable distribution of the goods and opportunities of the earth.

Obviously there is no formula by which such conduct can be mathematically demonstrated as unreasonable; but the proposition is as certain morally as any other proposition that is susceptible of rational defence in the field of distribution. No man who accepts the three fundamental principles stated some pages back, can deny the right of the labourer to a living wage. The man who does not accept them must hold that all property rights are the arbitrary creation of the State, or that there is no such thing as a moral right to material goods. In either supposition the distribution and possession of the earth's bounty are subject entirely to the arbitrament of might. There is nothing to be gained by a formal criticism of this assumption.

What persons, or group, or authority is charged with the obligation which corresponds to the right to a living wage? We have referred to "the community" in this connection, but we do not mean the community in its corporate capacity, i.e., the State. As regards private employments, the State is not obliged to pay a living wage, nor any other kind of wage, since it has not assumed the wage-paying function with respect to these labourers. As protector of natural rights, and as the fundamental determiner of industrial institutions, the State is obliged to enact laws which will enable the labourer to obtain a living wage; but the duty of actually providing this measure of remuneration rests upon that class which has assumed the wage-paying function. This is the employers. In our present industrial system, the employer is society's paymaster. He, not the State, receives the product out of which all the agents of production must be rewarded. Where the labourer is engaged in rendering personal services to his employer, the latter is the only beneficiary of the labourer's activity. In either case the employer is the only person upon whom the obligation of paying a living wage can primarily fall.

John Augustine Ryan

If the State were in receipt of the product of industry, the wage-paying fund, it would naturally be charged with the obligation that now rests immediately upon the employer. If any other class in the community were the owners of the product that class would be under this specific obligation. As things are, the employer is in possession of the product, and discharges the function of wage payer; consequently he is the person who is required to perform this function in a reasonable manner.

When the Employer is Unable to Pay a Living Wage

Evidently the employer who cannot pay a living wage is not obliged to do so, since moral duties suppose a corresponding physical capacity. In such circumstances the labourer's right to a living wage becomes suspended and hypothetical, just as the claim of a creditor when the debtor becomes insolvent. Let us see, however, precisely what meaning should reasonably be given to the phrase, "inability to pay a living wage."

An employer is not obliged to pay a full living wage to all his employés so long as that action would deprive himself and his family of a decent livelihood. As active director of a business, the employer has quite as good a right as the labourer to a decent livelihood from the product, and in case of conflict between the two rights, the employer may take advantage of that principle of charity which permits a man to prefer himself to his neighbour, when the choice refers to goods of the same order of importance. Moreover, the employer is justified in taking from the product sufficient to support a somewhat higher scale of living than generally prevails among his employés; for he has become accustomed to this higher standard, and would suffer a considerable hardship if compelled to fall notably below it. It is reasonable, therefore, that he should have the means of maintaining himself and family in moderate conformity with their customary standard of living; but it is unreasonable that they should indulge in anything like luxurious expenditure, so long as any of the employés fail to receive living wages.

Suppose that an employer cannot pay all his employés living wages and at the same time provide the normal rate of interest on the capital in the business. So far as the borrowed capital is concerned, the business man has no choice; he must pay the stipulated rate of interest, even though it prevents him from giving a living wage to all his employés. Nor can it be reasonably contended that the loan capitalist in that case is obliged to forego the interest due him. He cannot be certain that this interest payment, or any part of it, is really necessary to make up what is wanting to a complete scale of living wages. The employer would be under great temptation to defraud the loan capitalist on the pretext of doing justice to the labourer, or to conduct his business inefficiently at the expense of the loan capitalist. Anyhow, the latter is under no obligation to leave his money in a concern that is unable to pay him interest regularly. The general rule, then, would seem to be that the loan capitalist is not obliged to refrain from taking interest in order that the employés may have living wages.

Is the employer justified in withholding the full living wage from his employés to provide himself with the nomral rate of interest on the capital that he has invested in the enterprise? Speaking generally, he is not. In the first place, the right to any interest at all, except as a return for genuine sacrifices in saving, is not certain but only presumptive. Consequently it has no such firm and definite basis as the right to a living wage. In the second place, the right to interest, be it ever so definite and certain, is greatly inferior in force and urgency. It is an axiom of ethics that when two rights conflict, the less important must give way to the more important. Since all property rights are but means to the satisfaction of human needs, their relative importance is determined by the relative importance of the ends that they serve; that is, by the relative importançe of the dependent needs. Now the needs that are supplied through interest on the employer's capital are slight and not essential to his welfare; the needs that are supplied through a living wage are essential to a reasonable life for the labourer. On the assumption that the employer had already taken from the product sufficient to provide a decent livelihood, interest on his capital will be expended for luxuries or converted into new investments; a living wage for the labourer will all be required for the fundamental goods of life, physical, mental, or moral. Evidently, then the right to interest is inferior to the right to a living wage. To proceed on the contrary theory is to reverse the order of nature and reason, and to subordinate essential needs and welfare to unessential needs and welfare.

Nor can it be maintained that the capitalist-employer's claim to interest is a claim upon the product prior to and independent of the claim of the labourer to a living wage. That would be begging the question. The product is in a fundamental sense the common property of employer and employés. Both parties have co-operated in turning it out, and they have equal claims upon it, in so far as it is necessary to yield them a decent livelihood. Having taken therefrom the requisites of a decent livelihood for himself, the employer who appropriates interest at the expense of a decent livelihood for his employés, in effect treats their claims upon the common and joint product as essentially inferior to his own. If this assumption were correct it would mean that the primary and essential needs of the employés are of less intrinsic importance than the superficial needs of the employer, and that the employés themselves are a lower order of being than the employer. The incontestable fact is that such an employer deprives the labourers of access to the goods of the earth on reasonable terms, and gives himself an access thereto that is unreasonable.

Suppose that all employers who found themselves unable to pay full living wages and obtain the normal rate of interest, should dispose of their businesses and become mere loan capitalists, would the condition of the underpaid workers be improved? Two effects would be certain: an increase in the supply of loan capital relatively to the demand, and a decrease in the number of active business men. The first would probably lead to a decline in the rate of interest, while the second might or might not result in a diminution of the volume of products. If the rate of interest were lowered the employing business men would be able to raise wages; if the prices of products rose a further increase of wages would become possible. However, it is not certain that prices would rise; for the business men who remained would be the more efficient in their respective classes, and might well be capable of producing all the goods that had been previously supplied by their eliminated competitors. Owing to their superior efficiency and their larger output, the existing business men would be able to pay considerably higher wages than those who had disappeared from the field of industrial direction. As things are to-day, it is the less efficient business men who are unable to pay living wages and at the same time obtain the prevailing rate of interest on their capital. The ultimate result, therefore, of the withdrawal from business of those who could not pay a living wage, would probably be the universal establishment of a living wage.

Of course, this supposition is purely fanciful. Only a small minority of the business men of to-day are likely to be driven by their consciences either to pay a living wage at the cost of interest on their capital, or to withdraw from business when they are confronted with such a situation. Is this small minority under moral obligation to adopt either of these alternatives, when the effect of such action upon the great mass of the underpaid workers is likely to be very slight? The question would seem to demand an answer in the affirmative. Those employers who paid a living wage at the expense of interest would confer a concrete benefit of great value upon a group of human beings. Those who shrank from this sacrifice, and preferred to go out of business, would at least have ceased to co-operate in an unjust distribution of wealth, and their example would not be entirely without effect upon the views of their fellow employers.

An Objection and Some Difficulties

Against the foregoing argument it may be objected that the employer does his full duty when he pays the labourer the full value of the product or service. Labour is a commodity of which wages are the price; and the price is just if it is the fair equivalent of the labour. Like any other onerous contract, the sale of labour is governed by the requirements of commutative justice; and these are satisfied when labour is sold for its moral equivalent. What the employer is interested in and pays for, is the labourer's activity. There is no reason why he should take into account such an extrinsic consideration as the labourer's livelihood.

Most of these assertions are correct, platitudinously correct, but they yield us no specific guidance because they use language vaguely and even ambiguously. The contention underlying them

14

was adequately refuted in the last chapter, under the heads of theories of value and theories of exchange equivalence. At present it will be sufficient to repeat summarily the following points: if the value of labour is to be understood in a purely economic sense it means market value, which is obviously not a universal measure of justice; if by the value of labour we mean its ethical value we cannot determine it in any particular case merely by comparing labour and compensation; we are compelled to have recourse to some extrinsic ethical principle; such an extrinsic principle is found in the proposition that the personal dignity of the labourer entitles him to a wage adequate to a decent livelihood; therefore, the ethical value of labour is always equivalent to at least a living wage, and the employer is morally bound to give this much remuneration.

Moreover, the habit of looking at the wage contract as a matter of commutative justice in the mere sense of contractual justice, is radically defective. The transaction between employé and employer involves other questions of justice than that which arises immediately out of the relation between the things exchanged. When a borrower repays a loan of ten dollars, he fulfils the obligation of justice because he returns the full equivalent of the article that he received. Nothing else is pertinent to the question of justice in this transaction. Neither the wealth nor the poverty, the goodness nor the badness, nor any other quality of either lender or borrower, has a.bearing on the justice of the act of repayment. In the wage contract, and in every other contract that involves the distribution of the common bounty of nature, or of the social product, the juridical situation is vitally different from the transaction that we have just considered. The employer has obligations of justice, not merely as the receiver of a valuable thing through an onerous contract, but as the *distributor* of the common heritage of nature. His duty is not merely contractual, but social. He fulfils not only an individual contract, but a social function. Unless he performs this social and distributive function in accordance with justice, he does not adequately discharge the obligation of the wage contract. For the product out of which he pays wages is not his in the same sense as the personal income out of which he repays a loan. His claim upon the product is subject to the obligation of just distribution; the obligation of so distributing the product that the labourers who have contributed to the product shall not be denied their right to a decent livelihood on reasonable terms from the bounty of the earth. On the other hand, the activity of the labourer is not a mere commodity, as money or pork; it is the output of a *person*, and a person who has no other means of realising his inherent right to a livelihood. Consequently, both terms of the contract, the labour and the compensation, involve other elements of justice than that which arises out of their assumed mutual equivalence.

In a word, justice requires the employer not merely to give an equivalent for labour (an equivalent which is determined by some arbitrary, conventional, fantastic, or impossible attempt to compare work and pay) but to fulfill his obligation of justly distributing that part of the common bounty of the earth which comes into his hands by virtue of his social function in the industrial process. How futile, then, to endeavour by word juggling to describe the employer's obligation in terms of mere equivalence and contractual justice!

Some difficulties occur in connection with the wage rights of adult males whose ability is below the average, and female and child workers. Since the dignity and the needs of personality constitute the moral basis of the claim to a decent livelihood, it would seem that the inefficient worker who does his best is entitled to a living wage. Undoubtedly he has such a right if it can be effectuated in the existing industrial organisation. As already noted, the right of the workman of average ability to a living wage does not become actual until he finds an employer who would rather give him that much pay than do without his services. Since the obligation of paying a living wage is not an obligation to employ any particular worker, an employer may refrain from hiring or may discharge any labourer who does not add to the product sufficient value to provide his wages. For the employer cannot reasonably be expected to employ any one at a positive loss to himself. Whence it follows that he may pay less than living wages to any worker whose services he would rather dispense with than remunerate at that figure.

Women and young persons who regularly perform a full day's work, have a right to compensation adequate to a decent livelihood. In the case of minors, this means living at home, since this is the normal condition of all, and the actual condition of almost all. Adult females have a right to a wage sufficient to maintain them away from home, because a considerable proportion of them live in this condition. If employers were morally free to pay home-dwelling women less than those adrift, they would endeavour to employ only the former. This would create a very undesirable social situation. The number of women away from home who are forced to earn their own living is sufficiently large (20 to 25 per cent. of the whole) to make it reasonable that for their sakes the wage of all working women should be determined by the cost of living outside the parental precincts. This is one of the social obligations that reasonably falls upon the employer on account of his function in the present industrial system. In all the American minimum wage laws, the standard of payment is determined by the cost of living away from home. Besides, the difference between the living costs of women in the two conditions is not nearly as great as is commonly assumed. Probably it never amounts to a dollar a week.

The Family Living Wage

Up to the present we have been considering the right of the labourer to a wage adequate to a decent livelihood for himself as an individual. In the case of an adult male, however, this is not sufficient for normal life, nor for the reasonable development of personality. The great majority of men cannot live well balanced lives, cannot attain a reasonable degree of self development outside the married state. Therefore, family life is among the essential needs of a normal and reasonable existence. It is not, indeed, so vitally necessary as the primary requisites of individual life, such as food, clothing, and shelter, but it is second only to these. Outside the family man cannot, as a rule, command that degree of contentment, moral strength, and moral safety which are necessary for reasonable and efficient living. It is unnecessary to labour this point further, as very few would assert that the average man can live a normal and complete human life without marriage.

Now, the support of the family falls properly upon the husband and father, not upon the wife and mother. The obligation of the father to provide a livelihood for the wife and young children is quite as definite as his obligation to maintain himself. If he has not the means to discharge this obligation he is not justified in getting married. Yet, as we have just seen, marriage is essential to normal life for the great majority of men. Therefore, the material requisites of normal life for the average adult male, include provision for his family. In other words, his decent livelihood means a family livelihood. Consequently, he has a right to obtain such a livelihood on reasonable terms from the bounty of the earth. In the case of the wage earner, this right can be effectuated only through wages; therefore, the adult male labourer has a right to a family living wage. If he does not get this measure of remuneration his personal dignity is violated, and he is deprived of access to the goods of the earth, quite as certainly as when his wage is inadequate to personal maintenance. The difference between family needs and personal needs is a difference only of degree. The satisfaction of both is indispensable to his reasonable life.

Just as the woman worker who lives with her parents has a right to a wage sufficient to maintain her away from home, so the unmarried adult male has a right to a family living wage. If only married men get the latter wage they will be discriminated against in the matter of employment. To prevent this obviously undesirable condition, it is necessary that a family living wage be recognised as the right of all adult male workers. No other arrangement is reasonable in our present industrial system. In a competitive régime the standard wage for both the married and the unmarried man is necessarily the same. It will be determined by the living costs of either the one class or the other. At present the wage of the unskilled is unfortunately adjusted to the subsistence cost of the man who is not married. Since two prevailing scales of wages are impossible, the remuneration of the unmarried must in the interests of justice to the married be raised to the living costs of the latter. Moreover, the unmarried labourer needs more than an individual living wage in order to save sufficient money to enter upon the responsibilities of matrimony.

Only two objections of any importance can be brought against the male labourer's claim to a family living wage. The first is that just wages are to be measured by the value of the labour performed, and not by such an extrinsic consideration as the needs of a family. It has already been answered in this and the preceding chapters. Not the economic but the ethical value of the service rendered, is the proper determinant of justice in the matter of wages; and this ethical value is always the equivalent of at least a decent livelihood for the labourer and his family. According to the second objection, the members of the labourer's family have no claim upon the employer, since they do not participate in the work that is remunerated. This contention is valid, but it is also irrelevant. The claim of the labourer's family to sustenance is directly upon him, not upon his employer; but the labourer has a just claim upon the employer for the means of meeting the claims of his family. His right to this amount of remuneration is directly based neither upon the needs nor the rights of his family, but upon his own needs, upon the fact that family conditions are indispensable to his own normal life. If the wife and young children were self supporting, or were maintained by the State, the wage rights of the father would not include provision for the family. Since, however, family life involves support by the father, the labourer's right to such a life necessarily includes the right to a wage adequate to family support.

Other Arguments in Favour of a Living Wage

Thus far, the argument has been based upon individual natural rights. If we give up the doctrine of natural rights, and assume that all the rights of the individual come to him from the State, we must admit that the State has the power to withhold and withdraw all rights from any and all persons. Its grant of rights will be determined solely by considerations of social utility. In the concrete this means that some citizens may be regarded as essentially inferior to other citizens, that some may properly be treated as mere instruments to the convenience of others. Or it means that all citizens may be completely subordinated to the aggrandisement of an abstract entity, called the State. Neither of these positions is logically defensible. No group of persons has less intrinsic worth than another; and the State has no rational significance apart from its component individuals.

Nevertheless, a valid argument for the living wage can be set up on grounds of social welfare. A careful and comprehensive examination of the evil consequences to society and the State from the underpayment of any group of labourers, would show that a universal living wage is the only sound social policy. Among competent social students, this proposition has become a commonplace. It will not be denied by any intelligent person who considers seriously the influence of low wages in diminishing the efficiency, physical, mental, and moral, of the workers; in increasing the volume of crime, and the social cost of meeting it; in the immense social outlay for the relief of unnecessary poverty, sickness, and other forms of distress; and in the formation of a large and discontented proletariat.

The living wage doctrine also receives strong support from various kinds of authority. Of these the most important and best known is the famous encyclical, "On the Condition of Labour," May 15, 1891, by Pope Leo XIII. "Let it then be granted that workman and employer should, as a rule, make free agreements, and in particular should agree freely as to wages; nevertheless, there is a dictate of natural justice more imperious and ancient than any bargain between man and man; namely, that the remuneration should be sufficient to maintain the wage earner and reasonable and frugal comfort." Although the Pope refrained from specifying whether the living wage that he had in mind was one adequate merely to an individual livelihood, or sufficient to support a family, other passages in the Encyclical leave no room for doubt that he regarded the latter as the normal and equitable measure of remuneration. Within a dozen lines of the sentence quoted above, he made this statement: "If the workman's wages be sufficient to maintain himself, his wife, and his children in reasonable comfort, he will not find it difficult, if he be a sensible man, to practise thrift; and he will not fail, by cutting down expenses, to put by some little savings and thus secure a small income."

All lesser Catholic authorities hold that the adult male labourer has some kind of moral claim to a family living wage. In all probability the majority of them regard this claim as one of strict justice, while the minority would put it under the head of legal justice, or natural equity, or charity. The differences

20

between their views are not as important as the agreements; for all the Catholic writers maintain that the worker's claim is strictly moral in its nature, and that the corresponding obligation upon the employer is likewise of a moral character.

The Federal Council of the Churches of Christ in America, representing the principal Protestant denominations, has formally declared in favour of "a living wage as a minimum in every industry."

Public opinion likewise accepts the principle of a living wage as the irreducible minimum of fair treatment for all workers. Indeed, it would be difficult to find any important person in any walk of life to-day who would have the temerity to deny that the labourer is entitled to a wage sufficient for reasonable family life. Among employers the opinion is fairly general that the narrow margin of profit in competitive industries renders the burden of paying a family living wage to all adult males unfairly heavy; but the assertion that the wage contract is merely an economic transaction, having no relation to justice, is scarcely ever uttered publicly.

The Money Measure of a Living Wage

For self-supporting women a living wage is not less than eight dollars per week in any city of the United States, and in some of our larger cities it is from one to two dollars above this figure. The state minimum wage commissions that have acted in the matter, have fixed the rates not lower than eight nor higher than ten dollars per week. These determinations are in substantial agreement with a large number of other estimates, both official and unofficial.

When the present writer was making an estimate of the cost of decent living for a family about eleven years ago, he came to the conclusion that six hundred dollars per year was the lowest amount that would maintain a man and wife and four or five small children in any American city, and that this sum was insufficient in some of the larger cities. Since that time retail prices seem to have risen at least twenty-five and possibly forty-five per cent. If the six hundred dollar minimum were correct in 1905 it should, therefore, be increased to seven hundred and fifty dollars to meet the present range of prices. That this estimate is too low for some of the more populous cities, has been fully proved by several recent investigations. In 1915 the Bureau of Standards put the minimum cost of living for a family of five in New York City at $840.18. About the same time the New York Factory Investigating Commission gave the estimate of $876.43 for New York City, and $772.43 for Buffalo. In 1908, when the cost of living was from ten to thirty per cent. cheaper than to-day, the United States Bureau of Labour found that, "according to the customs prevailing in the communities selected for study," a fair standard of living for a family of five persons among mill workers was $600.74 in the South, and from $690.60 to $731.64 in Fall River, Massachusetts.

According to the "Manly Report" of the Federal Commission on Industrial Relations, between two-thirds and three-fourths of the adult male labourers of the United States receive less than $750.00 a year, and the same proportion of women workers are paid under eight dollars a week. A considerable majority, therefore, of both male and female labourers fail to obtain living wages. We are still very far from having actualised even the minimum measure of wage justice.

Pope Pius XI
1857-1939

*The years of the pontificate of Pope Pius XI (1922-1939)
both separate and link together the two great wars of the
twentieth century. They were years scarred by the worst catastrophe known to mankind up to that time, World War I. Some
of the consequences of the war were the collapse of the western
structures of morality and religion, international economic
crises, an increase of human misery throughout the entire world,
and the build up for World War II. It is astounding that one
man, a quiet, simple man of God, was capable of sustaining
throughout that entire period the pressure that it created for
the church and of responding to such tragic conditions with
incredible courage and integrity. For the role that he played
during these difficult years, Pius XI must be recognized as one
of the most competent popes of the modern church.*

*His name was Ambrogio Damiano Achille Ratti, born
May 31, 1857. He earned doctoral degrees in philosophy, theology and canon law by the age of 25 and was a professor at
the seminary in Milan. After serving as director of the Ambrosian
Library in Milan, he moved on to the Vatican Library in Rome.
In 1918 Ratti was sent to Poland as apostolic visitator. He was
appointed titular archbishop of Lepanto in 1919, archbishop
of Milan and a cardinal in 1921. On February 6, 1922, he was
elected pope, successor to Pope Benedict XV. Pius XI guided*

the church for 17 years and died on February 10, 1939, shortly before the outbreak of the second World War.

In the face of a world that was obviously in turmoil and pain, Pius XI issued a message of Christian love, of the sacredness of the family unit, of the radical dignity of the individual. He labored incessantly for a peace among nations that would be established on the gospel of Christ, for he realized that the end of the war had not established true peace but a mere stalemate. He challenged the modern state's attempt to monopolize education and defended the rights of the family and the church to educate. Pius internationalized the Catholic Church by creating bishops in mission countries and training native clergies for them. He concluded concordats with at least ten states and agreements with four others. In his effort to achieve world peace, he wrote against racialism, nationalism and persecution, and encouraged the nations of the world to organize.

On May 15, 1931, Pius XI issued the encyclical Quadragesimo anno, *forty years after Leo XIII's* Rerum Novarum. *Considered to be the second great social encyclical, it was issued when world depression was at its worst. Pius developed three topics in his encyclical, viz., the benefits deriving from* Rerum Novarum, *the authority of the church in social and economic affairs, and the many changes since the time of Leo XIII. The encyclical clarified church teaching on the right to own property, capital and labor, the principle of just distribution and the just wage. Pius observes that power and despotic economic domination are concentrated in the hands of a minority and warns that this can lead only to fierce struggle. Communism, which advocates merciless class warfare and abolition of private ownership is strongly condemned. In his conclusion, Pius reminds all mankind that there can be no serious renewal of society without moral reform and a revitalizatin of the Christian spirit.*

QUADRAGESIMO ANNO

Forty years have passed since Leo XIII's peerless Encyclical, *On the Condition of Workers*, first saw the light, and the whole Catholic world, filled with grateful recollection, is undertaking to commemorate it with befitting solemnity.

2. Other Encyclicals of Our Predecessor had in a way prepared the path for that outstanding document and proof of pastoral care: namely, those on the family and the Holy Sacrament of Matrimony as the source of human society, on the origin of civil authority and its proper relations with the Church, on the chief duties of Christian citizens, against the tenets of Socialism, against false teachings on human liberty, and others of the same nature fully expressing the mind of Leo XIII. Yet the Encyclical, *On the Condition of Workers*, compared with the rest had this special distinction that at a time when it was most opportune and actually necessary to do so, it laid down for all mankind the surest rules to solve aright that difficult problem of human relations called "the social question."

3. For toward the close of the nineteenth century, the new kind of economic life that had arisen and the new developments of industry had gone to the point in most countries that human society was clearly becoming divided more and more into two classes. One class, very small in number, was enjoying almost all the advantages which modern inventions so abundantly provided; the other, embracing the huge multitude of working people, oppressed by wretched poverty, was vainly seeking escape from the straits wherein it stood.

4. Quite agreeable, of course, was this state of things to those who thought it in their abundant riches the result of inevitable economic laws and accordingly, as if it were for charity to veil the violation of justice which lawmakers not only tolerated but at times sanctioned, wanted the whole care of supporting the poor committed to charity alone. The workers,

on the other hand, crushed by their hard lot, were barely enduring it and were refusing longer to bend their necks beneath so galling a yoke; and some of them, carried away by the heat of evil counsel, were seeking the overturn of everything, while others, whom Christian training restrained from such evil designs, stood firm in the judgment that much in this had to be wholly and speedily changed.

5. The same feeling those many Catholics, both priests and laymen, shared, whom a truly wonderful charity had long spurred on to relieve the unmerited poverty of the non-owning workers, and who could in no way convince themselves that so enormous and unjust an inequality in the distribution of this world's goods truly conforms to the designs of the all-wise Creator.

6. Those men were without question sincerely seeking an immediate remedy for this lamentable disorganization of States and a secure safeguard against worse dangers. Yet such is the weakness of even the best of human minds that, now rejected as dangerous innovators, now hindered in the good work by their very associates advocating other courses of action, and, uncertain in the face of various opinions, they were at a loss which way to turn.

7. In such a sharp conflict of minds, therefore, while the question at issue was being argued this way and that, nor always with calmness, all eyes as often before turned to the Chair of Peter, to that sacred depository of all truth whence words of salvation pour forth to all the world. And to the feet of Christ's Vicar on earth were flocking in unaccustomed numbers, men well versed in social questions, employers, and workers themselves, begging him with one voice to point out, finally, the safe road to them.

8. The wise Pontiff long weighed all this in his mind before God; he summoned the most experienced and learned to counsel; he pondered the issues carefully and from every angle. At last, admonished "by the consciousness of His Apostolic Office" lest silence on his part might be regarded as failure in his duty he decided, in virtue of the Divine Teaching Office entrusted to him to address not only the whole Church of Christ but all mankind.

9. Therefore on the fifteenth day of May, 1891, that long awaited voice thundered forth; neither daunted by the arduousness of the problem nor weakened by age but with vigorous energy, it taught the whole human family to strike out in the social question upon new paths.

10. You know, Venerable Brethren and Beloved Children, and understand full well the wonderful teaching which has made the Encyclical, *On the Condition of Workers*, illustrious forever. The Supreme Pastor in this Letter, grieving that so large a portion of mankind should "live undeservedly in miserable and wretched conditions," took it upon himself with great courage to defend "the cause of the workers whom the present age had handed over, each alone and defenseless, to the inhumanity of employers and the unbridled greed of competitors." He sought no help from either Liberalism or Socialism, for the one had proved that it was utterly unable to solve the social problem aright, and the other, proposing a remedy far worse than the evil itself, would have plunged human society into greater dangers.

11. Since a problem was being treated "for which no satisfactory solution" is found "unless religion and the Church have been called upon to aid," the Pope, clearly exercising his right and correctly holding that the guardianship of religion and the stewardship over those things that are closely bound up with it had been entrusted especially to him and relying solely upon the unchangeable principles drawn from the treasury of right reason and Divine Revelation, confidently and *as one having authority*, declared and proclaimed "the rights and duties within which the rich and the proletariat—those who furnish material things and those who furnish work—ought to be restricted in relation to each other," and what the Church, heads of States and the people themselves directly concerned ought to do.

12. The Apostolic voice did not thunder forth in vain. On the contrary, not only did the obedient children of the Church hearken to it with marvelling admiration and hail it with the greatest applause, but many also who were wandering far from the truth, from the unity of the faith, and nearly all who since then either in private study or in enacting legislation have concerned themselves with the social and economic question.

13. Feeling themselves vindicated and defended by the Supreme Authority on earth, Christian workers received this Encyclical with special joy. So, too, did all those noble-hearted men who, long solicitous for the improvement of the condition of the workers, had up to that time encountered almost nothing but indifference from many, and even rankling suspicion, if not open hostility, from some. Rightly, therefore, have all these groups constantly held the Apostolic Encyclical from that time in such high honor that to signify their gratitude they are wont, in various places and in various ways, to commemorate it every year.

14. However, in spite of such great agreement, there were some who were not a little disturbed; and so it happened that the teaching of Leo XIII, so noble and lofty and so utterly new to worldly ears, was held suspect by some, even among Catholics, and to certain ones it even gave offense. For it boldly attacked and overturned the idols of Liberalism, ignored long-standing prejudices, and was in advance of its time beyond all expectation, so that the slow of heart disdained to study this new social philosophy and the timid feared to scale so lofty a height. There were some also who stood, indeed, in awe at its splendor, but regarded it as a kind of imaginary ideal of perfection more desirable than attainable.

15. Venerable Brethren and Beloved Children, as all everywhere and especially Catholic workers who are pouring from all sides into this Holy City, are celebrating with such enthusiasm the solemn commemoration of the fortieth anniversary of the Encyclical *On the Condition of Workers*, We deem it fitting on this occasion to recall the great benefits this Encyclical has brought to the Catholic Church and to all human society; to defend the illustrious Master's doctrine on the social and economic question against certain doubts and to develop it more fully as to some points; and lastly, summoning to court the contemporary economic regime and passing judgment on Socialism, to lay bare the root of the existing social confusion and at the same time point the only way to sound restoration: namely, the Christian reform of morals. All these matters which we undertake to treat will fall under three main headings, and this entire Encyclical will be devoted to their development.

16. To begin with the topic which we have proposed first to discuss, We cannot refrain, following the counsel of St. Ambrose who says that "no duty is more important than that of returning thanks," from offering our fullest gratitude to Almighty God for the immense benefits that have come through Leo's Encyclical to the Church and to human society. If indeed We should wish to review these benefits even cursorily, almost the whole history of the social question during the last forty years would have to be recalled to mind. These benefits can be reduced conveniently, however, to three main points, corresponding to the three kinds of help which Our Predecessor ardently desired for the accomplishment of his great work of restoration.

17. In the first place Leo himself clearly stated what ought to be expected from the Church: "Manifestly it is the Church which draws from the Gospel the teachings through which the struggle can be composed entirely, or, after its bitterness is removed, can certainly become more tempered. It is the Church, again, that strives not only to instruct the mind, but to regulate by her precepts the life and morals of individuals, and that ameliorates the condition of the workers through her numerous and beneficent institutions."

18. The Church did not let these rich foundations lie quiescent in her bosom, but from them drew copiously for the common good of the longed-for peace. Leo himself and his Successors, showing paternal charity and pastoral constancy always, in defense especially of the poor and the weak, proclaimed and urged without ceasing again and again by voice and pen the teaching on the social and economic question which *On the Condition of Workers* presented, and adapted it fittingly to the needs of time and of circumstance. And many bishops have done the same, who in their continual and able interpretation of this same teaching have illustrated it with commentaries and in accordance with the mind and instructions of the Holy See provided for its application to the conditions and institutions of diverse regions.

19. It is not surprising, therefore, that many scholars, both priests and laymen, led especially by the desire that the unchanged and unchangeable teaching of the Church should

meet new demands and needs more effectively, have zealously undertaken to develop, with the Church as their guide and teacher, a social and economic science in accord with the conditions of our time.

20. And so, with Leo's Encyclical pointing the way and furnishing the light, a true Catholic social science has arisen, which is daily fostered and enriched by the tireless efforts of those chosen men whom We have termed auxiliaries of the Church. They do not, indeed, allow their science to lie hidden behind learned walls. As the useful and well attended courses instituted in Catholic universities, colleges, and seminaries, the social congresses and "weeks" that are held at frequent intervals with most successful results, the study groups that are promoted, and finally the timely and sound publications that are disseminated everywhere and in every possible way, clearly show, these men bring their science out into the full light and stress of life.

21. Nor is the benefit that has poured forth from Leo's Encyclical confined within these bounds; for the teaching which *On the Condition of Workers* contains has gradually and imperceptibly worked its way into the minds of those outside Catholic unity who do not recognize the authority of the Church. Catholic principles on the social question have as a result, passed little by little into the patrimony of all human society, and We rejoice that the eternal truths which Our Predecessor of glorious memory proclaimed so impressively have been frequently invoked and defended not only in non-Catholic books and journals but in legislative halls also and courts of justice.

22. Furthermore, after the terrible war, when the statesmen of the leading nations were attempting to restore peace on the basis of a thorough reform of social conditions, did not they, among the norms agreed upon to regulate in accordance with justice and equity the labor of the workers, give sanction to many points that so remarkably coincide with Leo's principles and instructions as to seem consciously taken therefrom? The Encyclical *On the Condition of Workers*, without question, has become a memorable document and rightly to it may be

applied the words of Isaias: "He shall set up a standard to the nations."

23. Meanwhile, as Leo's teachings were being widely diffused in the minds of men, with learned investigations leading the way, they have come to be put into practice. In the first place, zealous efforts have been made, with active good will, to lift up that class which on account of the modern expansion of industry had increased to enormous numbers but not yet had obtained its rightful place or rank in human society and was, for that reason, all but neglected and despised—the workers, We mean—to whose improvement, to the great advantage of souls, the diocesan and regular clergy, though burdened with other pastoral duties, have under the leadership of the Bishops devoted themselves. This constant work, undertaken to fill the workers' souls with the Christian spirit, helped much also to make them conscious of their true dignity and render them capable, by placing clearly before them the rights and duties of their class, of legitimately and happily advancing and even of becoming leaders of their fellows.

24. From that time on, fuller means of livelihood have been more securely obtained; for not only did works of beneficence and charity begin to multiply at the urging of the Pontiff, but there have also been established everywhere new and continuously expanding organizations in which workers, craftsmen, farmers, and employees of every kind, with the counsel of the Church and frequently under the leadership of her priests, give and receive mutual help and support.

25. With regard to civil authority, Leo XIII, boldly breaking through the confines imposed by Liberalism, fearlessly taught that government must not be thought a mere guardian of law and of good order, but rather must put forth every effort so that "through the entire scheme of laws and institutions . . . both public and individual well-being may develop spontaneously out of the very structure and administration of the State." Just freedom of action must, of course, be left both to individual citizens and to families, yet only on condition that the common good be preserved and wrong to any individual be abolished. The function of the rulers of the State, moreover, is to watch over the community and its parts; but in protecting

private individuals in their rights, chief consideration ought to be given to the weak and the poor. "For the nation, as it were, of the rich is guarded by its own defences and is in less need of governmental protection, whereas the suffering multitude, without the means to protect itself relies especially on the protection of the State. Wherefore, since wage-workers are numbered among the great mass of the needy, the State must include them under its special care and foresight."

26. We, of course, do not deny that even before the Encyclical of Leo, some rulers of the peoples had provided for certain of the more urgent needs of the workers and curbed more flagrant acts of injustice inflicted upon them. But after the Apostolic voice had sounded from the Chair of Peter throughout the world, rulers of nations, more fully alive at last to their duty, devoted their minds and attention to the task of promoting a more comprehensive and fruitful social policy.

27. And while the principles of Liberalism were tottering, which had long prevented effective action by those governing the State, the Encyclical *On the Condition of Workers* in truth impelled peoples themselves to promote a social policy on truer grounds and with greater intensity, and so strongly encouraged good Catholics to furnish valuable help to heads of States in this field that they often stood forth as illustrious champions of this new policy even in legislatures. Sacred ministers of the Church, thoroughly imbued with Leo's teaching, have, in fact, often proposed to the votes of the peoples' representatives the very social legislation that has been enacted in recent years and have resolutely demanded and promoted its enforcement.

28. A new branch of law, wholly unknown to the earlier time, has arisen from this continuous and unwearied labor to protect vigorously the sacred rights of the workers that flow from their dignity as men and as Christians. These laws undertake the protection of life, health, strength, family, homes, workshops, wages and labor hazards, in fine, everything which pertains to the condition of wage workers, with special concern for women and children. Even though these laws do not conform exactly everywhere and in all respects to Leo's recommendations, still it is undeniable that much in them savors of the Encyclical, *On the Condition of Workers*, to which great credit

must be given for whatever improvement has been achieved in the workers' condition.

29. Finally, the wise Pontiff showed that "employers and workers themselves can accomplish much in this matter, manifestly through those institutions by the help of which the poor are opportunely assisted and the two classes of society are brought closer to each other." First place among these institutions, he declares, must be assigned to associations that embrace either workers alone or workers and employers together. He goes into considerable detail in explaining and commending these associations and expounds with a truly wonderful wisdom their nature, purpose, timeliness, rights, duties, and regulations.

30. These teachings were issued indeed most opportunely. For at that time in many nations those at the helm of State, plainly imbued with Liberalism, were showing little favor to workers' associations of this type; nay, rather they openly opposed them, and while going out of their way to recognize similar organizations of other classes and show favor to them, they were with criminal injustice denying the natural right to form associations to those who needed it most to defend themselves from ill treatment at the hands of the powerful. There were even some Catholics who looked askance at the efforts of workers to form associations of this type as if they smacked of a socialistic or revolutionary spirit.

31. The rules, therefore, which Leo XIII issued in virtue of his authority, deserve the greatest praise in that they have been able to break down this hostility and dispel these suspicions; but they have even a higher claim to distinction in that they encouraged Christian workers to found mutual associations according to their various occupations, taught them how to do so, and resolutely confirmed in the path of duty a goodly number of those to whom socialist organizations strongly attracted by claiming to be the sole defenders and champions of the lowly and oppressed.

32. With respect to the founding of these societies, the Encyclical *On the Condition of Workers* most fittingly delcared that "workers' associations ought to be so constituted and so governed as to furnish the most suitable and most convenient means to attain the object proposed, which consists in this, that

the individual members of the association secure, so far as is possible, an increase in the goods of body, of soul, and of property," yet it is clear that "moral and religious perfection ought to be regarded as their principal goal, and that their social organization as such ought above all to be directed completely by this goal." For "when the regulations of associations are founded upon religion, the way is easy toward establishing the mutual relations of the members, so that peaceful living together and prosperity will result."

33. To the founding of these associations the clergy and many of the laity devoted themselves everywhere with truly praiseworthy zeal, eager to bring Leo's program to full realization. Thus associations of this kind have molded truly Christian workers who, in combining harmoniously the diligent practice of their occupation with the salutary precepts of religion, protect effectively and resolutely their own temporal interests and rights, keeping a due respect for justice and a genuine desire to work together with other classes of society for the Christian renewal of all social life.

34. These counsels and instructions of Leo XIII were put into effect differently in different places according to varied local conditions. In some places one and the same association undertook to attain all the ends laid down by the Pontiff; in others, because circumstances suggested or required it, a division of work developed and separate associations were formed. Of these, some devoted themselves to the defense of the rights and legitimate interests of their members in the labor market; others took over the work of providing mutual economic aid; finally, still others gave all their attention to the fulfillment of religious and moral duties and other obligations of like nature.

35. This second method has especially been adopted where either the laws of a country, or certain special economic institutions, or that deplorable dissension of minds and hearts so widespread in contemporary society and an urgent necessity of combating with united purpose and strength the massed ranks of revolutionarists, have prevented Catholics from founding purely Catholic labor unions. Under these conditions, Catholics seem almost forced to join secular labor unions. These unions, however, should always profess justice and equity and

give Catholic members full freedom to care for their own conscience and obey the laws of the Church. It is clearly the office of bishops, when they know that these associations are on account of circumstances necessary and are not dangerous to religion, to approve of Catholic workers joining them, keeping before their eyes, however, the principles and precautions laid down by Our Predecessor, Pius X of holy memory. Among these precautions the first and chief is this: Side by side with these unions there should always be associations zealously engaged in imbuing and forming their members in the teaching of religion and morality so that they in turn may be able to permeate the unions with that good spirit which should direct them in all their activity. As a result, the religious associations will bear good fruit even beyond the circle of their own membership.

36. To the Encyclical of Leo, therefore, must be given this credit, that these associations of workers have so flourished everywhere that while, alas, still surpassed in numbers by socialist and communist organizations, they already embrace a vast multitude of workers and are able, within the confines of each nation as well as in wider assemblies, to maintain vigorously the rights and legitimate demands of Catholic workers and insist also on the salutary Christian principles of society.

37. Leo's learned treatment and vigorous defense of the natural right to form associations began, furthermore, to find ready application to other associations also and not alone to those of the workers. Hence no small part of the credit must, it seems, be given to this same Encyclical of Leo for the fact that among farmers and others of the middle class most useful associations of this kind are seen flourishing to a notable degree and increasing day by day, as well as other institutions of a similar nature in which spiritual development and economic benefit are happily combined.

38. But if this cannot be said of organizations which Our same Predecessor intensely desired established among employers and managers of industry—and We certainly regret that they are so few—the condition is not wholly due to the will of men but to far graver difficulties that hinder associations of this kind which We know well and estimate at their full value. There is, however, strong hope that these obstacles also will be removed

soon, and even now We greet with the deepest joy of Our soul, certain by no means insignificant attempts in this direction, the rich fruits of which promise a still richer harvest in the future.

39. All these benefits of Leo's Encyclical, Venerable Brethren and Beloved Children, which We have outlined rather than fully described, are so numerous and of such import as to show plainly that this immortal document does not exhibit a merely fanciful, even if beautiful, ideal of human society. Rather did our Predecessor draw from the Gospel and, therefore, from an ever-living and life-giving fountain, teachings capable of greatly mitigating, if not immediately terminating that deadly internal struggle which is rending the family of mankind. The rich fruits which the Church of Christ and the whole human race have, by God's favor, reaped therefrom unto salvation prove that some of this good seed, so lavishly sown forty years ago, fell on good ground. On the basis of the long period of experience, it cannot be rash to say that Leo's Encyclical has proved itself the *Magna Charta* upon which all Christian activity in the social field ought to be based, as on a foundation. And those who would seem to hold in little esteem this Papal Encyclical and its commemoration either blaspheme what they know not, or understand nothing of what they are only superficially acquainted with, or if they do understand convict themselves formally of injustice and ingratitude.

40. Yet since in the course of these same years, certain doubts have arisen concerning either the correct meaning of some parts of Leo's Encyclical or conclusions to be deduced therefrom, which doubts in turn have even among Catholics given rise to controversies that are not always peaceful; and since, furthermore, new needs and changed conditions of our age have made necessary a more precise application of Leo's teaching or even certain additions thereto, We most gladly seize this fitting occasion, in accord with Our Apostolic Office through which We are debtors to all, to answer, so far as in Us lies, these doubts and these demands of the present day.

II

41. Yet before proceeding to explain these matters, that principle which Leo XIII so clearly established must be laid

down at the outset here, namely, that there resides in Us the right and duty to pronounce with supreme authority upon social and economic matters. Certainly the Church was not given the commission to guide men to an only fleeting and perishable happiness but to that which is eternal. Indeed "the Church holds that it is unlawful for her to mix without cause in these temporal concerns;" however, she can in no wise renounce the duty God entrusted to her to interpose her authority, not of course in matters of technique for which she is neither suitably equipped nor endowed by office, but in all things that are connected with the moral law. For as to these, the deposit of truth that God committed to Us and the grave duty of disseminating and interpreting the whole moral law, and of urging it in season and out of season, bring under and subject to Our supreme jurisdiction not only social order but economic activities themselves.

42. Even though economics and moral science employs each its own principles in its own sphere, it is, nevertheless, an error to say that the economic and moral orders are so distinct from and alien to each other that the former depends in no way on the latter. Certainly the laws of economics, as they are termed, being based on the very nature of material things and on the capacities of the human body and mind, determine the limits of what productive human effort cannot, and of what it can attain in the economic field and by what means. Yet it is reason itself that clearly shows, on the basis of the individual and social nature of things and of men, the purpose which God ordained for all economic life.

43. But it is only the moral law which, just as it commands us to seek our supreme and last end in the whole scheme of our activity, so likewise commands us to seek directly in each kind of activity those purposes which we know that nature, or rather God the Author of nature, established for that kind of action, and in orderly relationship to subordinate such immediate purposes to our supreme and last end. If we faithfully observe this law, then it will follow that the particular purposes, both individual and social, that are sought in the economic field will fall in their proper place in the universal order of purposes, and We, in ascending through them, as it were by steps, shall

attain the final end of all things, that is God, to Himself and to us, the supreme and inexhaustible Good.

44. But to come down to particular points, We shall begin with ownership or the right of property. Venerable Brethren and Beloved Children, you know that Our Predecessor of happy memory strongly defended the right of property against the tenets of the Socialists of his time by showing that its abolition would result, not to the advantage of the working class, but to their extreme harm. Yet since there are some who calumniate the Supreme Pontiff, and the Church herself, as if she had taken and were still taking the part of the rich against the non-owning workers—certainly no accusation is more unjust than that—and since Catholics are at variance with one another concerning the true and exact mind of Leo, it has seemed best to vindicate this, that is, the Catholic teaching on this matter from calumnies and safeguard it from false interpretations.

45. First, then, let it be considered as certain and established that neither Leo nor those theologians who have taught under the guidance and authority of the Church have ever denied or questioned the twofold character of ownership, called usually individual or social according as it regards either separate persons or the common good. For they have always unanimously maintained that nature, rather the Creator Himself, has given man the right of private ownership not only that individuals may be able to provide for themselves and their families but also that the goods which the Creator destined for the entire family of mankind may through this institution truly serve this purpose. All this can be achieved in no wise except through the maintenance of a certain and definite order.

46. Accordingly, twin rocks of shipwreck must be carefully avoided. For, as one is wrecked upon, or comes close to, what is known as "individualism" by denying or minimizing the social and public character of the right of property, so by rejecting or minimizing the private and individual character of this same right, one inevitably runs into "collectivism" or at least closely approaches its tenets. Unless this is kept in mind, one is swept from his course upon the shoals of that moral, juridical, and social modernism which We denounced in the Encyclical issued at the beginning of Our Pontificate. And, in particular,

let those realize this who, in their desire for innovation, do not scruple to reproach the Church with infamous calumnies, as if she had allowed to creep into the teachings of her theologians a pagan concept of ownership which must be completely replaced by another that they with amazing ignorance call "Christian."

47. In order to place definite limits on the controversies that have arisen over ownership and its inherent duties there must be first laid down as a foundation a principle established by Leo XIII: The right of property is distinct from its use. That justice called commutative commands sacred respect for the division of possessions and forbids invasion of others' rights through the exceeding of the limits of one's own property; but the duty of owners to use their property only in a right way does not come under this type of justice, but under other virtues, obligations of which "cannot be enforced by legal action." Therefore, they are in error who assert that ownership and its right use are limited by the same boundaries; and it is much farther still from the truth to hold that a right to property is destroyed or lost by reason of abuse or non-use.

48. Those, therefore, are doing a work that is truly salutary and worthy of all praise who, while preserving harmony among themselves and the integrity of the traditional teaching of the Church, seek to define the inner nature of these duties and their limits whereby either the right of property itself or its use, that is, the exercise of ownership, is circumscribed by the necessities of social living. On the other hand, those who seek to restrict the individual character of ownership to such a degree that in fact they destroy it are mistaken and in error.

49. It follows from what We have termed the individual and at the same time social character of ownership, that men must consider in this matter not only their own advantage but also the common good. To define these duties in detail when necessity requires and the natural law has not done so, is the function of those in charge of the State. Therefore, public authority, under the guiding light always of the natural and divine law, can determine more accurately upon consideration of the true requirements of the common good, what is permitted and what is not permitted to owners in the use of their property. Moreover, Leo XIII wisely taught "that God has left

the limits of private possessions to be fixed by the industry of men and institutions of peoples." That history proves ownership, like other elements of social life, to be not absolutely unchanging, We once declared as follows: "What divers forms has property had, from that primitive form among rude and savage peoples, which may be observed in some places even in our time, to the form of possession in the patriarchal age; and so further to the various forms under tyranny (We are using the word tyranny in its classical sense); and then through the feudal and monarchial forms down to the various types which are to be found in more recent times." That the State is not permitted to discharge its duty arbitrarily is, however, clear. The natural right itself both of owning goods privately and of passing them on by inheritance ought always to remain intact and inviolate, since this indeed is a right that the State cannot take away: "For man is older than the state," and also "domestic living together is prior both in thought and in fact to uniting into a polity." Wherefore the wise Pontiff declared that it is grossly unjust for a State to exhaust private wealth through the weight of imposts and taxes. "For since the right of possessing goods privately has been conferred not by man's law, but by nature, public authority cannot abolish it, but can only control its exercise and bring it into conformity with the common weal." Yet when the state brings private ownership into harmony with the needs of the common good, it does not commit a hostile act against private owners but rather does them a friendly service; for it thereby effectively prevents the private possession of goods, which the Author of nature in His most wise providence ordained for the support of human life, from causing intolerable evils and thus rushing to its own destruction; it does not destroy private possessions, but safeguards them; and it does not weaken private property rights, but strengthens them.

50. Furthermore, a person's superfluous income, that is, income which he does not need to sustain life fittingly and with dignity, is not left wholly to his own free determination. Rather the Sacred Scriptures and the Fathers of the Church constantly declare in the most explicit language that the rich are bound by a very grave precept to practice almsgiving, beneficence, and munificence.

51. Expending larger incomes so that opportunity for gainful work may be abundant, provided, however, that this work is applied to producing really useful goods, ought to be considered, as We deduce from the principles of the Angelic Doctor, an outstanding exemplification of the virtue of munificence and one particularly suited to the needs of the times.

52. That ownership is originally acquired both by occupancy of a thing not owned by any one and by labor, or, as is said, by specification, the tradition of all ages as well as the teaching of Our Predecessor Leo clearly testifies. For, whatever some idly say to the contrary, no injury is done to any person when a thing is occupied that is available to all but belongs to no one; however, only that labor which a man performs in his own name and by virtue of which a new form or increase has been given to a thing grants him title to these fruits.

53. Far different is the nature of work that is hired out to others and expended on the property of others. To this indeed especially applies what Leo XIII says is "incontestible," namely, that "the wealth of nations originates from no other source than from the labor of workers." For is it not plain that the enormous volume of goods that makes up human wealth is produced by and issues from the hands of the workers that either toil unaided or have their efficiency marvelously increased by being equipped with tools or machines? Every one knows, too, that no nation has ever risen out of want and poverty to a better and nobler condition save by the enormous and combined toil of all the people, both those who manage work and those who carry out directions. But it is no less evident that, had not God the Creator of all things, in keeping with His goodness, first generously bestowed natural riches and resources—the wealth and forces of nature—, such supreme efforts would have been idle and vain, indeed could never even have begun. For what else is work but to use or exercise the energies of mind and body on or through these very things? And in the application of natural resources to human use the law of nature, or rather God's will promulgated by it, demands that right order be observed. This order consists in this: that each thing have its proper owner. Hence it follows that unless a man is expending labor on his own property, the labor of one person and the

41

property of another must be associated, for neither can produce anything without the other. Leo XIII certainly had this in mind when he wrote: "Neither capital can do without labor, nor labor without capital." Wherefore it is wholly false to ascribe to property alone or to labor alone whatever has been obtained through the combined effort of both, and it is wholly unjust for either, denying the efficacy of the other, to arrogate to itself whatever has been produced.

54. Property, that is, "capital," has undoubtedly long been able to appropriate too much to itself. Whatever was produced, whatever returns accrued, capital claimed for itself, hardly leaving to the worker enough to restore and renew his strength. For the doctrine was preached that all accumulation of capital falls by an absolutely insuperable economic law to the rich, and that by the same law the workers are given over and bound to perpetual want, to the scantiest of livelihoods. It is true, indeed, that things have not always and everywhere corresponded with this sort of teaching of the so-called Manchesterian Liberals; yet it cannot be denied that economic-social institutions have moved steadily in that direction. That these false ideas, these erroneous suppositions, have been vigorously assailed, and not by those alone who through them were being deprived of their innate right to obtain better conditions, will surprise no one.

55. And therefore, to the harassed workers there have come "intellectuals," as they are called, setting up in opposition to a fictitious law the equally fictitious moral principle that all products and profits, save only enough to repair and renew capital, belong by very right to the workers. This error, much more specious than that of certain of the Socialists who hold that whatever serves to produce goods ought to be transferred to the State, or, as they say "socialized," is consequently all the more dangerous and the more apt to deceive the unwary. It is an alluring poison which many have eagerly drunk whom open Socialism had not been able to deceive.

56. Unquestionably, so as not to close against themselves the road to justice and peace through these false tenets, both parties ought to have been forewarned by the wise words of Our Predecessor: "However the earth may be apportioned among private owners, it does not cease to serve the common

interest of all." This same doctrine We ourselves also taught above in declaring that the division of goods which results from private ownership was established by nature itself in order that created things may serve the needs of mankind in fixed and stable order. Lest one wander from the straight path of truth, this is something that must be continually kept in mind.

57. But not every distribution among human beings of property and wealth is of a character to attain either completely or to a satisfactory degree of perfection the end which God intends. Therefore, the riches that economic-social developments constantly increase ought to be so distributed among individual persons and classes that the common advantage of all, which Leo XIII had praised, will be safeguarded; in other words, that the common good of all society will be kept inviolate. By this law of social justice, one class is forbidden to exclude the other from sharing in the benefits. Hence the class of the wealthy violates this law no less, when, as if free from care on account of its wealth, it thinks it the right order of things for it to get everything and the worker nothing, than does the non-owning working class when, angered deeply at outraged justice and too ready to assert wrongly the one right it is conscious of, it demands for itself everything as if produced by its own hands, and attacks and seeks to abolish, therefore, all property and returns or incomes, of whatever kind they are or whatever the function they perform in human society, that have not been obtained by labor, and for no other reason save that they are of such a nature. And in this connection We must not pass over the unwarranted and unmerited appeal made by some to the Apostle when he said: "If any man will not work neither let him eat." For the Apostle is passing judgment on those who are unwilling to work, although they can and ought to, and he admonishes us that we ought diligently to use our time and energies of body and mind and not be a burden to others when we can provide for ourselves. But the Apostle in no wise teaches that labor is the sole title to a living or an income.

58. To each, therefore, must be given his own share of goods, and the distribution of created goods, which, as every discerning person knows, is laboring today under the gravest evils due to the huge disparity between the few exceedingly

rich and the unnumbered propertyless, must be effectively called back to and brought into conformity with the norms of the common good, that is, social justice.

59. The redemption of the non-owning workers—this is the goal that Our Predecessor declared must necessarily be sought. And the point is the more emphatically to be asserted and more insistently repeated because the commands of the Pontiff, salutary as they are, have not infrequently been consigned to oblivion either because they were deliberately suppressed by silence or thought impracticable, although they both can and ought to be put into effect. And these commands have not lost their force and wisdom for our time because that "pauperism" which Leo XIII beheld in all its horror is less widespread. Certainly the condition of the workers has been improved and made more equitable especially in the more civilized and wealthy countries where the workers can no longer be considered universally overwhelmed with misery and lacking the necessities of life. But since manufacturing and industry have so rapidly pervaded and occupied countless regions, not only in the countries called new, but also in the realms of the Far East that have been civilized from antiquity, the number of the non-owning working poor has increased enormously and their groans cry to God from the earth. Added to them is the huge army of rural wage workers, pushed to the lowest level of existence and deprived of all hope of ever acquiring "some property in land," and, therefore, permanently bound to the status of non-owning worker unless suitable and effective remedies are applied.

60. Yet while it is true that the status of non-owning worker is to be carefully distinguished from pauperism, nevertheless the immense multitude of the non-owning workers on the one hand and the enormous riches of certain very wealthy men on the other establish an unanswerable argument that the riches which are so abundantly produced in our age of "industrialism," as it is called, are not rightly distributed and equitably made available to the various classes of the people.

61. Therefore, with all our strength and effort we must strive that at least in the future the abundant fruits of production will accrue equitably to those who are rich and will be

distributed in ample sufficiency among the workers—not that these may become remiss in work, for man is born to labor as the bird to fly—but that they may increase their property by thrift, that they may bear, by wise management of this increase in property, the burdens of family life with greater ease and security, and that, emerging from that insecure lot in life in whose uncertainties non-owning workers are cast, they may be able not only to endure the vicissitudes of earthly existence but have also assurance that when their lives are ended they will provide in some measure for those they leave after them.

62. All these things which Our Predecessor has not only suggested but clearly and openly proclaimed, We emphasize with renewed insistence in our present Encyclical; and unless utmost efforts are made without delay to put them into effect, let no one persuade himself that public order, peace, and the tranquility of human society can be effectively defended against agitators of revolution.

63. As We have already indicated, following in the footsteps of Our Predecessor, it will be impossible to put these principles into practice unless the non-owning workers through industry and thrift advance to the state of possessing some little property. But except from pay for work, from what source can a man who has nothing else but work from which to obtain food and the necessaries of life set anything aside for himself through practicing frugality? Let us, therefore, explaining and developing wherever necessary Leo XIII's teachings and precepts, take up this question of wages and salaries which he called one "of very great importance."

64. First of all, those who declare that a contract of hiring and being hired is unjust of its own nature, and hence a partnership-contract must take its place, are certainly in error and gravely misrepresent Our Predecessor whose Encyclical not only accepts working for wages or salaries but deals at some length with its regulation in accordance with the rules of justice.

65. We consider it more advisable, however, in the present condition of human society that, so far as is possible, the work-contract be somewhat modified by a partnership-contract, as is already being done in various ways and with no small advantage to workers and owners. Workers and other employees thus

become sharers in ownership or management or participate in some fashion in the profits received.

66. The just amount of pay, however, must be calculated not on a single basis but on several, as Leo XIII already wisely declared in these words: "To establish a rule of pay in accord with justice, many factors must be taken into account."

67. By this statement he plainly condemned the shallowness of those who think that this most difficult matter is easily solved by the application of a single rule or measure—and one quite false.

68. For they are greatly in error who do not hesitate to spread the principle that labor is worth and must be paid as much as its products are worth, and that consequently the one who hires out his labor has the right to demand all that is produced through his labor. How far this is from the truth is evident from what We have already explained in treating of property and labor.

69. It is obvious that, as in the case of ownership, so in the case of work, especially work hired out to others, there is a social aspect also to be considered in addition to the personal or individual aspect. For man's productive effort cannot yield its fruits unless a truly social and organic body exists, unless a social and juridical order watches over the exercise of work, unless the various occupations, being interdependent, cooperate with and mutually complete one another, and, what is still more important, unless mind, material things, and work combine and form as it were a single whole. Therefore, where the social and individual nature of work is neglected, it will be impossible to evaluate work justly and pay it according to justice.

70. Conclusions of the greatest importance follow from this two-fold character which nature has impressed on human work, and it is in accordance with these that wages ought to be regulated and established.

71. In the first place, the worker must be paid a wage sufficient to support him and his family. That the rest of the family should also contribute to the common support, according to the capacity of each is certainly right, as can be observed especially in the families of farmers, but also in the families of many craftsmen and small shopkeepers. But to abuse the years

of childhood and the limited strength of women is grossly wrong. Mothers, concentrating on household duties, should work primarily in the home or in its immediate vicinity. It is an intolerable abuse, and to be abolished at all cost, for mothers on account of the father's low wage to be forced to engage in gainful occupations outside the home to the neglect of their proper cares and duties, especially the training of children. Every effort must therefore be made that fathers of families receive a wage large enough to meet ordinary family needs adequately. But if this cannot always be done under existing circumstances, social justice demands that changes be introduced as soon as possible whereby such a wage will be assured to every adult workingman. It will not be out of place here to render merited praise to all, who with a wise and useful purpose, have tried and tested various ways of adjusting the pay for work to family burdens in such a way that, as these increase, the former may be raised and indeed, if the contingency arises, there may be enough to meet extraordinary needs.

72. In determining the amount of the wage, the condition of a business and of the one carrying it on must also be taken into account; for it would be unjust to demand excessive wages which a business cannot stand without its ruin and consequent calamity to the workers. If, however, a business makes too little money, because of lack of energy or lack of initiative or because of indifference to technical and economic progress, that must not be regarded a just reason for reducing the compensation of the workers. But if the business in question is not making enough money to pay the workers an equitable wage because it is being crushed by unjust burdens or forced to sell its product at less than a just price, those who are thus the cause of the injury are guilty of grave wrong, for they deprive workers of their just wage and force them under the pinch of necessity to accept a wage less than fair.

73. Let, then, both workers and employers strive with united strength and counsel to overcome the difficulties and obstacles and let a wise provision on the part of public authority aid them in so salutary a work. If, however, matters come to an extreme crisis, it must be finally considered whether the business can continue or the workers are to be cared for in some other

way. In such a situation, certainly most serious, a feeling of close relationship and a Christian concord of minds ought to prevail and function effectively among employers and workers.

74. Lastly, the amount of the pay must be adjusted to the public economic good. We have shown above how much it helps the common good for workers and other employees, by setting aside some part of their income which remains after necessary expenditures, to attain gradually to the possession of a moderate amount of wealth. But another point, scarcely less important, and especially vital in our times, must not be over-looked: namely, that the opportunity to work be provided to those who are able and willing to work. This opportunity de-pends largely on the wage and salary rate, which can help as long as it is kept within proper limits, but which on the other hand can be an obstacle if it exceeds these limits. For every one knows that an excessive lowering of wages, or their increase beyond due measure, causes unemployment. This evil, indeed, especially as we see it prolonged and injuring so many during the years of Our Pontificate, has plunged workers into misery and temptations, ruined the prosperity of nations, and put in jeopardy the public order, peace, and tranquillity of the whole world. Hence it is contrary to social justice when, for the sake of personal gain and without regard for the common good, wages and salaries are excessively lowered or raised; and this same social justice demands that wages and salaries be so managed, through agreement of plans and wills, insofar as can be done, as to offer to the greatest possible number the opportunity of getting work and obtaining suitable means of livelihood.

75. A right proportion among wages and salaries also con-tributes directly to the same result; and with this is closely connected a right proportion in the prices at which the goods are sold that are produced by the various occupations, such as agriculture, manufacturing, and others. If all these relations are properly maintained, the various occupations will combine and coalesce into, as it were, a single body and like members of the body mutually aid and complete one another. For then only will the social economy be rightly established and attain its purposes when all and each are supplied with all the goods that the wealth and resources of nature, technical achievement, and

the social organization of economic life can furnish. And these goods ought indeed to be enough both to meet the demands of necessity and decent comfort and to advance people to that happier and fuller condition of life which, when it is wisely cared for, is not only no hindrance to virtue but helps it greatly.

76. What We have thus far stated regarding an equitable distribution of property and regarding just wages concerns individual persons and only indirectly touches social order, to the restoration of which according to the principles of sound philosophy and to its perfection according to the sublime precepts of the law of the Gospel, Our Predecessor, Leo XIII, devoted all his thought and care.

77. Still, in order that what he so happily initiated may be solidly established, that what remains to be done may be accomplished, and that even more copious and richer benefits may accrue to the family of mankind, two things are especially necessary: reform of institutions and correction of morals.

78. When we speak of the reform of institutions, the State comes chiefly to mind, not as if universal well-being were to be expected from its activity, but because things have come to such a pass through the evil of what we have termed "individualism," that, following upon the overthrow and near extinction of that rich social life which was once highly developed through associations of various kinds, there remain virtually only individuals and the State. This is to the great harm of the State itself; for, with a structure of social governance lost, and with the taking over of all the burdens which the wrecked associations once bore, the State has been overwhelmed and crushed by almost infinite tasks and duties.

79. As history abundantly proves, it is true that on account of changed conditions many things which were done by small associations in former times cannot be done now save by large associations. Still, that most weighty principle, which cannot be set aside or changed, remains fixed and unshaken in social philosophy: Just as it is gravely wrong to take from individuals what they can accomplish by their own initiative and industry and give it to the community, so also it is an injustice and at the same time a grave evil and disturbance of right order to assign to a greater and higher association what

lesser and subordinate organizations can do. For every social activity ought of its very nature to furnish help to the members of the body social, and never destroy and absorb them.

80. The supreme authority of the State ought, therefore, to let subordinate groups handle matters and concerns of lesser importance, which would otherwise dissipate its efforts greatly. Thereby the State will more freely, powerfully, and effectively do all those things that belong to it alone because it alone can do them: directing, watching, urging, restraining, as occasion requires and necessity demands. Therefore, those in power should be sure that the more perfectly a graduated order is kept among the various associations, in observance of the principle of "subsidiary function," the stronger social authority and effectiveness will be and the happier and more prosperous the condition of the State.

81. First and foremost, the State and every good citizen ought to look to and strive toward this end: that the conflict between the hostile classes be abolished and harmonious co-operation of the Industries and Professions be encouraged and promoted.

82. The social policy of the State, therefore, must devote itself to the reestablishment of the Industries and Professions. In actual fact, human society now, for the reason that it is founded on classes with divergent aims and hence opposed to one another and therefore inclined to enmity and strife, continues to be in a violent condition and is unstable and uncertain.

83. Labor, as Our Predecessor explained well in his Encyclical, is not a mere commodity. On the contrary, the worker's human dignity in it must be recognized. It therefore cannot be bought and sold like a commodity. Nevertheless, as the situation now stands, hiring and offering for hire in the so-called labor market separate men into two divisions, as into battle lines, and the contest between these divisions turns the labor market itself almost into a battlefield where face to face the opposing lines struggle bitterly. Everyone understands that this grave evil which is plunging all human society to destruction must be remedied as soon as possible. But complete cure will not come until this opposition has been abolished and well-ordered members of the social body—Industries and Professions—are

constituted in which men may have their place, not according
to the position each has in the labor market but according to
the respective social functions which each performs. For under
nature's guidance it comes to pass that just as those who are
joined together by nearness of habitation establish towns, so
those who follow the same industry of profession—whether in
the economic or other field—form guilds or associations, so that
many are wont to consider these self-governing organizations,
if not essential, at least natural to civil society.

84. Because order, as St. Thomas well explains, is unity
arising from the harmonious arrangement of many objects, a
true, genuine social order demands that the various members of
a society be united together by some strong bond. This unifying force is present not only in the producing of goods or the
rendering of services—in which the employers and employees of
an identical Industry or Profession collaborate jointly—but
also in that common good, to achieve which all Industries and
Professions together ought, each to the best of its ability, to
cooperate amicably. And this unity will be the stronger and
more effective, the more faithfully individuals and the Industries and Professions themselves strive to do their work and
excel in it.

85. It is easily deduced from what has been said, that the
interests common to the whole Industry or Profession should
hold first place in these guilds. The most important among these
interests is to promote the cooperation in the highest degree of
each industry and profession for the sake of the common good
of the country. Concerning matters, however, in which particular points, involving advantage or detriment to employers or
workers, may require special care and protection, the two
parties, when these cases arise, can deliberate separately or as
the situation requires reach a decision separately.

86. The teaching of Leo XIII on the form of political
government, namely, that men are free to choose whatever form
they please, provided that proper regard is had for the requirements of justice and of the common good, is equally applicable
in due proportion, it is hardly necessary to say, to the guilds of
the various industries and professions.

87. Moreover, just as inhabitants of a town are wont to found associations with the widest diversity of purposes, which each is quite free to join or not, so those engaged in the same industry or profession will combine with one another into associations equally free for purposes connected in some manner with the pursuit of the calling itself. Since these free associations are clearly and lucidly explained by Our Predecessor of illustrious memory, We consider it enough to emphasize this one point: People are quite free not only to found such associations, which are a matter of private order and private right, but also in respect to them "freely to adopt the organization and the rules which they judge most appropriate to achieve their purpose." The same freedom must be asserted for founding associations that go beyond the boundaries of individual callings. And may these free organizations, now flourishing and rejoicing in their salutary fruits, set before themselves the task of preparing the way, in conformity with the mind of Christian social teaching, for those larger and more important guilds, Industries and Professions, which We mentioned before, and make every possible effort to bring them to realization.

88. Attention must be given also to another matter that is closely connected with the foregoing. Just as the unity of human society cannot be founded on an opposition of classes, so also the right ordering of economic life cannot be left to a free competition of forces. For from this source, as from a poisoned spring, have originated and spread all the errors of individualist economic teaching. Destroying through forgetfulness or ignorance the social and moral character of economic life, it held that economic life must be considered and treated as altogether free from and independent of public authority, because in the market, i.e., in the free struggle of competitors, it would have a principle of self-direction which governs it much more perfectly than would the intervention of any created intellect. But free competition, while justified and certainly useful provided it is kept within certain limits, clearly cannot direct economic life—a truth which the outcome of the application in practice of the tenets of this evil individualistic spirit has more than sufficiently demonstrated. Therefore, it is most necessary that economic life be again subjected to and governed

by a true and effective directing principle. This function is one that the economic dictatorship which has recently displaced free competition can still less perform, since it is a headstrong power and a violent energy that, to benefit people, needs to be strongly curbed and wisely ruled. But it cannot curb and rule itself. Loftier and nobler principles—social justice and social charity—must, therefore, be sought whereby this dictatorship may be governed firmly and fully. Hence, the institutions themselves of peoples and, particularly those of all social life, ought to be penetrated with this justice, and it is most necessary that it be truly effective, that is, establish a juridical and social order which will, as it were, give form and shape to all economic life. Social charity, moreover, ought to be as the soul of this order, an order which public authority ought to be ever ready effectively to protect and defend. It will be able to do this the more easily as it rids itself of those burdens which, as We have stated above, are not properly its own.

89. Furthermore since the various nations largely depend on one another in economic matters and need one another's help, they should strive with a united purpose and effort to promote by wisely conceived pacts and institutions a prosperous and happy international cooperation in economic life.

90. If the members of the body social are, as we said, reconstituted, and if the directing principle of economic-social life is restored, it will be possible to say in a certain sense even of this body what the Apostle says of the mystical body of Christ: "The whole body (being closely joined and knit together through every joint of the system according to the functioning in due measure of each single part) derives its increase to the building up of itself in love."

91. Recently, as all know, there has been inaugurated a special system of syndicates and corporations of the various callings which in view of the theme of this Encyclical it would seem necessary to describe here briefly and comment upon appropriately.

92. The civil authority itself constitutes the syndicate as a juridical personality in such a manner as to confer on it simultaneously a certain monopoly-privilege, since only such a syndicate, when thus approved, can maintain the rights (accord-

ing to the type of syndicate) of workers or employers, and since it alone can arrange for the placement of labor and conclude so-termed labor agreements. Anyone is free to join a syndicate or not, and only within these limits can this kind of syndicate be called free; for syndical dues and special assessments are exacted of absolutely all members of every specified calling or profession, whether they are workers or employers; likewise all are bound by the labor agreements made by the legally recognized syndicate. Nevertheless, it has been officially stated that this legally recognized syndicate does not prevent the existence, without legal status however, of other associations made up of persons following the same calling.

93. The associations, or corporations, are composed of delegates from the two syndicates (that is, of workers and employers) respectively of the same industry or profession and, as true and proper organs and institutions of the State, they direct the syndicates and coordinate their activities in matters of common interest toward one and the same end.

'94. Strikes and lock-outs are forbidden; if the parties cannot settle their dispute, public authority intervenes.

95. Anyone who gives even slight attention to the matter, will easily see what are the obvious advantages in the system We have thus summarily described: The various classes work together peacefully, socialist organizations and their activities are repressed, and a special magistracy exercises a governing authority. Yet lest We neglect anything in a matter of such great importance and that all points treated may be properly connected with the more general principles which We mentioned above and with those which We intend shortly to add, We are compelled to say that to Our certain knowledge there are not wanting some who fear that the State, instead of confining itself as it ought to the furnishing of necessary and adequate assistance, is substituting itself for free activity; that the new syndical and corporative order savors too much of an involved and political system of administration; and that (in spite of those more general advantages mentioned above, which are of course fully admitted) it rather serves particular political ends than leads to the reconstruction and promotion of a better social order.

96. To achieve this latter lofty aim, and in particular to promote the common good truly and permanently, We hold it is first and above everything wholly necessary that God bless it and, secondly, that all men of good will work with united effort toward that end. We are further convinced, as a necessary consequence, that this end will be attained the more certainly the larger the number of those ready to contribute toward it their technical, occupational, and social knowledge and experience; and also, what is more important, the greater the contribution made thereto of Catholic principles and their application, not indeed by Catholic Action (which excludes strictly syndical or political activities from its scope) but by those sons of Ours whom Catholic Action imbues with Catholic principles and trains for carrying on an apostolate under the leadership and teaching guidance of the Church—of that Church which in this field also that We have described, as in every other field where moral questions are involved and discussed, can never forget or neglect through indifference its divinely imposed mandate to be vigilant and to teach.

97. What We have taught about the reconstruction and perfection of social order can surely in no wise be brought to realization without reform of morality, the very record of history clearly shows. For there was a social order once which, although indeed not perfect or in all respects ideal, nevertheless, met in a certain measure the requirements of right reason, considering the conditions and needs of the time. If that order has long since perished, that surely did not happen because the order could not have accommodated itself to changed conditions and needs by development and by a certain expansion, but rather because men, hardened by too much love of self, refused to open the order to the increasing masses as they should have done, or because, deceived by allurements of a false freedom and other errors, they became impatient of every authority and sought to reject every form of control.

98. There remains to Us, after again calling to judgment the economic system now in force and its most bitter accuser, Socialism, and passing explicit and just sentence upon them, to search out more thoroughly the root of these many evils and

to point out that the first and most necessary remedy is a reform of morals.

III

99. Important indeed have the changes been which both the economic system and Socialism have undergone since Leo XIII's time.

100. That, in the first place, the whole aspect of economic life is vastly altered, is plain to all. You know, Venerable Brethren and Beloved Children, that the Encyclical of Our Predecessor of happy memory had in view chiefly that economic system, wherein, generally, some provide capital while others provide labor for a joint economic activity. And in a happy phrase he described it thus: "Neither capital can do without labor, nor labor without capital."

101. With all his energy Leo XIII sought to adjust this economic system according to the norms of right order; hence, it is evident that this system is not to be condemned in itself. And surely it is not of its own nature vicious. But it does violate right order when capital hires workers, that is, the non-owning working class, with a view to and under such terms that it directs business and even the whole economic system according to its own will and advantage, scorning the human dignity of the workers, the social character of economic activity and social justice itself, and the common good.

102. Even today this is not, it is true, the only economic system in force everywhere; for there is another system also, which still embraces a huge mass of humanity, significant in numbers and importance, as for example, agriculture, wherein the greater portion of mankind honorably and honestly procures its livelihood. This group, too, is being crushed with hardships and with difficulties, to which Our Predecessor devotes attention in several places in his Encyclical and which We Ourselves have touched upon more than once in Our present Letter.

103. But, with the diffusion of modern industry throughout the whole world, the "capitalist" economic regime has spread everywhere to such a degree, particularly since the publication of Leo XIII's Encyclical, that it has invaded and pervaded the economic and social life of even those outside its

orbit and is unquestionably impressing on it its advantages, disadvantages and vices, and, in a sense, is giving it its own shape and form.

104. Accordingly, when directing Our special attention to the changes which the capitalist economic system has undergone since Leo's time, We have in mind the good not only of those who dwell in regions given over to "capital" and industry, but of all mankind.

105. In the first place, it is obvious that not only is wealth concentrated in our times but an immense power and despotic economic dictatorship is consolidated in the hands of a few, who often are not owners but only the trustees and managing directors of invested funds which they administer according to their own arbitrary will and pleasure.

106. This dictatorship is being most forcibly exercised by those who, since they hold the money and completely control it, control credit also and rule the lending of money. Hence they regulate the flow, so to speak, of the life-blood whereby the entire economic system lives, and have so firmly in their grasp the soul, as it were, of economic life that no one can breathe against their will.

107. This concentration of power and might, the characteristic mark, as it were, of contemporary economic life, is the fruit that the unlimited freedom of struggle among competitors has of its own nature produced, and which lets only the strongest survive; and this is often the same as saying, those who fight the most violently, those who give least heed to their conscience.

108. This accumulation of might and of power generates in turn three kinds of conflict. First, there is the struggle for economic supremacy itself; then there is the bitter fight to gain supremacy over the State in order to use in economic struggles its resources and authority; finally there is conflict between States themselves, not only because countries employ their power and shape their policies to promote every economic advantage of their citizens, but also because they seek to decide political controversies that arise among nations through the use of their economic supremacy and strength.

109. The utimate consequences of the individualist spirit in economic life are those which you yourselves, Venerable Brethren and Beloved Children, see and deplore: Free competition has destroyed itself; economic dictatorship has supplanted the free market; unbridled ambition for power has likewise succeeded greed for gain; all economic life has become tragically hard, inexorable, and cruel. To these are to be added the grave evils that have resulted from an intermingling and shameful confusion of the functions and duties of public authority with those of the economic sphere—such as, one of the worst, the virtual degradation of the majesty of the State, which although it ought to sit on high like a queen and supreme arbitress, free from all partiality and intent upon the one common good and justice, is become a slave, surrendered and delivered to the passions and greed of men. And as to international relations, two different streams have issued from the one fountain-head: On the one hand, economic nationalism or even economic imperialism; on the other, a no less deadly and accursed internationalism of finance or international imperialism whose country is where profit is.

110. In the second part of this Ecyclical where We have presented Our teaching, We have described the remedies for these great evils so explicitly that We consider it sufficient at this point to recall them briefly. Since the present system of economy is founded chiefly upon ownership and labor, the principles of right reason, that is, of Christian social philosophy, must be kept in mind regarding ownership and labor and their association together, and must be put into actual practice. First, so as to avoid the reefs of individualism and collectivism, the two-fold character, that is individual and social, both of capital or ownership and of work or labor must be given due and rightful weight. Relations of one to the other must be made to conform to the laws of strictest justice—commutative justice, as it is called—with the support, however, of Christian charity. Free competition, kept within definite and due limits, and still more economic dictatorship, must be effectively brought under public authority in these matters which pertain to the latter's function. The public institutions themselves, of peoples, moreover, ought to make all human society conform to the needs of

the common good; that is, to the norm of social justice. If this is done, that most important division of social life, namely, economic activity, cannot fail likewise to return to right and sound order.

111. Socialism, against which Our Predecessor, Leo XIII, had especially to inveigh, has since his time changed no less profoundly than the form of economic life. For Socialism, which could then be termed almost a single system and which maintained definite teachings reduced into one body of doctrine, has since then split chiefly into two sections, often opposing each other and even bitterly hostile, without either one however abandoning a position fundamentally contrary to Christian truth that was characteristic of Socialism.

112. One section of Socialism has undergone almost the same change that the capitalistic economic system, as We have explained above, has undergone. It has sunk into Communism. Communism teaches and seeks two objectives: Unrelenting class warfare and absolute extermination of private ownership. Not secretly or by hidden methods does it do this, but publicly, openly, and by employing every and all means, even the most violent. To achieve these objectives there is nothing which it does not dare, nothing for which it has respect or reverence; and when it has come to power, it is incredible and portent-like in its cruelty and inhumanity. The horrible slaughter and destruction through which it has laid waste vast regions of eastern Europe and Asia are the evidence; how much an enemy and how openly hostile it is to Holy Church and to God Himself is, alas, too well proved by facts and fully known to all. Although We, therefore, deem it superfluous to warn upright and faithful children of the Church regarding the impious and iniquitous character of Communism, yet We cannot without deep sorrow contemplate the heedlessness of those who apparently make light of these impending dangers and with sluggish inertia allow the wide-spread propagation of doctrine which seeks by violence and slaughter to destroy society altogether. All the more gravely to be condemned is the folly of those who neglect to remove or change the conditions that inflame the minds of peoples, and pave the way for the overthrow and destruction of society.

113. The other section, which has kept the name Socialism, is surely more moderate. It not only professes the rejection of violence, but modifies and tempers to some degree, if it does not reject entirely, the class struggle and the abolition of private ownership. One might say that, terrified by its own principles and by the conclusions drawn therefrom by Communism, Socialism inclines toward and in a certain measure approaches the truths which Christian tradition has always held sacred; for it cannot be denied that its demands at times come very near those that Christian reformers of society justly insist upon.

114. For if the class struggle abstains from enmities and mutual hatred, it gradually changes into an honest discussion of differences founded on a desire for justice, and if this is not that blessed social peace which we all seek, it can and ought to be the point of departure from which to move forward to the mutual cooperation of the Industries and Professions. So also the war declared on private ownership, more and more abated, is being so restricted that now, finally, not the possession itself of the means of production is attacked but rather a kind of sovereignty over society which ownership has, contrary to all right, seized and usurped. For such sovereignty belongs in reality not to owners but to the public authority. If the foregoing happens, it can come even to the point that imperceptibly these ideas of the more moderate socialism will no longer differ from the desires and demands of those who are striving to remold human society on the basis of Christian principles. For certain kinds of property, it is rightly contended, ought to be reserved to the State since they carry with them a dominating power so great that cannot without danger to the general welfare be entrusted to private individuals.

115. Such just demands and desires have nothing in them now which is inconsistent with Christian truth, and much less are they special to Socialism. Those who work solely toward such ends have, therefore, no reason to become socialists.

116. Yet let no one think that all the socialist groups or factions that are not communist have, without exception, recovered their senses to this extent either in fact or in name. For the most part they do not reject the class struggle or the aboli-

tion of ownership, but only in some degree modify them. Now if these principles are modified and to some extent erased from the program, the question arises, or rather is raised without warrant by some, whether the principles of Christian truth cannot perhaps be also modified to some degree and be tempered so as to meet Socialism half-way and, as it were, by a middle course, come to agreement with it. There are some allured by the foolish hope that socialists in this way will be drawn to us. A vain hope! Those who want to be apostles among socialists ought to profess Christian truth whole and entire, openly and sincerely, and not connive at error in any way. If they truly wish to be heralds of the Gospel, let them above all strive to show to socialists that socialist claims, so far as they are just, are far more strongly supported by the principles of Christian faith and much more effectively promoted through the power of Christian charity.

117. But what if Socialism has really been so tempered and modified as to the class struggle and private ownership that there is in it no longer anything to be censured on these points? Has it thereby renounced its contradictory nature to the Christian religion? This is the question that holds many minds in suspense. And numerous are the Catholics who, although they clearly understand that Christian principles can never be abandoned or diminished seem to turn their eyes to the Holy See and earnestly beseech Us to decide whether this form of Socialism has so far recovered from false doctrines that it can be accepted without the sacrifice of any Christian principle and in a certain sense be baptized. That We, in keeping with Our fatherly solicitude, may answer their petitions, We make this pronouncement: Whether considered as a doctrine, or an historical fact, or a movement, Socialism, if it remains truly Socialism, even after it has yielded to truth and justice on the points which we have mentioned, cannot be reconciled with the teachings of the Catholic Church because its concept of society itself is utterly foreign to Christian truth.

118. For, according to Christian teaching, man, endowed with a social nature, is placed on this earth so that by leading a life in society and under an authority ordained of God he may fully cultivate and develop all his faculties unto the praise and

glory of his Creator; and that by faithfully fulfilling the duties of his craft or other calling he may obtain for himself temporal and at the same time eternal happiness. Socialism, on the other hand, wholly ignoring and indifferent to this sublime end of both man and society, affirms that human association has been instituted for the sake of material advantage alone.

119. Because of the fact that goods are produced more efficiently by a suitable division of labor than by the scattered efforts of individuals, socialists infer that economic activity, only the material ends of which enter into their thinking, ought of necessity to be carried on socially. Because of this necessity, they hold that men are obliged, with respect to the producing of goods, to surrender and subject themselves entirely to society. Indeed, possession of the greatest possible supply of things that serve the advantages of this life is considered of such great importance that the higher goods of man, liberty not excepted, must take a secondary place and even be sacrificed to the demands of the most efficient production of goods. This damage to human dignity, undergone in the "socialized" process of production, will be easily offset, they say, by the abundance of socially produced goods which will pour out in profusion to individuals to be used freely at their pleasure for comforts and cultural development. Society, therefore, as Socialism conceives it, can on the one hand neither exist nor be thought of without an obviously excessive use of force; on the other hand, it fosters a liberty no less false, since there is no place in it for social authority, which rests not on temporal and material advantages but descends from God alone, the Creator and last end of all things.

120. If Socialism, like all errors, contains some truth (which, moreover, the Supreme Pontiffs have never denied), it is based nevertheless on a theory of human society peculiar to itself and irreconcilable with true Christianity. Religious socialism, Christian socialism, are contradictory terms; no one can be at the same time a good Catholic and a true socialist.

121. All these admonitions which have been renewed and confirmed by Our solemn authority must likewise be applied to a certain new kind of socialist activity, hitherto little known but now carried on among many socialist groups. It devotes itself

above all to the training of the mind and character. Under the guise of affection it tries in particular to attract children of tender age and win them to itself, although it also embraces the whole population in its scope in order finally to produce true socialists who would shape human society to the tenets of Socialism.

122. Since in Our Encyclical, *The Christian Education of Youth,* We have fully taught the principles that Christian education insists on and the ends it pursues, the contradiction between these principles and ends the activities and aims of this socialism that is pervading morality and culture is so clear and evident that no demonstration is required here. But they seem to ignore or underestimate the grave dangers that it carries with it who think it of no importance courageously and zealously to resist them according to the gravity of the situation. It belongs to Our Pastoral Office to warn these persons of the grave and imminent evil: let all remember that Liberalism is the father of this Socialism that is pervading morality and culture and that Bolshevism will be its heir.

123. Accordingly, Venerable Brethren, you can well understand with what great sorrow We observe that not a few of Our sons, in certain regions especially, although We cannot be convinced that they have given up the true faith and right will, have deserted the camp of the Church and gone over to the ranks of Socialism, some to glory openly in the name of socialist and to profess socialist doctrines, others through thoughtlessness or even, almost against their wills to join associations which are socialist by profession or in fact.

124. In the anxiety of Our paternal solicitude, We give Ourselves to reflection and try to discover how it could happen that they should go so far astray and We seem to hear what many of them answer and plead in excuse: The Church and those proclaiming attachment to the Church favor the rich, neglect the workers and have no concern for them; therefore, to look after themselves they had to join the ranks of socialism.

125. It is certainly most lamentable, Venerable Brethren, that there have been, nay, that even now there are men who, although professing to be Catholics, are almost completely unmindful of that sublime law of justice and charity that binds

us not only to render to everyone what is his but to succor brothers in need as Christ the Lord Himself, and—what is worse—out of greed for gain do not scruple to exploit the workers. Even more, there are men who abuse religion itself, and under its name try to hide their unjust exactions in order to protect themselves from the manifestly just demands of the workers. The conduct of such We shall never cease to censure gravely. For they are the reason why the Church could, even though undeservedly, have the appearance of and be charged with taking the part of the rich and with being quite unmoved by the necessities and hardships of those who have been deprived, as it were, of their natural inheritance. The whole history of the Church plainly demonstrates that such appearances are unfounded and such charges unjust. The Encyclical itself, whose anniversary we are celebrating, is clearest proof that it is the height of injustice to hurl these calumnies and reproaches at the Church and her teaching.

126. Although pained by the injustice and downcast in fatherly sorrow, it is so far from Our thought to repulse or to disown children who have been miserably deceived and have strayed so far from the truth and salvation that We cannot but invite them with all possible solicitude to return to the maternal bosom of the Church. May they lend ready ears to Our voice, may they return whence they have left, to the home that is truly their Father's, and may they stand firm there where their own place is, in the ranks of those who, zealously following the admonitions which Leo promulgated and We have solemnly repeated, are striving to restore society according to the mind of the Church on the firmly established basis of social justice and social charity. And let them be convinced that nowhere, even on earth, can they find full happiness save with Him who, being rich, became poor for our sakes that through His poverty we might become rich, Who was poor and in labors from His youth, Who invited to Himself all that labor and are heavily burdened that He might refresh them fully in the love of His heart, and Who, lastly, without any respect for persons will require more of them to whom more has been given and "will render to everyone according to his conduct."

127. Yet, if we look into the matter more carefully and more thoroughly, we shall clearly perceive that, preceding this ardently desired social restoration, there must be a renewal of the Christian spirit, from which so many immersed in economic life have, far and wide, unhappily fallen away, lest all our efforts be wasted and our house be builded not on a rock but on shifting sand.

128. And so, Venerable Brethren and Beloved Sons, having surveyed the present economic system, We have found it laboring under the gravest of evils. We have also summoned Communism and Socialism again to judgment and have found all their forms, even the most modified, to wander far from the precepts of the Gospel.

129. "Wherefore," to use the words of our Predecessor, "if human society is to be healed, only a return to Christian life and institutions will heal it." For this alone can provide effective remedy for that excessive care for passing things that is the origin of all vices; and this alone can draw away men's eyes, fascinated by and wholly fixed on the changing things of the world, and raise them toward Heaven. Who would deny that human society is in most urgent need of this cure now?

130. Minds of all, it is true, are affected almost solely by temporal upheavals, disasters, and calamities. But if we examine things critically with Christian eyes, as we should, what are all these compared with the loss of souls? Yet it is not rash by any means to say that the whole scheme of social and economic life is now such as to put in the way of vast numbers of mankind most serious obstacles which prevent them from caring for the one thing necessary, namely, their eternal salvation.

131. We, made Shepherd and Protector by the Prince of Shepherds, Who Redeemed them by His Blood, of a truly innumerable flock, cannot hold back Our tears when contemplating this greatest of their dangers. Nay rather, fully mindful of Our pastoral office and with paternal solicitude, We are continually meditating on how We can help them; and We have summoned to Our aid the untiring zeal also of others who are concerned on grounds of justice or charity. For what will it profit men to become expert in more wisely using their wealth, even to gaining the whole world, if thereby they suffer the loss

of their souls? What will it profit to teach them sound principles of economic life if in unbridled and sordid greed they let themselves be swept away by their passion for property, so that "hearing the commandments of the Lord they do all things contrary."

132. The root and font of this defection in economic and social life from the Christian law, and of the consequent apostasy of great numbers of workers from the Catholic faith, are the disordered passions of the soul, the sad result of original sin which has so destroyed the wonderful harmony of man's faculties that, easily led astray by his evil desires, he is strongly incited to prefer the passing goods of this world to the lasting goods of Heaven. Hence arises that unquenchable thirst for riches and temporal goods, which has at all times impelled men to break God's laws and trample upon the rights of their neighbors, but which, on account of the present system of economic life, is laying far more numerous snares for human frailty. Since the instability of economic life, and especially of its structure, exacts of those engaged in it most intense and unceasing effort, some have become so hardened to the stings of conscience as to hold that they are allowed, in any manner whatsoever, to increase their profits and use means, fair or foul, to protect their hard-won wealth against sudden changes of fortune. The easy gains that a market unrestricted by any law opens to everybody attracts large numbers to buying and selling goods, and they, their one aim being to make quick profits with the least expenditure of work, raise or lower prices by their uncontrolled business dealings so rapidly according to their own caprice and greed that they nullify the wisest forecasts of producers. The laws passed to promote corporate business, while dividing and limiting the risk of business, have given occasion to the most sordid license. For We observe that consciences are little affected by this reduced obligation of accountability; that furthermore, by hiding under the shelter of a joint name, the worst of injustices and frauds are perpetrated; and that, too, directors of business companies, forgetful of their trust, betray the rights of those whose savings they have undertaken to administer. Lastly, We must not omit to mention those crafty men who, wholly unconcerned about any honest usefulness of their work,

do not scruple to stimulate the baser human desires and, when they are aroused, use them for their own profit.

133. Strict and watchful moral restraint enforced vigorously by governmental authority could have banished these enormous evils and even forestalled them; this restraint, however, has too often been sadly lacking. For since the seeds of a new form of economy were bursting forth just when the principles of rationalism had been implanted and rooted in many minds, there quickly developed a body of economic teaching far removed from the true moral law, and, as a result, completely free rein was given to human passions.

134. Thus it came to pass that many, much more than ever before, were solely concerned with increasing their wealth by any means whatsoever, and that in seeking their own selfish interests before everything else they had no conscience about committing even the gravest of crimes against others. Those first entering upon this broad way that leads to destruction easily found numerous imitators of their iniquity by the example of their manifest success, by their insolent display of wealth, by their ridiculing the conscience of others, who, as they said, were troubled by silly scruples, or lastly by crushing more conscientious competitors.

135. With the rulers of economic life abandoning the right road, it was easy for the rank and file of workers everywhere to rush headlong also into the same chasm; and all the more so, because very many managements treated their workers like mere tools, with no concern at all for their souls, without indeed even the least thought of spiritual things. Truly the mind shudders at the thought of the grave dangers to which the morals of workers (particularly younger workers) and the modesty of girls and women are exposed in modern factories; when we recall how often the present economic scheme, and particularly the shameful housing conditions, create obstacles to the family bond and normal family life; when we remember how many obstacles are put in the way of the proper observance of Sundays and Holy Days; and when we reflect upon the universal weakening of that truly Christian sense through which even rude and unlettered men were wont to value higher things, and upon its substitution by the single preoccupation of getting

in any way whatsoever one's daily bread. And thus bodily labor, which Divine Providence decreed to be performed, even after original sin, for the good at once of man's body and soul, is being everywhere changed into an instrument of perversion; for dead matter comes forth from the factory ennobled, while men there are corrupted and degraded.

136. No genuine cure can be furnished for this lamentable ruin of souls, which, so long as it continues, will frustrate all efforts to regenerate society, unless men return openly and sincerely to the teaching of the Gospel, to the precepts of Him Who alone has the words of everlasting life, words which will never pass away, even if Heaven and earth will pass away. All experts in social problems are seeking eagerly a structure so fashioned in accordance with the norms of reason that it can lead economic life back to sound and right order. But this order, which We Ourselves ardently long for and with all Our efforts promote, will be wholly defective and incomplete unless all the activities of men harmoniously unite to imitate and attain, insofar as it lies within human strength, the marvelous unity of the Divine plan. We mean that perfect order which the Church with great force and power preaches and which right human reason itself demands, that all things be directed to God as the first and supreme end of all created activity, and that all created good under God be considered as mere instruments to be used only insofar as they conduce to the attainment of the supreme end. Nor is it to be thought that gainful occupations are thereby belittled or judged less consonant with human dignity; on the contrary, we are taught to recognize in them with reverence the manifest will of the Divine Creator Who placed man upon the earth to work it and use it in a multitude of ways for his needs. Those who are engaged in producing goods, therefore, are not forbidden to increase their fortune in a just and lawful manner; for it is only fair that he who renders service to the community and makes it richer should also, through the increased wealth of the community, be made richer himself according to his position, provided that all these things be sought with due respect for the laws of God and without impairing the rights of others and that they be employed in accordance with faith and right reason. If these principles are

observed by every one, everywhere, and always, not only the production and acquisition of goods but also the use of wealth, which now is seen to be so often contrary to right order, will be brought back soon within the bounds of equity and just distribution. The sordid love of wealth, which is the shame and great sin of our age, will be opposed in actual fact by the gentle yet effective law of Christian moderation which commands man to seek first the Kingdom of God and His justice, with the assurance that, by virtue of God's kindness and unfailing promise, temporal goods also, insofar as he has need of them, shall be given him besides.

137. But in effecting all this, the law of charity, "which is the bond of perfection," must always take a leading role. How completely deceived, therefore, are those rash reformers who concern themselves with the enforcement of justice alone—and this, commutative justice—and in their pride reject the assistance of charity! Admittedly, no vicarious charity can substitute for justice which is due as an obligation and is wrongfully denied. Yet even supposing that everyone should finally receive all that is due him, the widest field for charity will always remain open. For justice alone can, if faithfully observed, remove the causes of social conflict but can never bring about union of minds and hearts. Indeed all the institutions for the establishment of peace and the promotion of mutual help among men, however perfect these may seem, have the principal foundation of their stability in the mutual bond of minds and hearts whereby the members are united with one another. If this bond is lacking, the best of regulations come to naught, as we have learned by too frequent experience. And so, then only will true cooperation be possible for a single common good when the constituent parts of society deeply feel themselves members of one great family and children of the same Heavenly Father; nay, that they are one body in Christ, "but severally members one of another," so that "if one member suffers anything, all the members suffer with it." For then the rich and others in positions of power will change their former indifference toward their poorer brothers into a solicitous and active love, listen with kindliness to their just demands, and freely forgive their possible mistakes and faults. And the workers, sincerely putting

aside every feeling of hatred or envy which the promoters of social conflict so cunningly exploit, will not only accept without rancor the place in human society assigned them by Divine Providence but rather will hold it in esteem, knowing well that every one according to his function and duty is toiling usefully and honorably for the common good and is following closely in the footsteps of Him Who, being in the form of God, willed to be a carpenter among men and be known as the son of a carpenter.

138. Therefore, out of this new diffusion throughout the world of the spirit of the Gospel, which is the spirit of Christian moderation and universal charity, We are confident there will come that longed-for and full restoration of human society in Christ, and that "Peace of Christ in the Kingdom of Christ," to accomplish which, from the very beginning of Our Pontificate, We firmly determined and resolved within Our heart to devote all Our care and all Our pastoral solicitude; and toward this same highly important and most necessary end now, you also, Venerable Brethren who with Us rule the Church of God under the mandate of the Holy Ghost, are earnestly toiling with wholly praiseworthy zeal in all parts of the world, even in the regions of the holy missions to the infidels. Let well merited acclamations of praise be bestowed upon you and at the same time upon all those, both clergy and laity, who We rejoice to see, are daily participating and valiantly helping in this same great work, Our beloved sons engaged in Catholic Action, who with a singular zeal are undertaking with Us the solution of the social problem insofar as by virtue of her divine institution this is proper to and devolves upon the Church. All these We urge in the Lord, again and again, to spare no labors and let no difficulties conquer them, but rather to become day by day more courageous and more valiant. Arduous indeed is the task which We propose to them, for We know well that on both sides, both among the upper and the lower classes of society, there are many obstacles and barriers to be overcome. Let them not, however, lose heart; to face bitter combats is a mark of Christians, and to endure grave labors to the end is a mark of them who, as good soldiers of Christ, follow Him closely.

139. Relying therefore solely on the all-powerful aid of Him "Who wishes all men to be saved," let us strive with all our strength to help those unhappy souls who have turned from God and, drawing them away from the temporal cares in which they are too deeply immersed, let us teach them to aspire with confidence to the things that are eternal. Sometimes this will be achieved much more easily than seems possible at first sight to expect. For if wonderful spiritual forces lie hidden, like sparks beneath ashes, within the secret recesses of even the most abandoned man—certain proof that his soul is naturally Christian—, how much the more in the hearts of those many upon many who have been led into error rather through ignorance or environment.

140. Moreover, the ranks of the workers themselves are already giving happy and promising signs of a social reconstruction. To Our soul's great joy, We see in these ranks also the massed companies of young workers, who are receiving the counsel of Divine Grace with willing ears and striving with marvelous zeal to gain their comrades for Christ. No less praise must be accorded to the leaders of workers' organizations who, disregarding their own personal advantage and concerned solely about the good of their fellow members, are striving prudently to harmonize the just demands of their members with the prosperity of their whole occupation and also to promote these demands, and who do not let themselves be deterred from so noble a service by any obstacle or suspicion. Also, as anyone may see, many young men, who by reason of their talent or wealth will soon occupy high places among the leaders of society, are studying social problems with deeper interest, and they arouse the joyful hope that they will dedicate themselves wholly to the restoration of society.

141. The present state of affairs, Venerable Brethren, clearly indicates the way in which We ought to proceed. For We are now confronted, as more than once before in the history of the Church, with a world that in large part has almost fallen back into paganism. That these whole classes of men may be brought back to Christ Whom they have denied, we must recruit and train from among them, themselves, auxiliary soldiers of the Church who know them well and their minds and

wishes, and can reach their hearts with a tender brotherly love. The first and immediate apostles to the workers ought to be workers; the apostles to those who follow industry and trade ought to be from among them themselves.

142. It is chiefly your duty, Venerable Brethren, and of your clergy, to search diligently for these lay apostles both of workers and of employers, to select them with prudence, and to train and instruct them properly. A difficult task, certainly, is thus imposed on priests, and to meet it, all who are growing up as the hope of the Church, must be duly prepared by an intensive study of the social question. Especially is it necessary that those whom you intend to assign in particular to this work should demonstrate that they are men possessed of the keenest sense of justice, who will resist with true manly courage the dishonest demands or the unjust acts of anyone, who will excel in the prudence and judgment which avoids every extreme, and, above all, who will be deeply permeated by the charity of Christ, which alone has the power to subdue firmly but gently the hearts and wills of men to the laws of justice and equity. Upon this road so often tried by happy experience, there is no reason why we should hesitate to go forward with all speed.

143. These Our Beloved Sons who are chosen for so great a work, We earnestly exhort in the Lord to give themselves wholly to the training of the men committed to their care, and in the discharge of this eminently priestly and apostolic duty to make proper use of the resources of Christian education by teaching youth, forming Christian organizations, and founding study groups guided by principles in harmony with the Faith. But above all, let them hold in high esteem and assiduously employ for the good of their disciples that most valuable means of both personal and social restoration which, as We taught in Our Encyclical, *Mens Nostra,* is to be found in the Spiritual Exercises. In that Letter We expressly mentioned and warmly recommended not only the Spiritual Exercises for all the laity, but also the highly beneficial Workers' Retreats. For in that school of the spirit, not only are the best of Christians developed but true apostles also are trained for every condition of life and are enkindled with the fire of the heart of Christ.

From this school they will go forth as did the Apostles from the Upper Room of Jerusalem, strong in faith, endowed with an invincible steadfastness in persecution, burning with zeal, interested solely in spreading everywhere the Kingdom of Christ.

144. Certainly there is the greatest need now of such valiant soldiers of Christ who will work with all their strength to keep the human family safe from the dire ruin into which it would be plunged were the teachings of the Gospel to be flouted, and that order of things permitted to prevail which tramples underfoot no less the laws of nature than those of God. The Church of Christ, built upon an unshakable rock, has nothing to fear for herself, as she knows for a certainty that the gates of hell shall never prevail against her. Rather, she knows full well, through the experience of many centuries, that she is wont to come forth from the most violent storms stronger than ever and adorned with new triumphs. Yet her maternal heart cannot but be moved by the countless evils with which so many thousands would be afflicted during storms of this kind, and above all by the consequent enormous injury to spiritual life which would work eternal ruin to so many souls redeemed by the Blood of Jesus Christ.

145. To ward off such great evils from human society nothing, therefore, is to be left untried; to this end may all our labors turn, to this all our energies, to this our fervent and unremitting prayers to God! For with the assistance of Divine Grace the fate of the human family rests in our hands.

146. Venerable Brethren and Beloved Sons, let us not permit the children of this world to appear wiser in their generation than we who by the Divine Goodness are the children of the light. We find them, indeed, selecting and training with the greatest shrewdness alert and resolute devotees who spread their errors ever wider day by day through all classes of men and in every part of the world. And whenever they undertake to attack the Church of Christ more violently, We see them put aside their internal quarrels, assembling in full harmony in a single battle line with a completely united effort, and work to achieve their common purpose.

147. Surely there is not one that does not know how many and how great are the works that the tireless zeal of Catholics is striving everywhere to carry out, both for social and economic welfare as well as in the fields of education and religion. But this admirable and unremitting activity not infrequently shows less effectiveness because of the dispersion of its energies in too many different directions. Therefore, let all men of good will stand united, all who under the Shepherds of the Church wish to fight this good and peaceful battle of Christ; and under the leadership and teaching guidance of the Church let all strive according to the talent, powers, and position of each to contribute something to the Christian reconstruction of human society which Leo XIII inaugurated through his immortal Encyclical, *On the Condition of Workers,* seeking not themselves and their own interests, but those of Jesus Christ; not trying to press at all costs their own counsels, but ready to sacrifice them, however excellent, if the greater common good should seem to require it, so that in all and above all Christ may reign, Christ may command, to Whom be "honor and glory and dominion forever and ever."

148. That this may happily come to pass, to all of you, Venerable Brethren and Beloved Children, who are members of the vast Catholic family entrusted to Us, but with the especial affection of Our heart to workers and to all others engaged in manual occupations, committed to us more urgently by Divine Providence, and to Christian employers and managements, with paternal love We impart the Apostolic Benediction.

149. Given at Rome, at Saint Peter's, the fifteenth day of May, in the year 1931, the tenth year of Our Pontificate.

Dorothy Day

1898-

It is difficult, for one who did not live them, to understand the decades of suffering and abuse experienced by the laboring classes of America during the first half of the twentieth century. Dorothy Day's autobiography, The Long Loneliness *(1952), takes the reader back into that unhappy period in our history and reveals the inhuman atmosphere in which the poor, the unemployed and the lower class workers were forced to dwell.*

Dorothy Day, born in Brooklyn Heights, New York City in 1898, lived through these difficult years in a most unusual way. Her father's employment as a sports journalist and editor in different cities of the United States exposed her to a variety of attitudes and social conditions. Besides New York, she lived in Berkeley and Oakland, California, and in Chicago, Illinois. The religious atmosphere of her youth was basically agnostic. As a teenager she became interested in and joined the Episcopal church. After completing high school in Chicago, she entered the University of Illinois in 1914. While there she joined the Socialist Party. The family returned to New York in 1916. There, Dorothy took an active role as a columnist with several Socialist and radical newspapers. In 1927 she had a daughter by her common-law husband, Forster Batterham. Contacts with Catholic friends had led Dorothy to the Catholic church. Her daughter, Tamar, was baptized in July 1927 and Dorothy herself entered the Church in December of the same year.

On May Day 1933, with the first issue of the Catholic Worker, *Dorothy Day's commitment to the social issues of America took a specific direction. The paper, for which she was co-publisher, addressed the major social questions of the day—unemployment, poverty, racism, war. But the poor, for whose cause the paper was published, expected more. They wanted food, clothing and housing. Dorothy and her fellow workers responded with St. Joseph's House of Hospitality and, during the 1930's, with at least thirty other hospitality houses.*

Dorothy traveled throughout the entire nation, speaking, writing, supporting strikers, encouraging labor movements. At times her unpopular stands earned her a short term in a House of Detention on the disagreement of individual members of the Catholic Hierarchy. Yet, quietly and gently she moved on, demonstrating how the layperson can and must channel religious convictions toward the society in which he or she dwells.

Persons such as Dorothy Day are integral to the process by which Christianity becomes relevant to a society. They are sensitive to the tragic aspects of the human condition, yet have the courage, talent and creativity not only not to be destroyed by what they see but also to take the steps necessary to ameliorate social conditions. They are not frightened nor paralyzed by injustice, poverty, hunger, and death. Such persons dwell mysteriously in time, anchored in the dynamism of true community that is answer to lonliness.

The reader will find this brief selection from The Long Loneliness *both disturbing and comforting, for it describes simply and directly some of the horrors of our own America only forty years ago, but then shows how dedicated humans can overcome all of this with Christian love.*

THE LONG LONELINESS

PART THREE

LOVE IS THE MEASURE

LABOUR

The *Catholic Worker*, as the name implied, was directed to the worker, but we used the word in its broadest sense, meaning those who worked with hand or brain, those who did physical, mental or spiritual work. But we thought primarily of the poor, the dispossessed, the exploited.

Every one of us who was attracted to the poor had a sense of guilt, of responsibility, a feeling that in some way we were living on the labor of others. The fact that we were born in a certain environment, were enabled to go to school, were endowed with the ability to compete with others and hold our own, that we had few physical disabilities—all these things marked us as the privileged in a way. We felt a respect for the poor and destitute as those nearest to God, as those chosen by Christ for His compassion. Christ lived among men. The great mystery of the Incarnation, which meant that God became man that man might become God, was a joy that made us want to kiss the earth in worship, because His feet once trod that same earth. It was a mystery that we as Catholics accepted, but there were also the facts of Christ's life, that He was born in a stable, that He did not come to be a temporal King, that He worked with His hands, spent the first years of His life in exile, and the rest of His early manhood in a crude carpenter shop in Nazareth. He fulfilled His religious duties in the synagogue and the temple. He trod the roads in His public life and the first men He called were fishermen, small owners of boats and nets. He was familiar with the migrant worker and the proletariat, and some of His parables dealt with them. He spoke of the living wage, not equal pay for equal work, in the parable of those who came at the first and the eleventh hour.

He died between two thieves because He would not be made an earthly King. He lived in an occupied country for thirty years without starting an underground movement or trying to get out from under a foreign power. His teaching transcended all the wisdom of the scribes and pharisees, and taught us the most effective means of living in this world while preparing for the next. And He directed His sublime words to the poorest of the poor, to the people who thronged the towns and followed after John the Baptist, who hung around, sick and poverty-stricken at the doors of rich men.

He had set us an example and the poor and destitute were the ones we wished to reach. The poor were the ones who had jobs of a sort, organized or unorganized, and those who were unemployed or on work-relief projects. The destitute were the men and women who came to us in the breadlines and we could do little with them but give what we had of food and clothing. Sin, sickness and death accounted for much of human misery. But aside from this, we did not feel that Christ meant we should remain silent in the face of injustice and accept it even though He said, "The poor ye shall always have with you."

In the first issue of the paper we dealt with Negro labor on the levees in the South, exploited as cheap labor by the War Department. We wrote of women and children in industry and the spread of unemployment. The second issue carried a story of a farmers' strike in the Midwest and the condition of restaurant workers in cities. In the third issue there were stories of textile strikes and child labor in that industry; the next month coal and milk strikes. In the sixth issue of the paper we were already combatting anti-Semitism. From then on, although we wanted to make our small eight-page tabloid a local paper, that is, covering the American scene, we could not ignore the issues abroad. They had their repercussions at home. We could not write about these issues without being drawn out on the streets on picket lines, and we found ourselves in 1935 with the Communists picketing the German consulate at the Battery.

It was not the first time we seemed to be collaborators. During the Ohrbach Department Store strike the year before I ran into old friends from the Communist group, but I felt then, and do now, that the fact that Communists made issue of Negro exploitation and labor trouble was no reason why we should stay out of the situation. "The truth is the truth," writes St. Thomas, "and proceeds from the Holy Ghost, no matter from whose lips it comes."

There was mass picketing every Saturday afternoon during the Ohrbach strike, and every Saturday the police drove up with patrol wagons and loaded the pickets into them with their banners and took them to jail. When we entered the dispute with our slogans drawn from the writings of the Popes regarding the condition of labor, the police around Union Square were taken aback and did not know what to do. It was as though they were arresting the Holy Father himself, one of them said, were they to load our pickets and their signs into their patrol wagons. The police contented themselves with giving us all injunctions. One seminarian who stood on the side lines and cheered was given an injunction too, which he cherished as a souvenir.

Our readers helped us when they responded to our call not to trade with a store which paid poor wages and forced workers to labor long hours, and we helped defeat the injunction, one of the usual weapons used by employers to defeat picketing, which was handed down against the strikers. Now there is the Taft-Hartley law.

At that time one of the big Catholic high schools in the city each month received a bundle of three thousand copies of our paper for their students. I had spoken there of the work for the poor and some of the students had worked with us. When we picketed the Mexican consulate to protest the religious persecution which was revived in 1934, the students came and joined us more than two thousand strong. We had set out, half a dozen of us, and, although we had printed an invitation in the paper, we did not expect such a hearty response. The police again were stunned at this demonstration, having met only with Communists in such mass demonstrations before. The students sang, marched and rejoiced in the fact that their pictures appeared on the front page of the *Daily News* the next morning.

Among other readers who joined us that day was a young mate on a Standard Oil tanker who said he first read our paper while sailing in the Gulf. From then on he visited the office between trips and contributed half his salary to the work. Other picketers were Margaret, our cook, and her baby, and my daughter. Most belligerent was a young woman who had been sent to us from a hospital after an unsuccessful operation for tumor on the brain. She was not too well informed as to issues and principles, and when one of the passers-by asked her what the picketing was about, she answered tartly, "None of your business."

She was one of those who liked to get out on the streets and sell the paper with Big Dan and a few others. There were many protests from the young intellectuals that these should seem to the public to represent the work. But they were certainly a part of it—"they belonged"—and they felt it and were fiercely loyal, though often they could make no answer for the faith that was in them.

The picketing of the Mexican consulate went well with the good Sisters who taught in a great Catholic high school, but when the students wanted to go on a picket line in a strike for the unionization of workers and better wages and hours, and were logical enough to extend their sympathy by boycotting the National Biscuit Company products and to inform their family grocers and delicatessens of this intention, then it was time for a stop. We were politely told that individuals could take the paper, but that the bundle order of three thousand must be canceled. There were too many people protesting against our activities with the students.

(On another occasion when I spoke to a high school group in Philadelphia, before I even returned to New York, a cancelation came in. "You must have done a good job down there," our circulation manager said grimly. "They used to take two thousand copies and now they've dropped them.")

Other readers who owned stock in N.B.C. sold their shares and informed the corporation. These acts helped settle the strike. The most spectacular help we gave in a strike was during the formation of the National Maritime Union. In May, 1936, the men appealed to us for help in housing and feeding some of the strikers, who came off the ships with Joe Curran in a spontaneous strike against not only the shipowners but also the old union leaders.

Dorothy Day

We had then just moved St. Joseph's house to 115 Mott Street and felt that we had plenty of room. Everyone camped out for a time while seamen occupied the rooms which they made into dormitories. There were about fifty of them altogether during the course of the next month or so, and a number of them became friends of the work.

There were O'Toole, a cook on the United States Lines, and Mike, a Portuguese engineer who carried copies of *The Catholic Worker* to Spain when he shipped out later, bringing us back copies of papers and magazines from Barcelona. This same friend brought us a bag full of earth from Mount Carmel after his ship had touched at the Holy Land. Once he asked me what I wanted from India, and I told him the kind of a spindle which Gandhi had sent to Chiang Kai-shek, as a gift and a warning, perhaps against United States industrialism. He and a shipmate searched in several Indian ports for what I wanted and finally found three spindles in Karachi which they brought to me. One was a metal hand spinner shaped like those shown in old pictures which could be carried about in a little box; the other two were most peculiar contraptions, one of them looking like a portable phonograph.

The seamen came and went and most of them we never saw again, but three remained for years and joined in our work. That first strike was called off, but in the fall, after the men built up their organization, the strike call went out again. For the duration of the strike we rented a store on Tenth Avenue and used it as a reading room and soup kitchen where no soup was served, but coffee and peanut butter and apple butter sandwiches. The men came in from picket lines and helped themselves to what they needed. They read, they talked, and they had time to think. Charlie O'Rourke, John Cort, Bill Callahan and a number of seamen kept the place open all day and most of the night. There was never any disorder; there were no maneuverings, no caucuses, no seeking of influence or power; it was simply a gesture of help, the disinterested help of brothers, inspired in great part by our tanker friend, Jim McGovern, who had written an article for the paper telling how he had been treated as a seaman in Russia and the kind of treatment these same men got here.

Jim was a college graduate, had fallen away from his early faith but regained it by reading Claudel. He was so painfully shy that he was no good at all in contacts with the rank and file. He went to sea because he loved it; he loved the ship he served and the responsibility it entailed. Perhaps there was much of romance and youth in his attitude. He wrote to us of the clubs in the Russian port, and how the men were treated as men, capable of appreciating lectures, concerts, dances and meetings with student groups. In this country, he said, the seamen were treated as the scum of the earth; port towns and the port districts in these towns were slums and water-front streets made up of taverns and pawnshops and houses of prostitution. He felt that the Russians treated their American comrades as though they were creatures of body and soul, made in the image and likeness of God (though atheism was an integral part of Marxism) and here in our professedly Christian country they were treated like beasts, and often became beasts because of this attitude.

Our headquarters were a tribute to the seaman's dignity as a man free to form association with his fellows, to have some share in the management of the enterprise in which he was engaged.

On another occasion, when the Borden Milk Company attempted to force a company union on their workers, *The Catholic Worker* took up their cause, called public attention to the use of gangsters and thugs to intimidate the drivers and urged our readers to boycott the company's products while unfair conditions prevailed. As a result of the story the company attacked *The Catholic Worker* in paid advertisements in the Brooklyn *Tablet* and the *Catholic News*.

Many times we have been asked why we spoke of *Catholic* workers, and so named the paper. Of course it was not only because we who were in charge of the work, who edited the paper, were all Catholics, but also because we wished to influence Catholics. They were our own, and we reacted sharply to the accusation that when it came to private morality the Catholics shone but when it came to social and political morality, they were often conscienceless. Also Catholics were the poor, and most of them had little ambition or hope of bettering their condition to the extent of achieving ownership of home or business, or further education for their children. They accepted things as they were with humility and looked for a better life to come. They thought, in other words, that God meant it to be so.

At the beginning of the organizing drive of the Committee (now the Congress) for Industrial Organization, I went to Pittsburgh to write about the work in the steel districts. Mary Heaton Vorse was there at the time and we stayed at Hotel Pitt together in the cheapest room available, at a dollar and a half a day. It was before we had the house of hospitality in Pittsburgh which now stands on the top of a hill in the Negro district. A student reader of the paper drove us around to all the little towns, talking of his soul, much to Mary's distress; she was especially distracted when he told of practicing penances on our Easton farm by going out at night and rolling in some brambles. He had no interest in the struggles of the workers—it was the spiritual side of our work which appealed to him—and he was driving us through all the complicated districts on either side of rivers not so much to help us, as to help himself. He wanted to talk to us about his problems. There was not the quiet and peace on such trips to make such talk very fruitful.

There had been the big strike in 1919 led by William Z. Foster, which Mary had covered, and she knew some of the old priests who had helped the people by turning the basements of their churches into relief centers. We went to see them, and we attended open-air meetings along the Monongahela and the Allegheny and Ohio Rivers, where we distributed papers.

On that visit Bishop Hugh Boyle said to me, "You can go into all the parishes in the diocese with my blessing, but half the pastors will throw you out." He meant that they did not have that social consciousness which I was seeking among Catholics and that they felt all organizations of workers were dominated by Communists and were a danger to be avoided.

Later in the big steel strikes in Chicago and Cleveland, when "Little Steel" fought it out with the workers, there was tragedy on the picket lines. In what came to be called the Memorial Day massacre, police shot down hundreds out on the prairies in front of the Republic Steel plants in South Chicago. Ten men died, and others were disabled for life. I had just visited their soup kitchens and strike headquarters; in addition to recognizing that the majority of the workers were Catholics, I also recognized an old friend, Elizabeth, the wife of Jack Johnstone, one of the Communist party leaders in this country. Elizabeth and Jack had brought me roast chicken and ginger ale one night as I lay sick with influenza in New York, and Elizabeth had taken care of Tamar for me so that I could go to Mass, and I had taken care of her young son. Elizabeth, whom I had last seen in New York, was there to write a pamphlet on "Women in Steel," a call to the wives and mothers to help their men organize. Her husband had been organizing in India, and they were accustomed to long separations during which both of them worked for the party. Elizabeth used to tease me by saying that it was due to me that she had become a member of the party and had met Jack, because I had obtained a job for her with the Anti-imperialist League, where I was working at the time.

Elizabeth in Chicago, Jack in India—these wives of Communists, dedicated to revolution as Rayna was! Rayna's husband had worked in the Philippines while she was in Hankow. They went where they were sent, had a sense of their world mission and accepted any hardship that it entailed. If I could only arouse Catholics to such zeal, with the spiritual weapons at their disposal, I thought! If they could only be induced to accept voluntary poverty as a principle, so that they would not fear the risk of losing job, of losing life itself. Organizing sometimes meant just that.

It was not only the Communists, however, who had this courage. One winter I had a speaking engagement in Kansas and my expenses were paid, which fact enabled me to go to Memphis and Arkansas to visit the Tenant Farmers' Union, which was then and is still headed by a Christian Socialist group. The headquarters were a few rooms in Memphis, where the organizers often slept on the floor because there was no money for rent other than that of the offices. Those days I spent with them I lived on sandwiches and coffee because there was no money to spend on regular meals either. We needed to save money for gas to take us around to the centers where dispossessed sharecroppers and tenant farmers were also camping out, homeless, in railroad stations, schools and churches. They were being evicted wholesale because of the purchase of huge tracts of land by northern insurance agencies. The picture has been shown in *Tobacco Road, In Dubious Battle* and *Grapes of Wrath*—pictures of such desolation and poverty and in the latter case of such courage that my heart was lifted again to hope and love and admiration that human beings could endure so much and yet have courage to go on and keep their vision of a more human life.

During that trip I saw men, women and children herded into little churches and wayside stations, camped out in tents, their household goods heaped about them, not one settlement but many—farmers with no land to farm, housewives with no homes. They tried with desperate hope to hold onto a pig or some chickens, bags of seed, some little beginnings of a new hold on life. It was a bitter winter and frame houses there are not built to withstand the cold as they are in the north. The people just endure it because the winter is short—accept it as part of the suffering of life.

I saw children ill, one old man dead in bed and not yet buried, mothers weeping with hunger and cold. I saw bullet holes in the frame churches, and their benches and pulpit smashed up and windows broken. Men had been kidnaped and beaten; men had been shot and wounded. The month after I left, one of the organizers was killed by a member of a masked band of vigilantes who were fighting the Tenant Farmers' Union.

There was so little one could do—empty one's pockets, give what one had, live on sandwiches with the organizers, and write, write to arouse the public conscience. I telegraphed Eleanor Roosevelt and she responded at once with an appeal to the governor for an investigation. The papers were full of the effrontery of a northern Catholic social worker, as they called me, who dared to pay a four-day visit and pass judgment on the economic situation of the state. The governor visited some of the encampments, and sarcastic remarks were made in some of the newspaper accounts about the pigs and chickens. "If they are starving, let them eat their stock," they wrote.

I spoke to meetings of the unemployed in California, to migrant workers, tenant farmers, steelworkers, stockyard workers, auto workers. The factory workers were the aristocrats of labor. Yet what a struggle they had!

There was that migrant worker I picked up when I drove in a borrowed car down through the long valley in California, writing about government aid to the agricultural workers. "Nothing I love so much as jest to get out in a field and chop cotton," he said wistfully.

There was that old Negro living in a little shack in Alabama where the rain fell through on the rags that covered him at night. While I talked to him a little boy ran up and gave him a bone and some pieces of cornbread; the old man was so excited talking to me and the priest who was with me that he dropped the bone on the ground and a hound dog started licking it. The little boy stood by him, pulling at his sleeve and crying. It was his dinner too, his only dinner, and it was being devoured by a dog. If the old man had more, the children would have less. And there was so little.

There was that little girl in Harrisburg, and another in Detroit, sent out by their parents to prostitute themselves on the street. While I talked to the family in Harrisburg, all of whom lived in one room, the little girl sat reading a tattered book, *Dorothy Vernon of Haddon Hall.*

There was Paul St. Marie, who was president of the first Ford local, a tool and die maker, with a wife and eight children. He suffered from unemployment, from discrimination when he was hired. He worked the graveyard shift from twelve to eight, walked a mile from gate to plant, and worked in the cold on stone floors. He fell ill with rheumatic fever at the age of forty-five and died. He knew poverty and insecurity and living on relief—he and his wife were heroic figures in the labor movement, thinking of their fellows more than of themselves. Paul took me around the auto plants and showed me what the assembly line meant. I met the men who were beaten to a pulp when they tried to distribute literature at plant gates, and I saw the unemployed who had fire hoses turned on them during an icy winter when they hung around the gates of the Ford plant looking for work.

"How close are you to the worker?" Pitirim Sorokin asked me when I was talking with him at Harvard. He himself was the son of a peasant woman and a migrant worker and was imprisoned three times under the Czars and three times under the Soviets. He too had suffered exile in the forests, hunger and imprisonment; he had lived under the sentence of death and was, through some miracle, and probably because of his doctrine of love in human behavior, allowed to go abroad. He had a right to ask such a question and it was a pertinent one.

Going around and seeing such sights is not enough. To help the organizers, to give what you have for relief, to pledge yourself to voluntary poverty for life so that you can share with your brothers is not enough. One must live with them, share with them their suffering too. Give up one's privacy, and mental and spiritual comforts as well as physical.

Our Detroit house of hospitality for women is named for St. Martha. We are always taking care of migrant families in that house, southern families who are lured to the North because they hear of the high wages paid. It is a house of eight large rooms, and each of the bedrooms has housed a family with children, but the congestion has meant that the husbands had to go to the men's house of hospitality named for St. Francis. Sometimes the families overflow into a front parlor and living room downstairs. The colored take care of the while children, and the white the colored, while the parents hunt for homes and jobs. Such an extreme of destitution makes all men brothers.

Yes, we have lived with the poor, with the workers, and we know them not just from the streets, or in mass meetings, but from years of living in the slums, in tenements, in our hospices in Washington, Baltimore, Philadelphia, Harrisburg, Pittsburgh, New York, Rochester, Boston, Worcester, Buffalo, Troy, Detroit, Cleveland, Toledo, Akron, St. Louis, Chicago, Milwaukee, Minneapolis, Seattle, San Francisco, Los Angeles, Oakland, even down into Houma, Louisiana where Father Jerome Drolet worked with Negroes and whites, with shrimp shellers, fishermen, longshoremen and seamen.

Just as the Church has gone out through its missionaries into the most obscure towns and villages, we have gone too. Sometimes our contacts have been through the Church and sometimes through readers of our paper, through union organizers or those who needed to be organized.

We have lived with the unemployed, the sick, the unemployables. The contrast between the worker who is organized and has his union, the fellowship of his own trade to give him strength, and those who have no organization and come in to us on a breadline is pitiable.

They are stripped then, not only of all earthly goods, but of spiritual goods, their sense of human dignity. When they are forced into line at municipal lodging houses, in clinics, in our houses of hospitality, they are then the truly destitute. Over and over again in our work, many young men and women who come as volunteers have not been able to endure it and have gone away. To think that we are forced by our own lack of room, our lack of funds, to perpetuate this shame, is heart-breaking.

"Is this what you meant by houses of hospitality," I asked Peter.

"At least it will arouse the conscience," he said.

Many left the work because they could see no use in this gesture of feeding the poor, and because of their own shame. But enduring this shame is part of our penance.

"All men are brothers." How often we hear this refrain, the rallying call that strikes a response in every human heart. These are the words of Christ, "Call no man master, for ye are all brothers." It is a revolutionary call which has even been put to music. The last movement of Beethoven's Ninth Symphony has that great refrain—"All men are brothers." Going to the people is the purest and best act in Christian tradition and revolutionary tradition and is the beginning of world brotherhood.

Never to be severed from the people, to set out always from the point of view of serving the people, not serving the interests of a small group or oneself. "To believe in the infinite creative power of the people," Mao Tse-tung, the secretary of the Communist party in China, wrote with religious fervor. And he said again in 1943, "The maxim 'three common men will make a genius' tells us that there is great creative power among the people and that there are thousands and thousands of genius-es among them. There are geniuses in every village, every city." It is almost another way of saying that we must and will find Christ in each and every man, when we look on them as brothers.

At a group meeting in New York, part of the Third Hour movement, made up of Catholics, Russian Orthodox, and Prot-estants of all denominations, a Socialist said to me that the gesture of going to the people was futile and that it had been tried in Russia and failed. We had a long discussion on the validity of such efforts to achieve brotherhood, and I kept repeating that the Christian point of view was to keep in mind the failure of the Cross. Then thinking I might be talking to someone with a Jewish background, I spoke of the natural order itself, how the seed must fall into the ground and die in order to bear fruit. In the labor movement every strike is considered a failure, a loss of wages and man power, and no one is ever convinced that understanding between employer and worker is any clearer or that gains have been made on either side; and yet in the long history of labor, certainly there has been a slow and steady bettering of conditions. Women no longer go down into the mines, little children are not fed into the mills. In the long view the efforts of the workers have achieved much.

At the close of the evening, I learned that I had been talking to Alexander Kerensky, one of the greatest failures in history.

My trips around the country were usually to visit our houses of hospitality, which were springing up everywhere, and also to speak at schools. I took advantage of these trips to cover strikes and the new organizational drive of the Congress of Industrial Organizations.

Father James G. Keller, head of the Christopher Movement, called me one day and said that Archbishop McNicholas would like to talk to me, so I took a train to Cincinnati. Usually I travel by bus in order to economize. But this time the Archbishop sent a ticket and I traveled comfortably. I spent the day with him and with several other bishops of the Midwest, discussing the condition of the unemployed and the strikes that were going on in the auto plants. We were served magnificently at the bishops' table but the Archbishop himself dined modestly on a few vegetables and milk. I could not help thinking, of course, of our breadlines, and our cramped quarters. It is not only the Archbishop's palace which is a contrast, but every rectory in our big cities, and even in country sections. Only in the mission fields is the rectory as poor as the homes of the workers round about. One can understand the idea of a functional society and the needs of doctors for cars and telephones and of the lawyer and teacher for books and space, but the ordinary family has need of space too for his little church which is his family.

For Christ Himself, housed in the tabernacles in the Church no magnificence is too great, but for the priest who serves Christ, and for the priesthood of the laity, no such magnificence, in the face of the hunger and homelessness of the world, can be understood.

And yet I do know too that if any bishop or archbishops started to take the poor into his palace, or moved out of his palace to live with the poor, he would be considered mad. And he would suffer the fate of the fool.

Bishops and priests may long to make that gesture, but their own humility no doubt restrains them. Some day may God put His hand upon them so unmistakably that they know they are called to this gesture, to this madness. We begin to see a little of it in Archbishop Stepinac, who told C. L. Sulzberger of the *New York Times* that he would not be other than where he was, in a prison cell, doing penance for the Church.

"The Church is the Cross on which Christ was crucified, and who can separate Christ from His cross," Guardini has written.

On that happy occasion when I enjoyed the day with the Archbishop, who, like so many others, lived in poverty in the midst of wealth, Father Keller and I listened to him read a pastoral letter he had just written. It was about the condition of capital and labor, and I felt it was a noble piece of writing. But Father Keller thought the archbishop was a trifle harsh to the rich.

That night when I discussed going to Detroit to cover the situation of the sit-down strikers in the Flint auto plants, the Archbishop urged me to go to them, to write about them. He had one of his priests reserve and pay for a Pullman berth for me so that I would be fresh the next day for my work.

It was a friendly and a happy day of talk about the needs of the workers and the poor. It made me unhappy when the Archbishop became so uneasy about *The Catholic Worker's* editorial position on the Spanish Civil War that he asked pastors in his diocese to discontinue getting it for their churches or schools, though he did not suggest that they cease taking it themselves.

On another occasion he issued a call in one of his public statements, for a mighty army of conscientious objectors if we embarked upon a war with Russia as an ally. Those of our associates around the country who swelled the ranks of the Catholic conscientious objectors looked ruefully on the anything-but-mighty army. They also felt that they were conscientious objectors for the same reason that they opposed the war in Spain, or class war or race war or imperialist war, not because Russia was our ally.

The Archbishop gave us three hundred dollars as a contribution toward our camp for conscientious objectors, and we deeply appreciated this first gesture of ecclesiastical friendship in our hitherto unheard-of position. Before he died he sent us his blessing again.

But I am trying to write about the bishops in connection with the labor movement. Archbishop Schrembs of Cleveland was always friendly when I visited him at those times I was invited to speak at congresses and social-action meetings. I visited strike headquarters during the Little Steel strike and talked with the men. They were worn with the protracted conflict and worried about losing the homes they had managed to buy after years of saving, and the food and clothing needed for their children if they lost both strike and job as had happened on other occasions in the past. The next day when I visited Archbishop Schrembs he told me that during the morning a representative of Associated Industries had called on him and told him of my presence at strike headquarters the day before.

In New York the Chancery office had also been informed of our activities, and when a priest came to see us in our Tenth Avenue headquarters during the seamen's strike the visit was immediately reported. This happened often enought to indicate to me that there were spies from the employers among the strikers and that the employers felt that the Church was on their side in any industrial dispute. The worker present at Mass was in the eyes of bishop and priest just like any member of Knights of Columbus or Holy Name Society, but as soon as he went on strike he became a dangerous radical, and the publicity he got linked him with saboteurs and Communists.

We met other bishops who visited our offices and told us about the work in their dioceses, in the co-operative movement, parish credit unions, circulating libraries and other activities among the laity. They sat down to eat with us—Bishop O'Hara, Bishop Waters, Bishop Busch—and abbots of monasteries, who are also princes of the Church, came too. Every six months when we sent out our appeals, there were a number of bishops who always responded, even those who disagreed so strongly on some aspects of our work that they would not permit meetings in their dioceses and certainly not houses of hospitality. However, some houses opened up not specifically associated with *The Catholic Worker,* but owing their inspiration to it. Those who run these houses feel themselves to be children of the movement since they work with the poor and dispossessed. However, they do not hold to the distributist or anarchist or pacifist positions that are taken editorially in *The Catholic Worker.* They leave the discussion of these issues to others, and do the immediate work of showing their love for their brothers in the simple practical method of the corporal works of mercy.

The spiritual works of mercy include enlightening the ignorant, rebuking the sinner, consoling the afflicted, as well as bearing wrongs patiently, and we have always classed picket lines and the distribution of literature among these works.

During the course of writing about labor and capital, we began a study club at the Mott Street headquarters. It was an outgrowth of the seamen's strike and was started by John Cort, a young Harvard graduate who was working with us at the time, and Martin Wersing, a union official in the electrical workers. Father John Monaghan and a group of other union men joined with them in forming what they called the Association of Catholic Trade Unionists. After it had obtained its start under our auspices, the group moved to Canal Street so that they would have room for their meetings and could handle the avalanche of inquiry which came to them, once they were under way.

Their aim and endeavor was to assist the worker to organize and to enlighten the Catholic in the existing unions as to the teachings of the Popes in regard to labor. They set out at once to oppose the Communist and gangster elements (two separate problems) in the longshoreman and other unions, and their policy came into conflict with ours.

As Peter pointed out, ours was a long-range problem, looking for ownership by the workers of the means of production, the abolition of the assembly line, decentralized factories, the restoration of crafts and ownership of property. This meant, of course, an accent on the agrarian and rural aspects of our economy and a changing of emphasis from the city to the land.

The immediate job at hand was enough for the Association. They disagreed too with our indiscriminate help in strikes where there was strong Communist influence, and our loss of the opportunity to get our own men into positions of vantage in order to influence others.

Peter, however, talked about Christ's technique, of working from the bottom and with the few, of self-discipline and self-organization, of sacrifice rather than enlightened self-interest, and of course, of the synthesis of cult, culture and cultivation. How he loved the roll of that phrase. Once when he spoke to the seamen at the Tenth Avenue strike headquarters he attacked communism, but it was by reviewing a book by André Gide and by talking of his disillusionment with the Russian regime. I supposed he considered the meeting from the standpoint of culture, most of the seamen never having heard of André Gide, or if they had, only of the unsavory aspects of his erotic life. Sometimes we used to sigh over Peter's idea as to what would be dynamic thought for the workers.

There is so much more to the Catholic Worker Movement than labor and capital. It is people who are important, not the masses. When I read Pope Pius XII's Christmas message, in which he distinguished between the masses and the people, I almost wished I had named our publication *The People*, instead of *The Catholic Worker*.

We published many heavy articles on capital and labor, on strikes and labor conditions, on the assembly line and all the other evils of industrialism. But it was a whole picture we were presenting of man and his destiny and so we emphasized less, as the years went by, the organized-labor aspect of the paper.

It has been said that it was *The Catholic Worker* and its stories of poverty and exploitation that aroused the priests to start labor schools, go out on picket lines, take sides in strikes with the worker, and that brought about an emphasis on the need to study sociology in the seminaries.

And many a priest who afterward became famous for his interest in labor felt that we had in a way deserted the field, had left the cause of the union man. Bishops and priests appearing on the platforms of the A.F. of L. and C.I.O. conventions felt that we had departed from our original intention and undertaken work in the philosophical and theological fields that might better have been left to the clergy. The discussion of the morality of modern war, for instance, and application of moral principle in specific conflicts. Labor leaders themselves felt that in our judgment of war, we judged them also for working in the gigantic armaments race, as indeed we did. Ours is indeed an unpopular front.

When we began our work there were thirteen million unemployed. The greatest problem of the day was the problem of work and the machine.

The state entered in to solve these problems by dole and work relief, by setting up so many bureaus that we were swamped with initials. NIRA gave plan to NRA, and as NRA was declared unconstitutional another organization, another administration was set up. The problem of the modern state loomed up as never before in American life. The Communists, stealing our American thunder, clamored on the one hand for relief and on the other set up Jeffersonian schools of democracy.

Peter also quoted Jefferson—"He governs best who governs least." One of his criticisms of labor was that it was aiding in the creation of the Welfare State, the Servile State, instead of aiming for the ownership of the means of production and acceptance of the responsibility that it entailed.

COMMUNITY

One of the great German Protestant theologians said after the end of the last war that what the world needed was community and liturgy.

The desire for liturgy, and I suppose he meant sacrifice, worship, a sense of reverence, is being awakened in great masses of people throughout the world by the new revolutionary leaders.

A sense of individual worth and dignity is the first result of the call made on them to enlist their physical and spiritual capacities in the struggle for a life more in keeping with the dignity of man. One might almost say that the need to worship grows in them with the sense of reverence, so that the sad result is giant-sized posters of Lenin and Stalin, Tito and Mao. The dictator becomes divine.

We had a mad friend once, a Jewish worker from the East Side, who wore a rosary around his neck and came to us reciting the Psalms in Hebrew. He stayed with us for weeks at a time, for although mad, he had the gentleness of St. Francis. He helped Hergenhan in our garden on Staten Island, and he liked to walk around in his bare feet. "I can feel things growing," he said. "I look at the little plants, and I draw them up out of the earth with the power of love in my eyes."

He sat at the table with us once and held up a piece of dark rye bread which he was eating. "It is the black bread of the poor. It is Russian Jewish bread. It is the flesh of Lenin. Lenin held bread up to the people and he said, 'This is my body, broken for you.' So they worship Lenin. He brought them bread."

There is nothing lukewarm about such worship, nothing tepid. It is the crying out of a great hunger. One thinks of the words of Ezekiel, condemning the shepherds who did not feed their sheep. I know that my college friend Rayna never heard the word of God preached and she never met a Christian. The failure is ours, and that of the shepherds.

Peter was not so much interested in labor as he was in work and community. He felt that as long as men sought jobs and wages, and accepted the assembly line and the material comforts the factory system brought, they would not think in terms of community, except for that which the union brought them. They might be gathered together in time of crisis, during strikes, but would they listen to what he said about the need for ownership and responsibility?

Every talk of Peter's about the social order led to the land. He spoke always as a peasant, but as a practical one. He knew the craving of the human heart for a toehold on the land, for a home of one's own, but he also knew how impossible it was to attain it except through community, through men banding together in farming communes to live to a certain extent in common, work together, own machinery together, start schools together.

He held the collective farms in Palestine up for our consideration. Since Peter's death, Martin Buber's book, *Paths in Utopia,* has told of the experiments in Israel, and Thomas Sugrue has written a book, *Watch for the Morning,* on these great adventures in building up a place in the desert for a dispossessed people. Claire Huchet Bishop has written about the communities in Europe in her books, *France Alive* and *All Things Common,* showing how men can become owners of the means of production and build up a community of work together.

But these books were not written when Peter started to talk, and he knew that people were not ready to listen. He was a prophet and met the ususal fate of the prophet. The work of the co-operatives in Nova Scotia had attracted the attention of the world, but Father Jimmy Tomkins said, "People must get down to rock bottom before they have the vision and the desperate courage to work along these lines and to overcome their natural individualism."

Community—that was the social answer to the long loneliness. That was one of the attractions of religious life and why couldn't lay people share in it? Not just the basic community of the family, but also a community of families, with a combination of private and communal property. This could be a farming commune, a continuation of the agronomic university Peter spoke of as a part of the program we were to work for. Peter had vision and we all delighted in these ideas.

"But not a five-year plan," he would say. He did not believe in blueprints or a planned economy. Things grow organically.

A parish priest in Canada, Father John McGoey, had a vision of a community of families. From a poor parish in Toronto, he inspired a number of families who were jobless and living on relief to band together and study the problems of getting back to the land. He secured a tract of land for them, obtained the co-operation of the city's relief bureau, and moved the families out of the slums. A school for the children was started, a weaving project set up, gardens put in, small animals cared for, and the families got on their feet again. With the ending of the depression and the beginning of preparations for war, some of them moved back to the factory neighborhoods again.

Monsignor Luigi Ligutti, head of the Catholic Rural Life Conference, did the same with a group of unemployed miners in Iowa. He obtained land and funds from the government, and the settlement he established has prospered. In both these cases government help was needed. Peter did not wish to turn to the government for funds. "He who is a pensioner of the state is a slave of the state," he felt. Neither Father McGoey nor Monsignor Liguitti felt enslaved, but they did admit there had been red tape and many headaches involved in getting the help needed.

Peter's plan was that groups should borrow from mutual-aid credit unions in the parish to start what he first liked to call agronomic universities, where the worker could become a scholar and the scholar a worker. Or he wanted people to give the land and money. He always spoke of giving. Those who had land and tools should give. Those who had capital should give. Those who had labor should give that. "Love is an exchange of gifts," St. Ignatius had said. It was in these simple, practical, down-to-earth ways that people could show their love for each other. If the love was not there in the beginning, but only the need, such gifts made love grow.

"To make love." Peter liked to study phrases, and to use them as though they were newly discovered. (*Honest to God* was the title of one of his series of essays.)

The strangeness of the phrase "to make love" strikes me now and reminds me of that aphorism of St. John of the Cross, "Where there is no love, put love and you will find love." I've thought of it and followed it many times these eighteen years of community life.

Peter set much store on labor as a prime requisite for a new order. "Work, not wages." That was an I.W.W. slogan and a Communist slogan too, and Peter liked it. During the days of the depression the Communists and our Catholic Workers often collided in street demonstrations. *Down with Chiang Kai-Shek!* said one of their posters, when we were demonstrating against evictions. *Work, not Wages* was another picket sign, when what the Communists were demanding was more relief, unemployment insurance, and every other benefit they could get from the state. Packed in that one tight little phrase is all the dynamite of revolution. Men wanted work more than they wanted bread, and they wanted to be responsible for their work, which meant ownership.

I know that as this is read, it will be questioned. "This is how people should be, but are they? Give them relief checks and they will sit back and do nothing for the rest of their days. When they do have jobs they see how much they can get away with in giving as little labor as possible for the highest pay they can get." One hears these complaints from householders and even from heads of religious orders, who complain that postulants enter without the slightest knowledge of any skills that will help the order. And girls do not know how to cook or sew or keep house. With the lack of knowledge of how to work has come a failure in physical strength too.

Peter was no dreamer but knew men as they were. That is why he spoke so much of the need for a philosophy of work. Once they had that, once their desires were changed, half the battle was won. To make men desire poverty and hard work, that was the problem. It would take example, and the grace of God, to do it.

The word philosophy is bandied around a great deal today. John Cogley, who formerly headed our house of hospitality in Chicago and is now an editor of *The Commonweal*, told us about one of his professors at Fribourg who lectured on Russian philosophy. "In all their schools, whether of law, medicine, art, engineering or agriculture, philosophy is required study," he said. And that is right, because in order to achieve integration, the whole man, there must be an underlying philosophy that directs and lends meaning to his life.

During World War II, a French Communist wrote an article reprinted in the *New Masses* which emphasized the need for a Communist in the Sorbonne or any other college to teach history or science from a Communist point of view. The party never misses the dominant importance of philosophy.

Peter's Christian philosophy of work was this. God is our creator. God made us in His image and likeness. Therefore we are creators. He gave us a garden to till and cultivate. We become co-creators by our responsible acts, whether in bringing forth children, or producing food, furniture or clothing. The joy of creativeness should be ours.

But because of the Fall the curse is laid on us of having to earn our bread by the sweat of our brows, in labor. St. Paul said that since the Fall nature itself travaileth and groaneth. So man has to contend with fallen nature in the beasts and in the earth as well as in himself. But when he overcomes the obstacles, he attains again to the joy of creativity. Work is not then all pain and drudgery.

All of us know these things instinctively, like Tom Sawyer whose example led others to covet his whitewashing job—or the workman, healthy tired, after a good day's toil like Levin reaping with the peasants in *Anna Karenina*.

Craftsmen, not assembly-line workers, know this physical, but not nervous, fatigue and the joy of rest after labor. Peter was never a craftsman but he was an unskilled laborer who knew how to use an ax, a pick and a shovel, how to break rocks and mend roads.

Peter and his slogans! "Fire the bosses" meant "Call no man master, for all ye are brothers." It meant "Bear ye one another's burdens."

"Eat what you raise and raise what you eat" meant that you ate the things indigenous to the New York climate, such as tomatoes, not oranges; honey, not sugar, etc. We used to tease him because he drank coffee, chocolate or tea, but "he ate what was set before him." Had he been a young husband raising a family he would have done without tea, or coffee, as indeed such a disciple as Larry Heaney did. Larry was in charge of the Holy Family House in Milwaukee until he married and was able with another Catholic Worker family to buy a fine farm in Missouri.

Peter liked to talk about the four-hour day. Four hours for work, four hours for study and discussion; but he didn't practice it. Knowing that people could not fit into neat categories he would seize upon them whenever he could for discussion and indoctrination.

Everyone, of course, wished to indoctrinate. They no sooner had a message than they wished to give it. Ideas which burst upon them like a flood of light made the young people want to get out and change the world.

We always had the war of the worker and scholar when the former accused the latter of side-stepping work. The joke went around the country that the Catholic Worker crowd lived on lettuce one bright summer of discussion at Maryfarm when students from ten universities around the country arrived for long visits. One young politician active in public life in Ohio, spent months with Peter and then returned to the Midwest to teach, eventually starting the Christ the King Center for Men at Herman, Pennsylvania.

Farms like ours began to dot the country. In Aptos, California, in Cape May, New Jersey, in Upton, Massachusetts, in Avon, Ohio, in South Lyon, Michigan—a dozen sprang up as Catholic Worker associates. Many others consisted of young married groups trying to restore the idea of community.

Some were started and abandoned as too isolated, or because of lack of water, lack of funds, lack of people who knew how to work. Men found out the reasons for cities and relief rolls when they ventured onto the land and sought to do manual labor. How to work in industry so as not to compromise oneself and yet earn a living for a family?

The problem did not really become acute until the family entered in. The family thought Peter's farming commune idea was solely for them. The scholars thought the agronomic university idea was for them. The sick and unemployed thought the Catholic Worker farms in general were for women and children and the helpless.

We all wrote a great deal about it in the paper and found interest in the most unlikely places. When I went to visit Tom Mooney, the labor leader who was imprisoned for twenty years for the Preparedness Day bombing in San Francisco, I found him and other prisoners in San Quentin interested in the land. Ramsey, King and Connor—I do not remember their first names— were officials of the Marine Firemen's Union who had also been imprisoned, as all the labor movement believed, on a framed charge of murder. I saw them too at that time and found them interested in the land.

"There's never a seaman wants to settle in the city," one of them said. "What they want is a little chicken farm of their own."

The desire was strong for private property, but even stronger for community. Man is not made to live alone. We all recognized that truth. But we were not truly communitarian, Peter said—we were only gregarious, as most people in cities are. Peter knew that most of us not only had not been trained to disciplined work, but we did not know how to work together. I remember seeing one seaman who was washing our kitchen floor throw down his mop when another man started to help him, saying, "Well, if you want to do it, go ahead and do it. The job is yours."

We had a number of seamen in our first years, so many in fact that one sarcastic sociologist wrote of our efforts on the land as being not farming communes for families but rest houses for celibate seamen. There were many such comments those first few years but the interest was widespread because we actually were trying to put into effect the ideas that Peter talked about. We were learning through grim experience, "the hard way" everyone said, but I never knew any other way. We consoled ourselves that we might not be establishing model communities, but many a family was getting a vacation, many a sick person was nursed back to health, crowds of slum children had the run of the woods and fields for weeks, and groups of students spent happy hours discussing the green revolution.

We write a great deal about the farms in *The Catholic Worker* to share experiences with our readers and to get their advice. Realizing that we were poor like themselves, without equipment, unskilled, floundering along, we have found friends who were not afraid to tell us of their own poverty and their hard-won knowledge. We have printed letters from owners of small farms as well as from farm laborers.

I myself traveled through the Southwest from Arkansas, down through Texas and Arizona and southern California, and visited the migrant camps through the state of California. In fact, I probably covered the route of the Joad family in *Grapes of Wrath*. After seeing that movie and the dilapidated old car that carried their poor household things across mountain and desert, I have never since been afraid to travel in our Catholic Worker cars, which are mostly discards from our readers. I have had clutches come out of the floor into my hands, the gas pedal fall down through the floor board, the battery fall out of the car, and innumerable tires go flat. And these mishaps always occurred miraculously enough within a step of home. Often at the end of a long trip just as I was pulling into the home stretch, the car would go dead. On one such occasion I was driving a man who had just been operated on for cancer to our retreat house for a convalescent period.

With one of these cars, but the best of them, bought for us by Harold McKinnon, a San Francisco lawyer, I made a trip down the long valley in California and visited each of the camps established by the government for the protection of the migrants. Certainly whenever we have written in *The Catholic Worker* about the conditions through the country we have tried to see and study them first hand, and to work out a solution that would be within the means and the capacities of all.

And what are these means and capacities?

As Peter saw it, to live according to Gospel simplicity meant that you begged when you were in need and by this you gave the opportunity to the rich to become poor for Christ's sake. "Appeals, not demands," was another of his slogans.

And since he was most often talking of the destitute, the unemployed, this was the line he usually took. But our young married couples did not fit into this category. "Man should earn his living by the sweat of his brow," Peter repeated, "and a gentleman, truly speaking, is one who does not live on the sweat of someone else's brow." In other words, he worked.

Our Catholic Worker retreats advocated detachment from unnecessary luxuries. The savings of those who do not smoke, drink beer, go to movies, use cosmetics, buy radios, cars, television sets, should be enough to buy a farm to enable them to make a start. And yet it did not always work out in this way. Men might not indulge themselves in any way, and yet be made destitute by sickness· and death. And there was many a form of sickness that stalked in our midst.

I wrote one long leading article for *The Catholic Worker* a few years ago which one of the girls in the office entitled, "What Dream Did They Dream—Utopia or Suffering," in which this mystery of suffering is discussed. Recently I have heard from friends in China, missionaries, who asked for more copies of that issue to send to their friends because I emphasized so much the necessity of suffering, and the glory of suffering for a cause. I read over that article recently and I noticed that I left out many of the specific sufferings that our friends in the apostolate have endured, the death of children, the loss of wife or husband, the mental breakdowns.

People tried to save for some purpose. But often their savings had to be spent for doctors or hospital bills, or to help others. How could one save when people were in need? And were not the two ideas contradictory, to perform the works of mercy at a personal sacrifice, and to save to provide for one's own? But one's own family of course came first. These were the arguments of those who wished to marry. They were not the problems of the single.

The Heaney family worked and saved to buy a farm, and joined with the Martin Paul family and Ruth Ann Heaney's brother to make a down payment and to stock the place. Martie Paul had already failed once, because of the war and his years in the army. He had been given a piece of land in northern Minnesota and with the help of Al Reser and his wife from the Chicago *Catholic Worker* had built a few cabins and made a start at a farming commune, calling it after St. Isadore, the patron of farmers. Don Humphrey and his wife from the Milwaukee *Catholic Worker* and their children lived and starved on the place for a while too. It was a grim experience, though all seem now to look back on their days there with nostalgia.

In the case of the St. Isadore's farm, Martie was drafted, the Resers lost a child from some obscure pancreatic disorder, and Al nearly died with asthma. The Humphreys stayed on the farm for a while, Mary with four children and Don away working on the road to Alaska. Later they moved into St. Cloud so that he could make a living for his growing family.

In the case of the Holy Family farm in Missouri, Larry died suddenly after a bout with pneumonia. He had an abscessed lung and died from the anesthetic, leaving a wife and six children. The farm is still in operation, with Ruth Ann's brother and other young men helping Martie with their labor, and contributing financially too.

The Detroit farm was given for our use by a priest's father who lost one son during the war and bore the suffering of his priest son's life for four years in a concentration camp. St. Benedict's farm, at S. Lyon, Michigan, is run for the benefit of the men who live at St. Francis House in Detroit. Produce is raised there, and the hundred acres provide living quarters for a number of the men. There is also Marybrook, a retreat house farm for week-end groups of students and workers.

Our Lady of the Wayside farm in Avon, Ohio, was given to us also, and Bill Gauchat, his wife and their five children share the land and the buildings with another Catholic Worker couple and their children, a Mexican family, and others who fall by the wayside and need help. They have sheltered unmarried girls who were having babies, have cared for sick children, taken in migrant families until they found work and homes, and with the most limited space and facilities have had summer schools and Sunday conferences for the readers of *The Catholic Worker* in that area.

St. Benedict's farm at Upton, Massachusetts was a bargain. We paid a thousand dollars for one hundred acres and an old farmhouse which was big enough to shelter many visitors as well as the families and single people who built it up. It got off to a bad start, with two young men in charge, one of whom wished to have a farming commune and the other a house of hospitality on the land. The farming commune idea won out; then with the first two families there was another conflict over the division of labor. Both men were hard workers. One of them wanted to farm and let the other work in a neighboring institution to raise the cash needed for seed and tools. The one who worked outside St. Benedict's thought that both should share this responsibility. The man who originally wished to remain and farm left to return to Boston. The young man who remained moved not much later for job and health considerations, turning over the house which he had built out of an abandoned schoolhouse to a man whose wife was ill. This schoolhouse home was later leased to a father and seven sons who have lived there for the last ten years.

There are three other families on St. Benedict's now and twenty-five children. The second to settle at Upton was a mother whose artist husband was imprisoned as a conscientious objector during World War II. She had her baby while her husband was in prison and returned to her one-room farmhome to wait patiently for his release some years later. The husband is a fine craftsman.

Since his release he has received many a commission for stained glass so that he has been able to employ others on the farm to help him. There are four children in that family now. The chap who returned to the city then came back to the farm, where he now lives with his wife and eight children. Another family in the village of Upton was burned out, and came to live in the original farmhouse, now used for guests. They have decided to join the community and build. The farm is held in the name of Ade Bethune and John Magee, the former head of the Boston Catholic Worker group, as trustees for *The Catholic Worker*, and plots of land of varying sizes are leased for fifty years to the families.

On our Easton farm, where we also had this trustee ownership, deeds of three acres each were given to families until the revolt occurred of the two families who wished twenty acres, not three. This resulted in our deeding them the original farm of twenty-seven acres. When Tamar was married to David Hennessy, they remained there for two years before buying a farm of their own in Stotler's Crossroads, West Virginia, where they lived for three years. This started out to be a community of three families, but that too was a failure, the first two families leaving after a year. One family indeed stayed only a few months and then moved back to the city. Right now Tamar and David are purchasing a farm on Staten Island so they can be near his New York job.

One of the main difficulties of all these farm ventures is the lack of skills, money and equipment; lack of leadership too is a factor. There could be, I believe, groups of families on the land, surrounding a chapel, disciplined by family life and daily attendance at Mass, all subject to one another, with a division of skills and labor and accepting too the authority of one co-ordinator. Ideally speaking, this should be as successful as any community of monks who maintain themselves by the labor of their hands.

It is no use comparing such a community of families, however, to a community of monks, because the latter are often maintained by the alms of the faithful. Land is often left to a monastery and usually there is income from schools. If lay communities were given the start, if young families were given an

105

initial subsidy, free and clear, and left to work out their way of life, great things could be done.

At Peter Maurin farm, on Staten Island, we have a three-acre asparagus bed which might eventually bring in enough money to pay the taxes of five hundred dollars a year. Our bakery there could make the place self-sustaining if we did not give away all the bread.

Through the skill of David Mason, former head of the house of hospitality in Philadelphia, proofreader and writer by profession, a "surplus commodity" oven from a battleship was set up in a little outer kitchen in the rear of the farmhouse. We can bake a hundred loaves at a time and several of us have learned to bake. Now we have the satisfaction of feeding our two houses, on Staten Island and Chrystie Street, and the breadline of hundreds of men who come twice a day for meals, with the best of whole wheat bread, made from whole-grain flour which we buy by the half ton.

What a delightful thing it is to be boldly profligate, to ignore the price of coffee and go on serving the long line of destitute men who come to us, good coffee and the finest of bread.

"Nothing is too good for the poor," our editor Tom Sullivan says, and he likes that aphorism especially when he is helping himself to something extra good.

Tom is the "co-ordinator" of the house of hospitality on Chrystie Street, New York, though we never use that title. He is in charge of the house, and his is a gentle and unobtrusive authority. He has won the respect of the men and their co-operation so that many of them take on jobs in the house and kitchen and keep the work going. There are a number who have worked with us in the past, who have been willing to take responsibility but unwilling for others to use initiative. Tom keeps the books, divides the money up in paying the bills, watches every expenditure scrupulously, writes a column for the paper, keeps a quiet eye on the men in the house and does a great deal of praying. People love him because he loves God, and for love of God loves the poor. They feel this in him and trust him.

John LaFarge
1835-1910

Civil Rights is one of the major social issues of the twentieth century in America. For many people, the term evokes the struggles during the 1950s for equality in education; the marches, riots and demonstrations through the 1960s which created the Civil Rights Act of 1964 and subsequent legislation; the life and death of Martin Luther King who crystallized the black American dream and who served for so many years as the focal point of the civil rights movement. Yet the protestations, explosions and laws of the last three decades had roots that go back through the previous century. Unfortunately most Americans were unprepared for the recent civil rights movement because they were ignorant of those roots.

One of the outstanding persons who helped pave the way for modern civil rights legislation was Father John LaFarge who dedicated a great part of the 85 years of his life to achieving interracial justice. John was born in Newport, Rhode Island, in 1880 and, after completing his elementary and secondary education in private schools, went to Harvard. He obtained the bachelor's degree in 1901, then studied at Innsbruck, Austria, for the Catholic priesthood. In 1905, the year of his ordination, he entered the Society of Jesus.

LaFarge started his apostolate for interracial justice in 1926. By way of constant lecturing, the writing of several books, and numberless articles in America *and the* Interracial Review, *he brought his message to the Catholics of America. Without question he rightly deserves the title of founder of the Catholic interracial movement in the United States. The various interracial councils and conferences that he helped create have become significant forces in the civil rights world. Father LaFarge died in 1963.*

The passage below is taken from Interracial Justice: A Study of the Catholic Doctrine of Race Relations, *written by LaFarge in 1937. It is a clear, concise statement of what he calls the Catholic teaching on the subject of human rights, with particular reference to racial relations. The statement anchors human rights on several fundamental theses: that there is a God; that Christ is the supreme representative of the human race; that all humans are united both naturally as children of God and supernaturally through Christ's redemptive work. The essential rights common to all humans are conveniently grouped together in the phrase "life, liberty and the pursuit of happiness (opportunity)." The opportunity for education, worship, a decent living and housing, recreation, self-development and peace must be as available to blacks as to whites.*

The American society has hardly begun to face the question of interracial justice in a mature manner. Prejudices, injustices and ignorance still exist in many parts of America. One of the most obvious obstacles to progress is the fact that America enacted civil rights legislation without establishing a sound philosophical basis for the legislation. As we begin to search for such a basis, insights such as those developed by John LaFarge can serve as a guide.

INTERRACIAL JUSTICE

CHAPTER V

HUMAN RIGHTS

We may discuss race relations descriptively: what the actual social conditions are like; or sociologically: what contemporary factors bring about these conditions? or historically: to what in the past are these conditions due? or practically: what are we going to do about it (methods and technique)? But as a basis to any such discussions we need to ask ourselves what the relations between the races *should be*, which is primarily an ethical discussion, and is founded on our concept of human rights. Our ideas on human rights, however, are conditioned by our ideas on man himself, his nature, destiny, and obligations. The following is a brief summary of the main points of Catholic teaching on this subject, with particular reference to racial relations.

Basis of Human Rights

1. We believe in the first place, as rationally demonstrable, that there is a personal God.

2. This God created the world as a sphere of activity wherein His sons and daughters might perfect, develop, and evolve to the full that nature which they derived from their Creator.

They would thereby fulfil the sublime destiny which He planned for them from eternity, which destiny consists in a participation in His own Divine life, as the source of all happiness in the life to come and of all genuine and lasting happiness in this life.

In order to accomplish this destiny, man is endowed with a certain nature comprising a spiritual soul gifted with intelligence and will, and a physical body provided with powers of sensation, imagination, and reproduction.

It is this our nature, spiritual and material; our condition, as children of God; this our destiny, as participants in the Divine life, which determines the conduct of our life. It determines our attitude towards the material goods of this world, of which we are stewards, not absolute owners. It also determines our relationships with one another.

3. Through the study of his nature in reference to his condition and destiny man arrives at a certain norm of conduct, which is entitled the *natural law*. This law while it receives the Divine sanction, and even a Divine promulgation, as in the case of the Ten Commandments, and the Sermon on the Mount, is nevertheless attainable by the operation of man's reason alone. It is distinguished from the positive Divine law, which is of its nature unattainable by human reasoning, and can be known only through Divine Revelation.

4. That man's unaided reason has frequently failed to discover the correct application of the natural law as for instance, in the matter of human relationships, is attributable to the fact that human passions are too strong, human selfishness too deeply rooted, to permit us an unprejudiced judgment. We see, therefore, the greatest minds of pagan antiquity falling into the grossest errors in the matter of human rights: Aristotle, Plato, Cicero, Seneca, Epictetus defending slavery and oppression. We see the Jews of the Old Testament fiercely nationalistic and denying Divine Providence to those of other races than their own. We see kindred phenomena in the pagan rebirth of today, as the Nazi racialist doctrine in Germany.

It was not until the Son of God appeared, as the Great Teacher of mankind, that mankind learned the true logical consequence, in the field of human relationships, of those simple truths enumerated above.

Christ spoke not only as the Son of God, not only as the Great Teacher, but also as the supreme representative of the human race itself, who in His own person made all things one, as our Leader, in the practical *work* of achieving these relationships.

5. The teachings of Christ proclaimed the moral unity of the human race, based upon men's natural unity as children by creation, of a common Father and as sharing a common physical

origin. This moral unity was immortally symbolized by Christ in the expression "neighbor," as applied to all men, regardless of supposed racial or national limitations. The opening words of the Lord's Prayer, "Our Father," reminded men of that natural unity upon which all human neighborliness was based.

From this moral unity of all mankind the Saviour drew positive lessons of human relationships of justice, mercy, patience, forgiveness, charity, respect for the young and the weak, etc., which had escaped the attention of moralists whether theistic or pagan.

6. Christ preached moreover a unity based not on man's natural life alone but upon the prerogatives of the supernatural life conferred upon mankind by the Redemption, and the prerogatives formed by the personal relationships of all individuals sharing in that supernatural life with His own Divine Person. Through the institution of His Church as a universal, perpetual, supra-national Society, all mankind was offered participation in a unity infinitely higher than that which the mere fact of common creation and common anthropological origin afforded. This higher unity is symbolized in the figure of the Mystical Body of Christ. As members of the one Body of which Christ is the Head the children of God enter into a unique relationship not only with one another but with the whole of mankind as well.

In Chapter VIII a brief summary is given, by means of famous texts, of the teaching of Scripture and Catholic tradition as to the moral and supernatural unity of mankind.

7. *Following the teachings of Christ,* we hold that the relationships of mankind are not matters of mere adjustment, for comfort or for material profit or for expediency's sake, but a vital question of the life and death, perfection or destruction of humanity. The guarantee of these relationships is human rights.

Nature of Human Rights

1. As is seen by the preceding, human rights originate from man's nature, as a being endowed with intelligence and free will (so that an animal, for instance, cannot properly be said to possess *rights,* though we have certain obligations toward ourselves to treat it humanely): and from man's destiny, by which an

obligation is laid on him to employ the intelligence and free will in the service of God and the perfection of his nature.

2. Human rights therefore are *natural,* they are something created with man and inherent in him; they are not something conferred on him as a privilege. For this reason no man can of himself *forego* his human rights. He may be obliged to deny himself the *exercise* of certain rights in order to preserve those even yet more fundamental. But his rights remain. Though prudence may dictate the manner and sequence of his assertion of his rights, so that he may claim one right in preference to another here and now, he is obliged to assert his rights as a human being, and it is immoral to deny *that* basic right.

3. By the same token, human rights are not conferred or taken away by social custom or *mores,* no matter how much these social customs may have developed into social institutions.

4. Still less are human rights *conferred* by the civil state, by its constitutions or its laws. The Constitution of the United States of America, with its Amendments, does not bestow or confer natural rights upon the United States citizens, although it asserts that they enjoy certain civic rights. It is not the *source* or origin of our natural rights. It is the governmental instrument by which the national sovereignty *guarantees* to each individual citizen, by conferring certain positive rights, those natural rights which the citizen enjoys by virtue of the very fact that he *is* a citizen and as such is vested with certain rights as he is bound by certain duties. Civic rights and civic duties alike spring, as from their ultimate source, not from any human instrument but from the citizen's relation to the Creator, as the Author and the supreme Ruler of human society.

The doctrine of human rights, as based upon objective ethical principles flowing from the spiritual nature of man, is necessarily *presupposed* by our American theory of stable government. It is the basis of the authority vested in our Constitution, and in the Supreme Court as the authorized interpreter of the Constitution, however imperfectly this authority may be exercised.

For this reason, a blow aimed at the exercise of *any one right* or set of rights is a blow aimed at all rights. For such an attack can be justified only by setting aside the ethical doctrine as to the objectivity and primacy of all and every form of human rights *as rights* which alone gives validity to any individual claim.

If, therefore, the right of jury trial or of legal procedure or of equitable share in the expenditure of public funds is denied to any *one* individual or group of people for any reason whatsoever, an assault is committed upon the rights of *every* citizen to enjoy jury trial or due process of law or such equitable expenditures. And further: the foundations are undermined of many other basic citizens' rights such as religious freedom or immunity from unlawful seizure. For this reason, the impairment of the civic rights of a single group implies a subversive, indeed a revolutionary policy toward the maintenance, under the American Constitution, of our civic and religious liberties.

The Protestant, Catholic, or Jew, therefore, who denounces a violation of religious freedom perpetrated in the name of discriminatory taxation or administrative measures, cannot, if he is consistent, look with indifference upon attacks, in the name of racial theory, upon the bodily or civic security of groups of citizens. In like manner, those who clamor for free speech are equally inconsistent, when they cynically ignore, in the name of social expediency, the claim of any group of citizens for the free exercise of religion.

Equality of Rights

5. Human rights, as human rights, are equal, since all men are equally called to perfect their moral nature. It is, therefore, against human rights to impose *unequal opportunities* of moral perfection where rights are equal, as it would be to provide unequal nourishment for equally healthy children of the same household.

The question naturally follows: is it unjust to deprive a person of equal opportunities, who is unable to make use of them? There is no injustice, for instance, in barring a cripple from the opportunity to compete for the Olympic Games; or a mentally defective from the opportunity for a higher education; or debarring a minor from the vote. In proportion as such inability was temporary (as in the case of the minor) or permanent (as in the case of the mentally defective), there would be just ground for temporary or permanent restriction.

Such a limitation, however, implies a *hypothesis,* viz., *a real* inability or inferiority, temporary or permanent. If any population group, racial or otherwise, *were* of its very nature, or essentially, unable to benefit by the opportunities common to the rest of mankind, it would evidently not be unjust to deprive them of what they could not use.

Even in the case of an individual such an hypothesis is harder to verify than at first sight appears. The blind man, for instance, unable to read ordinary books, may be able to read Braille. On that ground he may reasonably ask that a portion of the public funds which are set aside for libraries and adult education be allotted to the printing and distribution of books in Braille, and that the blind be educated to avail themselves of it. His very need creates a specialized right. Today it is universally assumed, even by the most conservative, that all citizens in their normal senses, without exception, can profit by a knowledge of reading and writing, and therefore have a claim on elementary education.

But can the infinitely more questionable proposition be maintained of fastening such a stigma of essential inability upon a population group comprising millions? Yet *this* is the hypothesis on which denial of equal opportunity to the Negro in America is based. The only ground that can be found for denying equal opportunity to the Negro group *as a group*, is the hypothesis that the membership in such a population group implies an essential inferiority in each and every member of the same.

This hypothesis is entirely distinct from the hypothesis that may attach to any *individual* person in the group. Evidently, in the case of Negro defectives, or Negro cripples, or Negro criminals, these individual Negroes suffer the same inabilities to profit by certain opportunities as do individual defectives, or cripples, or criminals of the white race. Their ground for disability is not their racial affiliation, but their individual deficiencies.

Just as the possible cure of such disabilities imposes upon society a certain duty to expend efforts upon the remedy of these disabilities, for any race, so does it impose upon society an obligation to attempt to remedy them in the case of Negro delinquents or defectives. All that can be deduced from such reasoning is that the presence of defectives or retarded or under-privileged persons among the Negroes imposes just so much a heavier claim upon the justice and charity of the community: that, and nothing more. But it in no way sanctions the denial of equal opportunity to the group as a whole.

Whether this hypothesis of essential inferiority *can* be maintained, was discussed in the preceding chapters (Chapters II-IV), where the reader could form his own conclusions. What is important now is to observe just what the hypothesis means, in its relation to human rights and equal opportunities.

Interracial Justice

6. As the essential rights of *individuals,* according to Christian ethics, are equal, so are the rights equal of the various *groups* that make up society. Equal rights, for instance, exist between the different industrial groups—worker, producer, consumer—and it is therefore against *industrial justice* to permit conditions to prevail which prevent one industrial group from obtaining its full rights in the industrial field.

Equal rights exist between the national groups that make up the international society; and it is therefore against international justice to deny, by wars of aggression, imperialism, or violation of treaties, equality of rights among nations.

Equal rights exist among population groups, such as those which make up the so-called racial groups in the United States. It is therefore a violation of interracial (or inter-group) justice, to deny any such group their rights in their relations with one another.

Interracial justice requires that:

(a) individuals and groups shall deal with one another in such manner that equality of opportunity shall not be denied because of the attribution to any group, *as a group,* of that inferiority which attaches only to certain individuals;

(b) society (or the social community) shall be so constituted that no such considerations shall be allowed to interfere with the practice of equal justice.

Interracial justice, in the opinion of the writer, *applies* primarily and *per se* to the *family,* since the family is primarily and *per se* the unit of social justice, of which interrracial justice (like industrial or international justice), is a part.

CHAPTER VI

SPECIFICATION OF HUMAN RIGHTS

As has already been shown, human rights are correlative with human *duties*. Rights bring duties, and duties bring rights. So that the classification of rights follows the classification of duties. A head of a family, for instance, has the obligation to bring up his children, not only physically, but mentally and spiritually as well. As a consequence of this obligation, therefore, he has a right to obtain some help from society, or from his neighbors, in the task of education, since he is unable to do all of it himself.

Rights are also specified by the *conditions* under which a man must perform his duties. In order that society may fulfil its obligations to help a man in educating his children, schools must be provided. Therefore he has a right (under the present conditions of human society), a human right, not a state-accorded right, to demand schools from the civil authority, which in the United States is the State Government. As a consequence of this right, he has a right to ask for competent teachers, which means equal salaries to be paid them with those of other races, equal equipment, equal protection from fire hazards, etc.

"There is a minimum of goods," observed the Rev. Francis J. Gilligan, S.T.D., of St. Paul Seminary, at the Twenty-First National Conference of Catholic Charities in Seattle, June, 1936, "which all men both white and black need and upon which they have a claim. That minimum includes the right to life and the right to liberty. It involves in return for honest labor, the right to remuneration sufficient to maintain the worker and his family in health and comfort. It involves the right to reasonable opportunities for recreation and education. It involves the opportunity to seek a home in an environment which is conducive to wholesome moral living. To all of those rights every Negro has a claim. To deny him less is to degrade him, to treat him less than a man."

Following a time-honored nomenclature, human rights may be conveniently grouped under the headings: *life, liberty,* and the *pursuit of happiness* (or opportunity). These headings are not mutually exclusive since much of what is included under

116

life and liberty may also be considered as belonging to the pursuit of happiness or opportunity.

Right to Life

The right to exist, and to use the means that are necessary for the sustenance of one's existence is the most elementary of human rights, correlative with the most elementary of human duties. This basic and general right includes the following specific rights:

1. The right to the protection of the law against the unjust taking of human life: just legal procedure, according to the law of the land (which in this country includes trial by a jury of one's peers); protection against mob violence or lynching; police protection, etc.

2. The right to public protection from insanitary living conditions, which menace the health and the life of the family and of the individual.

3. The right to exercise the means of livelihood, which under our modern economic conditions is accomplished only through the enjoyment of adequate return for one's labor.

Where individuals are so circumstanced, as in the case of the industrial or salaried worker, that they can obtain such adequate return for labor only through the wages paid to them by an employer, this implies the right to a living wage, and "to that degree of comfort which, morally speaking, is necessary if the worker is to live in accordance with his dignity as a human being, to practice virtue, and thus attain the end for which God made him." This implies, as is pointed out by Pope Leo XIII and Pope Pius XI in the Social Encyclicals, that labor shall not be treated as a commodity, to be bought and sold on the open market, but is a matter to be fixed by free contract.

The nature of the wage contract, however, in turn brings about certain conditions which are necessary to guarantee its freedom, such as the right to collective bargaining and the right to such forms of labor organization as are necessary to ensure collective bargaining.

It is against human rights, therefore, against justice, and specifically against interracial justice:

(a) To deprive a person or the member of a group of a means of livelihood to which they are naturally entitled, merely because of their race. Since the natural title to the means of livelihood is vested primarily and fundamentally in the head of the family (or the person who is acting, from necessity, as head of the family), such deprivation is particularly aimed at social justice when it concerns the head of the household, as the primary unit of social justice.

(b) To exclude a person on merely racial grounds from participation in such union organizations as is necessary for the maintenance of his and his family's livelihood.

Right to Liberty

The Law of God as well as the fundamental laws of the American Republic guarantee the following rights pertaining to liberty:

1. Liberty of conscience and of the free practice of religion, as long as the latter does not interfere with peace and public order.

2. Liberty to exercise natural *rights concerning children and the home.* It was against human rights, for instance, under slavery to separate husbands from wives or parents from their children, or to deny the right of matrimony. Similar practices under the forced-labor system prevailing today in certain parts of the world are equally unjust.

It is against such a type of liberty for the State to compel parents to send their children to State schools or any school contrary to their parents' choice, as long as such schools chosen by the parents fulfil the educational requirements demanded by the common good. And as has been noted before, the preservation of one set of liberties, educational or otherwise, is correlative with other sets of liberties. No one set can be completely isolated, and defended without reference to the other.

3. *Liberty of political suffrage.* While the exercise of the vote is in itself not an *inherent* human right—it cannot be claimed by those who have agreed to live under an absolute monarchy— it is *an adventitious* human right when circumstances are such that other human rights are obtained and secured by the right of franchise. Thus in the case of American citizens, including

those of racial groups, ordinary opportunities are assured, in most cases, through the exercise of the ballot.

4. *Liberty of speech and assembly.* The validity of this right depends not upon any supposedly self-justifying claim of the individuals to enjoy unlimited freedom of utterance, but upon the individual's relation to the common good. Where the individual finds it impossible to fulfil his duties as a citizen, to assist in promoting the common good and to provide for his own family if he is deprived of the power of free speech and assembly, it is evident that he has a right to the same, since civic rights flow from civic duties. Under the conditions of our modern civilization, however, such an impossibility prevails. Hence the need for civil authority to guarantee this right to the individual if it expects him to do his duty. In proportion as the individual is charged with greater and greater responsibilities towards the community, e.g., as a head of a family, as a custodian of a public trust, as an official of the public welfare, as an elected representative of the people his right and claim to the enjoyment of free speech and free assembly increases in gravity, according to any organic concept of government.

Pursuit of Happiness

The right to the pursuit of happiness springs from the social nature of man. Men are obliged to unify their activities. "The purpose of this unification of activities is to render the community more productive, and consequently to secure a peace and prosperity more complete than if each individual were to try to take care of many activities, especially in the economic order. Therefore there should be great advantages to the whole community of men resulting from this unification of effort. And so a distinguishing characteristic of the virtue of social justice should be an admission of the right of the entire cooperating community to a fair participation in the progressive advantages of the united human effort." (Joseph F. MacDonnell, S.J., "Approach to Social Justice.") Pius XI, in *Quadragesimo Anno,* insists upon the right of the working man to share in the progress of the community.

"Social justice may be defined as the harmonious conjunction of rights and duties assigned to persons, groups or persons

119

and to the entire community, in any given era of social life, in so far as each and all should attain the common good, should share with due proportion in the benefits of social activity." (*Ibid.*) Social justice, therefore, is not static but is progressive. While certain basic elements remain unchanged for all time, with the development of civilization new rights ensue, so that individuals who contribute to the progress of the common good may share in the benefits of that progress.

The implications of this principle as applied to the situation of an underprivileged group like the American Negro are evident and profound. The Negro has contributed, and still contributes, his blood, brain, and brawn to the progress of American civilization. But as civilization offers a higher standard of living, economically or culturally, so he naturally expects a share in that progress to which he has contributed. Neither for the Negro, nor for any other ethnic group, is it enough to say: "Your fathers were content with this minimum. Should it not be enough for you?" Even if the fathers were content with that minimum, which is by no means as evident as is stated, the Negro today has no idea of foregoing his rights.

"Catholic moralists teach that in addition to the minimum, men have some rights to other goods and privileges, such as, to seek employment in a variety of businesses, to seek promotion, to seek higher remuneration, to seek higher education, to be free from unfair and unreasonable restrictions when pursuing other legitimate goods. The basis and measures of the right to more goods than the minimum are the peculiar needs, capacities, and abilities of the individual. Catholic moralists vindicate such rights because the arbitrary denial of all opportunity and progress, renders men bitter and destroys the contentment which is necessary to reasonable human living. In harmony with this opinion of moralists is the moral sentiment of Americans who regard as evil any system in which goods above the minimum and positions of trust in the economic and commercial life are distributed solely upon the basis of nationality or family associations.

"If these principles are applied to the American race problem it would seem to follow that the Negro has a claim to goods and positions above the minimum in our economic and commercial life, proportionate to his ability and efforts. . . .

John LaFarge

"The only serious objections which may be raised against these assertions must be founded upon one of two assumptions: either all Negroes are inferior to whites, or, the Negro ghetto offers complete economic and cultural opportunities." (Rev. F.J. Gilligan, *loc. cit.*)

Opportunity

Under the title of opportunity, some of the more elementary claims are included which any group has to share in the progress of our times.

1. *Opportunity for education,* as the principal gateway to earthly happiness.

2. According to certain Catholic ethicists, man has an inherent *duty* to develop his faculties of mind and will. The right to an education is correlative to this duty.

At any rate, education is an absolutely indispensable condition for the enjoyment of nearly every other opportunity for moral perfection that our modern American civilization boasts: such as the vote, protection in the courts, decent living and recreation, livelihood and physical existence, health, etc. Hence the denial of equal rights in the field of education is one of the most vital denials possible of human opportunity.

This denial is made particularly flagrant by:

(a) the tremendous *de facto* emphasis, whether for right or wrong, placed upon free, equal, and universal education in our American scheme of citizenship;

(b) the peculiar handicaps of an under-privileged race, which has a special need of education; and

(c) the stress placed by the Catholic Church upon education, as an indispensable condition not for temporal welfare alone, but for eternal welfare and spiritual progress.

2. *Opportunity for worship;* both by our *nature*, as human beings, and by our *membership in a Church,* with the rights that it confers.

3. *Opportunity for decent living,* which includes the whole field of *housing.* Here again we see that the exercise of *one* human right is a condition for the exercise of other human rights, or opportunities, and vice versa. The denial of the opportunity for decent living causes crime, etc.

121

4. For wholesome *recreation;* both for young and old.

5. For *self-development* along humane and cultural lines. Such development cannot be characterized as mere "ambition," but is recognized by the Church as an inherent right of humanity. The *Osservatore Romano,* Vatican City daily which reflects the the policies of the Holy See, describing in its issue of January 28, 1927, the civilizing work of the Sacred Congregations de Propaganda Fide, in Rome, stated that its three great aims were: the abolition of castes; the liberation of slaves; and the social elevation of all colored races without distinction.

6. *Peace.*

Individuals as well as groups have the right to lead a peaceful, orderly existence; and to enjoy the protection, legal and administrative that will ensure such peace and order. Negroes find themselves in certain instances not only deprived of such protection, but subject to influences which tend directly to create lawlessness, as for instance the petty-magistrate system in some of our rural communities, various local devices resorted to in order to "keep the Negro in his place," and mob violence or lynching.

CHAPTER VII

GUARANTEES OF HUMAN RIGHTS

Christian social philosophy, as the custodian and champion of human rights, rejects as *sinful* the violation of human right. To greed's plea of necessity Christianity replies with conscience, warning of sin.

Christian social philosophy regards as sinful not only actual violations of right, but those *states of mind* which by inflaming human passion and clouding human intellect encourage such violations. For this reason Christian social philosophy looks upon racial prejudices, deliberately fostered, as a sin.

Human rights, speaking in general, find their guarantee in three major types of institutions: government and law; organic social structure; religion. In our American scheme of life the separation between these three types of institution is sharp and profound. Jealously maintained, this separation is held to be essential to social peace and national progress. Without attempting to dispute this point, it may still be noted that by the very strictness of this separation, which has been found necessary because of the diversity of peoples and of religious beliefs in the Republic, something is lost of the influence in behalf of human rights which society might otherwise exercise upon government, government upon society, and religion upon both.

There is no automatic guarantee of human rights. Their realization, as a moral matter, cannot be entrusted to the mere course of nature, not to any form of merely mechanical adjustment, not to merely pious wishes and humanitarian sentiments. The maintenance of human rights, whether for one's own benefit or for the benefit of others, depends upon voluntary effort. Since this effort, to be effective, must be organized, it places that heavy toll upon patience, intelligence, mutual forebearance, and perseverance, that all successful organized effort demands. Due to the lack of these requisites, and of personal ethical ideals, the mortality in schemes and plans for the attainment of human rights rivals the casualties of Gettysburg or Verdun.

Neither government, nor social structure, nor religion, as a present and concrete institution, of themselves, secure the exercise of human rights. Each type of institution presupposes an appropriate type of human activity. Each provides a field in which human activity, guided by motives of justice and charity, may profitably operate in behalf of one's neighbor. They do not claim to perform an automatic process. As the same abuses creep up in each suceeding generation, in spite of all social progress, due to the ever recurring weaknesses of human nature, renewed efforts are needed to secure for later generations the benefits which, throught the same agencies, were secured in earlier periods for their predecessors.

For this reason it is as unreasonable to say: "Christianity has been in existence all these centuries, yet we still find strife, war, prejudice, or other abuses!" as it is to say: "Schools, libraries, and physicians have existed for the last 3,000 years, yet we still find ignorance and sickness!"

Under the terms government and law are understood in the United States the protection afforded to human rights by

1. The fundamental law of the land: the Constitution of the United States, with its Amendments, as well as the Constitutions of the individual States.

2. Statutory laws and enactments: Federal, State, and municipal.

3. Specific legal decisions affecting human rights, which fall again into two main categories: decisions of the Supreme Court of the United States; decisions of lesser courts.

A brief resumé of some guarantees, as they affect the interracial situation, is furnished in the *Negro Year Book*, pp. 98-112.

Social Structure

History shows that abuses in the matter of human rights tend to shape themselves into *anti-social institutions.* What began as a mere matter of private enterprise, ambition, or gain *took permanent form* by receiving legal sanctions. A rationalized philosophic justification arose; new governmental and cultural forms developed in accord with the legal and philosophic structure.

This is seen in the history of the slave trade, of commercial exploitation, of financial manipulation.

The remedy, therefore, for anti-social institutions is to be found not in the merely collective activity of large number of individuals, but in the organized *reconstruction of society* upon an ethical basis.

In order to safeguard society against abuses of human rights which are specifically aimed at racial groups, the *establishment of such social institutions is needed as are based upon principles directly contrary to the false principles that have led to these abuses.*

Modern Catholic historians and sociologists, following the guidance of Pope Pius XI in his Encyclical, *Quadragesimo Anno*, see in the tendency of our times to subordinate all considerations of the dignity of the human person to the unbridled quest of material gain, as the primary source of interracial, as well as of economic, industrial, and international injustice.

When the human personality is cheapened, when human life is set at naught, it makes little difference whether this is done in the field of finance, industry, war, or race relations. The root of the evil in each instance is the same. Cheap labor brings cheap lives. And from cheap lives follow customs and maxims sanctioning the cheapening of lives.

To exploitations of the human personality in the unbridled pursuit of gain, Christianity opposes not class warfare, which merely aggravates the disease, but cooperation and collaboration for the sake of the common good.

Such cooperation, in the Christian idea, applies to individual (producer and consumer, lender and borrower, labor and capital, etc.); to nations with one another; to the State itself; and to relations between the races.

The *type of social structure*, therefore, which is the principle guarantee of relations between racial groups based upon human rights is the structure which will *embody* the principle of collaboration or cooperation in our society; not as a mere passing set of activities, but as a regeneration of our entire system of living.

How shall the principle of collaboration or cooperation be embodied in modern society? The main lines thereof are laid down by Pope Pius in *Quadragesimo Anno* in the vocational or occupational groups therein proposed. The establishment of such groups presupposes an organic or functional idea of society.

If racial diversifications *were* the real basis of human differences, then the more organically society were constructed, the more these racial differences would be made the basis of discrimination. But since, as is shown elsewhere, it is not race, but other, very different factors that really diversify men in relation to society, a truly organic concept of society will see its members functioning therein not according to the unreal and artifical standards by which one ethnic group is set off against another, but operating according to their real capacities, based upon the contribution that each person can best make to society.

"Negro Rights"

The essential human rights of Negroes do not appertain to them as Negroes, but simply as members of the human family. Human rights are not Negro rights, any more than they are white rights or red-haired persons' rights. They flow from the essential constituents of our nature, not from its accidental characteristics.

125

Negro insistence on human rights as *Negro rights* can only have the effect of provoking white insistence upon supposed "white rights," which are equally baseless.

On the other hand, it is consistent with the foregoing doctrine, that Negroes insists, *as a matter of general human rights,* that due regard be given, in educational or other welfare programs for the peculiar difficulties, situations, and capacities of their race. Also that where public programs of welfare (spiritual or temporal), or educational, afford, as a matter of general policy special recognition to the merits of the various population groups that make up the community, the Negro group should have its share in such recognition. If, for instance, special attention is paid in the schools to the history and culture of the various groups that make up a mixed population—English history—Polish history—Slovak history, etc.—it is only reasonable that the Negro group should enjoy recognition of the cultural heritage that belongs to the race.

Charity or Justice?

Charity supposes justice. There can be no real exercise of charity which does not first take into consideration the claims of justice. Before giving alms to a man we pay him our debts, if any such be owing to him.

Disastrous experience, in various modern forms of government, of the substitution of an arbitrary governmental benevolence (e.g. under Socialism) for a constitutional regime based upon adequate recognition of human rights is a severe warning to those who would attempt, with any group or condition of men, to *substitute* mere benevolence for justice. Such an erroneous principle, if admitted in any one instance, all too readily admits of transfer to a wider field.

It is equally disastrous, however, to attempt to substitute justice for charity. The dynamics of justice are not to be found in justice alone, but in the impelling power of love, which alone can provide adequate motivation and spiritual force for the realization of human rights.

The use of terms is frequently a matter of practical expediency, considering the temper of those addressed. So narrow, so confused a notion prevails among a large body of our citizens concerning the matter of human rights, that their mention frequently has no effect but to provoke a blind resistance not to justice alone, but any form of humanity. Comparatively few persons, however, are so inhuman that they will wish to deny opportunity to their fellowman, once they realize his needs. For the attainment, therefore, of immediate, practical good, the preaching of opportunity is apt to be more effective than the preaching of abstract rights. At the same time, however, in order that basic misunderstandings may be cleared up, and the foundation laid solidly for a lasting and constructive social program, the author believes that together with the discussion of specific racial problems there should be a program of education in the general nature of human rights.

CHAPTER VIII

CHRISTIAN TEACHING ON HUMAN UNITY

The Christian religion, as mentioned in Chapter V, has never ceased to lay stress upon the fact all men are brothers, as descendants from a common earthly ancestor and as children of the same Heavenly Father. Flowing from this community of origin, as well as from our need of one another in the task of fulfilling our temporal and eternal destiny, are those obligations of the natural law which are characterized as human rights. Far from destroying or ignoring this natural unity of mankind, the supernatural unity of the Kingdom of God perfects and transforms natural unity into a corporate spiritual communion, governed by the law of charity, but at the same time teaching explicitly those implications of the natural law which remained unnoticed when man trusted to his unaided reason.

Following are some texts from the Gospels and the Epistles illustrating these truths, and a few of the many utterances thereon of Popes and theologians. For a number of these citations I am indebted to John Eppstein: *The Catholic Tradition of the Law of Nations,* through kind arrangement of Robert Wilberforce.

The Voice of Scripture

Christ the Saviour of All Peoples. "He [Simeon] took him into his arms and blessed God and said: Now thou dost dismiss thy servant, O Lord, according to thy word in peace; because my eyes have seen thy salvation which thou has prepared before the face of all peoples: a light to the revelation of the Gentiles and the glory of thy people Israel." (St. Luke: 28-32.) Cf. St. Matthew, chapter ii, account of the Epiphany.

Children of One Father. "But I say to you, love your enemies: do good to them that hate you: and pray for them that persecute and caluminate you; that you may be the children of your Father who is in Heaven, who maketh his sun to rise upon the good and the bad, and raineth upon the just and the unjust." (St. Matthew v: 44-45.)

The Apostles Sent to All Races of Men. "You are the salt of the earth. But if the salt lose its savour wherewith shall it be salted? It is good for nothing any more than to be cast out and to be trodden on by men. You are the light of the world. A city seated on a mountain cannot be hid." (St. Matthew v: 13-14.)

"And this gospel of the kingdom shall be preached in the whole world for a testimony to all nations: and then shall the consummation come." (St. Matthew xxiv: 14.)

To Teach All Nations. "And Jesus coming, spoke to them, saying: All power is given to me in heaven and earth. Going, therefore, teach ye all nations, baptizing them in the name of the Father and of the Son and of the Holy Ghost. Teaching them to observe all things whatsoever I have commanded you. And behold I am with you all the days even to the consummation of the world." (St. Matthew xxviii: 18-20.)

"And that penance and remission of sins should be preached in his name unto all nations, beginning at Jerusalem." (St. Luke xxiv: 47.)

"And he said to them: Go ye into the whole world and preach the gospel unto every creature." (St. Mark xvi: 15.)

Mystical Union. "Abide in me: and I in you. As the branch cannot bear fruit of itself, unless it abide in the vine, so neither can you, unless you abide in me. I am the vine; you the branches. . . ." (St. John xv: 4-12.)

Christ's Prayer for Unity. "And not for them only do I pray, but for them also who through their word shall believe in me: That they all may be one, as thou, Father, in me and I in thee: that they may be one in us: that the world may believe that thou hast sent me. . . ." (St. John xvii: 20-23.)

Love of Brethren. "Let us therefore love God, because God hath first loved us. If any man say, I love God, and hateth his brother; he is a liar. For he that loveth not his brother, whom he seeth, how can he love God, whom he seeth not? And this commandment we have from God, that he, who loveth God, loveth also his brother." (I. Epistle St. John iv: 19-21.)

Birth of the Christian Community. "And when the days of Pentecost were accomplished, they were all together in one place. . . . Now there were dwelling at Jerusalem Jews, devout men out of every nation under heaven. . . . And how have we heard, every man in our own tongue wherein we were born? . . .

"But Peter said to them: Do penance: and be baptized every one of you in the name of Jesus Christ, for the remission of your sins, and you shall receive the gift of the Holy Ghost. For the promise is to you and to your children and to all that are afar off whomsoever the Lord our God shall call. . . . (Acts ii: 1-11; 38-39.)

"And the multitude of believers had but one heart and one soul." (Acts iv: 32.)

Universality of the Church. "And Peter opening his mouth said: In every deed I perceive that God is not a respecter of persons. But in every nation he that heareth him and worketh justice is acceptable to him. God sent the word to the children of Isreal, preaching peace by Jesus Christ (he is Lord of all)." (Acts. x: 34-36.)

The Mystical Body. "For as the body is one, and hath many members; and all the members of the body, whereas they are many, yet are one body, so also *is* Christ. For in one spirit were we all baptized into one body, whether Jews or Gentiles, whether bond or free; and in one spirit have we been all made to drink. . . . But now there are many members indeed, but one body." (I. Cor. xii: 12-14, 20.)

"God hath tempered the body together, giving to that which wanted the more abundant honor. That there might be no schism in the body; but the members might be mutually careful one for another. And if one member suffer anything, all the members suffer with it: or if one member glory, all the members rejoice with it. Now you are the body of Christ and members of member." (I. Cor. xii: 24-27.)

"But now in Christ Jesus, you who some time were afar off are made nigh by the blood of Christ. For he is our peace, who hath made both one, and breaking down the middle wall of partition, the enmities in his flesh; making void the law of commandments *contained* in decrees; that he might make the two in himself into one new man, making peace; and might reconcile both to God in one body by the cross, killing the enmities in himself. And coming, he preached peace to you that were afar off, and peace to them that were nigh. For by him we have access both in one Spirit to the Father. Now therefore you are no more strangers and foreigners; but you are fellow citizens with the saints, and the domestics of God, built upon the foundation of the apostles and prophets, Jesus Christ himself being the chief corner stone: in whom all the building, being framed together, groweth up into an holy temple in the Lord. In whom also ye are built together into an habitation of God in the Spirit." (Ephesians ii: 13-22.)

Cf. Colossians i: 12-22.

"One body and one Spirit: as you are called in one hope of your calling. One Lord, one faith, one baptism. One God and Father of all, who is above all and through all, and in us all. . . . Until we all meet into the unity of faith and of the knowledge of the Son of God, unto a perfect man into the measure of the age of the fulness of Christ. . . . But doing the truth in charity, we may in all things grow up in him who is the head, even Christ." (Eph. iv: 5-15.)

The Voice of the Church

The Common Human Family. "Who would imagine, as we see them thus filled with a hatred of one another, that they are all of one common stock, all of the same nature, all members of the same human society? Who would recognize brothers whose Father is in Heaven?" (Pope Benedict XV: Encyclical Letter, *Ad Beatissimi*, on the World War, November 1, 1914.)

"The Church will certainly not refuse her zealous aid to States united under the Christian law in any of their undertakings inspired by justice and charity, inasmuch as she is herself the most perfect type of universal society. She possesses in her organization and institutions a wonderful instrument for bringing this brotherhood among men, not only for their eternal salvation but also for their material well-being in this world; she leads them through temporal well-being to the sure acquisition of eternal blessings. It is the teaching of history that when the Church pervaded with her spirit the ancient and barbarous nations of Europe, little by little the many and varied differences that divided them were diminished and their quarrels extinguished; in time they formed a homogeneous society from which sprang Christian Europe which, under the guidance and auspices of the Church, whilst preserving a diversity of nations, tended to a unity that favored its prosperity and glory. On this point St. Augustine well says: 'This celestial city, in its life here on earth, calls to itself citizens of every nation, and forms out of all the peoples one varied society; it is not harassed by differences in customs, laws, and institutions, which serve to the attainment or the maintenance of peace on earth; it neither rends nor detroys anything but rather guards all and adapts itself to all; however these things may vary among the nations, they are all directed to the same end of peace on earth as long as they do not hinder the exercise of religion, which teaches the worship of the true supreme God.' And the same holy Doctor thus addresses the Church: 'Citizens, peoples, and all men, thou, recalling their common origin, shalt not only unite among themselves, but shall make them brothers.' " (Pope Benedict XV, Encyclical Letter, *Pacem Dei Munus Pulcherrimum,* May 23, 1920.)

"Then only will it be possible to unite all in harmonious striving for the common good, when all sections of society have the intimate conviction that they are members of a single family and children of the same Heavenly Father, and further, that they are 'one body in Christ, and everyone members one of another,' so that 'if one member suffer anything all members suffer with it.' " (Pope Pius XI, Encyclical, *On the Reconstruction of the Social Order.*)

Love Is the Order of Nature. "Holy Church of God, knowing how sweet is charity and how delectable is concord, thou preachest the alliance of the nations; thou longest for the union of peoples. . . . The order of nature wills that all the nations, descended as they are from a single man, should be bound together by a mutual love." (St. Leander of Seville, A.D. 589, at the Third Council of Toledo. Migne *Pat. Lat. LXII:* 895.)

Men Created Free. "It is a noble act by the benefit of manumission to give freedom back to men, whom nature from the beginning created and brought forth free, but whom the Law of Nations has subjected to the yoke of slavery." (Pope St. Gregory the Great: *Liberation of Two Slaves,* v. Ep. 12.)

Unity of the Race. "The human race, though divided into no matter how many different peoples and nations, has for all that a certain unity, a unity not merely physical, but also in a sense political and moral. This is shown by the natural precept of mutual love and mercy, which extends to all men, including foreigners of every way of thinking." (Francisco Suarez, *De Legibus,* Lib. ii, cap. 19, par. 9.)

All Men Capable of the Faith. "Whoever, therefore, has the nature of man is capable of receiving the Faith of Christ. . . . Hence Our Lord, who is truth itself, and can neither deceive nor be deceived, said to the first preachers of the Faith, when He appointed them to their office: 'Go and teach all nations.' He said all nations, without exception, because all men are capable of the Faith." (Pope Paul III, Bull *Sublimis Deus Sic Dilexit,* June 17, 1537. Against the enslavement of the Indians.)

" 'Every animal loveth its kind' (*Ecclesiasticus* xv). Therefore, it appears that friendship among men exists by natural law and it is against nature to shun the society of harmless folk." (Francisco de Vitoria, *Relectio de Indis.*)

"The Spaniards are the neighbors of the barbarians, as appears from the Gospel parable of the Samaritan (St. Luke x). But they are bound to love their neighbors as themselves (St. Matthew xxii). Therefore they may not keep them away from their country without cause: 'When it is said "Love thy neighbor" it is clear that every man is our neighbor.' (St. Augustine's *De doctrina Christiana*.)" (Vitoria, *ib.*)

"And, as is said in *Dig.* i, 1, 3: 'Nature has established a bond of relationship between all men,' and so it is contrary to natural law for one man to dissociate himself from another without good reason. 'Man,' says Ovid, 'is not a wolf to his fellow-man, but a man.' " (Vitoria, *ib.*)

Against Racial Particularism. "If we consider the element in human nature that makes the nations, on the one hand, and universal human society on the other, we see that the latter derives from an essential trait of human nature: its identity in the whole race, and the duty of mutual aid and support which flows from it. The nation, on the other hand, owes its foundation to particular qualities of land, race, or history, contingent or variable, which add to, and are secondary to, the essential in human nature. Hence the order of relation between the two societies; the national groups are subordinate to universal society.

". . . Under all natural differentiations there exist a natural right of human sociability, in virtue of which no local group can cut itself off from communication and exchange, commercial, industrial, intellectual and moral. Natural law demands this widening of human life and *racial particularism has no prescriptive right against it.*" (Rev. J.T. Delos, O.P., *La société internationale.*)

Natural Unity Is Helped by Progress. "Every constant factor which brings any two nations into touch with one another, establishes a positive society between them. The society is subject to the universal laws of justice and love, for these nations are equals and are destined to the same end. But it is in the very nature of things that every nation should have continuous relations with its neighbors. Settled by its agriculture in a limited area, it extends first up to the frontiers of other nations. Then trade, which is a true social blessing, makes it tend further, almost instinctively, to establish relations with the most distant peoples. Thus it is that, in the design of the Creator, commerce becomes the great social link which unites all nations into one single society, and brings many and varied advantages to peoples and individuals. Material advantages, through the common usage of the products of the whole world, intellectual advantages through the spread of ideas and the progress of the sciences; moral advantages, through the mutual guarantee of order or the unity of religious beliefs. Thus it is nature itself, that eloquent interpreter of the Divine will, which calls all people to form among themselves one universal association and at the same time makes it their duty so to do." (Taparelli, *Essai Théorique du Droit Naturel.* Book VI, Chap. iii.)

Against Class Warfare. "Sons of the same race, all descendants of the one same primitive pair, called by God the Father to a supernatural vocation and to participation in the Divine Life, all men without exception are brothers. We should be penetrated with this idea of brotherhood and should make it the inspiration of our conduct toward our neighbor. Since we are brethren, we should repudiate class warfare and in the same way all systematic hostility between peoples. The law which brotherhood imposes upon us all is that of mutual benevolence, of confidence and collaboration in every field so as to assure families and peoples of material prosperity, the cultural goods of mind and heart, and religious liberty." (Most Rev. Msgr. Chollet, Archbishop of Cambrai, France: Pastoral Letter of October 24, 1936.)

Emmanuel Mounier
1905-1950

*Individualism and socialism are the two intellectual struc-
tures that dominate modern society. They permeate politics,
economics, religion, science, morality, art forms and education.
The one glorifies the individual around whom the whole of
existence revolves; the other recognizes only the communal
aspect of man and places all value in the society. Both structures
are operative at present. Both have proven themselves to be
tragically inadequate. Where does one turn after seeing their
limitations?*

*One effort to correct the course of mankind and to make
a worthwhile third option available is the movement known as
personalism. It is a style of philosophy, a way of handling existence. Among its foremost modern proponents is the Frenchman,
Emmanuel Mounier.*

*He was born in Grenoble, France, in 1905. After complet-
ing his studies in Grenoble and at the Sorbonne in Paris, he
taught philosophy for a few years. During the 1930s he was part
of a generation of young French intellectuals who challenged
the value systems and social structures of the French establishment. They called for revolution and an end to the status quo.
Mounier established a journal called* Esprit, *his vehicle for
criticizing the contemporary world. During World War II he was
a member of the French Resistance and was imprisoned in 1941.*

After the war he resumed publication of Esprit. *Mounier wrote several books as well. He died suddenly in 1950, at the age of 45.*

Mounier's criticism was not simply negative. He developed a positive theory of personalism which he believed could serve as the structure for a new social order. His book, Personalism, *is an excellent introduction to this type of thinking. Part One of the book explores the structure of the personal universe. Man is totally body and totally spirit. The tendency to divide man into two independent beings, body and spirit, is rejected from the start by personalist realism. The person is radically a being oriented toward other, a communicating being, whose primary action is to sustain, together with others, a society of persons, the structure, the customs, the sentiments and the institutions of which are shaped by their nature as persons. Freedom, happiness, truth, and moral values all take on a specific meaning within the personalist framework.*

In Part Two, which is the reading presented below, Mounier relates his personalism to the revolution of the twentieth century. He discusses and rejects the phenomenon of nihilism that swept across Europe during the early decades of this century. He then treats various aspects of society: the economy, the family, sexuality, national and international outlooks, education, and culture.

The philosophy of personalism is rich and refreshing. There is no doubt that a society established on such a philosophy would be unique in the history of man. Sadly, its beauty is tempered by the feeling that to existentialize such a philosophy would demand too much of modern man. Everything that nations and individuals have built up in our time in the name of socialism or rugged individualism would be submitted to critique—the military powers and weapon stockpiles, political intrigue and power, industrial and private fortunes. It is not yet evident that man has grown to the point of sacrificing all that insanity in order to become a person.

PERSONALISM

PART ONE
CHAPTER I
EMBODIED EXISTENCE

Modern philosophies of spirit divide man and the world between two independent series, material and spiritual. Sometimes they accept, as brute fact, the independence of the two series (psycho-physical parallelism) abandoning matter to its determinism, whilst safeguarding the absolute right of the spirit to legislate within its own domain: the connection between the two worlds then remains unexplained. Sometimes they deny any reality to the material world, to the point of making it a mere reflection of the spirit: the importance of such an apparent world then becomes somewhat of a paradox.

Such schema are rejected from the start by personalist realism.

The person immersed in nature

Man is a body in the same degree that he is a spirit, wholly body and wholly spirit. His most fundamental instincts, eating and reproduction, he has elaborated into the subtle arts of gastronomy and courtship. Yet the great philosopher is attacked by headaches, and St. John of the Cross used to vomit during his ecstasies. My moods and my ideas are shaped by the climate, by geography, by my situation upon the crust of the earth, by my heredity and perhaps beyond all this by unfathomable currents of cosmic rays. Into these influences the supervening psychological and collective determinants are interwoven; there is nothing in me that is not mingled with the earth and the blood. Research has shown us that the great religions spread along the same routes as the great epidemics. Why should we be shocked at this? Missionaries also go on legs, and have to follow the contours of the landscape.

So much for the truth, and it is considerable, of the materialist analysis. But it is nothing new. The indissoluble union of the soul and the body is the pivot of Christian thinking. It does not oppose 'spirit' to 'the body' or to 'matter' in the modern acceptation of the terms. In Christianity the 'spirit'—in the composite meaning of modern spiritualism, which signifies at once the thought ($\nu o \upsilon \varsigma$) the soul ($\psi \upsilon \chi \acute{\eta}$) and the breath of life—is fused with the body in existence. When both together strive in the direction opposed to the supernatural vocation of man, Christianity calls this movement 'the flesh', and means by that the downward drag of the soul as much as of the body; when it strives towards God, body and soul together collaborate with the power of the spirit ($\Pi \nu \epsilon \upsilon \mu a$) in the substantial kingdom of God and not in some ethereal realm of spirit. Though original sin has wounded human nature, it is the composite man in his totality who is stricken; and ever since the time of the Gospels the malice and the perversities of the spirit have attracted more anathemas than those of the flesh in the narrower sense of the word. The Christian who speaks of the body or of matter with contempt does so against his own most central tradition. According to mediaeval theology, we cannot normally attain to the highest spiritual realities or to God himself except by thwarting matter, and by the force we exert against it. But in truth this is the Greek contempt for the material, that has been transmitted from century to century down to our own days, under false Christian credentials.

We have today to overcome this dualism in our way of life as in our thinking. Man is a natural being: by his body he is a part of nature, and the body is everywhere with him: we must now consider what this implies.

Nature—exterior, pre-human, unconscious psychological nature, including impersonal involvement in society—is not the human evil; man's incarnation is not a fall. But since it is the ground of the impersonal and the objective, it is an abiding *occasion* of perversity. Poverty, like abundance, can undo us. Man is beleaguered as it were between the one and the other. Marxism is right in thinking that the ending of material poverty is the ending of an aberration, and a necessary stage to the development of humanity. But it is not the ending of all aberration, even upon the natural plane.

The person transcends nature

Man is a natural being. But is he no more than that? Is he altogether a sport of nature? Or does he, plunged into and emerging out of nature, transcend it?

The difficulty is how rightly to think this notion of transcendence. Our minds resist the representation of a reality whose concrete existence is wholly immersed in another but which nevertheless exists on a higher plane. One cannot be on the ground floor and on the sixth story at the same time, as Léon Brunschvig said. But this is using a spatial image to ridicule an experience that is not imaginable in space. The universe is full of men going through the same motions in the same surroundings, but carrying within themselves, and projecting around them, universes as mutually remote as the constellations.

Then let us look at nature. Let us dismiss the materialist myth of an impersonal Being of Nature, with limitless powers. We will also dismiss the romantic myth of a benevolent Mother, sacrosanct and unchangeable, from whom one dare not separate oneself on pain of sacrilege and disaster: both of these myths subject active and personal man to an impersonal fiction. In truth, nature reveals nothing to our rational understanding but an infinitely tangled web of tendencies, and we cannot even tell whether this is reducible, beyond the systems we construct in order to grasp it, to any logical unity at all. By what authority are we ourselves to be reduced to such systems?—to Pavlov's chains of associated reflexes, for instance?

If we are to render an account of humanity, we must grasp the living reality of man in his total activity. Pavlov's experiments are artificial creations of the laboratory: their results present us with a mechanistic view because they isolate the subject under conditions that are in themselves wholly mechanical. The man escapes them. "Man is a natural being, but a natural human being," and the singularity of man is his dual capacity for breaking with nature. He alone knows the universe that enfolds him, and he alone transforms it—he, the most defenceless and the least powerful of the larger animals. What is infinitely more, man is capable of love. The Christian will add, that he is capable of co-operation with God. We must not ignore the salivary reflexes, but neither should we be obsessed by them.

The determinisms that surround us are indeed no idle word. But the notion of determinism, though it has not been dismissed from science as some imagine, is now limited to the description of large-scale material phenomena. Infra-atomic phenomena escape it; biological phenomena surpass it. At the sub-atomic level the physicist finds no more than a "pseudo-causality", which is such that "the same cause may produce one or another of several possible effects with only a certain probability that such-and-such an effect will be produced and not another." (L. de Broglie). Man is no longer cramped in a vice of determinism. Though we remain concretely involved in, and restricted by many determinisms, every new law that a scientist discovers adds another note to the gamut of our liberty. So long as the laws of aerodynamics remained unknown, men dreamed of flying: when their dream inserted itself into a system of necessities, they flew. Seven notes make but a restricted register; yet those seven notes have made musical invention possible for several centuries already. Whoever argues from necessities of nature to the denial of human potentialities is either bowing down before a myth or trying to justify his own fatalism.

The emergence of creative personality can be read throughout the history of the world. It appears as a struggle between two contrary tendencies, of which one is *a constant trend towards depersonalization*. This is seen not only in matter itself, which indeed is impersonality, passivity and indifference, for it subsides into entropy (degradation of energy) and into sameness or repetition as its natural end. It attacks life, reduces its urge, degrades species to the monotonous repetition of the typical, makes discovery degenerate into automatism, curbs vital audacity within systems of security from which inventiveness disappears, prolongs many movements by inertia till they work against their own purpose. Finally, it lowers the tension of social life and the life of the spirit by the relaxations of habit, of routine, of generalized ideas, and of diurnal gossip.

The other tendency is the *movement of personalization,* which strictly speaking, begins only with man, though one may discern a preparation for it throughout the history of the universe. The phenomena of radio-activity are already announcing a break in the rigid fatalities of matter. Henceforth life takes on the appearance of an accumulation of energy progressively organized into more and more complex nuclei of indeterminacy: a fan of possibilities is thus opened to the free choice of the individual, according to biological predisposition, for the formation of centres of personality. The atomic particle, emptied of all qualities, is no longer identifiable even by its position in space, since the quantum theory forbids us to accord it any precise or lasting localization. An embryonic individuality thus appears even in the atom itself, in the very structure of matter. In the animal, individuality attains to a clearer definition; although nature treats it with scant consideration, multiplying it with prodigality and expending it in massive waste. Two out of two million eggs of a fly hatch and grow into mature individuals. Animals know nothing of reflective consciousness or of conscious reciprocity. The good of the individual is subordinated to that of the species whenever the two conflict. It is in the human person that this series of forms finds, not indeed its explanation but its significance.

The emergence of the personal universe does not arrest the course of natural history, but takes it up into the history of man, without wholly bending it thereto. We sometimes speak of 'primitive man' as if he were a being long lost in the mists of prehistory; but if we attained to the vivid and searching experience of personal reality, we should find our origins still very near to us. The worldly and moralistic comedy in which we play our parts is secretly designed by our instincts, our interests and our needs; even what we call the 'life of the spirit' devotes a great part of its activity to concealing these unacknowledged actors behind the arras of justification and prestige. Materialism is partly right, so long as it is historical and gives its references, though wrong in the realm of values.

For at the stage which humanity has so far attained, and for the great majority, and except for the individual conversions which are always possible (that makes three restrictive conditions), our biological and economic situation still massively manages our behaviour. Numerous individuals and the great movements that some of them have inspired in ages past, doubtless ever since man became man, have broken out of this servitude; again and again, alone or in fellowship, man reaches by a leap the heights of humanity; but man in the mass continues, step by step, his earthbound way towards them. The personal universe does not yet exist except in individual or collective exceptions, in promises yet to be redeemed; yet its progressive conquest is the essential history of mankind.

The consequences of this condition

Certain important consequences follow from the condition we have just defined.

(1) It is pointless to approach either the science of 'matter' or the science of 'spirit' with disparagements or idealizations that are ineffectual on the plane of reality.

(2) Personalism is not a kind of spiritual doctrine, but rather the reverse. It includes every human problem in the entire range of concrete human life, from the lowliest material conditions to the highest spiritual possibilites. The crusades were at one and the same time, and with differing degrees of justification in each case, outstanding expressions of religious sentiment and economic convulsions in a declining feudalism. It is therefore true that the explanation by instinct (Freud) and by economic analysis (Marx) are valid ways of approach to *all* human phenomena, including the highest. On the other hand none, not even the most elementary, can be understood apart from the values, the systems and the vicissitudes of that personal universe which is the immanent goal of every human spirit and of the whole travail of nature. Spiritual and moralist doctrines are impotent because they neglect biological and economic necessities; but materialism is no less futile for the opposite reason. As Marx himself said, 'abstract materialism' and 'abstract spiritualism' come to the same thing; it is not a case of choosing the one or the other, but 'the truth which

unites them both' beyond their separation. More and more clearly, science and reflection are confronting us with a world that cannot do without man, and with man who cannot do without the world.

(3) We must apply to the plane of action what we have just said about the sphere of understanding. In every practical problem, the solution must be verified at the level of the biological and economic substructures, if the measures proposed for higher reason are to be viable. Is this child abnormally idle or indolent? Examine his endocrines before you start lecturing him. Do the people grumble? Study their pay packets before denouncing their materialism. And if you want them to show more virtue, first give them that material security which you are passing on from father to son and without which—as you may forget—your own social moderation might be less conspicuous.

Reciprocally, the biological or economic solution of a human problem, closely though it may conform to elementary needs, will be imperfect and precarious if it does not take account of the profounder aspirations of man. The spiritual, too, is a substructure. Psychological and spiritual maladjustments linked to an economic disorder may gradually undermine any solution achieved on the economic plane alone. And the most rational of economic systems, if it be established in disregard of the fundamental requirements of personality, bears within it the germs of its own decay.

Embodied Existence

Personalism thus opposes idealism, whenever idealism: (a) reduces all matter (and the body) to a reflection of the human spirit, absorbing it into itself by a purely mental activity; or (b) resolves the personal subject into a diagram of geometrical or intellectual relations, whence its presence is excluded; or (c) reduces it to a mere receiving-station for objective findings. For personalism, on the contrary:

(1) With however powerful and subtle a light the human mind may be able to penetrate the structure of the material universe, even to its most delicate articulations, materiality still exists, with an existence that is irreducible, autonomous, and opposed to consciousness. It cannot be resolved into rela-

tions internal to consciousness. That is the affirmation that Marx-Engels called 'materialist'. Yet it is in line with the most traditional realism, with a realism which does not refuse to assimilate the valuable findings of idealist criticism. What is alone radically foreign to consciousness is dispersion, pure, blind and unknowable. One cannot speak of any object, still less of a world, except in relation to a consciousness that perceives it. It is therefore useless to seek to reduce matter to a network of relations. What could we make of the relations that were not perceived? The dialectical relation between matter and consciousness is as irreducible as is the existence of the one and of the other.

(2) I am a person from my most elementary existence upward, and my embodied existence, far from de-personalizing me, is a factor essential to my personal status. My body is not one object among others, nor even the nearest object—for how then could it be one with my experience as a subject? In fact the two experiences are not separate: *I exist subjectively, I exist bodily* are one and the same experience. I cannot think without being and I cannot be without my body, which is my *exposition*—to myself, to the world, to everyone else: by its means alone can I escape from the solitude of a thinking that would be only thought about thought. By its refusal to leave me wholly transparent to myself, the body takes me constantly out of myself into the problems of the world and the struggles of mankind. By the solicitation of the senses it pushes me out into space, by growing old it acquaints me with duration, and by its death, it confronts me with eternity. We bear the weight of its bondage, but it is also the basis of all consciousness and of all spiritual life, the omnipresent mediator of the life of the spirit. In this sense, we may acknowledge with Marx that "a being which is not objective is not a being"—immediately adding, however, that a being which was nothing but objective would fall short of the full achievement of being, the personal life.

The personalization of nature

It is not enough for personality to conform to nature, out of which it proceeds, or to react against nature's provocations.

144

Emmanuel Mounier

The person turns against nature to transform it, progressively to subdue nature to the sovereignty of a personal universe.

Up to a point, personal consciousness affirms itself by simple acceptance of its natural environment. Recognition of the real is the first stage in all creative life; whoever refuses this becomes unhinged and his purpose miscarries.

But this acceptance is only a first stage. To over-adapt oneself is to give oneself up to the bondage of things. The aim of comfort turns man into the domestic animal of the things that provide his comfort; it degrades his productive or social function to automatism. Man's exploitation of nature is not destined to erect upon the web of natural determinism another net-work of conditional reflexes; it is to open up, before the creative liberty of an ever-increasing number of men, the highest possibilities of human being. It is the force of personal affirmation which breaks down the obstacles and opens the way: and to this end we have to deny nature as it is given while affirming it as a task—a task which is both personal and the condition of all personality. Only then, when the *belonging* to nature turns into the *mastery* of nature, is the world joined to the body and man to his proper destiny.

But we must give its correct meaning to this action of man on nature.

Such action cannot, without disaster, give itself up to the frenzy of its own acceleration—to what Henry Ford was admitting in his reply to the question why he went on for ever developing his enterprise,—"Because I can't stop myself!"

It does not consist in subjecting things to the relationship of a slave under a master. The person achieves freedom only in conferring it: and is called to liberate things as well as humanity. Marx used to say of capitalism that its reduction of things to commodities degrades them: to be made merely instrumental to profit deprives the things themselves of the intrinsic dignity which poets, for example, see in them. We contribute to this degradation whenever we use things as mere obstacles to be overcome, as stuff to be possessed or dominated. The arbitrary power we then presume to exercise over things soon communicates itself to human relations, infusing them with tyranny; for tyranny originates always in man, never from things. The Marxist movement, with its belief that the mission of mankind is, on the contrary, to elevate the status of things through the humanization of nature, in this respect approaches the Christian doctrine that the destiny of man is to redeem, both by labour and through his own redemption, the nature that has been corrupted with his fall. The supreme value that is claimed, by Marxism, for man's practical activity (*praxis*), is a kind of secularization of the central value that the Christian tradition claims for work.

The relation of the person with nature is not, then, a purely exterior one, but is a dialectic of exchange, and of ascension. Man presses down upon nature to overcome nature, as the aeroplane rests its weight on the air in order to free itself from weight. Ever since man's first appearance upon the earth—'to cultivate and to tend it' (Genesis II. 15.) and to give names to all creatures—there has been no absolute nature, but only nature in process of humanization. So-called nature, is interspersed throughout with man's artifices. Yet we have hardly been able, since our history began, to do more than begin clumsily to learn how to understand and administer the world. We are now but beginning to enter into its secrets, those of matter, of life and of the psyche. This is a critical turning-point. As the *Essays of Feuerbach* announce in a tone of triumph, henceforth we are going to *transform* as much as to *explain*. Wisdom is to take up industry. Industry will make mistakes: but will it make more of them than philosophy has done? In this sense, *to produce* is indeed an essential activity of the person, for production is viewed in a perspective so sublime that the more menial activities are caught up in the wind of the spirit that lifts humanity above itself. Shackled at first to the immediate satisfaction of elementary needs, then loosened from them by parasitic interests or betrayed to its own infatuations, production should at last become an activity both liberated and liberating, shaped by *all* the requirements of personality. Upon that condition, the mandate of economics, wherever it rightly rules, is the mandate of mankind. But production has value only in regard to its highest end, which is the advent of the world of persons. It cannot derive value from the organization of techniques, nor from the accumulation of products, nor purely and simply as the means to prosperity.

By this light alone can we grasp the profound meaning of technical development. Man is unique in his invention of tools, and in his subsequent linking of them into systems of machinery that slowly frame a collective body for all humanity. The men of this twentieth century are bewildered to see this new and all powerful body they are constructing. The power of abstraction in the machine is indeed frightening: by its severance of human contacts, it can make us forget, more dangerously than anything else has ever done, what happens to those whose work it controls and whose bodies it may sacrifice. Perfectly objective, altogether explicable, it de-educates us from all that is intimate, secret or inexpressible. It puts undreamed-of powers into the hands of imbeciles: it entertains us by its excesses, only to distract us from its cruelties. Left to its own blind inertia, it is the most powerful of forces making for depersonalization. It is all these things, however, only when regarded apart from the spirit that is promoting it as a means to the liberation of man from natural servitude, and to the reconquest of nature. Any purely negative attitude towards technical development springs from inadequate analysis, or from some idealist notion of a destiny that we can only imagine as a subjection to the forces of the earth. The technical age will indeed menace man's progress towards personalization with the greatest possible dangers, just as the rapid growth of an adolescent's body threatens to upset his equilibrium. But this is a development immune to our maledictions. And far from being a disastrous error European particularism, it may yet prove to be the means by which man will one day invade the universe, extending his kingdom until his imagination is at last set free from the fear that his conscious mind, for all its glory, is only a paradox adrift in the infinite inane.

Checks upon the personalization of nature

The tragic optimism

When we trace, with a kind of triumphant amplitude, the vistas of destiny that are opened up by the urge of personalization, let us never forget that its future is by no means automatically assured. At every moment, some new difficulty refers this prospect back to the personal decision of each of us, and it is prejudiced by each and all of our derelictions. For matter is rebellious, not only passive, it is aggressive and not merely inert. Personalism, to borrow a phrase from Maurice Nédoncelle, is not 'a philosophy for Sunday afternoons'. Wherever the person directs its illumination, nature, the body or matter inserts its opacity, beclouding the formula of the scientist, the clarity of reason, or even the transparency of love. Whenever liberty spreads its wings, nature finds numerous ways to depress its flight. When we move towards intimate knowledge, nature externalizes, extends and generalizes. A gain in sensitivity can be a loss of sensation; species spring from a recession of life; habit and custom harden with the lack of invention and laws from the decline of love. Beset by the personal universe, nature ceaselessly threatens to besiege it in her turn. There is nothing in the relation between personal man and the world that suggests the 'pre-established harmony' of Leibnitz. Insecurity and trouble are our lot. Nor does anything suggest that the struggle will end in some predictable time or manner; we have no reason to doubt that it is constitutive of our condition. The perfection of the embodied personal universe, therefore, is not the perfection of an order, as it is in all the philosophic (and all the political) systems which pretend that man will one day totalise the world. It is the perfection of a liberty that is militant, locked in combat, subsisting indeed by the limits it overcomes. Between the impatient optimism of liberal and revolutionary illusion, and the impatient pessimism of the fascists, the right road for man is in this tragic optimism, where he finds his true destiny in a goal of greatness through unending struggle.

PART TWO

PERSONALISM AND THE REVOLUTION
OF THE TWENTIETH CENTURY

Thought and action being so inseparably united in personalist doctrine, the reader will expect some definition of action not only in general method and perspective, but in some precise lines of conduct. A personalism that was content with speculation about the structure of the personal universe would belie its name.

However, the links between ends and means are not immediate or obvious, on account of the complexity introduced into their relations by the transcendence of values. Two men who were in agreement with all that is in the preceding pages might disagree about the problems of the state schools in France, or which trade union they would prefer, or what economic associations ought to be encouraged. There is nothing unusual in that: Sorel was an inspiration to both Lenin and Mussolini. Action is thought-out by reflection upon certain concrete analyses and practical alternatives, viewed in the light of a spectrum of values. Values may be held in common while the analyses differ and expectations diverge. Even such a philosophy as Marxism, wholly subordinated to politico-social analysis, can guarantee no direct deductions from its analyses to its precepts: unless we are mistaken, both Trotsky and Léon Blum thought themselves as good Marxists as Stalin.

Since the 1930's, personalist principles have been applied to a certain historic situation, in a phase of militant thinking. We would not identify personalism in detail with these applications of it, which do not pretend to be exhaustive or definitive; but they are at least illustrative, and give outline to a movement which is not without unity. Let us examine them.

The European Nihilism

This reaction began in the crisis of 1929, which sounded the knell of Euope's happiness and directed attention to revolutions already under way. Of the troubles and miseries which ensued, some gave purely technical and others purely moral explanations. A few young men thought that the disease was at the same time economic and moral, both in the social structure and in the hearts of men; that no remedy was possible without both an economic and a spiritual revolution; and that, man having become what he is, we should have to find and loosen the knots that bind him in the one respect and in the other. First we had to analyse both crises in order to clear the way.

The spiritual crisis is that of classical European man, born into the bourgeois world. He had believed that he was realizing the ideal of the reasonable animal, that triumphant reason was successfully domesticating the animal in him whilst well-being neutralized its passions. Three shocks of warning were administered within a century to this civilization over-confident of its stability. Marx revealed, underneath its economic progress, the merciless struggle of profound social forces; Freud exposed, beneath its psychological complacencies, the witches' cauldron of rebellious instincts; Nietzsche, finally, proclaimed the nihilism of Europe before yielding the floor to Dostoievsky. Since then, their themes have been richly orchestrated by two world wars, the arrival of police states and an underworld of concentration camps. Today, European nihilism is spreading and organizing its forces in every field left vacant by the retreat of those substantial beliefs which kept our fathers in heart—the Christain faith, the culture of science, of reason and of duty. This desperate world has its philosophers, whose teaching is of absurdity and despair, its authors who sow mockery to the four winds. It has its masses, who are less destructive. 'The supreme despair,' wrote Kierkegaard, 'is not to feel desperate.' The reign of satisfied mediocrity is, without doubt, the contemporary basis of nihilism and, as Bernanos has it, of the demoniac.

One can no longer tell what man is, and as we watch him today undergoing such astonishing transformations, some think there is no such thing as human nature. For some people, this idea becomes translated into 'everything is *possible* for man', and in that they find some hope; for others, 'everything is *permissible* to man', and with that they abandon all restraint; for others, finally, 'everything is *permissible against* man', and with that we have arrived at Buchenwald. All the games that might divert us from our disarray have lost their savour, or have been indulged in to satiety. The play of ideas has yielded all it has to give in Hegel—he marks, in fact, the end of philosophy, inasmuch as philosophy is a scholarly architecture designed to conceal our suffering. The religious lunacy which worships the God of philosophers and bankers would indeed justify us in proclaiming that God is dead, if that idol were he. Could we have only a little respite from the wars, to carry on with our technical miracles, then, glutted with comfort, we should soon be able to declare that happiness was dead. Another fourteenth century, as it were, is crumbling away before our eyes: the time for 'a second Renaissance' is at hand.

A crisis in social organization is involved with this spiritual collapse. In the midst of a distracted economy, science continues serenely on its course, redistributing riches and altering social pressures, until social classes fall apart, and the most responsible classes sink into incompetence and indecision. The State has to collect its forces in this tumult: and in the end war or the preparation for war, which is the end-result of such ubiquitous conflict, has for thirty years paralysed both our progress towards the betterment of living conditions and the higher functions of our collective existence.

The rejection of nihilism

Three attitudes towards this total crisis are much in evidence.

Some people give way to fear, and its most usual symptom is the conservative appeal to pre-existing ideas and established powers. The stratagem of the conservative mind is to exalt the past as a pseudo-tradition, or even as pseudo-nature, and to condemn everything modern by the authority of this formal abstraction. It is a defence by prestige; nevertheless it compromises, by withdrawing them from life, the very values it purports to be saving. It is a move for security which exposes its flanks to vengeance and destruction.

Others seek refuge in the cult of catastrophe. They sound the apocalyptic trumpet, minimising every progressive effort with the argument that eschatology alone is worthy of noble souls: they inveigh against all the disorders of the times, or at least against all those that confirm their prejudices. This is a neurosis that is typical of periods of crisis, the inspiration of mystagogues innumerable.

There is one way out, and only one—that is, to confront the event, to invent, and to go ahead—the way which, since the dawn of life, has alone enabled life to cope with crises. The creatures whose effort to surmount danger were limited to withdrawals into sheltered quarters are those that burdened themselves with shell or carapace: they became mussels or oysters, the waifs and strays of life. It was the fish, who took the risk of a naked skin and the hazards of travel, whose initiative led at last to *homo sapiens*. But this affirmative line may be taken in different ways.

We do not disparage the conservative myth of stability in order to commend a myth of blind adventurousness. This, in the face of mediocrity, boredom and despair, has been the temptation of many young men, and of some of the best, in the earlier years of the twentieth century. Lawrence, Malraux and Jünger were among their teachers, as Nietzsche was their foundation. 'A man who is active and at the same time pessimistic' said Manuel in his *l'Espoir*, 'has the makings of a fascist in him, unless he has some fidelity behind him.' For in his solitariness overshadowed by death, what else is there to do, but to plunge into the intoxication of some vivid, unique career, defying all obstacles, rules and regulations; to seek in emotional paroxysms some substitute for a living faith, hoping to leave somewhere upon this accursed world at least a lasting scar? That way, at whatever cost in cruelty, he thinks to regain the sense that he exists, a feeling which frenzy itself no longer gives him. Existentialism has a certain bias in the same direction, but the swindling and brigandage of the years of war are at least equally responsible for mixing this cocktail of theatrical realism. Alcohol to drown all problems, but only for him who knows the way to get it—we have now seen how this ends, in collective crime.

Is it to avoid this fate, that so many others give themselves up body and soul to the instructions of a party? Rather suddenly, it has become the fashion to praise conformity. In so far as this shows a new sense of the collective task, tinged with a nostalgia for the churches of long ago, there is a certain modesty, a regard for community and sacrifice about it—something certainly more respectable than the intellectual anarchism that either ends at thirty years of age in a solicitor's office or goes on for ever from one café table to another. But of what use is it, without the spirit of freedom and the spirit of truth?

From all these observations one can, it would seem, deduce a few rules of personalist strategy.

(1) At least in the beginning, independence of established groups and parties is required, in order to find one's bearings. This does not connote any anarchism or rejection of politics in principle: indeed, wherever individual membership of a collective activity leaves one sufficient freedom of action, it is to be preferred to isolation.

(2) Although spirit is no wild or magical force, there is always a risk of mystification in the affirmation of spiritual values alone, unaccompanied by any precise statement of means and conditions for acting upon them.

(3) The solidarity of the 'spiritual' and the 'material' implies that, in every question, all its problematic aspects must be envisaged, ranging from the 'vilest' data to the 'noblest', with equal accuracy from the one pole to the other. Confusion of mind is the greatest enemy to comprehensive thinking.

(4) Regard for freedom and regard for reality alike demand that the required research should be on its guard against all *à priori* dogmatism, and be ready for anything, even for a change in its whole direction, in order to keep faith with reality and with its own spirit.

(5) The immense accumulation of disorders in our world has led some personalists to call themselves revolutionaries. Facile employment of this word too often renders it devoid of meaning. A sense of the great continuities of life forbids our acceptance of the *tabula rasa* myth of revolution: a real revolution is always a morbid crisis, and it never achieves any automatic solution. To be revolutionary means no more, and also no less, than that the disorders of this century are too intimate and obstinate to be eliminated without reversing the engines, without a profound revision of values, a reorganization of systems and a replacement of those who occupy the most socially responsible places. This having been said, there is no greater abuse of the word than to label yet another conformity with it, or to employ it as a trump in argument or as a substitute for thinking.

Economic society

Marxism is right in giving a certain primacy to economics. Few people despise economics, except those who have ceased to be harassed by any nervousness about their daily bread; and in order to convert the latter, a tour of slumland is preferable to any arguments. At the elementary stage of history which we have thus far attained, economic needs and habits, interests and frustrations do determine the behaviour and the opinions of men in the mass. But this does not mean that economic values are the only ones, or that they are superior to others: the primacy of economics marks a historic disorder from which we have to extricate ourselves.

To find the way out, it is not enough to persuade men, we have also to master material things. Economic disorder can only be cured with economic means if not by those means alone.

Upon the technical aspects of this disorder, personalism as such has nothing to say; it can only study and draw conclusions like anyone else. It concludes, broadly speaking, that capitalism in Europe, in all its diverse forms, is exhausted and at the end of its devices. American capitalism, still in its phase of expansion, can keep that of Europe alive a little longer by affording it transfusions of credit, but sooner or later, living as it does upon the same principles, it will encounter equally serious contradictions. This development needs however to be closely and critically watched; we must not apply the same stereotyped notion of 'capitalism' to every form it may take, regardless of what is in fact happening.

Such critical observation, brought into the personalist perspective, will coincide with Marxist analysis at several points. Liberal democracy has enabled man to become, politically, a subject, but for the most part he remains an object on the plane of economic existence. The anonymous power of money, by which he is privileged to participate in the profits and advantages this kind of world affords, hardens class distinctions and alienates the real man from them. He needs to recover his own disposition; his values, which the tyranny of production for profit has subverted; his sanity, unhinged by the follies of speculation. If he does not, financial imperialism, wherever it feels itself menaced, will not scruple to turn against the liberties it defended while they were useful to it, and will entrust its ultimate security to reigns of terror or to inexpiable wars.

Capitalism cannot be replaced by some new, fully-fledged régime: economic evolution is too continuous for that. It is within the full-grown body of capitalism itself that the embryonic forms of the socialist world first appear and it is these forms that we have to extend and develop, if by socialism we mean the following:—The abolition of the proletarian condition; the supersession of the anarchic economy of profit by an economy directed to the fulfilment of the totality of personal needs; the socialization, without state monopoly, of those sectors of industry which otherwise foster economic chaos; the development of co-operative life; the rehabilitation of labour; the promotion, in rejection of all paternalist compromises, of the worker to full personality; the priority of labour over capital; the abolition of class distinctions founded upon the division of labour or of wealth; the priority of personal responsibility over the anonymous organization.

From the adoption of socialism as the general directive idea for social reorganization, it does not follow that one must approve every measure that may be proposed in its name. Sometimes socialism goes to sleep, and sometimes it loses its way, or becomes perverted under bureaucratic or police systems. All the greater is the need for a re-edition of socialism, rigorous and at the same time democratic. That is the invention now required of Europe, towards which personalism seeks to contribute in its own way. The future will determine whether personalists ought to work in other ways, according to the lessons of experience.

From this point of view, human problems and the problems of social organization are indivisible: the great question of the twentieth century, without doubt, will be whether it can avoid that dictation by the technocrats, either from the right or the left, which loses sight of man in the organizing of his activities. But to keep the two series of problems in practical relation is far from easy. Certain thinkers are tempted to construct an economy *à priori* in the image of man, rather like the

155

first builders of the motor-car, who encumbered the development of its proper structure by designing it in the form of the horse-drawn carriage. Some of these imagine a corporative economy modelled upon the human organism, and postulate a harmony of workers, employers, nation and state by a mythical analogy which is in striking contradiction with the actual and enduring divergences of interests. Others, who pay attention to interpersonal relations, imagine a society in which economic relations would be man-to-man relations indefinitely multiplied into galaxies of little groups 'upon the human scale', as in the myth of Proudhon. But modern economy is a given reality, which seems to evolve rather like physics, towards the concrete by means of the abstract. It is the abstract equations of aerodynamics that have given the aeroplane its form, supple and beautiful as that of a bird; and no doubt it will be from formulas, at first far removed from the principles of corporative or contractual economics, that we shall evolve the simple but unforeseeable structures of a truly human economy.

There remains the question of means: how do we go from the present economic disorders to the order of tomorrow? The means will doubtless vary with circumstances. The extension of capitalism over the whole globe and its possible unification under one powerful empire render it improbable that this transition can be made without resistances and crises. Parliamentary democracy, which has shown itself incapable of effecting profound economic reforms upon the national scale, can hardly be expected to do so in a far vaster sphere. A 'labour policy without Labour', springing simply from the conciliatory good-will of the enlightened section of the middle classes, has demonstrated its impotence throughout the European resistance movements. The attainment of socialism must be, as it was originally formulated, a work of the workers themselves, of movements of peasants and workers organized with the more enlightened portions of the bourgeoisie. Whether it will be achieved piecemeal or in one piece, quickly or slowly, directly or in roundabout ways, are secrets of the future. But its visage will be that which these movements will have impressed upon it: hence the importance of vigilance, not only with regard to the success of these movements but to their integrity.

Emmanuel Mounier

Family and society. The relations of the sexes

To human affairs no exclusive categories apply. The family, which attains the status of a society in its biological aspect, is also in other aspects one of the most spiritual social forms. Its narrownesses and its evils have been denounced to satiety by modern writers, whilst others have extolled it only this side idolatry and cried sacrilege upon all who drew attention to its limitations. In truth it deserves neither such excess of praise nor such derogation.

It is primarily a biological structure, complicated, seldom wholly healthy, which gives rise to innumerable individual and collective dramas by its internal emotional disequilibria. Its carnal character, even when it is healthy, frequently obscures its spirituality; but on the other hand, also endows it with the substance and the intimate illumination which are its essential poesy.

It is a social cell, the first society known to the child, where it learns what human relations are: the family develops these relations as far as the heart is capable of them, and that is its grandeur: but also its weakness, for its members are often deprived of that degree of mutual distance which is necessary for intimacy itself; their spiritual vitality is menaced by the wear and tear of constant contact and by the passions of the tribe. In the end, its internal tensions communicate themselves to the society of which it is a cell: plenty of political and religious rebellions are revolts that were repressed in the familial past. The liabilities in which the family involves us are indeed too heavy to permit any excessive idealization. They make some people unable to see it as anything but a reactionary force.

Yet the family is not only biologically or socially useful, and many of those who defend it simply in its functional aspect miss its full significance. It is the place of contact between public and private affairs, combining a certain range of social relations with a certain intimacy. It socialises the private life while it interiorises the life of manners and customs. Through this mediatory function, the family becomes an essential factor in the personal universe. When it sinks down under the weight of the flesh, it devitalises those whom it was its duty to lead beyond itself, towards higher forms of society. And when it tries completely to socialize itself, infatuated with a kind of family imperialism, there are few more unseemly spectacles. The family with its hackles up, angrily asserting proprietary rights over all its members—whoever delights to see the family in this repulsive light has never understood anything of its miraculous but fragile fabric, woven by love, in which it is the greatest educator. On the other hand, the family can be stifled when it is confused with a stuffy intimacy, shutting-out every draught of fresh air. The charms of private life are the opium of the bourgeoisie, or its hiding-hole from the misery of the world. The values of privacy need rescuing from that profanation.

The family, a biological community, undergoes modifications of structure imposed by its environmental conditions which can profoundly alter its expression without touching its real being. The organization of youth, as an independent age-group, the increase of mobility and of removals, and the democratization of manners are slowly taking the old structure of the family to pieces. If it is true that the increasing laxity of morals and the expiring antics of individualism are dangerously undermining the family as an institution, and spoiling some of its greatest values, we must not confuse such decomposition with its needed ventilation, or with its promotion to a more universal status.

In the perspective we have just outlined, we should be able rightly to place the problems of the sexual life, upon which the great philosophies themselves are so peculiarly discreet. Sexual problems cannot be reduced, as a certain kind of family idealism gives us to understand, to the problems of the family itself; closely though they concern that interior order which the family manifests upon the social plane. Man and woman can only find fulfilment in one another, and their union only finds its fulfilment in the child; such is their inherent orientation towards a kind of abundance and overflow, not to an intrinsic and utilitarian end. Sexual isolation, and childlessness in marriage, engender a whole series of problems, which in part are of potential value and in part merely produced by the unnatural privation. To conceal these is to maintain, and often to provoke, the disorders that they are accused of fostering. But they can only be clearly understood when the particular conditions of privation are viewed in relation to the human condition as a whole.

It is too naive to indict bourgeois respectability for having invented sexual pharisaism, of which it has, however, developed some peculiarly odious forms both from fear and self-interest. Morality would be better served by a little more honesty and a less sordid view of sex.

This is no less true of the vast question of the position of women, in which pseudo-'mystery' we are still far from having disentangled the permanent from the merely historical. Neither masculine self-sufficiency nor the exasperation of vengeful feminism will ever elucidate this dilemma. It is nevertheless true that our social world is one that man has made for men, and that the resources of feminine being are among those which humanity still largely neglects. How these resources are to be fully developed and drawn upon without imprisoning woman in her functions; how to unite her with the world and the world with her; what new values and what new conditions this project calls for—these are questions and tasks inescapable for everyone who gives its full meaning to the affirmation that woman, also, is a person.

National and international society

The nation represents an element of mediation more universalising in its effects than the family. It educates and develops the rational man, enriches the social man by the complexity of the environment it offers him, and opens out before him the entire range of his possibilities. Its correlative danger lies in its greater generality, which renders it so little resistant to the appeals of impassioned verbalism, under the tutelage of vested interests or of the state. Nationalism today appears, in many respects, superannuated, ruinous and regressive. Nevertheless, the national sense is still a powerful corrective of the vital egoism of individuals and of families, of the domination of the state, and of servility towards cosmopolitan economic interests. Human equilibrium is in part regulated from this higher level, which concerns not only citizenship; the nation is one of the integrating factors in man's spiritual life. It may be destined one day to disappear, but its mediating role is still indispensable.

The nation becomes introverted, and a seed-bed of war, if it is not built into a community of nations. The mistake made by the best minds after 1918, was to believe, on liberal, ideological grounds, that this international community could be built simply upon the foundations of sentiment, juridical agreements and parliamentary institutions; whilst other passional, economic and social forces were arousing conflicts and leading to explosions. This illusion persists in the second after-war period (in the U.N.O.) with a more cynical attitude to force: thus evil is piled upon evil. Nevertheless, the world is in fact becoming more and more international: there are no more 'independent' nations in the old sense of the word. The prevailing winds are all making towards world unity, and will sooner or later bring it about, if three conditions can be fulfilled:—namely, that the nations give up their complete sovereignty, not for the benefit of some super-imperialism but to a democratic community of peoples; that this union be achieved between the peoples and their representatives, not between the several governments; and that the forces making for imperialism, especially the economic forces which act sometimes in national and sometimes in cosmopolitan disguise, can be kept under control by the united peoples. Until then, every international organization will be undermined from within by movements that tend to war. Federalism, as a utopian directive, is indeed an expression of personalism: but a directive utopia, whether its character be pacifist or federalist, ought never to be allowed to become an actual utopia, thereby hiding from itself the direction imposed upon it by circumstances, sometimes against its will.

In this epoch particular mention must be made of inter-racial society. The doctrine of the equality of persons obviously excludes every form of racialism, and of xenophobia: which is not in the least to say that it denies the gravity of the practical problems presented by ethnic differences. The colonial period is nearing its end, and justice requires that the metropolitan societies should effectively and loyally pilot towards independence those peoples whose education they have undertaken, and whom they have in some cases uprooted from a social equilibrium quite as valuable as their own. The slightest degree of clairvoyance should warn them not to throw back into chaos those peoples, by whose aid alone are they likely to be able to salvage and continue, their own past achievements in new communities of nations.

The State. Democracy. Sketch of a personalist doctrine of power

Politics is not an end in itself, over-ruling all other aims. Nevertheless, if politics is not everything, it enters into everything.

The first point of reference here should be the rightful place of the State. The State, let us repeat, is not the nation, nor even a condition that must be fulfilled before the nation can attain to veritable being. Only fascists openly proclaim their aim to be the good of the State. The State is that which gives objectivity, strength and concentration, to human rights; it emerges spontaneously from the life of organized groups (G. Gurvitch), and in this respect it is the institutional guarantee of the person. The State is meant for man, not man for the State.

The crucial problem for personalism is that of the legitimacy of power wielded by man over man, which seems to be incompatible with the interpersonal relation: the anarchists indeed think it is so. They believe that the affirmation of the individual, free of all constraint, would spontaneously and of itself bring about a collective order; and that power, on the other hand, is inevitably corrupt and oppressive, however it be constituted. The liberal thesis is not essentially different from this. At the very opposite extreme we have the theorists of absolute power, who think that man, being incurably egoistic, is incapable of raising himself to the level of a common law, and must be forcibly constrained to observe it. On the one side, then, we see optimism about the person but pessimism about power, and on the other pessimism about the person but optimism about power. In both these views of the relation between the personal and the collective one term is idealised and the other degraded. Anarchism and liberalism forget that since man's personality is deeply rooted in the natural world it is impossible to exercise power over things without exercising some constraint over men. However, if this necessity makes power inevitable, it does not endow it with authority. Authority can be founded only upon the final destiny of the person, which power ought to respect and promote. Several things follow from this:—

In the first place, that the person ought to be protected against abuses of power, and that all power not subject to a higher power tends to corrupt. The pre-requisites for this protection are—public and statutory recognition of the person and constitutional limitation of the powers of the State; a balance between the central and the local authorities; the established right of appeal by the citizen against the State; *habeas corpus;* limitation of the powers of the police, and the independence of the judicial authority.

Where the person has to be subordinate, it is the more essential to safeguard his sovereignty as a subject, and to reduce to the minimum such irresponsibility as the very condition of being governed imposes upon him. This is the real problem of *democracy,* a word surrounded with ambiguities. Sometimes it is the name of a form of government, at other times it is used for spontaneous arbitrament by the masses, but it is, in intention, the research for a form of government erected upon the spontaneity of the masses in order to ensure their participation as subjects in the objective structure of powers. Though the two things cannot be separated, they need to be distinguished: for either the 'mob-rule' at the one extreme or the irremovable one-party State at the other are but different kinds of irresponsible tyranny.

The sovereignty of the public cannot be based on the authority of numbers; the dictate of the many—or of the majority—is just as arbitrary as one person's good pleasure. Nor, as Rousseau rightly perceived, can authority be turned over to an anarchic sovereignty of free individuals; it is the attribute of a society rationally organized in a juridical order; the basis of authentic sovereignty lies in human rights. Rights, which constitute the middle term between freedom and organization, maintain the sphere of action in which it is possible for the collective drama to proceed, between individual liberties and the progressive personalization of powers. And here popular initiative is effective in two ways—

Indirectly through representatives, as sincere, public-spirited and able as are obtainable, of the citizens' will. This presupposes a preponderant concern with political education, a function for which political parties have long had the responsibility. When they become mere 'electoral machinery' for depersonalizing both reformers and electors by administrative delays, internal conformity and ideological petrifaction, these parties are dismissing themselves from their business. Unable to get beyond the liberal stage of democracy, diffident about their ideology, their tactics and the social classes for which they must still act, willy-nilly, as rubber-stamps, they will surely soon be superseded. Reform of the party system might palliate these evils, but could not now cure them. Only on the foundation of a new social structure will democracy be able to build up, not a single-party totalitarian system that would perpetuate and intensify its existing defects, but new systems of education and political procedure corresponding to the altered conditions of society. If representation is to be sincere it must also be incorruptible by the temptations of power. It presupposes that the political life is spontaneous as well as unrepressed; that the majority will govern always for the good of all citizens and their education, and will not seek the suppression of the minority.

The sovereignty of the people still finds expression, when its representatives fail in their function, in direct pressure upon the government—in meetings of protest, disturbances, seditious groups and associations, strikes, boycotts and, in the extreme case, in national insurrection. The State, itself born in strife but forgetful of its origins, usually regards such acts of pressure as illegal; they are nevertheless profoundly legitimate if a State is condoning injustice or oppression. We must never forget that during the century and a half that has elapsed since the beginning of the labour movement, many more wrongs have been righted by direct pressure than by the initiative of jurists or the good will of the powerful. Direct action may be about to enter a new field and bear its part in developing international justice. It is certainly one of the rights of citizenship, the hardest to exercise and the most liable to abuse, but inalienable.

In considering these enduring problems of power and of the State, one must always bear in mind the close correspondence between political forms and their underlying social contents. The Marxist criticism of formal democracy is on the whole unanswerable: many of the rights that the liberal State grants to its citizens are abrogated by the facts of their economic and social existence. The parliamentary machine of the State is already little more than a survival: its wheels are revolving in a void; its orators sow the wind and reap the whirlwind. Political democracy needs to be wholly reorganized in relation to an effectual economic democracy adapted to the contemporary systems of production.

Only upon this organic basis can the legitimate authority of the State be restored. To propose its restoration without saying by whom or with what ends in view, is merely to demand greater executive powers for established injustice. Ought the State then to disappear? Will the government of men be one day replaced by the administration of things? One may well doubt this, since men and things are inextricably involved and it becomes more and more impossible to leave affairs to their own drift. And what State could conceivably renounce its own unity? Advocates of personalism have sometimes felt that their aspiration ought to be expressed by a demand for a 'pluralist State', in which the division and balance of its constituent powers would mutually guarantee them against abuse. But the formula is in danger of appearing too contradictory; one should speak rather of a State articulated in the service of a pluralist society.

The education of the person

The development of the person in man, and the orientation of man towards the individual and collective requirements of the personal universe, begin from birth.

Our education has been described as a 'massacre of the innocents' on the largest scale. Misunderstanding the person in the child, it imposes upon his mind a synopsis of adult conceptions of life including a scale of social inequalities, and replaces his own discrimination between characters and vocations by an authoritarian formulation of knowledge. The new educational movement, which is a reaction against this, has been partly misguided by liberal optimism, with its exclusive ideal of the thriving, philanthropic and well-adapted man. It needs to be reformed, one might say made more virile, by bringing it into the full perspective of individual and social man.

How is a child's education actually effected? The question depends upon another—what is its aim? Not to *make*, but to *awaken* personality. By definition, personality awakens itself in response to an appeal, and cannot be fabricated from without. The purpose of education cannot therefore be to fashion the child in conformity with an environment, either familial, social or of the State, nor can it be restricted to adapting the child to the function or occupation that he is to fulfil as an adult. The transcendence of the person means that the person belongs to nobody else but to himself: the child is a subject, it is not a *RES societatis* nor a *RES familiae* nor a *RES Ecclesiae*. Not that it is purely subjective nor an isolated subject. Inserted into various collectivities the child is educated by them and within them; if they are not all-powerful in its eyes, they are its natural formative environments—the family and the nation and (the Christian adds) the Church, are all avenues that open out towards a wider humanity.

The educational question cannot be reduced to the problems of the school: the school is only one educational instrument among others; and even to make it the principal instrument is a dangerous error. The school is not charged with the duty of imparting 'instruction' in the abstract, but with scholarly education, which is but one sector of the whole. This kind of education being that which is most closely linked with the needs of the nation—the formation of the citizen and the producer—is that which the nation, represented by its administrative organs, has the most direct right to supervise and organize. Schools are not organs of the State, but in our modern countries they are national institutions and their methods have to be shaped in accordance with the needs and concrete situation of the nation, within the frame of natural educational rights. These conditions may sometimes require the dispersal, and at other times the concentration, of scholastic institutions, but never justify their becoming organs of the State. And the extra-scholastic areas of education ought to be allowed as complete freedom as possible. Finally, considered as a function of the nation as a whole, school education should be open to all, none of its higher degrees being reserved for a privileged section of the people. Its function is to impart to everyone the minimum of knowledge that the free person requires, but also to call forth, from whatever social environment, those individuals of talent who, given effectively equal opportunity, will be able to discharge the directive responsibilities of the nation for each new generation.

Culture

Culture is not one sector, but a comprehensive function, of the personal life. For a being who finds himself, and forms himself by a process of development, everything is culture, the management of a factory or the formation of a body no less than the conduct of a conversation or the cultivation of the soil. This is to say that there is not *a* culture, in distinction from which every other activity is uncultured (a 'cultured man') but there are as many kinds of culture as of activity. This point needs to be remembered against our bookish civilization.

Since the personal life is that of freedom and self-surpassing, not of accumulation and repetition, culture does not consist, in any of its domains, in the heaping-up of knowledge, but in a deep transformation of the subject, enabling him to fulfil ever new possibilities in response to ever-renewed calls from within. As someone has said, culture is that which remains when one no longer knows anything,—it is what the man himself has become.

It follows that, like everything else that is personal, culture is an awakening, it cannot be contrived or imposed. But neither can it develop, any more than anything else of a personal nature, in absolute liberty; or without being under pressure from a thousand solicitations and constraints which it finally turns to good account. Inventive even in its decline, culture elaborates orthodoxies and finally perishes under their tyranny. It is obvious that any culture, at a certain level of achievement, can and needs to be directed or, it would be better to say, sustained. But it will not endure being planned. And in its creative phases, it needs to go its own way alone, though in a loneliness freely responsive to every vibration of the great world without.

Some degree of support from the collective life is indispensable to the creations of culture; when it is vital they can flourish, when it is mediocre they are enfeebled. Yet the creative impulse always acts through the single person, though he may afterwards be lost in the crowd; every folk-song had its first original composer: and even were all men to become artists, there would not be one art, but as many varieties of art as there were men. All that is true in the collectivist doctrine of culture is that any one class tends to imprison culture in conventions, and that the inexhaustible resources of cultural renewal are in the people themselves.

Once again—all culture is a transcendence and a renewal. As soon as a cultural development is arrested, it becomes anti-cultural—academic, pedantic or commonplace: as soon as it loses its sense of the universal it begins to dry up into specialisms. And as soon as it confuses universality with a static notion of totality, it hardens into a system.

Most of these conditions obtain, more or less unrecognized in the culture of today; hence its disorder. The social cleavage between the horny-handed and the white-collared, and prejudiced ideas about the priority of 'the spiritual' lead people to confound culture with book-knowledge and technology. The deep class divisions that accompany this prejudice have imprisoned culture, or at least its means, its privileges and sometimes its illusions, within a minority, to its sophistication and impoverishment. Here, one social class subjects culture more and more to its own ends; there, a government does the same; everywhere it is abused. As a common term between a society and its spiritual life, it is submerged by conventions on one side and the latest fashions on the other. Creative artists have no longer a public, and where a public exists they lack the means to make an appearance. Economic and social conditions are largely responsible for these privations; they produce a cultural caste which seduces art (of the court, the salon or the church) into esotericism, snobbery or preciosity to flatter its importance; into academicism for its reassurance; into frivolity for its distraction; and into pungency, complexity or brutality to relieve its boredom. As technique widens the choice of means and multiplies the possibilities of artistic production, the products are commercialized and cheapened to the greater profit of the smaller number, to the detriment alike of the producer, the work and the public taste. The condition of the artist, the professional and the man of learning thus oscillates between the poverty of neglect and the servility of a tradesman. Many are the maladies so bound up with our social structure that its disappearance is the first condition for their cure. We must not therefore ignore two no less considerable factors in the enfeeblement of our culture: the bewilderment of the contemporary conscience, from which the vision of the great hierarchies of value (both religious and rationalist) are fading away; and the present obsession by mechanical and utilitarian ideas.

The position of Christianity

We sought to distinguish, in actual religious life, between the eternal reality, its expressions in temporal and perishable forms, and the compromises to which men reduce them. The religious spirit does not consist in the justification of all these together by apologetics, but in separating the authentic from the inauthentic, what will endure from what is obsolete. And here it makes contact with the spirit of personalism.

The compromises of contemporary Christianity include several movements that are historical revivals. There is the old theocratic temptation of state-control of the conscience; the sentimental conservatism which would link the defence of the faith with that of out-of-date class-systems; and a stubborn logic of money that would over-ride the interests it ought to serve. Elsewhere, in reaction against these nostalgias and survivals, there are frivolous attempts to curry favour with the latest ideological success. Whoever wishes to maintain Christian values in their vigour should rather seek, by all means, to separate Christianity from these established disorders.

But that, after all, is but a very external activity in relation to the crucial problem that this age presents to Christianity. Christianity no longer holds the field. There are other massive realities; undeniable values are emerging apparently without its help, arousing moral forces, heroisms and even kinds of saintliness. It does not seem, for its own part, able to combine with the modern world (with its consciousness, reason, science, technology, and its labouring masses) in a marriage such as it consummated with the mediaeval world. Is it, indeed, approaching its end, of which this divorce is the sign? A deeper study of the facts leads us to believe that this crisis is not the end of Christianity, but only of a kind of Christianity. Perhaps the decomposing hulk of a world that Christianity built, that has now slipped its moorings, is drifting away, and leaving behind it the pioneers of a new Christianity. Or it would seem that, having for many centuries flirted, as it were, with the Jewish temptation, of trying directly to establish the Kingdom of God upon the plane of terrestrial power, Christianity is slowly returning to its first position; renouncing government upon earth and the outward appearances of sanctification to achieve the unique work of the Church, the community of Christians in the Christ, mingled among all men in the secular work,— neither theocracy nor liberalism, but a return to the double rigours of transcendence and incarnation. Nevertheless one cannot say that the tendencies of today, any more than those of yesterday, give final definition to the relations between Christianity and the world, because no such definition is possible. What is essential to each, is that the living spirit should be fostered.

The crisis of Christianity is not only a historic crisis of the Church, it is a crisis of religious values throughout the white man's world. The philosophy of the Enlightenment believed that religious values were artificially maintained, and was persuaded that they would shortly disappear. For some time this illusion could be kept up upon the rising tide of scientific enthusiasm. But if one sure conclusion can already be drawn from the experiences of this twentieth century, it is that as fast as these values in Christian vestments disappear, they reappear under other, more obsessive images: the body is divinised, or the collectivity, or the evolutionary striving of the species; or the Leader, or the Party, and so forth. All the regulative ideals that are set forth in the 'phenomenology' of religion come back again in novel cults and in generally debased forms, decidedly retrograde in comparison with those of Christianity, precisely because the personal universe and its requirements are eliminated.

The positions indicated in these few pages are debatable and subject to revision. For these are not conclusions drawn from the application of a received ideology; they have the free, provisional character of a progressive disclosure of the human predicament in our time. It cannot but be the hope of every personalist that these positions will develop as discovery proceeds, until the word 'personalism' itself be one day forgotten, because there will no longer be any need to direct attention to what will have become the common and accepted knowledge of the situation of mankind.

Jacques Maritain
1882-1973

Jacques Maritain is clearly one of the most brilliant and influential intellectuals of the twentieth century. His entire life was dedicated to a careful, meditative search for absolute and eternal truth. The fruit of this search, lucidly expressed in more than fifty books, has played a significant role in shaping Christian, and especially Catholic, views of the modern world's most important problems. Born in Paris, November 18, 1882, Jacques Maritain grew up in a liberal Protestant atmosphere. He pursued his studies at the Sorbonne. While a student there, he met and married Raissa Oumancoff, a young woman of Russian Jewish origin, who was searching as seriously as was Maritain for meaning in life. In 1906, the Maritains became Catholics.

Maritain turned his attention to a thorough study of Thomas Aquinas, the great thirteenth century thinker. What he found in the Thomistic system of thought shaped the remainder of his life. He was convinced that his task was to use the principles of Aquinas in his effort to resolve the questions of art, science and society in the twentieth century. From 1913 through to 1960, Maritain taught philosophy at universities such as Louvain, Oxford, Chicago, Columbia and Princeton. After the death of his wife in 1960, he retired to Toulouse, where he lived with the community of the Little Brothers of Jesus. He died there April 28, 1973.

THE CATHOLIC TRADITION: Social Thought

The dignity of man, as an earthly and social being, is central to Maritain's thought. He rejected the philosophies of capitalism and socialism, both of which deny true human value, and called for a new vision of mankind, a vision that could sustain human liberties, enrich the person, and satisfy the basic human needs. Turning toward religion, he insisted decorative Christianity is insufficient and that Christians must go out into the highways to conquer the world through love and the gift of self. Maritain realized that the twentieth century Christian tended to divide his life into two halves, the Christian and the pagan. This he declared to be inadmissible. He urged the Church to take concrete steps toward healing the rift that had developed between herself and the working classes throughout the world.

Maritain's lifelong dedication to teaching and writing bore fruit. He must be recognized as one of the major personalities who prepared the Church for the Second Vatican Council. The ideas and positions developed by the Council owe much to Maritain's philosophy. At the close of the Council, Pope Paul VI, who referred to Maritain as his teacher, publicly embraced him in St. Peter's Square.

The reading below is taken from Man and the State, *in which Maritain explores the principles of democracy and calls for a redefinition of the essence of the democratic idea. Basic concepts such as nation, the people, sovereignty, human rights and world government are carefully reviewed. Maritain was aware that the terms common to all political groups change meaning according to each group's vision of man. Working from a rich model of the person, he exposes and critiques extreme individualism and socialism, and successfully proposes a healthy, balanced alternative.*

MAN AND THE STATE

MEN MUTUALLY OPPOSED IN THEIR THEORETICAL CONCEPTIONS CAN COME TO A MERELY PRACTICAL AGREEMENT REGARDING A LIST OF HUMAN RIGHTS

Owing to the historical development of mankind, to ever widening crises in the modern world, and to the advance, however precarious, of moral conscience and reflection, men have today become aware, more fully than before, though still imperfectly, of a number of practical truths regarding their life in common upon which they can agree, but which are derived in the thought of each of them—depending upon their ideological allegiances, their philosophical and religious traditions, their cultural backgrounds and their historical experiences—from extremely different, or even basically opposed, theoretical conceptions. As the International Declaration of Rights published by the United Nations in 1948 showed very clearly, it is doubtless not easy but it is possible to establish a common formulation of such *practical conclusions,* or in other words, of the various rights possessed by man in his personal and social existence. Yet it would be quite futile to look for a common *rational justification* of these practical conclusions and these rights. If we did so, we would run the risk of imposing arbitrary dogmatism or of being stopped short by irreconcilable differences. The question raised at this point is that of the practical agreement among men who are theoretically opposed to one another.

Here we are confronted by the paradox that rational justifications are *indispensable* and at the same time *powerless* to create agreement among men. They are indispensable, because each of us believes instinctively in truth and only wishes to give his consent to what he has recognized as true and rationally valid. Yet rational justifications are powerless to create agreement among men, because they are basically different, even opposed to each other; and is this surprising? The problems raised by rational justifications are difficult, and the philosophical traditions in which those justifications originate have been in opposition for a long time.

During one of the meetings of the French National Commission of UNESCO at which the Rights of Man were being discussed, someone was astonished that certain proponents of violently opposed ideologies had agreed on the draft of a list of rights. Yes, they replied, we agree on these rights, *providing we are not asked why*. With the "why," the dispute begins.

The subject of the Rights of Man provides us with an eminent example of the situation that I tried to describe in an address to the second International Conference of UNESCO, from which I take the liberty of quoting a few passages. "How," I asked, "is an agreement conceivable among men assembled for the purpose of jointly accomplishing a task dealing with the future of the mind, who come from the four corners of the earth and who belong not only to different cultures and civilizations, but to different spiritual families and antagonistic schools of thought? Since the aim of UNESCO is a practical aim, agreement among its members can be spontaneously achieved, not on common speculative notions, but on common practical notions, not on the affirmation of the same conception of the world, man, and knowledge, but on the affirmation of the same set of convictions concerning action. This is doubtless very little, it is the last refuge of intellectual agreement among men. It is, however, enough to undertake a great work; and it would mean a great deal to become aware of this body of common practical convictions.

"I should like to note here that the word *ideology* and the word *principle* can be understood in two very different ways. I have just said that the present state of intellectual division among men does not permit agreement on a common *speculative* ideology, nor on common *explanatory* principles. However, when it concerns, on the contrary, the basic *practical* ideology and the basic principles of *action* implicitly recognized today, in a vital if not a formulated manner, by the consciousness of free peoples, this happens to constitute *grosso modo* a sort of common residue, s sort of unwritten common law, at the point of practical convergence of extremely different theoretical ideologies and spiritual traditions. To understand that, it is sufficient to distinguish properly between the rational justifications, inseparable from the spiritual dynamism of a philosophical doctrine or religious faith, and the practical conclusions which, separately justified for each, are, for all, analogically common principles of action. I am fully convinced that my way of justifying the belief in the rights of man and the ideal of freedom, equality, and fraternity is the only one which is solidly based on truth. That does not prevent me from agreeing on these practical tenets with those who are convinced that their way of justifying them, entirely different from mine or even opposed to mine in its theoretical dynamism, is likewise the only one that is based on truth. Assuming they both believe in the democratic charter, a Christian and a rationalist will, nevertheless, give justifications that are incompatible with each other, to which their souls, their minds, and their blood are committed, and about these justifications they will fight. And God keep me from saying that it is not important to know which of the two is right! That is essentially important. They remain, however, in agreement on the practical affirmation of that charter, and they can formulate together common principles of action."

On the level of rational interpretations and justifications, on the speculative or theoretical level, the question of the rights of man brings into play the whole system of moral and metaphysical (or anti-metaphysical) certainties to which each individual subscribes. As long as there is no unity of faith or unity of philosophy in the minds of men, the interpretations and justifications will be in mutual conflict.

In the domain of practical assertion, on the contrary, an agreement on a common declaration is possible by means of an approach that is more pragmatic than theoretical, and by a collective effort of comparing, recasting, and perfecting the drafts in order to make them acceptable to all as points of practical convergence, regardless of the divergence in theoretical perspectives. Thus nothing prevents the attainment of formulations which would indicate notable progress in the process of world unification. It is not reasonably possible to hope for more than this practical convergence on a set of articles drafted in common. If a theoretical reconciliation, a truly philosophical synthesis, is desired, this could only come about as a result of a vast amount of probing and purification, which would require higher intuitions, a new systematization, and the radical criticism of a certain number of errors and confused ideas—which for these very reasons, even if it succeeded in exerting an important influence on culture, would remain one doctrine among many, accepted by a number and rejected by the rest, and could not claim to establish in actual fact universal ascendancy over men's minds.

Is there any reason to be surprised at seeing conflicting theoretical systems converge in their practical conclusions? The history of moral philosophy generally presents this very picture. This fact merely proves that systems of moral philosophy are the product of intellectual reflection on ethical data that precede and control them and reveal a very complicated type of geology of the conscience, in which the natural work of spontaneous, pre-scientific, and pre-philosophical reason is at every moment conditioned by the acquisitions, the servitudes, the structure and evolution of the social group. Thus there is a sort of vegetative development and growth, so to speak, of moral knowledge and moral feeling, which is in itself independent of the philosophical systems, although in a secondary way the latter in turn enter into reciprocal action with this spontaneous process. As a result these various sytems, while disputing about the "why," prescribe in their practical conclusions rules of behavior which appear on the whole as almost the same for any given period and culture. Thus, from a sociological point of view, the most important factor in the moral progress of humanity is the experiential development of awareness which takes place outside of systems and on another logical basis—at times facilitated by systems when they awaken consciousness to itself, at other times thwarted by them when they obscure the apperceptions of spontaneous reason or when they jeopardize an authentic acquisition of moral experience by linking it to some theoretical error or some false philosophy.

II

THE PHILOSOPHICAL ISSUE DEALS WITH THE RATIONAL FOUNDATION OF HUMAN RIGHTS

Yet, from the point of view of intelligence, what is essential is to have a true justification of moral values and moral norms. With regard to Human Rights, what matters most to a philosopher is the question of their rational foundations.

The philosophical foundation of the Rights of man is Natural Law. Sorry that we cannot find another word! During the rationalist era jurists and philosophers have misused the notion of natural law to such a degree, either for conservative or for revolutionary purposes, they have put it forward in so over-simplified and so arbitrary a manner, that it is difficult to use it now without awakening distrust and suspicion in many of our contemporaries. They should realize, however, that the history of the rights of man is bound to the history of Natural Law, and that the discredit into which for some time positivism brought the idea of Natural Law inevitably entailed a similar discrediting of the idea of the Rights of man.

As Mr. Laserson rightly said, "The doctrines of natural law must not be confused with natural law itself. The doctrines, may propound various arguments or theories in order to substantiate or justify natural law, but the overthrow of these theories cannot signify the overthrow of natural law itself, just as the overthrow of some theory or philosophy of law does not lead to the overthrow of law itself. The victory of judicial positivism in the XIXth Century over the doctrine of natural law did not signify the death of natural law itself, but only the victory of the conservative historical school over the revolutionary rationalistic school, called for by the general historical conditions in the first half of the XIXth Century. The best proof of this is the fact that at the end of that century, the so-called 'renaissance of natural law' was proclaimed."

From the XVIIth Century on, people had begun to think of Nature with a capital N and Reason with a capital R, as abstract divinities sitting in a Platonic heaven. As a result the consonance of a human act with reason was to mean that that act was traced from a ready-made, pre-existing pattern which infallible Reason had been instructed to lay down by infallible Nature, and which, consequently, should be immutably and universally recognized in all places of the earth and at all moments of time. Thus Pascal himself believed that justice among men should of itself have the same universal application as Euclid's propositions. If the human race knew justice, "the brilliance of true equity," he says, "would have subdued all nations, and legislators would not have taken as models, in place of this unchanging justice, the fantasies and caprices of Persians and Germans. One would see it established in all the states of the world and through all the ages. . . ." Which is, I need not say, a wholly abstract and unreal conception of justice. Wait a little more than a century and you will hear Condorcet promulgate this dogma, which at first glance seems self-evident, yet which means nothing: "A good law should be good for everyone"—say, for man of the age of cave-dwellers as well as for man of the age of the steam-engine, for nomadic tribes as well as for agricultural peoples,—"a good law should be good for everyone, just as a true proposition is true for everyone."

So the XVIIIth Century conception of the Rights of man presupposed, no doubt, the long history of the idea of natural law evolved in ancient and mediaeval times; but it had its immediate origins in the artificial systematization and rationalist recasting to which this idea had been subjected since Grotius and more generally since the advent of a geometrising reason. Through a fatal mistake, natural law—which is *within* the being of things as their very essence is, and which precedes all formulation, and is even known to human reason *not* in terms of conceptual and rational knowledge—natural law was thus conceived after the pattern of a *written* code, applicable to all, of which any just law should be a transcription, and which would determine *a priori* and in all its aspects the norms of human behaviour through ordinances supposedly prescribed by Nature and Reason, but in reality arbitrarily and artificially formulated. "As Warnkoenig has shown, eight or more new systems of natural law made their appearance at every Leipzig booksellers' fair since 1780. Thus Jean-Paul Richter's ironical remark contained no exaggeration: Every fair and every war brings forth a new natural law." Moreover, this philosophy of rights ended up, after Rousseau and Kant, by treating the individual as a god and making all the rights ascribed to him the absolute and unlimited rights of a god.

As to God himself, He had only been, from the XVIIth Century on, a superadded guarantor for that trine, self-subsistent absolute: Nature, Reason, Natural Law, which even if God did not exist would still hold sway over men. So that finally the human Will or human Freedom, also raised to Platonic self-subsistence in that intelligible, though unreachable, empyreal world which Kant inherited from Leibniz, was to replace God in actual fact as supreme source and origin of Natural Law. Natural Law was to be deduced from the so-called autonomy of the Will (there is a genuine notion of autonomy, that of St. Paul—unfortunately the XVIIIth Century had forgotten it). The rights of the human person were to be based on the claim that man is subject to no law other than that of his own will and freedom. "A person," Kant wrote, "is subject to no other laws than those which he (either alone or jointly with others) gives to himself." In other words, man must "obey only himself," as Jean-Jacques Rousseau put it, because every measure or regulation springing from the world of nature (and finally from creative wisdom) would destroy at one and the same time his autonomy and his supreme dignity.

This philosophy built no solid foundations for the rights of the human person, because nothing can be founded on illusion: it compromised and squandered these rights, because it led men to conceive them as rights in themselves divine, hence infinite, escaping every objective measure, denying every limitation imposed upon the claims of the ego, and ultimately expressing the absolute independence of the human subject and a so-called absolute right—which supposedly pertains to everything in the human subject by the mere fact that it is in him—to unfold one's cherished possibilities at the expense of all other beings. When men thus instructed clashed on all sides with the impossible, they came to believe in the bankruptcy of the rights of the human person. Some have turned against these rights with an enslaver's fury; some have continued to invoke them, while in their inmost conscience they are weighed down by a temptation to scepticism which is one of the most alarming symptoms of the crisis of our civilization.

III

NATURAL LAW

Shall we try to reestablish our faith in human rights on the basis of a true philosophy? This true philosophy of the rights of the human person is based upon the true idea of natural law, as looked upon in an ontological perspective and as conveying through the essential structures and requirements of created nature the wisdom of the Author of Being.

The genuine idea of natural law is a heritage of Greek and Christian thought. It goes back now only to Grotius, who indeed began deforming it, but, before him to Suarez and Francisco de Vitoria; and further back to St. Thomas Aquinas (he alone grasped the matter in a wholly consistent doctrine, which unfortunately was expressed in an insufficiently clarified vocabulary, so that its deepest features were soon overlooked and disregarded); and still further back to St. Augustine and the Church Fathers and St. Paul (we remember St. Paul's saying: "When the Gentiles who have not the Law, *do by nature* the things contained in the Law, these, having not the Law, are a law unto themselves . . ."); and even further back to Cicero, to the Stoics, to the great moralists of antiquity and its great poets, particularly Sophocles. Antigone, who was aware that in transgressing the human law and being crushed by it she was obeying a better commandment, the *unwritten and unchangeable laws,* is the eternal heroine of natural law: for, as she puts it, they were not, those unwritten laws, born out of today's or yesterday's sweet will, "but they live always and forever, and no man knows from where they have arisen."

The First Element (Ontological) in Natural Law

Since I have not time here to discuss nonsense (we can always find very intelligent philosophers, not to quote Mr. Bertrand Russell, to defend it most brilliantly) I am taking it for granted that we admit that there is a human nature, and that this human nature is the same in all men. I am taking it for granted that we also admit that man is a being gifted with intelligence, and who, as such, acts with an understanding of what he is doing, and therefore with the power to determine for himself the ends which he pursues. On the other hand, possessed of a nature, or an ontologic structure which is a locus of intelligible necessities, man possesses ends which necessarily correspond to his essential constitution and which are the same for all—as all pianos, for instance, whatever their particular type and in whatever spot they may be, have as their end the production of certain attuned sounds. If they do not produce these sounds they must be tuned, or discarded as worthless. But since man is endowed with intelligence and determines his own ends, it is up to him to put himself in tune with the ends necessarily demanded by his nature. This means that there is, by the very virtue of human nature, an order or a disposition which human reason can discover and according to which the human will must act in order to attune itself to the essential and necessary ends of the human being. The unwritten law, or natural law, is nothing more than that.

The example that I just used—taken from the world of human workmanship—was purposely crude and provocative: yet did not Plato himself have recourse to the idea of any work of human art whatever, the idea of the Bed, the idea of the Table, in order to make clear his theory (which I do not share) of eternal Ideas? What I mean is that every being has its own natural law, as well as it has its own essence. Any kind of thing produced by human industry has, like the stringed instrument that I brought up a moment ago, its own natural law, that is, the *normality of its functioning,* the proper way in which, by reason of its specific construction, it demands to be put into action, it *"should"* be used. Confronted with any supposedly unknown gadget, be it a corkscrew or a peg-top or a calculating machine or an atom bomb, children or scientists, in their eagerness to discover how to use it, will not question the existence of that inner typical law.

Any kind of thing existing in nature, a plant, a dog, a horse, has its own natural law, that is, the *normality of its functioning,* the proper way in which, by reason of its specific structure and specific ends, it *"should"* achieve fulness of being either in its growth or in its behaviour. Washington Carver, when he was a child and healed sick flowers in his garden, had an obscure knowledge, both by intelligence and congeniality, of that vegetative law of theirs. Horse-breeders have an experiential knowledge, both by intelligence and congeniality, of the natural law of horses, a natural law with respect to which a horse's behaviour makes him a *good horse* or a *vicious horse* in the herd. Well, horses do not enjoy free will, their natural law is but a part of the immense network of essential tendencies and regulations involved in the movement of the cosmos, and the individual horse who fails in that equine law only obeys the universal order of nature on which the deficiencies of his individual nature depend. If horses were free, there would be an ethical way of conforming to the specific natural law of horses, but that horsy morality is a dream because horses are not free.

When I said a moment ago that the natural law of all beings existing in nature is the proper way in which, by reason of their specific nature and specific ends, they *should* achieve fulness of being in their behaviour, this very word *should* had only a metaphysical meaning (as we say that a good or a normal eye "should" be able to read letters on a blackboard from a given distance.) The same word *should* starts to have a *moral* meaning, that is, to imply moral obligation, when we pass the threshold of the world of free agents. Natural law for man is *moral* law, because man obeys or disobeys it freely, not necessarily, and because human behaviour pertains to a particular, privileged order which is irreducible to the general order of the cosmos and tends to a final end superior to the immanent common good of the cosmos.

What I am emphasizing is the first basic element to be recognized in natural law, namely the *ontological* element; I mean the *normality of functioning* which is grounded on the essence of that being: man. Natural law in general, as we have just seen, is the ideal formula of development of a given being; it might be compared with an algebraical equation according to which a curve develops in space, yet with man the curve has freely to conform to the equation. Let us say, then, that in its ontological aspect, natural law is an *ideal order* relating to human actions, a *divide* between the suitable and the unsuitable, the proper and the improper, which depends on human nature or essence and the unchangeable necessities rooted in it. I do not mean that the proper regulation for each possible human situation is contained in the human essence, as Leibniz believed that every event in the life of Caesar was contained beforehand in the idea of Caesar. Human situations are something existential. Neither they nor their appropriate regulations are contained in the essence of man. I would say that they ask questions of that essence. Any given situation, for instance the situation of Cain with regard to Abel, implies a relation to the essence of man, and the possible murder of the one by the other is incompatible with the general ends and innermost dynamic structure of that rational essence. It is rejected by it. Hence the prohibition of murder is grounded on or required by the essence of man. The precept: thou shalt do no murder, is a precept of natural law. Because a primordial and most general end of human nature is to preserve being—the being of that existent who is a person, and a universe unto himself; and because man insofar as he is man has a right to live.

Suppose a completely new case or situation, unheard of in human history: suppose, for instance, that what we now call *genocide* were as new as that very name. In the fashion that I just explained, that possible behaviour will face the human essence as incompatible with its general ends and innermost dynamic structure: that is to say, as prohibited by natural law. The condemnation of genocide by the General Assembly of United Nations has sanctioned the prohibition of the crime in question by natural law—which does not mean that that prohibition was part of the essence of man as I know not what metaphysical feature eternally inscribed in it—nor that it was a notion recognized from the start by the conscience of humanity.

To sum up, let us say that natural law is something both *ontological* and *ideal*. It is something *ideal*, because it is grounded on the human essence and its unchangeable structure and the intelligible necessities it involves. Natural law is something *ontological*, because the human essence is an ontological reality, which moreover does not exist separately, but in every human being, so that by the same token natural law dwells as an ideal order in the very being of all existing men.

In that first consideration, or with regard to the basic *ontological* element it implies, natural law is coextensive with the whole field of natural moral regulations, the whole field of natural morality. Not only the primary and fundamental regulations but the slightest regulations of natural ethics mean conformity to natural law—say, natural obligations or rights of which we perhaps have now no idea, and of which men will become aware in a distant future.

An angel who knew the human essence in his angelic manner and all the possible existential situations of man would know natural law in the infinity of its extension. But we do not. Though the Eighteenth Century theoreticians believed they did.

The Second Element (Gnoseological) in Natural Law

Thus we arrive at the *second* basic element to be recognized in natural law, namely natural law *as known,* and thus as measuring in actual fact human practical reason, which is the measure of human acts.

Natural law is not a written law. Men know it with greater or less difficulty, and in different degrees, running the risk of error here as elsewhere. The only practical knowledge all men have naturally and infallibly in common as a self-evident principle, intellectually perceived by virtue of the concepts involved, is that we must do good and avoid evil. This is the preamble and the principle of natural law; it is not the law itself. Natural law is the ensemble of things to do and not to do which follow therefrom in *necessary* fashion. That every sort of error and deviation is possible in the determination of these things merely proves that our sight is weak, our nature coarse, and that innumerable accidents can corrupt our judgment. Montaigne maliciously remarked that, among certain peoples, incest and thievery were considered virtuous acts. Pascal was scandalized by this. All this proves nothing against natural law, any more than a mistake in addition proves anything against arithmetic, or the mistakes of certain primitive peoples, for whom the stars were holes in the tent which covered the world, prove anything against astronomy.

Natural law is an unwritten law. Man's knowledge of it has increased little by little as man's moral conscience has developed. The latter was at first in a twilight state. Anthropologists have taught us within what structures of tribal life and in the midst of what half-awakened magic it was primitively formed. This proves merely that the knowledge men have had of the unwritten law has passed through more diverse forms and stages than certain philosophers or theologians have believed. The knowledge which our own moral conscience has of this law is doubtless still imperfect, and very likely it will continue to develop and to become more refined as long as humanity exists. Only when the Gospel has penetrated to the very depth of human substance will natural law appear in its flower and its perfection.

So the law and the knowledge of the law are two different things. Yet the law has force of law only when it is promulgated. It is only insofar as it is known and expressed in assertions of practical reason that natural law has force of law.

At this point let us stress that human reason does not discover the regulations of natural law in an abstract and theoretical manner, as a series of geometrical theorems. Nay more, it does not discover them through the conceptual exercise of the intellect, or by way of rational knowledge. I think that Thomas Aquinas' teaching, here, should be understood in a much deeper and more precise fashion than is usual. When he says that human reason discovers the regulations of natural law through the guidance of the *inclinations* of human nature, he means that the very mode or manner in which human reason knows natural law is not rational knowledge, but knowledge *through inclination*. That kind of knowledge is not clear knowledge through concepts and conceptual judgments; it is obscure, unsystematic, vital knowledge by connaturality or congeniality, in which the intellect, in order to bear judgment, consults and listens to the inner melody that the vibrating strings of abiding tendencies make present in the subject.

When one has clearly seen this basic fact, and when, moreover, one has realized that St. Thomas' views on the matter call for an historical approach and a philosophical enforcement of the idea of development that the Middle Ages were not equipped to carry into effect, then at last one is enabled to get a completely comprehensive concept of Natural Law. And one understands that the human knowledge of natural law has been progressively shaped and molded by the inclinations of human nature, starting from the most basic ones. Do not expect me to offer an a priori picture of those genuine inclinations which are rooted in man's being as vitally permeated with the preconscious life of the mind, and which either developed or were released as the movement of mankind went on. They are evinced by the very history of human conscience. Those inclinations *were really genuine* which in the immensity of the human past have guided reason in becoming aware, little by little, of the regulations that have been most definitely and most generally recognized by the human race, starting from the most ancient social communities. For the knowledge of the primordial aspects of natural law was first expressed in social patterns rather than in personal judgments: so that we might say that that knowledge has developed within the double protecting tissue of human inclinations and human society.

With regard to the second basic element, the element of knowledge which natural law implies in order to have force of law, it thus can be said that natural law—that is, natural law *naturally known,* or, more exactly, natural law *the knowledge of which is embodied in the most general and most ancient heritage* of mankind—covers only the field of the ethical regulations of which men have become aware by virtue of knowledge *through inclination,* and which are *basic principles* in moral life—progressively recognized from the most common principles to the more and more specific ones.

All the previous remarks may help us to understand why, on the one hand, a careful examination of the data of anthropology would show that the fundamental *dynamic schemes* of natural law, if they are understood in their authentic, that is, still undetermined meaning (for instance: to take a man's life is not like taking another animal's life; or, the family group has to comply with some fixed pattern; or, sexual intercourse has to be contained within given limitations; or, we are bound to look at the Invisible; or, we are bound to live together under certain rules and prohibitions), are subject to a much more universal awareness—everywhere and in every time—than would appear to a superficial glance; and why, on the other hand, an immense amount of relativity and variability is to be found in the particular rules, customs, and standards in which, among all peoples of the earth, human reason has expressed its knowledge even of the most basic aspects of natural law: for, as I pointed out above, that spontaneous knowledge does not bear on moral regulations conceptually discovered and rationally deduced, but on moral regulations known through inclination, and, at the start, on general tendential forms or frameworks, I just said on *dynamic schemes* of moral regulations, such as can be obtained by the first, "primitive" achievements of knowledge through inclination. And in such tendential frameworks or dynamic schemes many various, still defective contents can occur,—not to speak of the warped, deviated, or perverted inclinations which can mingle with the basic ones.

We may understand at the same time why natural law essentially involves a dynamic development, and why moral conscience, or the knowledge of natural law, has progressed from the age of the cave-man in a double manner: first, as regards the way in which human reason has become aware in a less and less crepuscular, rough, and confused manner, of the primordial regulations of natural law; second, as regards the way in which it has become aware—always by means of knowledge through inclination—of its further, higher regulations. And such knowledge is still progressing, it will progress as long as human history endures. That progress of moral conscience is indeed the most unquestionable instance of progress in humanity.

I have said that natural law is unwritten law: it is unwrittne law in the deepest sense of that expression, because our knowledge of it is no work of free conceptualization, but results from a conceptualization *bound* to the essential inclinations of being, of living nature, and of reason, which are at work in man, and because it develops in proportion to the degree of moral experience and self-reflection, and of social experience also, of which man is capable in the various ages of his history. Thus it is that in ancient and mediaeval times attention was paid, in natural law, to the *obligations* of man more than to his *rights*. The proper achievement—a great achievement indeed—of the XVIIIth Century has been to bring out in full light the *rights* of man as also required by natural law. That discovery was essentially due to a progress in moral and social experience, through which the root *inclinations* of human nature as regards the rights of the human person were set free, and consequently, *knowledge through inclination* with regard to them developed. But, according to a sad law of human knowledge, that great achievement was paid for by the ideological errors, in the theoretical field, that I have stressed at the beginning. Attention even shifted from the obligations of man to his rights only. A genuine and comprehensive view would pay attention *both* to the obligations and the rights involved in the requirements of natural law.

IV

HUMAN RIGHTS AND NATURAL LAW

I need not apologize for having dwelt so long on the subject of natural law. How could we understand human rights if we had not a sufficiently adequate notion of natural law? The same natural law which lays down our most fundamental duties, and by virtue of which every law is binding, is the very law which assigns to us our fundamental rights. It is because we are enmeshed in the universal order, in the laws and regulations of the cosmos and of the immense family of created natures (and finally in the order of creative wisdom), and it is because we have at the same time the privilege of sharing in spiritual nature, that we possess rights vis-à-vis other men and all the assemblage of creatures. In the last analysis, as every creature acts by virtue of its Principle, which is the Pure Act; as every authority worthy of the name (that is to say, just) is binding in conscience by virtue of the Principle of beings, which is pure Wisdom: so too every right possessed by man is possessed by virtue of the right possessed by God, Who is pure Justice, to see the order of His wisdom in beings respected, obeyed, and loved by every intelligence. It is essential to law to be an order of *reason;* and natural law, or the normality of functioning of human nature known by knowledge through inclination, is *law,* binding in conscience, only because nature and the inclinations of nature manifest an order of reason,—that is of *Divine Reason.* Natural law is law only because it is a participation in Eternal Law.

At this point we see that a positivistic philosophy recognizing Fact alone—as well as either an idealistic or a materialistic philosophy of absolute Immanence—is powerless to establish the existence of rights which are naturally possessed by the human being, prior and superior to written legislation and to agreements between governments, rights which the civil society does not have to *grant* but to *recognize* and sanction as universally valid, and which no social necessity can authorize us even momentarily to abolish or disregard. Logically, the concept of such rights can seem only a superstition to these philosophies. It is only valid and rationally tenable if each existing individual has a nature or essence which is the locus of intelligible necessities and necessary truths, that is to say, if the realm of Nature taken as a constellation of facts and events envelops and reveals a realm of Nature taken as a universe of Essences transcending the fact and the event. In other words there is no right unless a certain order—which can be violated in fact— is inviolably required by *what things are* in their intelligible type or their essence, or by what the nature of man is, and is cut out for: an order by virtue of which certain things like life, work, freedom are due to the human person, an existent who is endowed with a spiritual soul and free will. Such an order, which is not a factual datum in things, but demands to be realized by them, and which imposes itself upon our minds to the point of binding us in conscience, exists in things in a certain way, I mean as a requirement of their essence. But that very fact, the fact that things participate in an ideal order which transcends their existence and requires to govern it, would not be possible if the foundation of this ideal order, like the foundation of essences themselves and eternal truths, did not exist in a separate Spirit, in an Absolute which is superior to the world, in what perennial philosophy calls the Eternal Law.

For a philosophy which recognizes Fact alone, the notion of Value,—I mean Value objectively true in itself—is not conceivable. How, then, can one claim rights if one does not believe in values? If the affirmation of the intrinsic value and dignity of man is nonsense, the affirmation of the natural rights of man is nonsense also.

V

ABOUT HUMAN RIGHTS IN GENERAL

Let us now discuss further some problems which deal with human rights in general. My first point will relate to the distinction between Natural Law and Positive Law. One of the main errors of the rationalist philosophy of human rights has been to regard positive law as a mere transcript traced off from natural law, which would supposedly prescribe in the name of Nature all that which positive law prescribes in the name of society. They forgot the immense field of human things which depend on the variable conditions of social life and on the free initiative of human reason, and which natural law leaves undetermined.

As I have pointed out, *natural law* deals with the rights and the duties which are connected in a *necessary* manner with the first principle: "Do good and avoid evil." This is why the precepts of the unwritten law are in themselves or in the nature of things (I am not saying in man's knowledge of them) universal and invariable.

Jus gentium, or the *Law of Nations,* is difficult to define exactly, because it is intermediary between natural law and positive law. Let us say that in its deepest and most genuine meaning, such as put forward by Thomas Aquinas, the law of nations, or better to say, the common law of civilization, differs from natural law because it is *known,* not through inclination, but through the *conceptual exercise of reason,* or through rational knowledge; in this sense it pertains to positive law, and formally constitutes a juridical order (though not necessarily written in a code). But as concerns its content, *jus gentium* comprises both things which belong also to natural law (insofar as they are not only known as rationally inferred, but also known through inclination) and things which—though obligatory in a universal manner, since concluded from a principle of natural law—are beyond the content of natural law (because they are *only* rationally inferred, and not known through inclination). In both cases *jus gentium* or the common law of civilization deals, like natural law, with rights and duties which are connected with the first principle in a *necessary* manner. And precisely because it is known through rational knowledge, and is itself a work of reason, it is more especially concerned with such rights and duties as exist in the realm of the basic natural work achieved by human reason, that is, the state of civil life.

Positive Law, or the body of laws (either customary law or statute law) in force in a given social group, deals with the rights and the duties which are connected with the first principle, but in a *contingent* manner, by virtue of the determinate ways of conduct set down by the reason and the will of man when they institute the laws or give birth to the customs of a particular society, thus stating of themselves that in the particular group in question certain things will be good and permissible, certain other things bad and not permissible.

But it is by virtue of natural law that the law of Nations and positive law take on the force of law, and impose themselves upon the conscience. They are a prolongation or an extension of natural law, passing into objective zones which can less and less be sufficiently determined by the essential inclinations of human nature. For it is *natural law itself which requires that whatever it leaves undetermined shall subsequently be determined,* either as a right or a duty existing for all men, and of which they are made aware, not by knowledge through inclination, but by conceptual reason—that's for *jus gentium*—or—this is for positive law—as a right or a duty existing for certain men by reason of the human and contingent regulations proper to the social group of which they are a part. Thus there are imperceptible transitions (at least from the point of view of historical experience) between Natural Law, the Law of Nations, and Positive Law. There is a dynamism which impels the unwritten law to flower forth in human law, and to render the latter ever more perfect and just in the very field of its contingent determinations. It is in accordance with this dynamism that the rights of the human person take political and social form in the community.

Man's right to existence, to personal freedom, and to the pursuit of the perfection of moral life, belongs, strictly speaking, to natural law.

The right to the private ownership of material goods pertains to natural law, insofar as mankind is naturally entitled to possess for its own common use the material goods of nature; it pertains to the law of Nations, or *jus gentium,* in so far as reason necessarily concludes that for the sake of the common good those material goods must be privately owned, as a result of the conditions naturally required for their management and for human work (I mean human work performed in a genuinely human manner, ensuring the freedom of the human person in the face of the community). And the particular modalities of the right to private ownership, which vary according to the form of a society and the state of the development of its economy, are determined by positive law.

The freedom of nations to live unburdened by the yoke of want or distress ("freedom from want") and the freedom for them to live unburdened by the yoke of fear or terror ("freedom from fear"), as President Roosevelt defined them in his Four Points, correspond to requirements of the law of Nations which are to be fulfilled by positive law and by a possible economic and political organization of the civilized world.

The right of suffrage granted to each one of us for the election of the officials of the State arises from positive law, determining the way in which the natural right of the people to self-government has to apply in a democratic society.

* * *

My second point will deal with the inalienable character of natural human rights. They are inalienable since they are grounded on the very nature of man, which of course no man can lose. This does not mean that they reject by nature any limitation, or that they are the infinite rights of God. Just as every law,—notably the natural law, on which they are grounded,—aims at the common good, so human rights have an intrinsic relation to the common good. Some of them, like the right to existence or to the pursuit of happiness, are of such a nature that the common good would be jeopardized if the body politic could restrict in any measure the possession that men naturally have of them. Let us say that they are absolutely inalienable. Others, like the right of association or of free speech, are of such a nature that the common good would be jeopardized if the body politic could not restrict in some measure (all the less as societies are more capable of and based upon common freedom) the possession that men naturally have of them. Let us say that they are inalienable only substantially.

* * *

Yet, even absolutely inalienable rights are liable to limitation, if not as to their possession, at least as to their exercise. So my third point will deal with the distinction between the *possession* and the *exercise* of a right. Even for the absolutely inalienable rights, we must distinguish between possession and exercise—the latter being subject to conditions and limitations dictated in each case by justice. If a criminal can be justly condemned to die, it is because by his crime he has deprived himself, let us not say of the right to live, but of the possibility of justly asserting this right: he has morally cut himself off from the human community, precisely as regards the use of this fundamental and "inalienable" right which the punishment inflicted upon him prevents him from exercising.

The right to receive the heritage of human culture through education is also a fundamental, absolutely inalienable right: the exercise of it is subject to a given society's concrete possibilities; and it can be contrary to justice to claim the use of this right for each and all *hic et nunc* if that can only be realized by ruining the social body, as in the case of the slave society of ancient Rome or the feudal society of the Middle Ages—though of course this claim to education for all remained legitimate, as something to be fulfilled in time. In such cases what remains is to endeavor to change the social state involved. We see from this example—and I note this parenthetically—that the basis for the secret stimulus which incessantly fosters the transformation of societies lies in the fact that man *possesses* inalienable rights but is deprived of the possibility of justly claiming the *exercise* of certain of these rights because of the inhuman element that remains in the social structure of each period.

This distinction between the possession and the exercise of a right is, in my opinion, of serious importance. I have just indicated how it enables us to explain the limitations that can be justly imposed upon the assertion of certain rights under certain circumstances, either by the guilt of some delinquent or criminal individual, or by social structures whose vice or primitiveness prevents the claim, legitimate in itself, from being immediately fulfilled without encroaching upon major rights.

I should like to add that this distinction also enables us to understand that it is fitting at times, as history advances, to forego the exercise of certain rights which we nevertheless continue to possess. These considerations apply to many problems concerning either the modalities of private property in a society that is in the process of economic transformation, or the limitations on the so-called "sovereignty" of States in an international community that is in the process of being organized.

VI

HUMAN RIGHTS IN PARTICULAR

Coming finally to the problems dealing with the enumeration of human rights taken in particular, I shall first recall to our minds what I have previously stated: namely the fact that in natural law there is immutability as regards things, or the law itself ontologically considered, but progress and relativity as regards human awareness of it. We have especially a tendency to inflate and make absolute, limitless, unrestricted in every respect, the rights of which we are aware, thus blinding ourselves to any other right which would counterbalance them. Thus in human history no "new" right, I mean no right of which common consciousness was becoming newly aware, has been recognized in actual fact without having had to struggle against and overcome the bitter opposition of some "old rights." That was the story of the right to a just wage and similar rights in the face of the right to free mutual agreement and the right to private ownership. The fight of the latter to claim for itself a privilege of divine, limitless absolutism was the unhappy epic of the XIXth Century. (Another unhappy epic was to follow, in which on the contrary the very principle of private ownership was under fire, and every other personal freedom with it.) Well! In 1850, when the law against fugitive slaves was enforced, was not any help given to a fugitive slave held by the conscience of many people to be a criminal attempt against the right to ownership?

Conversely "new" rights often wage war against the "old" ones, and cause them to be unfairly disregarded. At the time of the French Revolution, for instance, a law promulgated in 1791 prohibited as "an attack on freedom and on the Declaration of the Rights of Man" any attempt by workers to associate in trade unions and join forces in refusing to work except for a given wage. This was considered an indirect return to the old system of corporations.

As concerns the problems of the present time, it is obvious that human reason has now become aware not only of the rights of man as a human and a civic person, but also of his rights as a social person engaged in the process of production and consumption, especially of his rights as a working person.

Generally speaking, a new age of civilization will be called upon to recognize and define the rights of the human being in his social, economic, and cultural functions—producers' and consumers' rights, technicians' rights, rights of those who devote themselves to labor of the mind, rights of everyone to share in the educational and cultural heritage of civilized life. But the most urgent problems are conerned on the one hand with the rights of that primordial society which is family society, and which is prior to the political state; on the other hand with the rights of the human being as he is engaged in the function of labor.

I am alluding to rights such as the right to work and freely to choose one's work.—The right freely to form vocational groups or unions.—The right of the worker to be considered socially as an adult, and to have, some way or other, a share and active participation in the responsibilities of economic life.—The right of economic groups (unions and working communitites) and other social groups to freedom and autonomy.—The right to a just wage, that is, sufficient to secure the family's living.—The right to relief, unemployment insurance, sick benefits, and social security.—The right to have a part, free of charge, depending on the possibilities of the social body, in the elementary goods, both material and spiritual, of civilization.

What is involved in all this is first of all the dignity of work, the feeling for the rights of the human person in the worker, the rights in the name of which the worker stands before his employer in a relationship of justice and as an adult person, not as a child or as a servant. There is here an essential datum which far surpasses every problem of merely economic and social technique, for it is a *moral* datum, affecting man in his spiritual depths.

I am convinced that the antagonism between the "old" and the "new" rights of man—I mean the social rights to which I just alluded, especially those which relate to social justice and aim both at the efficacy of the social group and at the freedom from want and economic bondage of the working person—I am convinced that that antagonism, which many contemporary writers take pleasure in magnifying, is by no means insuperable. These two categories of rights seem irreconcilable only because of the clash between the two opposed ideologies and political systems which appeal to them, and of which they are independent in actual reality. Too much stress cannot be placed on the fact that the recognition of a particular category of rights is not the privilege of one school of thought at the expense of the others; it is no more necessary to be a follower of Rousseau to recognize the rights of the individual than it is to be a Marxist to recognize the economic and social rights. As a matter of fact, the universal Declaration of the Rights of Man adopted and proclaimed by the United Nations on December 10, 1948, makes room for the "old" and the "new" rights together.

If each of the human rights were by its nature absolutely unconditional and exclusive of any limitation, like a divine attribute, obviously any conflict between them would be irreconcilable. But who does not know in reality that these rights, being human, are, like everything human, subject to conditioning and limitation, at least, as we have seen, as far as their exercise is concerned? That the various rights ascribed to the human being limit each other, particularly that the economic and social rights, the rights of man as a person involved in the life of the community, cannot be given room in human history without restricting, to some extent, the freedoms and rights of man as an individual person, is only normal. What creates irreducible differences and antagonisms among men is the determination of the degree of such restriction, and more generally the determination of the scale of values that governs the exercise and the concrete organization of these various rights. Here we are confronted with the clash between incompatible political philosophies. Because here we are no longer dealing with the simple recognition of the diverse categories of human rights, but with the principle of dynamic unification in accordance with which they are carried into effect; we are dealing with the tonality, the specific key, by virtue of which different music is played on this same keyboard, either in harmony or in discord with human dignity.

We can imagine—in accordance with the views set forward in the first part of this chapter—that the advocates of a liberal-individualistic, a communistic, or a personalist type of society will lay down on paper similar, perhaps identical, lists of the rights of man. They will not, however, play that instrument in the same way. Everything depends upon the supreme value in accordance with which all these rights will be ordered and will mutually limit each other. It is by virtue of the hierarchy of values to which we thus subscribe that we determine the way in which the rights of man, economic and social as well as individual, should, in our eyes, pass into the realm of existence. Those whom, for want of a better name, I just called the advocates of a liberal-individualistic type of society, see the mark of human dignity first and foremost in the power of each person to appropriate individually the goods of nature in order to do freely whatever he wants; the advocates of a communistic type of society see the mark of human dignity first and foremost in the power to submit these same goods to the collective command of the social body in order to "free" human labor (by subduing it to the economic community) and to gain the control of history; the advocates of a personalistic type of society see the mark of human dignity first and foremost in the power to make these same goods of nature serve the common conquest of intrinsically human, moral, and spiritual goods and of man's freedom of autonomy. Those three groups inevitably will accuse each other of ignoring certain essential rights of the human being. It remains to be seen who makes a faithful image and who a distorted image of man. As far as I am concerned, I know where I stand: with the third of the three schools of thought I just mentioned.

John Courtney Murray
1904-1967

Christian thinkers for nineteen centuries have struggled with the questions of the true nature of the state and the relationship of religion to politics. These are serious and demanding questions, for they involve human lives supported by and directed by two powerful social structures, the Church and the State. The way that these two structures are related to one another by theologians goes far in determining how Christians live out their communal and individual histories.

Church and State can be pitted against one another; they can be set beside one another in either a friendly or a neutral co-existence; one can be set above the other; they can be made to coincide and become one another. Each of these approaches carries specific overtones for the Christian who is asked to develop both a life as believer in an eternal God and a life as citizen of a temporal society.

Father John Courtney Murray is one of the outstanding political theologians who has undertaken to rethink this basic Church-State question within the specific context of the American tradition. He was born in New York in 1904, studied at Boston College (B.A. and M.A.), Woodstock Seminary in Maryland (S.T.L.) and the Gregorian University in Rome (S.T.D.). He taught in the Philippines and at Woodstock, and during 1951-52 was Visiting Professor of Philosophy at Yale University.

Father Murray served as editor of Theological Studies *and as associate editor of* America.

The theological approach of Father Murray to public issues of concern for Christians has had significant influence in shaping recent Catholic theology. This is recognized, for example, that he played the major role in constructing the Second Vatican Council's decree on religious freedom, which was issued in 1965. Father Murray died in 1967.

We Hold These Truths, *from which the following selection is taken, was published in 1960. As the subtitle states, the book is a series of Catholic Reflections on the American proposition. They are the reflections by a Catholic citizen who, in the light of the principles of Catholic faith and morality, seeks to answer the basic civil question: "What are the truths we hold?"*

Father Murray visualized religion as having an indirect power in, rather than over, politics. The difference in prepositions reveals two totally different ways of living out one's civic obligations as a Catholic. He was convinced that his approach would allow both structures the maximum of healthy freedom and provide the Catholic with a realistic approach to religion and politics. Recognizing that old political structures die and give way to new ones, he sought to establish a relationship that would help religious beliefs and teachings to retain a continuity from one political structure to the next.

In the foreword to We Hold These Truths, *Father Murray warns Catholics that they may not merge religious and patriotic faith; nor submerge one in the other. The Catholic must reckon with his centuries old traditions and history and must, at the same time, recognize "that a new problem has been put to the universal Church by the American doctrine and project in the matter of pluralism, as stated in the First Amendment."*

WE HOLD THESE TRUTHS

INTRODUCTION

The "free society" seems to be a phrase of American coinage. At least it has no comparable currency in any other language, ancient or modern. The same is true of the phrase "free government." This fact of itself suggests the assumption that American society and its form of government are a unique historical realization. The assumption is generally regarded among us as unquestionable.

However, we have tended of late to pronounce the phrase, "the free society," with a rising interrogatory inflection. The phrase itself, it seems, now formulates a problem. This is an interesting new development. It was once assumed that the American proposition, both social and political, was self-evident; that it authenticated itself on simple inspection; that it was, in consequence, intuitively grasped and generally understood by the American people. This assumption now stands under severe question.

What is the free society, in its "idea"? Is this "idea" being successfully realized in the institutions that presently determine the pattern of American life, social and personal? The web of American institutions has altered, rapidly and profoundly, even radically, over the past few generations. Has the "idea" of the free society perhaps been strangled by the tightening intricacies of the newly formed institutional network? Has some new and alien "idea" subtly and unsuspectedly assumed the role of an organizing force in American society? Do we understand not only the superficial facts of change in American life but also the underlying factors of change—those "variable constants" that forever provide the dynamisms of change in all human life?

The very fact that these questions are being asked makes it sharply urgent that they be answered. What is at stake is

America's understanding of itself. Self-understanding is the necessary condition of a sense of self-identity and self-confidence, whether in the case of an individual or in the case of a people. If the American people can no longer base this sense on naive assumptions of self-evidence, it is imperative that they find other more reasoned grounds for their essential affirmation that they are uniquely a people, uniquely a free society. Otherwise the peril is great. The complete loss of one's identity is, with all propriety of theological definition, hell. In diminished forms it is insanity. And it would not be well for the American giant to go lumbering about the world today, lost and mad.

THE CIVIL MULTITUDE

At this juncture I suggest that the immediate question is not whether the free society is really free. This question may be unanswerable; it may even be meaningless as a question, if only for the reason that the norms of freedom seem to have got lost in a welter of confused controversy. Therefore I suggest that the immediate question is whether American society is properly civil. This question is intelligible and answerable, because the basic standard of civility is not in doubt: "Civilization is formed by men locked together in argument. From this dialogue the community becomes a political community." This statement, made by Thomas Gilby, O.P., in *Between Community and Society*, exactly expresses the mind of St. Thomas Aquinas, who was himself giving refined expression to the tradition of classic antiquity, which in its prior turn had given first elaboration to the concept of the "civil multitude," the multitude that is not a mass or a herd or a huddle, because it is characterized by civility.

The specifying note of political association is its rational deliberative quality, its dependence for its permanent cohesiveness on argument among men. In this it differs from all other forms of association found on earth. The animal kingdom is held together simply by the material homogeneity of the species; all its unities and antagonisms are of the organic and biological order. Wolves do not argue the merits of running in packs. The primal human community, the family, has its own distinctive bonds of union. Husband and wife are not drawn into the marital association simply by the forces of reason but by the forces of life itself, importantly including the mysterious dynamisms of sex. Their association is indeed founded on a contract, which must be a rational and free act. But the substance and finality of the contract is both infra- and suprarational; it is an engagement to become "two in one flesh." The marital relationship may at times be quarrelsome, but it is not argumentative. Similarly, the union of parents and children is not based on reason, justice, or power; it is based on kinship, love, and *pietas.*

It is otherwise with the political community. I am not, of course, maintaining that civil society is a purely rational form of association. We no longer believe, with Locke or Hobbes, that man escapes from a mythical "state of nature" by an act of will, by a social contract. Civil society is a need of human nature before it becomes the object of human choice. Moreover, every particular society is a creature of the soil; it springs from the physical soil of earth and from the more formative soil of history. Its existence is sustained by loyalties that are not logical; its ideals are expressed in legends that go beyond the facts and are for that reason vehicles of truth; its cohesiveness depends in no small part on the materialisms of property and interest. Though all this is true, nevertheless the distinctive bond of the civil multitude is reason, or more exactly, that exercise of reason which is argument.

Hence the climate of the City is likewise distinctive. It is not feral or familial but forensic. It is not hot and humid, like the climate of the animal kingdom. It lacks the cordial warmth of love and unreasoning loyalty that pervades the family. It is cool and dry, with the coolness and dryness that characterize good argument among informed and responsible men. Civic amity gives to this climate its vital quality. This form of friendship is a special kind of moral virtue, a thing of reason and intelligence, laboriously cultivated by the discipline of passion, prejudice, and narrow self-interest. It is the sentiment proper to the City. It has nothing to do with the cleavage of a David to a Jonathan, or with the kinship of the clan or with the charity, *fortis ut mors,* that makes the solidarity of the Church. It is in direct contrast with the passionate fanaticism of the

Jacobin: "Be my brother or I'll kill you!" Ideally, I suppose, there should be only one passion in the City—the passion for justice. But the will to justice, though it engages the heart, finds its measure as it finds its origin in intelligence, in a clear understanding of what is due to the equal citizen from the City and to the City from the citizenry according to the mode of their equality. This commonly shared will to justice is the ground of civic amity as it is also the ground of that unity which is called peace. This unity, qualified by amity, is the highest good of the civil multitude and the perfection of its civility.

THE PUBLIC ARGUMENT

If then society is civil when it is formed by men locked together in argument, the question rises, what is the argument about? There are three major themes.

First, the argument is about public affairs, the *res publica,* those matters which are for the advantage of the public (in the phrase as old as Plato) and which call for public decision and action by government. These affairs have their origin in matters of fact; but their rational discussion calls for the Socratic dialogue, the close and easy use of the habit of cross-examination, that transforms brute facts into arguable issues.

Second, the public argument concerns the affairs of the commonwealth. This is a wider concept. It denotes the affairs that fall, at least in decisive part, beyond the limited scope of government. These affairs are not to be settled by law, though law may be in some degree relevant to their settlement. They go beyond the necessities of the public order as such; they bear upon the quality of the common life. The great "affair" of the commonwealth is, of course, education. It includes three general areas of common interest: the school system, its mode of organization, its curricular content, and the level of learning among its teachers; the later education of the citizen in the liberal art of citizenship; and the more general enterprise of the advancement of knowledge by research.

The third theme of public argument is the most important and the most difficult. It concerns the constitutional consensus whereby the people acquires its identity as a people and the society is endowed with its vital form, its entelechy, its sense of purpose as a collectivity organized for action in history. The idea of consensus has been classic since the Stoics and Cicero; through St. Augustine it found its way into the liberal tradition of the West: *"Res publica, res populi; populus autem non omnis hominum coetus quoquo modo congregatus, sed coetus multitudinis iuris consensu et utilitatis communione sociatus"* (Scipio).

The state of civility supposes a consensus that is constitutional, *sc.,* its focus is the idea of law, as surrounded by the whole constellation of ideas that are related to the *ratio iuris* as its premises, its constituent elements, and its consequences. This consensus is come to by the people; they become a people by coming to it. They do not come to it accidentally, without quite knowing how, but deliberatively, by the methods of reason reflecting on experience. The consensus is not a structure of secondary rationalizations erected on psychological data (as the behaviorist would have it) or on economic data (as the Marxist would have it). It is not the residual minimum left after rigid application of the Cartesian axiom, *"de omnibus dubitandum."* It is not simply a set of working hypotheses whose value is pragmatic. It is an ensemble of substantive truths, a structure of basic knowledge, an order of elementary affirmations that reflect realities inherent in the order of existence. It occupies an established position in society and excludes opinions alien or contrary to itself. This consensus is the intuitional a priori of all the rationalities and technicalities of constitutional and statutory law. It furnishes the premises of the people's action in history and defines the larger aims which the action seeks in internal affairs and in external relations.

The whole premise of the public argument, if it is to be civilized and civilizing, is that the consensus is real, that among the people everything is not in doubt, but that there is a core of agreement, accord, concurrence, acquiescence. We hold certain truths; therefore we can argue about them. It seems to have been one of the corruptions of intelligence by positivism to assume that argument ends when agreement is reached. In a basic sense the reverse is true. There can be no argument except on the premise, and within a context, of agreement. *Mutatis mutandis,* this is true of scientific, philosophical, and theological argument. It is no less true of political argument.

On its most imperative level the public argument within the City and about the City's affairs begins with the agreement that there is a reality called, in the phrase of Leo XIII, *patrimonium generis humani,* a heritage of an essential truth, a tradition of rational belief, that sustains the structure of the City and furnishes the substance of civil life. It was to this patrimony that the Declaration of Independence referred: "These are the truths we hold." This is the first utterance of a people. By it a people establishes its identity, and under decent respect to the opinions of mankind declares its purposes within the community of nations.

In later chapters an effort will be made to state the contents of the public consensus in America. Briefly, its principles and doctrines are those of Western constitutionalism, classic and Christian. This is our essential patrimony, laboriously wrought out by centuries of thought, further refined and developed in our own land to fit the needs of the new American experiment in government. In addition, as will later appear, the consensus has a growing end, as American society itself has a growing end. My point at the moment, however, is that there are two reasons why the consensus furnishes the basic theme of the public argument whereby American society hopes to achieve and maintain the mark of civility.

Initially, we hold these truths because they are a patrimony. They are a heritage from history, through whose dark and bloody pages there runs like a silver thread the tradition of civility. This is the first reason why the consensus continually calls for public argument. The consensus is an intellectual heritage; it may be lost to mind or deformed in the mind. Its final depository is the public mind. This is indeed a perilous place to deposit what ought to be kept safe; for the public mind is exposed to the corrosive rust of skepticism, to the predatory moths of deceitful *doxai* (in Plato's sense), and to the incessant thieveries of forgetfulness. Therefore the consensus can only be preserved in the public mind by argument.

High argument alone will keep it alive, in the vital state of being "held."

Second, we hold these truths because they are true. They have been found in the structure of reality by that dialectic of observation and reflection which is called philosophy. But as the achievement of reason and experience the consensus again presents itself for argument. Its vitality depends on a constant scrutiny of political experience, as this experience widens with the developing—or possibly the decaying—life of man in society. Only at the price of this continued contact with experience will a constitutional tradition continue to be "held," as real knowledge and not simply as a structure of prejudice. However, the tradition, or the consensus, is not a mere record of experience. It is experience illumined by principle, given a construction by a process of philosophical reflection. In the public argument there must consequently be a continued recurrence to first principles. Otherwise the consensus may come to seem simply a projection of ephemeral experience, a passing shadow on the vanishing backdrop of some given historical scene, without the permanence proper to truths that are "held."

On both of these titles, as a heritage and as a public philosophy, the American consensus needs to be constantly argued. If the public argument dies from disinterest, or subsides into the angry mutterings of polemic, or rises to the shrillness of hysteria, or trails off into positivistic triviality, or gets lost in a morass of semantics, you may be sure that the barbarian is at the gates of the City.

The barbarian need not appear in bearskins with a club in hand. He may wear a Brooks Brothers suit and carry a ball-point pen with which to write his advertising copy. In fact, even beneath the academic gown there may lurk a child of the wilderness, untutored in the high tradition of civility, who goes busily and happily about his work, a domesticated and law-abiding man, engaged in the construction of a philosophy to put an end to all philosophy, and thus put an end to the possibility of a vital consensus and to civility itself. This is perennially the work of the barbarian, to undermine rational standards of judgment, to corrupt the inherited intuitive wisdom by which the people have always lived, and to do this not by spreading new beliefs but by creating a climate of doubt and bewilderment in which clarity about the larger aims of life is dimmed and the self-confidence of the people is destroyed, so that finally what you have is the impotent nihilism of the "generation of the third eye," now presently appearing on our university campuses. (One is, I take it, on the brink of impotence and nihilism when one begins to be aware of one's own awareness of what one is doing, saying, thinking. This is the paralysis of all serious thought; it is likewise the destruction of all the spontaneities of love.)

The barbarian may be the eighteenth-century philosopher, who neither anticipated nor desired the brutalities of the Revolution with its Committee on the Public Safety, but who prepared the ways for the Revolution by creating a vacuum which he was not able to fill. Today the barbarian is the man who makes open and explicit rejection of the traditional role of reason and logic in human affairs. He is the man who reduces all spiritual and moral questions to the test of practical results or to an analysis of language or to decision in terms of individual subjective feeling.

It is a Christian theological intuition, confirmed by all of historical experience, that man lives both his personal and his social life always more or less close to the brink of barbarism, threatened not only by the disintegrations of physical illness and by the disorganizations of mental imbalance, but also by the decadence of moral corruption and the political chaos of formlessness or the moral chaos of tyranny. Society is rescued from chaos only by a few men, not by the many. *Paucis humanum vivit genus.* It is only the few who understand the disciplines of civility and are able to sustain them in being and thus hold in check the forces of barbarism that are always threatening to force the gates of the City. To say this is not, of course, to endorse the concept of the fascist élite—a barbarous concept, if ever there was one. It is only to recall a lesson of history to which our own era of mass civilization may well attend. We have not been behind our forebears in devising both gross and subtle ways of massacring ancient civilities.

John Courtney Murray

Barbarism is not, I repeat, the forest primeval with all its relatively simple savageries. Barbarism has long had its definition, resumed by St. Thomas after Aristotle. It is the lack of reasonable conversation according to reasonable laws. Here the word "conversation" has its twofold Latin sense. It means living together and talking together.

Barbarism threatens when men cease to live together according to reason, embodied in law and custom, and incorporated in a web of institutions that sufficiently reveal rational influences, even though they are not, and cannot be, wholly rational. Society becomes barbarian when men are huddled together under the rule of force and fear; when economic interests assume the primacy over higher values; when material standards of mass and quantity crush out the values of quality and excellence; when technology assumes an autonomous existence and embarks on a course of unlimited self-exploitation without purposeful guidance from the higher disciplines of politics and morals (one thinks of Cape Canaveral); when the state reaches the paradoxical point of being everywhere intrusive and also impotent, possessed of immense power and powerless to achieve rational ends; when the ways of men come under the sway of the instinctual, the impulsive, the compulsive. When things like this happen, barbarism is abroad, whatever the surface impressions of urbanity. Men have ceased to live together according to reasonable laws.

Barbarism likewise threatens when men cease to talk together according to reasonable laws. There are laws of argument, the observance of which is imperative if discourse is to be civilized. Argument ceases to be civil when it is dominated by passion and prejudice; when its vocabulary becomes solipsist, premised on the theory that my insight is mine alone and cannot be shared; when dialogue gives way to a series of monologues; when the parties to the conversation cease to listen to one another, or hear only what they want to hear, or see the other's argument only through the screen of their own categories; when defiance is flung to the basic ontological principle of all ordered discourse, which asserts that Reality is an analogi-

209

cal structure, within which there are variant modes of reality, to each of which there corresponds a distinctive method of thought that imposes on argument its own special rules. When things like this happen, men cannot be locked together in argument. Conversation becomes merely quarrelsome or querulous. Civility dies with the death of the dialogue.

All this has been said in order to give some meaning to the immediate question before us, sc., whether American society, which calls itself free, is genuinely civil. In any circumstances it has always been difficult to achieve civility in the sense explained. A group of men locked together in argument is a rare spectacle. But within the great sprawling City that is the United States the achievement of a civil society encounters a special difficulty—what is called religious pluralism.

THE EXPERIENCE OF RELIGIOUS PLURALISM

The political order must borrow both from above itself and from below itself. The political looks upward to metaphysics, ethics, theology; it looks downward to history, legal science, sociology, psychology. The order of politics must reckon with all that is true and factual about man. The problem was complicated enough for Aristotle, for whom man in the end was only citizen, whose final destiny was to be achieved within the City, however much he might long to play the immortal. For us today man is still citizen; but at least for most of us his life is not absorbed in the City, in society and the state. In the citizen who is also a Christian there resides the consciousness formulated immortally in the second-century *Letter to Diognetes:* "Every foreign land is a fatherland and every fatherland is a foreign land." This consciousness makes a difference, in ways upon which we need not dwell here. What makes the more important difference is the fact of religious divisions. Civil discourse would be hard enough if among us there prevailed conditions of religious unity; even in such conditions civic unity would be a complicated and laborious achievement. As it is, efforts at civil discourse plunge us into the twofold experience of the religiously pluralist society.

The first experience is intellectual. As we discourse on public affairs, on the affairs of the commonwealth, and particularly on the problem of consensus, we inevitably have to move upward, as it were, into realms of some theoretical generality—into metaphysics, ethics, theology. This movement does not carry us into disagreement; for disagreement is not an easy thing to reach. Rather, we move into confusion. Among us there is a plurality of universes of discourse. These universes are incommensurable. And when they clash, the issue of agreement or disagreement tends to become irrelevant. The immediate situation is simply one of confusion. One does not know what the other is talking about. One may distrust what the other is driving at. For this too is part of the problem—the disposition amid the confusion to disregard the immediate argument, as made, and to suspect its tendency, to wonder what the man who makes it is really driving at.

This is the pluralist society as it is encountered on the level of intellectual experience. We have no common universe of discourse. In particular, diverse mental equivalents attach to all the words in which the constitutional consensus must finally be discussed—truth, freedom, justice, prudence, order, law, authority, power, knowledge, certainty, unity, peace, virtue, morality, religion, God, and perhaps even man. Our intellectual experience is one of sheer confusion, in which soliloquy succeeds to argument.

The second experience is even more profound. The themes touched upon in any discussion of Religion and the Free Society have all had a long history. And in the course of discussing them we are again made aware that only in a limited sense have we severally had the same history. We more or less share the short segment of history known as America. But all of us have had longer histories, spiritual and intellectual.

These histories may indeed touch at certain points. But I, for instance, am conscious that I do not share the histories that lie behind many of my fellow citizens. The Jew does not share the Christian history, nor even the Christian idea of history. Catholic and Protestant history may be parallel in a limited sense but they are not coincident or coeval. And the secularist is a latecomer. He may locate his ancestry in the eighteenth or nineteenth centuries, or, if his historic sense is strong, he may go back to the fourteenth century, to the rise of what Lagarde has called *l'esprit laïque*. In any case, he cannot go back to Athens, Rome, or Alexandria; for his laicism is historically conditioned. It must situate itself with regard to the Christian tradition. It must include denials and disassociations that the secularism of antiquity did not have to make; and it also includes the affirmation of certain Christian values that antiquity could not have affirmed.

The fact of our discrepant histories creates the second experience of the pluralist society. We are aware that we not only hold different views but have become different kinds of men as we have lived our several histories. Our styles of thought and of interior life are as discrepant as our histories. The more deeply they are experienced and the more fully they are measured, the more do the differences among us appear to be almost unbridgeable. Man is not only a creature of thought but also a vibrant subject of sympathies; and in the realm of philosophy and religion today the communal experiences are so divergent that they create not sympathies but alienations as between groups.

Take, for instance, the question of natural law, of which there will be much discourse in the pages that follow. For the Catholic it is simply a problem in metaphysical, ethical, political, and juridical argument. He moves into the argument naturally and feels relatively at ease amid its complexities. For the Protestant, on the contrary, the whole doctrine of natural law is a challenge, if not an affront, to his entire style of moral thought and even to his religiosity. The doctrine is alien to him, unassimilable by him. He not only misunderstands it; he also distrust it. "Thus," says Robert McAfee Brown in *American Catholics: a Protestant-Jewish View,* "Catholic appeals to natural law remain a source of friction rather than a basis of deeper understanding" as between Protestant and Catholic.

Another example might be the argument that has been made by Catholics in this country for more than a century with regard to the distribution of tax funds for the support of the school system. The structure of the argument is not complex. Its principle is that the canons of distributive justice ought to control the action of government in allocating funds that it coercively collects from all people in pursuance of its legitimate interest in universal compulsory schooling. The fact is that these canons are presently not being observed. The "solution" to the School Question reached in the nineteenth century reveals injustice, and the legal statutes that establish the injustice are an abuse of power. So, in drastic brevity, runs the argument. I shall return to it in a later chapter. For my part, I have never heard a satisfactory answer to it.

This is a fairly serious situation. When a large section of the community asserts that injustice is being done, and makes a reasonable argument to substantiate the assertion, either the argument ought to be convincingly refuted and the claim of injustice thus disposed of, or the validity of the argument ought to be admitted and the injustice remedied. As a matter of fact, however, the argument customarily meets a blank stare, or else it is "answered" by varieties of the fallacy known as *ignoratio elenchi.* At the extreme, from the side of the more careerist type of anti-Catholic, the rejoinder takes this form, roughly speaking (sometimes the rejoinder is roughly spoken): "We might be willing to listen to this argument about the rights of Catholic schools if we believed that Catholic schools had any rights at all. But we do not grant that they have any rights, except to tolerance. Their existence is not for the advantage of the public; they offend against the integrity of the democratic community, whose warrant is fidelity to Protestant principle (or secularist principle, as the case may be)." This "answer" takes various forms, more or less uncomplimentary to the Catholic Church, according to the temper of the speaker. But this is the gist of it. The statement brings me to my next point.

A STRUCTURE OF WAR

The fact is that among us civility—or civic unity or civic amity, as you will—is a thing of the surface. It is quite easy to break through it. And when you do, you catch a glimpse of the factual reality of the pluralist society. I agree with Prof. Eric Voegelin's thesis that our pluralist society has received its structure through wars and that the wars are still going on beneath a fragile surface of more or less forced urbanity. What

Voegelin calls the "genteel picture" will not stand the text of confrontation with fact.

We are not really a group of men singly engaged in the search for truth, relying solely on the means of persuasion, entering into dignified communication with each other, content politely to correct opinions with which we do not agree. As a matter of fact, the variant ideas and allegiances among us are entrenched as social powers; they occupy ground; they have developed interest; and they possess the means to fight for them. The real issues of truth that arise are complicated by secondary issues of power and prestige, which not seldom become primary.

There are numerous well-known examples. What they illustrate is that the entrenched segments of American pluralism claim influence on the course of events, on the content of the legal order, and on the quality of American society. To each group, of course, its influence seems salvific; to other groups it may seem merely imperialist. In any case, the forces at work are not simply intellectual; they are also passionate. There is not simply an exchange of arguments but of verbal blows. You do not have to probe deeply beneath the surface of civic amity to uncover the structure of passion and war.

There is the ancient resentment of the Jew, who has for centuries been dependent for his existence on the good will, often not forthcoming, of a Christian community. Now in America, where he has acquired social power, his distrust of the Christian community leads him to align himself with the secularizing forces whose dominance, he thinks, will afford him a security he has never known. Again, there is the profound distrust between Catholic and Protestant. Their respective conceptions of Christianity are only analogous; that is, they are partly the same and totally different. The result is *odium theologicum*, a sentiment that not only enhances religious differences in the realm of truth but also creates personal estrangements in the order of charity.

More than that, Catholic and Protestant distrust each other's political intentions. There is the memory of historic clashes in the temporal order; the Irishman does not forget Cromwell any more readily than the Calvinist forgets Louis

XIV. Neither Protestant nor Catholic is yet satisfied that the two of them can exist freely and peacefully in the same kind of City. The Catholic regards Protestantism not only as a heresy in the order of religion but also as a corrosive solvent in the order of civilization, whose intentions lead to chaos. The Protestant regards Catholicism not only as idolatry in the order of religion but as an instrument of tyranny in the order of civilization, whose intentions lead to clericalism. Thus an *odium civile* accrues to the *odium theologicum.*

This problem is particularly acute in the United States, where the Protestant was the native and the Catholic the immigrant, in contrast to Europe where the Catholic first held the ground and was only later challenged. If one is to believe certain socio-religious critics (Eduard Heimann, for instance), Protestantism in America has forged an identification of itself, both historical and ideological, with American culture, particularly with an indigenous secularist unclarified mystique of individual freedom as somehow the source of everything, including justice, order, and unity. The result has been Nativism in all its manifold forms, ugly and refined, popular and academic, fanatic and liberal. The neo-Nativist as well as the paleo-Nativist addresses to the Catholic substantially the same charge: "You are among us but you are not of us." (The neo-Nativist differs only in that he uses footnotes, apparently in the belief that reference to documents is a substitute for an understanding of them.) To this charge the Catholic, if he happens to set store, *pro forma,* on meriting the blessed adjective "sophisticated," will politely reply that this is Jacobinism, *nouveau style,* and that Jacobinism, any style, is out of style in this day and age. In contrast, the sturdy Catholic War Veteran is more likely to say rudely, "Them's fighten' words." And with this exchange of civilities, if they are such, the "argument" is usually over.

There is, finally, the secularist (I here use the term only in a descriptive sense). He too is at war. If he knows his own history, he must be. Historically his first chosen enemy was the Catholic Church, and it must still be the Enemy of his choice, for two reasons that will be further developed in a later chapter. First, it asserts that there is an authority superior to the authority of individual reason and of the political projection of individual reason, the state. But this assertion is the first object of the secularist's anathema. Second, it asserts that by divine ordinance this world is to be ruled by a dyarchy of authorities, within which the temporal is subordinate to the spiritual, not instrumentally but in dignity. This assertion is doubly anathema. It clashes with the socio-juridical monism that is always basic to the secularist position when it is consistently argued. In secularist theory there can be only one society, one law, one power, and one faith, a civic faith that is the "unifying" bond of the community, whereby it withstands the assaults of assorted pluralisms.

The secularist has always fought his battles under a banner on which is emblazoned his special device, "The Integrity of the Political Order." In the name of this thundering principle he would banish from the political order (and from education as an affair of the City) all the "divisive forces" of religion. At least in America he has traditionally had no quarrel with religion as a "purely private matter," as a sort of essence or idea or ambient aura that may help to warm the hidden heart of solitary man. He may even concede a place to religion-in-general, whatever that is. What alarms him is religion as a Thing, visible, corporate, organized, a community of thought that presumes to sit superior to, and in judgment on, the "community of democratic thought," and that is furnished somehow with an armature of power to make its thought and judgment publicly prevail. Under this threat he marshals his military vocabulary and speaks in terms of aggression, encroachment, maneuvers, strategy, tactics. He rallies to the defense of the City; he sets about the strengthening of the wall that separates the City from its Enemy. He too is at war.

THE CONSPIRACIES AND THEIR CONSPIRACY

What it comes to then is that the pluralist society, honestly viewed under abdication of all false gentility, is a pattern of interacting conspiracies. There are chiefly four—Protestant, Catholic, Jewish, secularist, though in each camp, to continue the military metaphor, there are forces not fully broken to the authority of the high command.

John Courtney Murray

I would like to relieve the word "conspiracy" of its invidious connotations. It is devoid of these in its original Latin sense, both literal and tropical. Literally it means unison, concord, unanimity in opinion and feeling, a "breathing together." Then it acquires inevitably the connotation of united action for a common end about which there is agreement; those who think alike inevitably join together in some manner of action to make their common thought or purpose prevail. The word was part of the Stoic political vocabulary; it was adopted by Cicero; and it has passed into my own philosophical tradition, the Scholastic tradition, that has been formative of the liberal tradition of the West. Civil society is formed, said Cicero, *"conspiratione hominum atque consensu,"* that is by action in concert on the basis of consensus with regard to the purposes of the action. Civil society is by definition a conspiracy, *"conspiratio plurium in unum."* Only by conspiring together do the many become one. *E pluribus unum.*

The trouble is that there are a number of conspiracies within American society. I shall not object to your calling Catholicism a conspiracy, provided you admit that it is only one of several. (Incidentally, I never have seen the validity of Prof. Sidney Hook's distinction: "Heresy, yes; conspiracy, no." The heresy that was not a conspiracy has not yet appeared on land or sea. One would say with greater propriety of word and concept: "Conspiracy, yes; heresy, no." Heresy, not conspiracy, is the bad word for the evil thing. No one would be bothered with the Communist conspiracy if its dynamism were not a civilizational heresy, or more exactly, an apostasy from civilization.)

Perhaps then our problem today is somehow to make the four great conspiracies among us conspire into one conspiracy that will be American society—civil, just, free, peaceful, one.

Can this problem be solved? My own expectations are modest and minimal. It seems to be the lesson of history that men are usually governed with little wisdom. The highest political good, the unity which is called peace, is far more an ideal than a realization. And the search for religious unity, the highest spiritual good, always encounters the "messianic necessity," so called: "Do you think that I have come to bring peace on earth? No, but rather dissension" (Luke 12:51). In the same text the dissension was predicted with terrible explicitness of the family. It has also been the constant lot of the family of nations and of the nations themselves. Religious pluralism is against the will of God. But it is the human condition; it is written into the script of history. It will not somehow marvelously cease to trouble the City.

Advisedly therefore one will cherish only modest expectations with regard to the solution of the problem of religious pluralism and civic unity. Utopianism is a Christian heresy (the ancient pagan looked backward, not forward, to the Golden Age); but it is a heresy nonetheless. We cannot hope to make American society the perfect conspiracy based on a unanimous consensus. But we could at least do two things. We could limit the warfare, and we could enlarge the dialogue. We could lay down our arms (at least the more barbarous kind of arms!), and we could take up argument.

Even to do this would not be easy. It would be necessary that we cease to project into the future of the Republic the nightmares, real or fancied, of the past. In Victorian England John Henry Newman noted that the Protestant bore "a stain upon the imagination," left there by the vivid images of Reformation polemic against the Church of Rome. Perhaps we all bear some stain or other upon our imaginations. It might be possible to cleanse them by a work of reason. The free society, I said at the outset, is a unique realization; it has inaugurated a new history. Therefore it might be possible within this new history to lay the ghosts of the past—to forget the ghettos and the autos-da-fé; the Star Chamber and the Committee on the Public Safety; Topcliffe with his "Bloody Question" and Torquemada with his rack; the dragonnades and the Black and Tans; Samuel F. B. Morse, the convents in Charleston and Philadelphia, the Know-Nothings and the Ku Klux Klan and what happened to Al Smith (whatever it was that did happen to him).

All this might be possible. It certainly would be useful. I venture to say that today it is necessary. This period in American history is critical, not organic (to use Prof. Toynbee's distinction). We face a crisis that is new in history. We would do well to face it with a new cleanliness of imagination, in the realization that internecine strife, beyond some inevitable human measure, is a luxury we can no longer afford. Serious issues confront us on all the three levels of public argument. Perhaps the time has come when we should endeavor to dissolve the structure of war that underlies the pluralistic society, and erect the more civilized structure of the dialogue. It would be no less sharply pluralistic, but rather more so, since the real pluralisms would be clarified out of their present confusion. And amid the pluralism a unity would be discernible—the unity of an orderly conversation. The pattern would not be that of ignorant armies clashing by night but of informed men locked together in argument in the full light of a new dialectical day. Thus we might present to a "candid world" the spectacle of a civil society.

PART I

CHAPTER 1

E PLURIBUS UNUM

The American Consensus

As it arose in America, the problem of pluralism was unique in the modern world, chiefly because pluralism was the native condition of American society. It was not, as in Europe and in England, the result of a disruption or decay of a previously existent religious unity. This fact created the possibility of a new solution; indeed, it created a demand for a new solution. The possibility was exploited and the demand was met by the American Constitution.

The question here concerns the position of the Catholic conscience in the face of the new American solution to a problem that for centuries has troubled, and still continues to trouble, various nations and societies. A new problem has been put to the universal Church by the fact of America—by the uniqueness of our social situation, by the genius of our newly conceived constitutional system, by the lessons of our singular national history, which has molded in a special way the con-

219

sciousness and temper of the American people, within whose midst the Catholic stands, sharing with his fellow citizens the same national heritage. The Catholic community faces the task of making itself intellectually aware of the conditions of its own co-existence within the American pluralistic scene. We have behind us a lengthy historical tradition of acceptance of the special situation of the Church in America, in all its differences from the situations in which the Church elsewhere finds herself. But it is a question here of pursuing the subject, not in the horizontal dimension of history but in the vertical dimension of theory.

The argument readily falls into two parts. The first part is an analysis of the American Proposition with regard to political unity. The effort is to make a statement, later to be somewhat enlarged, of the essential contents of the American consensus, whereby we are made "e pluribus unum," one society sub-sisting amid multiple pluralisms. Simply to make this statement is to show why American Catholics participate with ready conviction in the American consensus. The second part of the argument, to be pursued in the next chapter, is an analysis of the American Proposition with regard to religious pluralism, especially as this proposition is embodied in our fundamental law. Again, simply to make this analysis is to lay bare the reasons why American Catholics accept on principle the unique American solution to the age-old problem.

THE NATION UNDER GOD

The first truth to which the American Proposition makes appeal is stated in that landmark of Western political theory, the Declaration of Independence. It is a truth that lies beyond politics; it imparts to politics a fundamental human meaning. I mean the sovereignty of God over nations as well as over individual men. This is the principle that radically distinguishes the conservative Christian tradition of America from the Jacobin laicist tradition of Continental Europe. The Jacobin tradition proclaimed the autonomous reason of man to be the first and the sole principle of political organization. In contrast, the first article of the American political faith is that the political community, as a form of free and ordered human life, looks to the sovereignty of God as to the first principle of its organization. In the Jacobin tradition religion is at best a purely private concern, a matter of personal devotion, quite irrelevant to public affairs. Society as such, and the state which gives it legal form, and the government which is its organ of action are by definition agnostic or atheist. The statesman as such cannot be a believer, and his actions as a statesman are immune from any imperative or judgment higher than the will of the people, in whom resides ultimate and total sovereignty (one must remember that in the Jacobin tradition "the people" means "the party"). This whole manner of thought is altogether alien to the authentic American tradition.

From the point of view of the problem of pluralism this radical distinction between the American and the Jacobin traditions is of cardinal importance. The United States has had, and still has, its share of agnostics and unbelievers. But it has never known organized militant atheism on the Jacobin, doctrinaire Socialist, or Communist model; it has rejected parties and theories which erect atheism into a political principle. In 1799, the year of the Napoleonic *coup d'état* which overthrew the Directory and established a dictatorship in France, President John Adams stated the first of all American first principles in his remarkable proclamation of March 6:

> . . . it is also most reasonable in itself that men who are capable of social arts and relations, who owe their improvements to the social state, and who derive their enjoyments from it, should, as a society, make acknowledgements of dependence and obligation to Him who hath endowed them with these capacities and elevated them in the scale of existence by these distinctions. . . .

President Lincoln on May 30, 1863, echoed the tradition in another proclamation:

> Whereas the Senate of the United States, devoutly recognizing the supreme authority and just government of Almighty God in all the affairs of men and nations, has by a resolution requested the President to designate and set apart a day for national prayer

and humiliation; And whereas it is the duty of nations as well as of men to own their dependence upon the overruling power of God, to confess their sins and trespasses in humble sorrow, yet with the assured hope that genuine repentance will lead to mercy and pardon. . . .

The authentic voice of America speaks in these words. And it is a testimony to the enduring vitality of this first principle—the sovereignty of God over society as well as over individual men—that President Eisenhower in June, 1952, quoted these words of Lincoln in a proclamation of similar intent. There is, of course, dissent from this principle, uttered by American secularism (which, at that, is a force far different in content and purpose from Continental laicism). But the secularist dissent is clearly a dissent; it illustrates the existence of the American affirmation. And it is continually challenged. For instance, as late as 1952 an opinion of the United States Supreme Court challenged it by asserting: "We are a religious people whose institutions presuppose a Supreme Being." Three times before in its history—in 1815, 1892, and 1931—the Court had formally espoused this same principle.

THE TRADITION OF NATURAL LAW

The affirmation in Lincoln's famous phrase, "this nation under God," sets the American proposition in fundamental continuity with the central political tradition of the West. But this continuity is more broadly and importantly visible in another, and related, respect. In 1884 the Third Plenary Council of Baltimore made this statement: "We consider the establishment of our country's independence, the shaping of its liberties and laws, as a work of special Providence, its framers 'building better than they knew,' the Almighty's hand guiding them." The providential aspect of the matter, and the reason for the better building, can be found in the fact that the American political community was organized in an era when the tradition of natural law and natural rights was still vigorous. Claiming no sanction other than its appeal to free minds, it still commanded universal acceptance. And it furnished the basic materials for the American consensus.

John Courtney Murray

The evidence for this fact has been convincingly presented by Clinton Rossiter in his book, *Seedtime of the Republic,* a scholarly account of the "noble aggregate of 'self-evident truths' that vindicated the campaign of resistance (1765—1775), the resolution for independence (1776), and the establishment of the new state governments (1776—1780)." These truths, he adds, "had been no less self-evident to the preachers, merchants, planters, and lawyers who were the mind of colonial America." It might be further added that these truths firmly presided over the great time of study, discussion, and decision which produced the Federal Constitution. "The great political philosophy of the Western world," Rossiter says, "enjoyed one of its proudest seasons in this time of resistance and revolution." By reason of this fact the American Revolution, quite unlike its French counterpart, was less a revolution than a conservation. It conserved, by giving newly vital form to, the liberal tradition of politics, whose ruin in Continental Europe was about to be consummated by the first great modern essay in totalitarianism.

The force for unity inherent in this tradition was of decisive importance in what concerns the problem of pluralism. Because it was conceived in the tradition of natural law the American Republic was rescued from the fate, still not overcome, that fell upon the European nations in which Continental Liberalism, a deformation of the liberal tradition, lodged itself, not least by the aid of the Lodges. There have never been "two Americas," in the sense in which there have been, and still are, "two Frances," "two Italys," "two Spains." Politically speaking, America has always been one. The reason is that a consensus was once established, and it still substantially endures, even in the quarters where its origins have been forgotten.

Formally and in the first instance this consensus was political, that is, it embraced a whole constellation of principles bearing upon the origin and nature of society, the function of the state as the legal order of society, and the scope and limitations of government. "Free government"—perhaps this typically American shorthand phrase sums up the consensus. "A free people under a limited government" puts the matter more exactly. It is a phrase that would have satisfied the first Whig, St. Thomas Aquinas.

To the early Americans government was not a phenomenon of force, as the later legal positivists would have it. Nor was it a "historical category," as Marx and his followers were to assert. Government did not mean simply the power to coerce, though this power was taken as integral to government. Government, properly speaking, was the right to command. It was authority. And its authority derived from law. By the same token its authority was limited by law. In his own way Tom Paine put the matter when he said, "In America Law is the King." But the matter had been better put by Henry of Bracton (d. 1268) when he said, "The king ought not to be under a man, but under God and under the law, because the law makes the king." This was the message of Magna Charta; this became the first structural rib of American constitutionalism.

Constitutionalism, the rule of law, the notion of sovereignty as purely political and therefore limited by law, the concept of government as an empire of laws and not of men—these were ancient ideas, deeply implanted in the British tradition at its origin in medieval times. The major American contribution to the tradition—a contribution that imposed itself on all subsequent political history in the Western world—was the written constitution. However, the American document was not the *constitution octroyée* of the nineteenth-century Restorations—a constitution graciously granted by the King or Prince-President. Through the American techniques of the constitutional convention and of popular ratification, the American Constitution is explicitly the act of the people. It embodies their consensus as to the purposes of government, its structure, the extent of its powers and the limitations on them, etc. By the Constitution the people define the areas where authority is legitimate and the areas where liberty is lawful. The Constitution is therefore at once a charter of freedom and a plan for political order.

THE PRINCIPLE OF CONSENT

Here is the second aspect of the continuity between the American consensus and the ancient liberal tradition; I mean the affirmation of the principle of the consent of the governed. Sir John Fortescue (d. 1476), Chief Justice of the Court of King's Bench under Henry VI, had thus stated the tradition, in distinguishing between the absolute and the constitutional monarch: "The secounde king [the constitutional monarch] may not rule his people by other laws than such as thai assenten to. And therefore he may set uppon thaim non imposicions without their consent." The principle of consent was inherent in the medieval idea of kingship; the king was bound to seek the consent of his people to his legislation. The American consensus reaffirmed this principle, at the same time that it carried the principle to newly logical lengths. Americans agreed that they would consent to none other than their own legislation, as framed by their representatives, who would be responsible to them. In other words, the principle of consent was wed to the equally ancient principle of popular participation in rule. But, since this latter principle was given an amplitude of meaning never before known in history, the result was a new synthesis, whose formula is the phrase of Lincoln, "government by the people."

Americans agreed to make government constitutional and therefore limited in a new sense, because it is representative, republican, responsible government. It is limited not only by law but by the will of the people it represents. Not only do the people adopt the Constitution; through the techniques of representation, free elections, and frequent rotation of administrations they also have a share in the enactment of all subsequent statutory legislation. The people are really governed; American political theorists did not pursue the Rousseauist will-o'-the-wisp: how shall the individual in society come to obey only himself? Nevertheless, the people are governed because they consent to be governed; and they consent to be governed because in a true sense they govern themselves.

The American consensus therefore includes a great act of faith in the capacity of the people to govern themselves. The faith was not unrealistic. It was not supposed that everybody could master the technical aspects of government, even in a day when these aspects were far less complex than they now are. The supposition was that the people could understand the gen-

225

eral objectives of governmental policy, the broad issues put to the decision of government, especially as these issues raised moral problems. The American consensus accepted the premise of medieval society, that there is a sense of justice inherent in the people, in virtue of which they are empowered, as the medieval phrase had it, to "judge, direct, and correct" the processes of government.

It was this political faith that compelled early American agreement to the institutions of a free speech and a free press. In the American concept of them, these institutions do not rest on the thin theory proper to eighteenth-century individualistic rationalism, that a man has a right to say what he thinks merely because he thinks it. The American agreement was to reject political censorship of opinion as unrightful, because unwise imprudent, not to say impossible. However, the proper premise of these freedoms lay in the fact that they were social necessities. "Colonial thinking about each of these rights had a strong social rather than individualistic bias," Rossiter says. They were regarded as conditions essential to the conduct of free, representative, and responsible government. People who are called upon to obey have the right first to be heard. People who are to bear burdens and make sacrifices have the right first to pronounce on the purposes which their sacrifices serve. People who are summoned to contribute to the common good have the right first to pass their own judgment on the question, whether the good proposed be truly a good, the people's good, the common good. Through the technique of majority opinion this popular judgment becomes binding on government.

A second principle underlay these free institutions—the principle that the state is distinct from society and limited in its offices toward society. This principle too was inherent in the Great Tradition. Before it was cancelled out by the rise of the modern omnicompetent society-state, it had found expression in the distinction between the order of politics and the order of culture, or, in the language of the time, the distinction between *studium* and *imperium*. The whole order of ideas in general was autonomous in the face of government; it was immune from political discipline, which could only fall upon actions, not ideas. Even the medieval Inquisition respected this distinction of orders; it never recognized a crime of opinion, *crimen opinionis;* its competence extended only to the repression of organized conspiracy against public order and the common good. It was, if you will, a Committee on un-Christian Activities; it regarded activities, not ideas, as justiciable.

The American Proposition, in reviving the distinction between society and state, which had perished under the advance of absolutism, likewise renewed the principle of the incompetence of government in the field of opinion. Government submits itself to judgment by the truth of society; it is not itself a judge of the truth in society. Freedom of the means of communciation whereby ideas are circulated and criticized, and the freedom of the academy (understanding by the term the range of institutions organized for the pursuit of truth and the perpetuation of the intellectual heritage of society) are immune from legal inhibition or government control. This immunity is a civil right of the first order, essential to the American concept of a free people under a limited government.

A VIRTUOUS PEOPLE

"A free people": this term too has a special sense in the American Proposition. America has passionately pursued the ideal of freedom, expressed in a whole system of political and civil rights, to new lengths; but it has not pursued this ideal so madly as to rush over the edge of the abyss, into sheer libertarianism, into the chaos created by the nineteenth-century theory of the "outlaw conscience," *conscientia exlex,* the conscience that knows no law higher than its own subjective imperatives. Part of the inner architecture of the American ideal of freedom has been the profound conviction that only a virtuous people can be free. It is not an American belief that free government is inevitable, only that it is possible, and that its possibility can be realized only when the people as a whole are inwardly governed by the recognized imperatives of the universal moral law.

The American experiment reposes on Acton's postulate, that freedom is the highest phase of civil society. But it also reposes on Acton's further postulate, that the elevation of a people to this highest phase of social life supposes, as its condition that they understand the ethical nature of political freedom. They must understand, in Acton's phrase, that freedom is "not the power of doing what we like, but the right of being able to do what we ought." The people claim this right, in all its articulated forms, in the face of government; in the name of this right, multiple limitations are put upon the power of government. But the claim can be made with the full resonance of moral authority only to the extent that it issues from an inner sense of responsibility to a higher law. In any phase civil society demands order. In its highest phase of freedom it demands that order should not be imposed from the top down, as it were, but should spontaneously flower outward form the free obedience to the restraints and imperatives that stem from inwardly possessed moral principle. In this sense democracy is more than a political experiment; it is a spiritual and moral enterprise. And its success depends upon the virtue of the people who undertake it. Men who would be politically free must discipline themselves. Likewise institutions which would pretend to be free with a human freedom must in their workings be governed from within and made to serve the ends of virtue. Political freedom is endangered in its foundations as soon as the universal moral values, upon whose shared possession the self-discipline of a free society depends, are no longer vigorous enough to restrain the passions and shatter the selfish inertia of men. The American ideal of freedom as ordered freedom, and therefore an ethical ideal, has traditionally reckoned with these truths, these truisms.

HUMAN AND HISTORICAL RIGHTS

This brings us to the threshold of religion, and therefore to the other aspect of the problem of pluralism, the plurality of religions in America. However, before crossing this threshold one more characteristic of the American Proposition, as implying a consensus, needs mention, namely, the Bill of Rights. The philosophy of the Bill of Rights was also tributary to the tradition of natural law, to the idea that man has certain original responsibilities precisely as man, antecedent to his status as citizen. These responsibilities are creative of rights which inhere in man antecedent to any act of government; therefore they are not granted by government and they cannot be surrendered to government. They are as inalienable as they are inherent. Their proximate source is in nature, and in history insofar as history bears witness to the nature of man; their ultimate source, as the Declaration of Independence states, is in God, the Creator of nature and the Master of history. The power of this doctrine, as it inspired both the Revolution and the form of the Republic, lay in the fact that it drew an effective line of demarcation around the exercise of political or social authority. When government ventures over this line, it collides with the duty and right of resistance. Its authority becomes arbitrary and therefore nil; its act incurs the ultimate anathema, "unconstitutional."

One characteristic of the American Bill of Rights is important for the subject here, namely, the differences that separate it from the Declaration of the Rights of Man in the France of '89. In considerable part the latter was a parchment-child of the Enlightenment, a top-of-the-brain concoction of a set of men who did not understand that a political community, like man himself, has roots in history and in nature. They believed that a state could be simply a work of art, a sort of absolute beginning, an artifact of which abstract human reason could be the sole artisan. Moreover, their exaggerated individualism had shut them off from a view of the organic nature of the human community; their social atomism would permit no institutions or associations intermediate between the individual and the state.

In contrast, the men who framed the American Bill of Rights understood history and tradition, and they understood nature in the light of both. They too were individualists, but not to the point of ignoring the social nature of man. They did their thinking within the tradition of freedom that was their heritage from England. Its roots were not in the top of anyone's brain but in history. Importantly, its roots were in the medieval notion of the *homo liber et legalis,* the man whose freedom rests on law, whose law was the age-old custom in which the nature of man expressed itself, and whose lawful freedoms were possessed in association with his fellows. The rights for which the colonists contended against the English Crown were basically the rights of Englishmen. And these were substantially the rights written into the Bill of Rights.

Of freedom of religion there will be question later. For the rest, freedom of speech, assembly, association, and petition for the redress of grievances, security of person, home, and property—these were great historical as well as civil and natural rights. So too was the right to trial by jury, and all the procedural rights implied in the Fifth- and later in the Fourteenth-Amendment provision for "due process of law." The guarantee of these and other rights was new in that it was written, in that it envisioned these rights with an amplitude, and gave them a priority, that had not been known before in history. But the Bill of Rights was an effective instrument for the delimitation of government authority and social power, not because it was written on paper in 1789 or 1791, but because the rights it proclaims had already been engraved by history on the conscience of a people. The American Bill of Rights is not a piece of eighteenth-century rationalist theory; it is far more the product of Christian history. Behind it one can see, not the philosophy of the Enlightenment but the older philosophy that had been the matrix of the common law. The "man" whose rights are guaranteed in the face of law and government is, whether he knows it or not, the Christian man, who had learned to know his own personal dignity in the school of Christian faith.

THE AMERICAN CONSENSUS TODAY

Americans have been traditionally proud of the earlier phases of their history—colonial and Revolutionary, constitutional and Federalist. This pride persists today. The question is, whether the American consensus still endures—the consensus whose essential contents have been sketched in the foregoing. A twofold answer may be given. The first answer is given by Professor Rossiter:

"Perhaps Americans could achieve a larger measure of liberty and prosperity and build a more successful government if they were to abandon the language and assumptions of men who lived almost two centuries ago. Yet the feeling cannot be downed that rude rejection of the past, rather than level-headed respect for it, would be the huge mistake. Americans may eventually take the advice of their advanced philosophers and adopt a political theory that pays more attention to groups, classes, public opinion, power-élites, positive law, public administration, and other realities of twentieth-century America. Yet it seems safe to predict that the people, who occasionally prove themselves wiser than their philosophers, will go on thinking about the political community in terms of unalienable rights, popular sovereignty, consent, constitutionalism, separation of powers, morality, and limited government. The political theory of the American Revolution—a theory of ethical, ordered liberty—remains the political tradition of the American people."

This is a cheerful answer. I am not at all sure that it is correct, if it be taken to imply that the tradition of natural law, as the foundation of law and politics, has the same hold upon the mind of America today that it had upon the "preachers, merchants, planters, and lawyers who were the mind of colonial America." There is indeed talk today about a certain revival of this great tradition, notably among more thoughtful men in the legal profession. But the talk itself is significant. One would not talk of reviving the tradition, if it were in fact vigorously alive. Perhaps the American people have not taken the advice of their advanced philosophers. Perhaps they are wiser than their philosophers. Perhaps they still refuse to think of politics and law as their philosophers think—in purely positivist and pragmatist terms. The fact remains that this is the way the philosophers think. Not that they have made a "rude rejection of the past." They are never rude. And they can hardly be said to have rejected what they never knew or understood, because it was never taught to them and they never learned it. The tradition of natural law is not taught or learned in the American university. It has not been rejected, much less refuted. We do not refute our adversaries, said Santayana; we quietly bid them goodbye. I think, as I shall later say, that the American university long since bade a quiet goodbye to the whole notion of an American consensus, as implying that there are truths that we hold in common, and a natural law that makes known to all of us the structure of the moral universe in such wise that all of us are bound by it in a common obedience.

There is, however, a second answer to the question, whether the original American consensus still endures. It is certainly valid of a not inconsiderable portion of the American people, the Catholic community. The men of learning in it acknowledge certain real contributions made by positive sociological analysis of the political community. But both they and their less learned fellows still adhere, with all the conviction of intelligence, to the tradition of natural law as the basis of free and ordered political life. Historically, this tradition has found, and still finds, its intellectual home within the Catholic Church. It is indeed one of the ironies of history that the tradition should have so largely languished in the so-called Catholic nations of Europe at the same time that its enduring vigor was launching a new Republic across the broad ocean. There is also some paradox in the fact that a nation which has (rightly or wrongly) thought of its own genius in Protestant terms should have owed its origins and the stability of its political structure to a tradition whose genius is alien to current intellectualized versions of the Protestant religion, and even to certain individualistic exigencies of Protestant religiosity. These are special questions, not to be pursued here. The point here is that Catholic participation in the American consensus has been full and free, unreserved and unembarrassed, because the contents of this consensus—the ethical and political principles drawn from the tradition of natural law—approve themselves to the Catholic intelligence and conscience. Where this kind of language is talked, the Catholic joins the conversation with complete ease. It is his language. The ideas expressed are native to his own universe of discourse. Even the accent, being American, suits his tongue.

Another idiom now prevails. The possibility was inherent from the beginning. To the early American theorists and politicians the tradition of natural law was an inheritance. This was its strength; this was at the same time its weakness, especially since a subtle alteration of the tradition had already commenced. For a variety of reasons the intellectualist idea of law as reason had begun to cede to the voluntarist idea of law as will. One can note the change in Blackstone, for instance, even though he still stood within the tradition, and indeed drew whole generations of early American lawyers into it with him.

(Part of American folklore is Sandburg's portrait of Abraham Lincoln, sitting barefoot on his woodpile, reading Blackstone.) Protestant Christianity, especially in its left wing (and its left wing has always been dominant in America), inevitably evolved away from the old English and American tradition. Grotius and the philosophers of the Enlightenment had cast up their secularized versions of the tradition. Their disciples were to better their instruction, as the impact of the methods of empirical science made itself felt even in those areas of human thought in which knowledge is noncumulative and to that extent recalcitrant to the methods of science. Seeds of dissolution were already present in the ancient heritage as it reached the shores of America.

Perhaps the dissolution, long since begun, may one day be consummated. Perhaps one day the noble many-storeyed mansion of democracy will be dismantled, levelled to the dimensions of a flat majoritarianism, which is no mansion but a barn, perhaps even a tool shed in which the weapons of tyranny may be forged. Perhaps there will one day be wide dissent even from the political principles which emerge from natural law, as well as dissent from the constellation of ideas that have historically undergirded these principles—the idea that government has a moral basis; that the universal moral law is the foundation of society; that the legal order of society—that is, the state—is subject to judgment by a law that is not statistical but inherent in the nature of man; that the eternal reason of God is the ultimate origin of all law; that this nation in all its aspects—as a society, a state, an ordered and free relationship between governors and governed—is under God. The possiblity that widespread dissent from these principles should develop is not foreclosed. If that evil day should come, the results would introduce one more paradox into history. The Catholic community would still be speaking in the ethical and political idiom familiar to them as it was familiar to their fathers, both the Fathers of the Church and the Fathers of the American Republic. The guardianship of the original American consensus, based on the Western heritage, would have passed to the Catholic community, within which the heritage was elaborated long before America was. And it would be for others, not Catholics, to ask themselves whether they still shared the consensus which first fashioned the American people into a body politic and determined the structure of its fundamental law.

What has been said may suffice to show the grounds on which Catholics participate in the American consensus. These grounds are drawn from the materials of the consensus itself. It has been a greatly providential blessing that the American Republic never put to the Catholic conscience the questions raised, for instance, by the Third Republic. There has never been a schism within the American Catholic community, as there was among French Catholics, over the right attitude to adopt toward the established polity. There has never been the necessity for nice distinctions between the regime and the legislation; nor has there ever been the need to proclaim a policy of *ralliement*. In America the *ralliement* has been original, spontaneous, universal. It has been a matter of conscience and conviction, because its motive was not expediency in the narrow sense—the need to accept what one is powerless to change. Its motive was the evident coincidence of the principles which inspired the American Republic with the principles that are structural to the Western Christian political tradition.

Karl Rahner
1904-

The task of the theologian in the twentieth century is a
difficult and challenging one. His quest for the meaning of Christian reality must express fidelity to a tradition that has been
developing for two thousand years. At the same time he must
be equally faithful to the contemporary world of which he is
child, to its knowledge explosion in the natural and behavioral
sciences, to its many revolutions, to its philosophies. Today's
theologian, while sustaining a fidelity to both the traditional and
and the contemporary, must further have the capacity to communicate with the ordinary Christian.

Father Karl Rahner is all of this. He is known and respected
throughout the professional world for the richness and originality
of his insight, for his serious, reflective scholarship, and for his
capacity to blend the foundational truths of Christianity with
contemporary ideas and terminologies.

He was born in Freiburg, Germany, and received his early
schooling there. After entering the Society of Jesus in 1922, he
pursued his seminary studies for ten years and was ordained a
priest in Munich in 1932. Afterwards he returned to his home-
town of Freiburg to study philosophy; he was particularly influenced by the great German philosopher Martin Heidegger. He
earned a doctorate in theology from the University of Innsbruck

and since 1937, has led a life dedicated to theological investigations.

During the 1950's Rahner's work was looked upon by many with some suspicion. His "theological anthropology" was too novel an approach. But with the advent of Pope John XXIII it was only a matter of time until his theology began to be received more favorably.

It is difficult to evaluate the impact of Karl Rahner on the Church since the Second Vatican Council. His familiarity with modern thought as well as with the historical tradition, his pastoral commitment which colors his theological speculation, and his fearless confrontation with the major questions of our century have given him a central role in shaping Catholic thought.

The following selection is A Theological Interpretation of the Position of Christians in the Modern World. *Rahner originally presented it as a paper in 1954 to the conference of Catholic publicists at Cologne. It is now part of a three volume work entitled* Mission and Grace: Essays in Pastoral Theology.

Rahner argues that Christians, as Christians, simply do not have any ready-made programme for the conduct of the state, or of culture, or of economics, and in fact cannot have one. Such an insight shatters any claim on the part of modern Christianity to have the answers to the world's problems. It challenges the Christian to shake off the tendency toward dogmatism and to lose himself in the world. Though Christianity exists everywhere, it does so as a minority. Thus the characteristic of Christianity in our age is that of diaspora. Christians are spread thinly around the world, so that the modern age is not stamped with the Christian seal. Not only must the Christian avoid slipping into a ghetto mentality, he must also get ready to live Christianity in a whole new way. He must move forward and not try to salvage the unsalvageable. One can no longer be Christian by culture, by politics or by morals. A profound faith in eternal life is required.

Father Rahner's fresh approach to Christianity provides the Church with the freedom necessary to face modern society courageously and to fashion a response to the demands of contemporary life.

MISSION AND GRACE

A THEOLOGICAL INTERPRETATION OF THE POSITION
OF CHRISTIANS IN THE MODERN WORLD

There is a preliminary observation to be made before I embark on my real theme. I think that what I am going to say is, in itself, more or less right. But for this opinion, I should not be saying it. But this does not necessarily carry with it the conviction that this right thing that I want to say is the thing which here and now needs saying; that this right thing may not perhaps be out of place, so that it would be more right to say some other right thing. Suppose you say, "In twelve hours this house will be cut off by flood"; the information can scarcely fail to be of some interest to the inhabitants of the house. But it might, according to circumstances, be still more important to tell them that the roof was on fire and they had better get out. It is not easy both to say the right thing and to say it in the right place. I am not, from this point of view, altogether sure that my lecture has the necessary qualification of urgency, and that it does not fail to say things which would be much more important at the present moment. So if, at the end of it, it seems to you that I have for the time being gone off in the wrong direction, though still remaining on the ground of truth, i.e., of what is right in itself, I shall be glad to hear from you about it. It can, of course, also happen that one judges more immediate and urgent matters falsely through being unwilling to listen to something fundamental but less immediate and urgent.

My theme, as formulated by those in charge of this conference, is: The theological interpretation of the position of Christians in the modern world.

The wording requires me to speak not as a politician or a historian of ideas or a philosopher or a prophet, but as a theologian. A theologian speaks on the basis of Scripture and Tradition as interpreted by the teaching Church. This gives him a relatively easy basis for speaking of the position of Christians in the world. He can speak of the nature of man, of his destiny, of nature and grace, of what is included in the concept "the world", of the orders of creation and redemption, of the meaning of history, of sin and redemption, of the working out of both of them on the secular plane of man's existence, of the relationship between Church, people and State, of the relative self-subsistence of the different areas of cultural life, of the natural law, and of numerous similar things and norms which are always to be found in God's world, which is also the world of his Christ and of the Church. But my task is *not* to speak of these things. For I am to say something, as a theologian, about the *theological* interpretation of the position of Christians in the *modern* world. Can anything be said of this, *theologically*? It is a world which did not exist when there came forth that word of revelation which the Church preserves and proclaims and with which the theologian is concerned. Of course there still exists today the world of creation, sin, redemption, and movement towards the future things of God of which revelation speaks. The world of Scripture is our world too. And if we direct our gaze towards that in our world which revelation explicitly sees in it, which revelation expresses of it, then we are undoubtedly seeing what is most important in it, and something which always deserves and needs to be considered afresh. But we should not then be seeing the modern world *as modern,* i.e., that in it which makes our world different from any earlier one, that in it which has not always been the case, not even always and everywhere in the age, the *aion,* of Christ—precisely *our* situation, not that of any earlier generation of Christians. Can we, indeed, say anything theologically about *that*? We can of course, in regard to this present modality of the world, by which it is differentiated from preceding epochs, say all the things that Christians can always say; that it is something created and yet subject to evil, that it is subject to evil and yet redeemed and, in Christ, assumed by God into grace, that it is entrusted to human freedom and yet in the hand of God, that it has meaning and yet can only move onwards that fulfilled and real meaning which God will give in his future judgement. But to consider all this (and it would be an important consideration) would still be to fall back into that general kind of evaluation of which we have said already that it is not our present task. Are we to say then, that, in so far as the special character of our age is not simply one more instance of the general Christian interpretation of the world, it can only be, for the Christian as such, a matter of indifference, and hence not a theme for theological consideration? But in that case the world, in itself, is a matter of indifference, undifferentiated matter, in which the Christian, as such, operates according to his other-worldly Christianity, until, like the characters in *Everyman,* he strips off what is no more than the costume of the part he has played and goes into eternal life taking with him only that part of him which he could just as well have enacted in any other role. In that case, the universal is everything, and the particular, the historically unique, is nothing, is non-being. In that case, we should have nothing to say on our particular theme except that we have to recognize that we are always dealing with the same world, with the Christian always in the same relationship to it. But if this is not so—if the present world as such, in its historical uniqueness, is a concern of Christians—how is the theologian to know anything about this present world, precisely in its modernity, *from revelation?* At the time when that historic word of revelation, to which nothing can be added, was uttered in Christ, this present world did not exist.

If we are to suppose that anything was said *then* about this world of *today,* it can only have been by way of prediction. But is there any such prediction? Does the message of Christianity include any such prophecy of our age, enabling us to say something theologically about our age as such? Or are we, as Christians, able only to declare what is always and universally valid, and then apply it to the case in hand?—in which process we shall always be dogged by the feeling that our principles are assuredly sound and good, but the attempt to apply them can be successful only to a limited extent, with the most important point of all left open: it can never yield any unambiguous conclusions because, having regard to this age as a whole, any such application of principles would rest upon an interpretation and analysis of our situation itself made not by theological but

239

by purely personal means, thus always remaining our own, highly questionable work.

I am of the opinion that such a prediction does exist, and determines the Christian's position in our modern world. It is, obviously, not in the nature of an advance description of our time. This, for one thing, because divine prophecy is never a satisfaction of human curiosity about what is going to happen, but a help to steering a Christian course through a future which is unknown and remains unknown; an illumination of the meaning of the future which still leaves it dark, not history written in advance. Moreover, this applies particularly to our present case, since we cannot expect that so small a section of time as concerns us here will be described in advance by the predictive word of God in such fashion that we can gather from it any kind of soothsaying prognosis of the future. But that little which the word of God gives us can nevertheless illuminate our present situation, even though it still leaves us in darkness and does not relieve us either of our cares or of responsibility in decision.

But before we can attempt to say what it is that God has predicted concerning our time, there are one or two premises to be laid down which, while they are theologically valid for all periods, appear to be particularly important in our own situation.

In the sphere of secular, worldly living, there is never any period that can be called *the* Christian age, any culture which is *the* Christian culture, etc. This does not only mean that according to Catholic teaching there are always Church and State, redemptive history and secular history, nature and grace, and that these can never be adequately united in one thing. It means, rather, that it is never possible simply to deduce, from Christian principles of belief and morality, any one single pattern of the world as it ought to be. In principle, there is neither in respect of the State nor of economics nor of culture nor of history, any one clear, concrete imperative which can be deduced from Christian teaching as the one and only possible right course. It is possible to reject certain conditions, tendencies, endeavours and actions as contradicting the Christian law of faith and morality. In numerous *individual cases* it may be that man's area of freedom in choice and action is, in the concrete, so narrow that there is in fact only *one* line of action remaining open to him as permissible or obligatory, if he wants to avoid offending against the Christian law; further, Christian principles, which give the structure of reality itself as offered to man's freedom to work on, may be of the greatest and most beneficial significance for human activity, and any violation of them may have the direst consequences. But it is never, in principle, possible to say in the name of these principles that the world is or has got to be precisely "thus and so", when "thus and so" means something ultimate, positive and individual. In principle, there can in one and the same situation be several possibilities of action, not only practical but also justified. The choice between these possibilities, which has to be made and always involves an historical human decision, cannot, in principle, be settled in advance in the name of Christianity. To deny this would be not only to refuse that right and proper dualism of which we have already spoken its reality, or at least its right to reality; it would be, beyond this, an ontological heresy, since it would be an assertion that concrete events in the human sphere are *only* limiting instances of the universal, with no significance over and above that of the universal expressible in universal norms.

All this may seem a truism. But it is nevertheless extremely important in practical terms. It means, for instance, that nothing is ever *the* Christian culture, *the* Christian education, *the* Christian political system, *the* Christian party etc. There can at most, in principle at any rate, be things which are unchristian in so far as they definitely contradict general Christian norms; there can be Christian cultures, systems of education, parties etc. in so far as these are, in principle, in intention, and to some degree in practice, in harmony with these norms, but there can never (apart from the Church herself) be any single concrete thing in the sphere of world history and culture which can lay claim to be, in principle, uniquely and exclusively *the* Christian realization of anything. This implies that any earlier age which may have called itself Christian was not only often in fact very unchristian, but was also, even taking the most favourable possible view, only *a,* and not *the,* expression of the Christian spirit. Hence no aspect of it is binding on us; not only because "times have changed" (meaning the conditions surrounding human free action), but in any case, since it could, even at the time, have legitimately been otherwise. The fact that we do not always see this so easily—that, for instance, we speak with facile romanticism of the Christian Middle Ages and enthuse over "the West" in the name of Christianity (and not, as is permissible, in the name of our own historical freely chosen decision)—is because the area of free choice *then,* the creative possibilities historically existing *then,* were relatively restricted, not because of Christian principles but because of geographical, technical, economic and other factors; so that *at that time* any general desire to exist in a Christian fashion was probably almost bound to produce what in fact was then produced. But this was, to repeat, something done because of historical necessity, not (as often supposed) because of the essence of Christianity.

From this it follows that as soon as there is any appreciable widening of the area of practical human possibilities, as soon as any considerable number of things, hitherto impossible, become possible to human freedom, the Christian in this historical situation at once discovers the sharply painful nature of choice. That is to say, it is only in these circumstances that a Christian comes explicitly to realize that he cannot use his Christian principles to supply a clear imperative for his activity at the historical level. They leave him in the air; meaning that they demand to be respected and put into practice in whatever course of action he may decide upon, but they cannot tell him what to decide; for, given the circumstances we have described, he is suddenly, as never before, presented with a multiplicity of legitimate possibilities, all of which could be ways of being a Christian.

No-one would try to deny that this present age, the end-product of the modern period, does present us with this wide possibility of choice, carrying with it both the pain and the noble potentialities of freedom, or that it does so to an over-whelming degree. In the fields of technology, economics, sociology, mass psychology etc., things are possible today which were impossible in earlier centuries. It is the simple truth that we are beginning to live in an age in which all that lies before it seems to shrink together into a single period.

From these two things, among others, immediately follow. First, it will now become plain, in the clearest possible way, that Christians *as such* simply do not have any ready-made, concrete programme for the conduct of the State, or of culture, or of economics, and in fact *cannot* have one. This was indeed theoretically the case in earlier ages as well. But it did not appear so plainly, because the area of possibilities historically available for human realization was relatively narrow. It is now going to become gradually clear that the gap between universal Christian principles and the putting of them into practice in any one of a number of possible forms is a gap as wide as the possibilities now opening up before us. From this it follows that while we Christians should indeed rejoice that it is given to us to have the true standards by which human living can be shaped according to its meaning (their importance, and the importance of clearly recognizing them by the saving and searching light of revelation, have grown all the greater in face of the greater possibilities, now grown to monstrous proportions, of ignoring them to our own hurt), yet we cannot, *as Christians,* have any single, unitary programme, when it comes to planning in the concrete. It may be that in some given, temporary situation we have to stand together because of a radical threat to Christian and human values. It may also be that in some given situation Christians, in their historical activity as *human beings,* in making their decision on some particular thing, without being required to do so precisely in the name of Christianity, happen to decide, more or less together, on one particular course. But they cannot bolster up either of these unities by saying that the norms of Christian conduct clearly lay down this one particular way, which is alone to be approved and chosen as providing the right course among the bewildering profusion of possibilities stretching around us. What is immediately at work at the historical level is not the unchanging norms (though their effect, for good or ill, will indeed make itself felt at that level), but some one determinate, formative pattern and plan, as concrete as the actual activity which puts it into practice. This is what we Christians *as such* cannot have.

We never have had one, for even in earlier times the particular concrete form given to the Christian ideal was not determined by Christianity as such (though indeed by Christians) but by other historical forces and influences. But it was possible in earlier times to *confuse* the original principles, and the practice of them, with a particular ideal at work at the historical level, and to regard this synthesis as final and obligatory. On this matter we of today are disillusioned, or we ought to be. We Christians have grown poorer. What we have lost is, of course, merely the illusion that because we were the people who listened with faith to the Word of God, we therefore had a complete recipe for the world's problems in our pockets, and the only difficulty was to be accurate and faithful in putting it into practice. It is useless to commend our Christian principles to the world as its salvation. What it wants is to hear concrete proposals. We have got to have the courage to act as human beings with a task in the world of history, and so to come forward with such proposals. But we cannot propagate them in the name of Christianity. It is here that we find the really profound reason for the withdrawal of the Church from politics. Such a withdrawal involves neither opportunism nor a failure to proclaim and defend Christian principles. It arises from the realization that, in itself, fundamentally, if politics means having a concrete programme, then there cannot be any one Christian form of politics, whether in the economic, constitutional, cultural or any other field. We must acknowledge this poverty in ourselves, if we want to be honest; and even here, honesty is the best policy. If we are honest about this "impoverishment" of Christianity, due to the clarification of the *diastasis* between Christianity as such and any particular concrete form given in the past to it, then Christianity will be divested, in men's minds, of that responsibility for particular historical states of affairs with which it is still involuntarily burdened today. If we are not honest about it—i.e., if we make some synthesis of Christian principles and our own historical preferences and then propagate that as what Christianity itself unconditionally demands, to stand or fall by it—then people will take us at our word in this false declaration. They will then, unavoidably, combat Christianity itself if ever they take some other historical decision than ours and set about implementing it, for it is we who will have declared ours to be a pure and simple case of Christian principles in action.

There is this to consider, too: It is no doubt true that there do exist in this world forces of evil, of organized godlessness. There are not only differences of opinion and taste which can be settled by democratic compromise, being all equally justified in principle. There is, beyond these, a more and more concrete opposition between good and evil, and this does not mean a dialectical tension which ultimately makes harmonious sense because it keeps hauling the wagon-train of world history in one constant direction. But true though this is, and real though its consequences may often be, we Christians cannot for all that be Manichees and believe in a real, absolute Evil, still less in an incarnation of any such Evil. In other words, we see as Christians that evil has power only through the good which is in it, and which derives from God. So if we refuse to see the programmes and performances of anti-Christians, even the most extreme of them, simply as the embodiment of evil and nothing else; if we seek for the good in them, without which they would be powerless to achieve anything; if we refrain from committing ourselves, irrevocably and in advance, to the view that any such good is always adequately embodied already in our own admirable programmes and mediocre performances (for we are in fact often sinful and short-sighted), we are not then guilty of cowardly compromise or cloudy universal tolerance but are performing a Christian duty, since it would be heresy, not Christian firmness, to believe that there is an absolute evil as there is an absolute good.

The vast range of possibilities now opening out as a field of historical human decision calls for some active entity capable of availing itself of those possibilities; and the very width of the range confers upon any such entity an importance as new and as immeasurable as the new opportunities themselves, by comparison with earlier entities active in the historical process and with the possibilities open to them in earlier ages. This means that organized human society has taken on an importance, because of these new possibilities, which it has not had before. It is not for the Church to be that which actually and directly responds to such historical possibilities in the secular sphere. But something must be; such an entity is positively forced into existence (or into a new mode of existence) by the development of the possibilities themselves. It can only be the State, or the community of people organized at a planetary level. Any other entity would simply not be capable of exploiting these possibilities. But this implies, whether we like it or not, that the State (either individual or planetary) is taking on an importance which it has never had before. The opportunities for moulding human existence arbitrarily, according to plan and choice, used to represent a very small sector of human life in comparison with what was determined by natural conditions or done by smaller communities. The State, with its policies and its legislation, was able to bring relatively little to bear, in the way of conscious planning, on human life. Things have changed. Furthermore, the possibilities are such that the practical realization of them *cannot* be simply avoided. Hence they will in fact be realized. In other words, there will be a State (if indeed there is not already), whether regional or world-wide, in which the concentration of power will be gigantically vast in comparison with anything which has borne the name of State in the past. And this will happen even if Christian principles of subsidiarity and so on are respected. For the State has no need to take to itself anything which other, smaller corporations or individuals have *hitherto* disposed of, being capable of handling and controlling it themselves. It need only take to itself those possibilities, insistently clamouring to be used, which are entirely new developments, and which no-one and nothing else would be capable of handling. These alone are enough to make it such as to inspire fear at first sight; to make it, indeed, a very disquietingly dangerous structure, as dangerous as the potentialities which the modern age places at its disposal. It is quite impossible that the State (whether regional or world-wide) should continue to be what we have been accustomed to in the past in such matters as world population: the scope and needs of technology; problems of mass psychology in a vast and crowded population; ways of waging war; economic and cultural modifications in the way of life of individual peoples. Even with the most favourable possible outcome—i.e., maximum justice—the sphere of the State is going to outweigh that of private life; not because the sphere of private life has shrunk, but because that of the State has expanded, the increased potentialities offered by the present historical situation being such that nothing else but the State could possibly handle them.

We have to take account of all this when we come to ask ourselves: What, as shown forth in the prophetic word of God, is the present position of the Christian, through which the situation as so far described acquires its special character?

My thesis is this: In so far as our outlook is really based on today, and looking towards tomorrow, the present situation of Christians can be characterized as that of a *diaspora*; and this signifies, in terms of the history of salvation, a "must", from which we may and must draw conclusions about our behaviour as Christians.

Before I try to explain and demonstrate the real heart of this thesis, there is one concept which I must explain as being extremely important to it. I have said that the *diaspora* situation is, in terms of the history of salvation, a "must". This needs explaining. There are, on the one hand, things which ought to be, *a priori,* unconditionally; such things, for instance, as are expressed in the Ten Commandments. There are, on the other hand, things which simply are, though they ought not to be; whether they are due to guilt or to misfortune, one simply recognizes their existence, and that is all there is to it, except to bear them patiently if they cannot be changed and otherwise, at best, to try to eliminate them from the world. Between these two classes of things—things that ought to be, and things that ought not to be but simply are—there is a third, intermediate group of things and events and relationships. They ought not really to exist; that is to say, they are in contradiction with some rule of what should be, some ideal, some postulate; but they are not simply the factual contradiction of a rule. When they come into existence, and continue, they acquire, despite their conflict with what ought to be, a queer sort of justification and validity, a kind of inevitability, significance and value. It is impossible, and wrong, simply to endure them or simply to protest against them. Though they have not, properly speaking, any *right* to exist, yet one cannot simply eliminate them or struggle wildly against them. One ought rather to give them their due; to reckon with them; to draw certain conclusions from their existence (which "considered in themselves" they ought not to have, but which has, in the concrete, its own validity)—conclusions which will, in their turn, present us with an "ought", and this because these things, precisely *as existing* (and not simply as something to be grimly endured or fought against), have a significance for salvation. I should like to say of such things, conditions and events that, in terms of the history of salvation, they are things which *must be,* basing myself in this on scriptural usage. For the Scripture witnesses to such things. When for instance our Lord says, "The poor you have always with you", this is something more than a statement about the persistence of a distressing fact. It does not dispute the necessity "in itself" of continually striving to the end that there shall be no poor, that they shall no longer exist. Still less is it a denial that the mode of poverty can change enormously within the changing modes of social relationships. Nevertheless, the existence of poverty is not ranged amongst those mere facts whose sheer existence can only be acknowledged under protest. Although, in the last analysis, there are poor people only because there is guilt, yet this fact is acknowledged as something that *must* be, something to be reckoned with, so that to exclude it from the maxims of practical activity would be to commit the fault and error of unchristian idealistic utopianism. Anything that is in this sense a δεῖ in terms of the history of salvation is often spoken of in Scripture as willed by God, as "having" to be, as signifying salvation, as calling for man's active acknowledgment, even though "in itself" it ought not to be at all. The supreme instance of such a "must" in the history of salvation is the Cross of Christ, for it was necessary that the Son should suffer. He had to suffer, although it was by human guilt that he did suffer. He did not see his passion (although it was something that *ought* not to happen) as something which he should take all possible steps to avoid; he did not say to Peter, "Yes, you are right, it must not be, and we will do our utmost to avoid it, only unfortunately it will happen all the same." He said, "Go behind me, Satan . . . thou savourest not the things that are of God,

but the things that are of men." (Matt. 16.23.) So too elsewhere; scandals and schisms "must" come; not merely they
are coming, but they *must* come, for all that it is woe to them
by whom they come. Hence we conclude that it is possible and
permissible for a Christian to affirm a "must" of this sort
within the history of salvation, to reckon with it as such, and to
draw from it conclusions involving an "ought" for his own
conduct, even though it does not itself arise from any *a priori*
"ought", but from historical causes and even from human guilt
and failure. Fault and failure in our proper historical task need
not always consist in refusing the right kind of combat (which
is also our duty) against the facts of this world; it may consist in
combating them with an unchristian utopian radicalism, refusing
to acknowledge them for what they are. There is a wrong way
of working to eliminate poverty; there is a wrong kind of
obstinate, pseudo-heroic apostolate which refuses to shake the
dust from its feet and go into another city when the message
falls upon deaf ears. All the New Testament prophecies about
the hard time that the Church was to have in history were made
not only to prevent us from being too dismayed, but also so
that this historical situation of the Church, not "as it ought to
be" but nevertheless foreknown, should be something from
which we could draw conclusions for our own conduct.

We cannot here go on to provide a more precise ontological
and theological basis for this concept. Taking it for granted, we
proceed to the next assertion: that our situation as a *diaspora*
is for us today a "must" of this kind in the history of salvation.
This means that we have not only to acknowledge this *diaspora*
situation as unfortunately permitted by God, but can recognize
it as willed by God as a "must" (not as an "ought"), and go
freely on to draw our conclusions from this.

But first we have to look at the fact itself. The mere
fact of being a *diaspora* on this planet has had to be gradually
admitted. Whether it is a happy choice of words, or theologically
correct, to speak of the countries of Europe as mission countries, can be left an open question. But that there are no longer
any Christian countries (with the *possible* exception of the
Iberian peninsula) is a fact. Christianity (though in very varying
proportions) exists *everywhere* in the world, and everywhere as

a *diaspora*. It is effectually, *in terms of numbers,* a minority *everywhere*; nowhere does it fill such a role of effective leadership as would permit it to set upon the age with any force or clarity the stamp of a Christian ideal. Indeed, we are undoubtedly in an era which is going to see an increase in this *diaspora* character, no matter what causes we may assign to it. The new age of Jesus Christ, as prophesied by Fr. Lombardi, is certainly not going to dawn for some considerable while. On the contrary, the Christendom of the Middle Ages and after, peasant and individualistic petty-bourgeois Christendom, is going to disappear with ever-increasing speed. For the causes which have brought about this process in the West are still at work and have not yet had their full effect.

But that we are a *diaspora* throughout the world is not merely a fact to be recognized *a posteriori* and with dismay. It is something which, on the basis of our faith, we should have expected, in the sense of a "must" within the history of salvation. It is foretold, though of course only as an implication which could be made explicit only by reference to certain facts in the present world situation. It is a theological datum which can be interpreted according to faith. It is something which "ought not to be", in so far as all men ought to become Christians when the message of faith is preached to them (which to a certain measure has been done all over the world), and in so far as the peoples of the West ought not to have fallen away from Christianity. To this extent, the Christian desire *not* to be a *diaspora* remains, of course, an obligation on every Christian, a desire which cannot fail to inspire apostolic activity and witness, both active and passive. But between this grimly heroic desire and the merely dismayed recognition that it has very small success there can and should lie something intermediate: the knowledge of this *diaspora* situation as a "must" in the history of salvation, and the valid conclusions drawn from this historical knowledge.

Every earthly institution wants to make good; it measures its internal self-justification in terms of its palpable, immediate chances of total victory. But to Christianity and the Church her Founder promised not only that she would endure until the end of time, but, just as clearly, that his work would always be a sign of contradiction and persecution, of dire and (in secular terms) desperate combat; that love would grow cold; that he, in his disciples, would be persecuted in the name of God; that the struggle would narrow down to an ever more critical point; that the victory of Christianity would not be the fruit of immanent development and widening and a steady, progressive leavening of the world, but would come as the act of God coming in judgement to gather up world history into its wholly unpredictable and unexpected end. This permanent state of contradiction, foretold to the Church and the Christian as a "must", is something that we must not water down. It does not simply mean that each generation has to be christianized afresh, and that this always comes hard to every member of the human race. It is not only a matter of contradiction and friction in individual private existence, in which everyone, being a sinner, is capable of resisting the message of the Gospel. Scripture sees the contradiction as a fact of public life and universal history, a matter of peoples and politics. Hence this contradiction is a "must" in the history of salvation.

Why is the universal *diaspora* situation prophesied as a "must" in this sense? This needs explaining.

This is our starting-point: That the Church and Christianity will be to the end of time a stone of stumbling and a matter of contradiction; that this will not simply happen to be so as a matter of fact, but is a part of that mysterious "must" (appearing constantly in Scripture) in which human guilt, which ought not to exist, yet remains within God's plan; that God does not will man's guilt, and yet this guilt, which is not willed, is used even "in advance" as a means to the working out of the divine plan.

For a believer, who judges things from God's standpoint, a "must" of this sort is not merely something with which he *may* reckon, but something with which he *must* reckon; something that he must calmly expect and at which he must not be surprised.

Given this contradiction of the Church—permanent, public, to be expected from the start and not to be wondered at—how is it going to manifest itself?

As long as the Church was in practice limited to one cultural and historical sphere (e.g., the West), the contradiction could come "from outside", simply because there *was* an "outside". Hence the Church and Christianity could, within that restricted area, be "omnipotent", the unquestioned, uncontradicted leader and ruler, and still have her opponents "from outside"—heresies (ultimately of oriental origin), and Christendom's hereditary foe, the Turks.

From the very moment (a moment which may, of course, need centuries to develop its full potentialities) when there is no longer any such "outside", both because the Church has become actually world-wide and (the two interacting on each other) because the histories of separate peoples have merged into one single history of mankind, every people and every historical situation becoming from then on a force *within* every other one—from the very moment when this happens, the contradiction of the Church, in terms of theological history, can no longer come from "outside" and *must* (in that mysterious sense of "must" which is our present concern) arise within Christendom as such, in the form of schism and apostasy. For otherwise, either the Church would be uncontradicted or else she would still be to some extent an historically insular Church, belonging to one particular separate culture. Neither is possible.

In fact, we see that the beginnings of schism and the dechristianization of the West through the Reformation and the Renaissance and Enlightenment do in fact appear at just that moment when, on a substratum of European expansion, the Church begins to be in actuality a world-wide Church. In the moment when she begins to be a Church of *all* the heathen, she also begins, everywhere, to be a Church *among the heathen*. The actual combination of these events is, of course, loaded with guilt and tragedy; but seeing it at the higher level of theology, and of a theology of history, it is nevertheless included within a mysterious "must"; something that should not be a surprise or a scandal to a believing Christian, because it was in fact to be expected, as indeed he has to expect the continuance of guilt and of rejection of Christ even to the end of time. The loss of the Church's medieval omnipotence in public life (it is best in this sense to reckon the Middle Ages as ending with the French Revolution) was, then, theologically, something to be expected, however much it may have involved guilt as well. The value given to the Church in the public life of society, state and culture in the Middle Ages cannot be regarded as something demanded by the very nature of the Church; not if the Church is bound to be, permanently, the Church of contradiction, and if it was also to be, and had in fact become, a world-wide Church. The medieval form was possible only so long as the Church was the Church of a more or less closed culture. It became impossible from the moment when the West became an integral part of world history. From then on the contradiction had to be either everywhere or nowhere. Since it cannot be nowhere—it has to *be*—it must be everywhere. "O foolish and slow of heart . . . ought not Christ to have suffered these things?" applies to his sufferings in world history as well.

Furthermore, the value set upon the Church in public life, in its medieval form, is not attributable, as a phenomenon, simply and solely to the supernatural power of the Church and Christianity. That particular form (not the Church's essential theological value) was also, at least in its factual, existential realization, the result of temporal, secular combinations of historical forces. It was a fact of cultural history rather than of theology. One might say that every "Middle Ages" (i.e., every culture resting on a peasant and small-city foundation, and remaining historically stationary for a whole period) has its ruling religion, established in unchallenged supremacy; this without reference to whether such religion be true or false, from below or from above, medieval Islam, or medieval feudal Shintoism in Japan, or anything else. What reveals the supernatural power of Christianity is not so much the mere fact that it, like other cultural religions, did in one particular culture and one particular, necessarily passing, stage of that culture, exercise a practically unchallenged ruling power over the hearts of men and their cultural institutions. This argument, dear though it is to many apologists, will not seem entirely convincing to an historian or a philosopher of history. It is rather that, on the one hand, when this secular and temporary historical situation disappears, Christianity then manifests, even empirically, and despite all apostasies and other losses, an incomparably greater power of resistance and endurance than other religions which have also known their similarly favourable "Middle Ages"; and, on the other hand, that the Church's position in the Middle Ages can be seen as having had a providential significance in enabling Christianity to make as powerful an entrance as it did, both moving *out of* and moving *with* that limited culture, into the world at large, and so become, empirically, a world religion.

Hence we have a full right, indeed almost a duty, to take account of the fact, without any sense of shock, that the form of the Church's existence in public life is changing. The fact that the Church is becoming a *diaspora everywhere,* that she is a Church surrounded by non-Christians and hence living in a culture, in a State, amidst political movements, economic activity, science and art which are conducted *not* simply and solely by Christians—all this is a "must" in the history of salvation. From this "must" we are permitted and indeed enjoined to draw sane and sober conclusions, in the shape of maxims to be applied to our pastoral work for the offensive and defensive activities of the Church and of Christians. Such conclusions bear a dialectical relationship to the maxim (which is at the level of "ought") which we apply to the spread and defence of Christianity, which demands that we try with all available means to win all men and all aspects of culture for Christ. Nothing less than the dialectical unity of both sets of maxims can constitute the full law governing our positions as Christians in the present age.

Before we go on to the implications for our attitude as Christians to be drawn from this *diaspora* situation as a prospective characteristic of the present age of the Church and a "must" in the history of salvation, we must give some consideration to the elements of the *diaspora* situation itself.

Let us simply ask ourselves: What happens, what is bound to happen, when a Christian has to live his Christianity amongst a large number of non-Christians? A great many things follow of themselves:

(*a*) His faith is constantly threatened from without. Christianity receives no support, or very little, from institutional morality, custom, civil law, tradition, public opinion, normal conformism etc. Each individual has to achieve it afresh for himself; it is no longer simply "a heritage from our fathers". Each individual must be won to it afresh, and such a recruitment can appeal only to personal decision, to what is independent and individual in a man, not to that in him which makes him a homogeneous part of the masses, a product of his situation, of "public opinion" and of his background. Christianity ceases to be a religion of growth and becomes a religion of choice. Obviously Christians will still give institutional form to their lives, over and above the institutional element in the Church herself; they will try to transmit to their children the faith that they have themselves won in a personal decision, they will develop and try to preserve Christian habits of morality, customs, practices, associations and organizations. But by and large the situation will remain one of choice, not of natural growth; of a personal achievement constantly renewed amid perilous surroundings.

(b) A considerable part of the riches of culture—literary, artistic, scientific—upon which a Christian, too, lives, and *must* live, unless he wants to become a hopeless outsider in the intellectual life of this world, will not be specifically Christian nor bear the stamp of Christianity. Much of what is institutional in social, civic, political and cultural life will be such as to exercise a negative influence on a Christian's moral life, and will bring his life into almost unavoidable conflict with his Christian morality. The non-Christian world, which (though we love to assert such things of it) is *not* a sheer mass of decomposition and deterioration, will even seek to develop its own forces, its own institutions of a social, intellectual, educational and moral kind, and these will certainly not be so obliging as to prove a mere series of desperate and unsuccessful efforts. These things will then make an impression on Christians, and refute our cheaply repetitious (and theologically false) propaganda to the effect that anywhere where the Church and the clergy are not in control and do not supply the principles of action, there can be nothing but disintegration and decay.

(c) The Church of the *diaspora*, if it is to remain alive at all, will be a Church of active members, a Church of the laity:

a laity conscious of itself as bearing the Church in itself, as constituting her, and not being simply an object for her, i.e., the clergy, to look after. Wherever this new kind of Church exists or comes to be, the laity will have to be given this possibility in fact, and not only on paper; the laity will have ecclesiastical duties which they, as a matter of course, carry out, and rights, as they did in the early Church; they will not be simply people to whom such-and-such orders are given in such-and-such a case, and who are expected to count it an honour to be allowed to do something for the hierarchical Church, meaning the clergy. *Sociologically* speaking, the Church of the *diaspora* has the character of a sect, in contrast to that of a Church of the vast mass of people, a Church *in possession,* and hence, sociologically, confronting the individual not as something constituted and sustained by himself but as independent of him and over against him; the *diaspora* Church has the advantages that her "sect" character gives her, and the duty constantly to overcome the dangers inherent in it. The Church of the *diaspora* rests permanently on the goodwill of her ordinary members. The Church of the *diaspora* will be the Church of an age in which other institutions, state and cultural, will be exercising functions in the fields of education, research, creative culture etc. which were formerly exercised by the Church; for the *diaspora* Church will be, to a large extent, quite unable to exercise such functions any longer, since these functions address themselves to the *whole* population, and for this reason, and others too, cannot devolve upon what is only a *part* of civil society. It follows that the Church of the *diaspora* will be more immediately religious in aspect. This is not because this Church of the future will not have her principles, applicable to every cultural field, which she will seek to realize through the Christians working in these fields; it is because as a sect (sociologically speaking) she cannot directly set the tone in the realm of culture in the way that she could when the vast mass of people belonged to her. Hence, in what she directly does she will of her own accord concentrate on what is her own most vital sphere, even if no-one confines her by force to the church and sacristy or drives her into the catacombs.

(d) The clergy will no longer belong automatically to the upper, privileged levels of society. To be a member of the clergy will not, in the long run, continue to be, to the extent and in the sense that it has been hitherto, a "status" in the sociological sense. It remains a status in the Church, but it will not always be, to the extent that it has been, a status in secular society.

(e) In general, we shall not have so much of *the* Church and *the* State confronting each other, whether in conflict or concordat. For this relationship of the past was based upon the fact that everyone (or nearly everyone) was simultaneously both a citizen and a member of the Church. In the future, contacts between Church and State will tend to take place within the individual and his conscience. For the State is no longer so much the Government or a monarch, but rather the, precisely *non*-Christian (for the most part) population (no matter what the constitution may be: the patriarchal State is in any case a thing of the past). And this population is, for the most part, uninterested in the particular Christian interests of one part of it; nor is the Church any longer an organization whose direct political power could be of any great significance.

It would be possible to enumerate many more things of a similar sort which can be seen to follow, given a little psychology and sociology, from the fact of a religious communion living, growing and preserving itself in an indifferent or hostile environment; a Church of the *diaspora,* now and for the foreseeable future. It seems to me that much depends on our fully and freely recognizing this fact and courageously accepting its consequences. Such an outcome is not so much a matter of course as might be supposed. We have still not fully wakened from our dream of a homogeneous Christian West. It often leads us to react furiously and in a false context when something happens to shake us out of the dream; we often seek, again in a false context and with inappropriate means, to realize this dream-ideal, and so apply ourselves to the wrong point altogether. I had better refrain from giving examples. For it would inevitably be possible to discuss each of them *in utramque partem,* since any particular effort aimed at a *limited* objective, and intended as a *partial* realization of a homogeneous Christian West, could well be *both,* as such, misconceived *and* nevertheless, in the circumstances, correctly regarded as justified and necessary on other grounds. I can only ask you to think over what I have said (supposing it to be new to you, which I expect it is not) and then, as occasion arises, to test by it the manifestations of Catholic life which you encounter; must they be, ought they to be, what they are, if we are to regard the *diaspora* situation not only as a sheer disaster (calling for one legitimate response and one only, that of grim resistance) but also as a preordained "must" (not "ought"!) in the history of salvation?

If we now go on to ask what follows from this situation, we are going beyond the theme as originally set, since it referred to the situation, not to its consequences. But since the rest of this conference has been concerned with other problems, we have sufficient grounds for thus overstepping the bounds of our theme. So:

(*a*) We must first stress once more that our *diaspora* situation is not just a fact but a "must" in the history of salvation. This means that we cannot simply approve of it as something justified in advance. Our relationship to it is not that of the ancient Jewish people to the Gentiles, who were from the start, i.e., by the will of God in advance of any guilt, left out of the Covenant. We cannot cease to be missionary; we have to want the number of Christians to increase, to want their influence, their importance, the concrete realization of a Christian spirit in public affairs and social institutions to grow; we have to try to diminish the contrary of these things. But despite all this, our growing *diaspora* situation is something to be expected, something foretold, something we can count on and which need not cause us any inner conflict or missionary defeatism. It is foolishness, not high principle, to suppose that because something was brought about by guilt in the first place, its effects must necessarily be removable; to think that there is a permanent and universal duty to aim deliberately and directly at eliminating something by, so to speak, fanatically intolerant frontal attack, merely because its coming into existence involved guilt. This is wrong in the sphere of individual life, and equally wrong in the wider sphere of history. Though we must keep our missionary fervour, there is nevertheless a right sense in which we must adjust ourselves to the *diaspora* situation and come to terms with it. Not only interiorly, with faith and serene trust in God's direction of all things, and reverence for his will, positive and permissive, by which good is brought out of evil. It has to be in our outward behaviour as well. The objection might be made that if as Christians we are supposed to remain missionary, and even on the offensive, what is all this about coming to terms with the *diaspora* situation as a "must" in the history of salvation? Isn't this demanding coexistence and covalidity for principles of Christian behaviour in public life which are in fact incompatible? No, the principle of coming to terms with the fact of the *diaspora* does not contradict the duty to maintain a positive missionary spirit, and it does have a practical bearing on outward behaviour. It makes us realize that there can be points over which we do *not* need to take the offensive, where we can let things take their course and come to terms with them, precisely so as to work away with all our available and limited resources, interior and exterior, at other points where it makes sense to do so, and thus not waste our energies in the wrong place. Throughout her history the Church has constantly come to terms with unavoidable situations, once they were established, without thereby betraying God or herself. But how many times she has tried to go on too long fighting the inevitable, and so wasted her energies in the wrong place when they were wanted elsewhere! The theoretical realization that the *diaspora* situation is a "must" in the history of salvation should be a help in guarding against this danger.

What, after all, does a person do if he sees the *diaspora* situation coming and thinks of it as something which simply and absolutely must not be? He makes himself a closed circle, an artificial situation inside which it looks as if the inward and outward *diaspora* isn't one; he makes a ghetto. This, I think, is the *theological* starting-point for an approach to the ghetto idea. The old Jewish ghetto was the natural expression of an idea, such that orthodox Judaism was ultimately bound to produce it from within itself; the idea, namely, of being the one and only Chosen People, wholly autonomous, as of right, in every respect, including secular matters, and of all other nations as not only not belonging in practice to this earthly, social community of the elect and saved, but as not in any sense called to it, not an object towards which there is a missionary duty. But a Christian cannot regard his Church as autonomous in secular, cultural and social matters; his Church is not a theocracy in worldly affairs; nor can he look upon non-Christians as not called; nor can he with inopportune or inordinate means aim to get rid of the "must" with which the history of salvation presents him, namely, that there are now non-Christians in amongst the Christians or real Christians in amongst the non-Christians. His life has to be open towards the non-Christians. If he incapsulates himself in a ghetto, whether in order to defend himself or to leave the world to the judgement of wrath as the fate which it deserves, or with the feeling that it has nothing of any value or importance to offer him anyway, he is falling back into the Old Testament. But this is our temptation, this ghetto idea. For a certain type of deeply convinced, rather tense, militant Catholic at a fairly low (petty-bourgeois) cultural level, the idea of entrenching oneself in a ghetto is rather alluring; it is even religiously alluring: it looks like seeking only the Kingdom of God. Here we are, all together, and we can behave as though there were nothing in the world but Christians. The ghetto policy consists in thinking of the Church not only as the autonomous community of salvation (which she is) but as an autonomous society in every field. So a Christian has to consider Linden-Weber a greater poet than Goethe, and have no opinion of any magazine except *Feuerreiter* (I imply of course no criticism of this magazine nor of those who promote it); any statesman who makes his Easter duties is a great statesman, any other is automatically a bit suspect; Christian-Democratic parties are always right, Socialists always wrong, and what a pity we haven't got a Catholic party. The insistence, for the sake of the ghetto, on integrating everything into an ecclesiastical framework naturally means that the clergy have to be in control of everything. This results in anti-clerical feeling, which is not always an effect of malice and hatred for God. The interior structure of the ghetto conforms, inevitably, to the style of that period which it is, in make-believe, preserving; its human types are those sociological, intellectual and cultural types which belong to that period and feel comfortable in the ghetto; in our case, the petty-bourgeois in contrast to the worker of today or the man of tomorrow's atomic age. It is no wonder, then, if people outside identify Christianity with the ghetto, and have no desire to get inside it; it is the sheer grace of God if anyone ever manages to recognize the Church as the house of God, all cluttered up as she is with pseudo-Gothic décor and other kinds of reactionary petty-bourgeois stuff. We may be preserved from this danger, which has become a reality only too often during the last few centuries, by a clear-sighted and courageous recognition of the fact that the *diaspora* situation is a "must" in the history of salvation, with which it is right to come to terms in many aspects of our practical conduct.

(*b*) If I now try, as I must, to give a few practical applications of this principle, by way of illustration, these are simply in the nature of samples, and the samples are not in themselves of great importance. If, for instance, we, in our mid-European German-speaking world, clamour for a Catholic university, complete with all faculties, on the lines of the Italian universities, then we are asking, *rebus sic stantibus,* for a ghetto-university, and refusing to realize that we do and must live in a *diaspora.* If, again, we cry out for the Government to make laws to check the decline in moral standards, we are forgetting that we live in a *diaspora* and that all that this will do, in the long run, is to generate anticlerical feeling in people who don't want to be burdened with enforced regulations laid on them by us. (I hope I do not need to stress that there are, of course, laws in this respect that are justified; but they have to be well motivated, well proportioned and introduced with tact and intelligence.) Again, we shall simply have to accept, in many respects, the feelings that people have about life, of a cultural or uncultural nature. If people who like to go and roar in chorus at football matches on Sunday (I don't happen to be one of them) are considered by us to be pretty well lost souls already, then our pastoral attitude is at least as distorted as their mentality is, perhaps, infantile and superficial. If people today regard the evening as the time for cultural activities, then we must have evening masses; and attempts to convince them of the superior excellence of getting up early in the morning had better be left unmade. If people of today are, in moral matters, influenced by their environment, because they lived in the *diaspora* and must live in it and, without thereby putting themselves in the wrong, *want* to live in it, then the Christian education and formation of their moral conscience—which is, inevitably, somewhat coarsened by their environment—has to start from some point where there is still an understanding tending towards a higher level, not at points where any such understanding is—unfortunately—simply not available, nor merely with the Church's formal authority in moral matters.

If our presentation of Christian principles is to be effective, then what applies to the winning of an individual must also apply to our public presentation of ideas amongst the masses; we must begin with things for which we can expect some understanding, and go on slowly step by step. A man's ability genuinely and existentially to grasp particular values (which is a necessary condition for *subjectively* grave sin) is very largely the product of his environment. We cannot countenance any departure from the objective moral norm. But our proclamation of Christian principles ought not to ignore the fact that there are not only in individual cases *causae excusantes a peccato formali* but, among Catholics living in the *diaspora*, general sociological causes; a hardness of heart which is socially conditioned and generally present. Have we asked ourselves searchingly enough what follows from this?—not, indeed, as regards moral norms, but as regards our practical pastoral attitude to people who were or are Christians according to their baptismal certificates but perhaps, because of the *diaspora* situation, have never been so in practice, interiorly, even if they do, for social reasons, pay their tax to the Church and send their children for religious instruction. What, for instance, am I to do with a Catholic whose second "marriage" (invalid because of the divorce of one party) has been of moral benefit to him, because he does not see this second marriage as immoral, on account of his socially, culturally, historically conditioned hardness of heart (cf. the Old Testament situation), and its consequences for him, morally as well as in other ways, have been entirely happy? We are not going to assume, *a priori*, that in questions of this sort all further thought on more practically useful methods of applying general principles is bound to be entirely superfluous. If we live in the *diaspora,* then—just another example—it is as important to teach young people how to read non-Christian books, periodicals and magazines, which they are going to read anyway, as to instruct them to take the Catholic papers. If we live in the *diaspora,* we cannot allow ourselves to produce, educationally, and to hail as the best, the type of layman who has the mentality of a *bien-pensant* of the year something-or-other. If we live in the *diaspora,* then the office-job type of pastor will have to die out. For the only service available from the bureaucrat mentality, which does still exist, is one that has no real care for the public: a service of an institution, not of people. Have we the courage to break away from bureaucracy, office hours, routine, impersonal, non-functional organizational clutter and clerical machinery—and just do pastoral work? If a man can find in us another man, a real Christian, with a heart, someone who cares about him and is really delivering the message of God's mercy towards us sinners, then more is happening than if we can hear the impressive and unmistakable hum of bureaucratic machinery. Let us get away from the tyranny of statistics. For the next hundred years they are always going to be against us, if we ever let them speak out of turn. *One* real conversion in a great city is something more splendid than the spectacle of a whole remote village going to the sacraments. The one is an essentially religious event, a thing of grace; the other is to a large extent a sociological phenomenon, even though it may be a means of God's grace.

When today all of us, clergy and laity together, in our different ways, do our pastoral work in the *diaspora,* we find ourselves, *mutatis mutandis,* facing the same problem as in the foreign missions. We may, in *our* mission, be guilty of the same sorry fault as is represented there by Europeanism. When we are trying to convert people to Christ, we want to convert them to the cultural style which we have inherited; which is perhaps something that belongs to us, but not to them. Think of the appearance of the inside of many religious houses; of the level of many of the product of "folk" religion; of the unctuous tones of our religious talk; the narrowness of our bourgeois horizons; our censorious attitude to a thousand and one things in everyday life (hair-styles and lipstick, for a start)—and you will understand what I mean by this equivalent in the home mission to Europeanism in the foreign missions. We cannot afford this kind of thing in the *diaspora* situation.

If we are living in the *diaspora,* when we say or write anything on Church matters we must do so in the recollection that non-Christians can hear and read as well as ourselves. It is not all right to write, as did one prominent Catholic newspaper, just *one day* after the announcement that the Pope intended to define a new dogma, that the whole Catholic world had rejoiced at the news; it is not all right to say (as the same paper did) that the Pope was throwing open access to God's grace and mercy when he granted an indulgence to travellers by sea; it is not all right to put up notices on church doors in a Holy Year saying that to gain the latest indulgence the minimum requirement is to be in a state of grace, as though it were not particularly requisite in other circumstances.

If we live in the *diaspora,* it is not all right for the Catholic Press, out of pure devotion, to give the impression that there is no public opinion in the Church or ought to be none; that every criticism of anything the Hierarchy does, however correctly expressed, is necessarily uncatholic; that it is, *a priori,* quite impossible that the Hierarchy's actions should arise from human motives, mistaken information or a failure to recognize the needs of the day. It *is* uncatholic to be always assuming, on a basis of general anti-Hierarchy feeling, that such things are so (and this does happen); but it is, equally, theologically false to assume that such things simply cannot be so. Something that A. Koch once wrote applies here: the time is past when it was possible to hope that real wrongs could be systematically hushed up and concealed, because suppressed truths turn poisonous and, living in the *diaspora,* we cannot afford to have a loyal opposition inside the Church perverted into a crypto-heretical underground movement.

(c) When we say that we have the right to make a cool, dispassionate reckoning with the fact that the Church is a *diaspora,* we mean, understanding it rightly, the very opposite of resignation and defeatism. If we once have the courage to give up our defence of the old facades which have nothing or very little behind them; if we cease to maintain, in public, the pretence of a universal Christendom; if we stop straining every nerve to get *everybody* baptized, to get *everybody* married in church and onto our registers (even when success means only, at bottom, a victory for tradition, custom and ancestry, not for true faith and interior conviction); if, by letting all this go, we visibly relieve Christianity of the burdensome impression that it accepts responsibility for everything that goes on under this Christian top-dressing, the impression that Christianity is *nutura sua* a sort of Everyman's Religious Varnish, a folk-religion (at the same level as that of folk-costumes)—*then* we can be free for real missionary adventure and apostolic self-confidence. Then we should not need to sigh and say, "We *still* have 15 per cent"; we could say, "We're up to 17 per cent already". Just where is it written that *we* must have the whole 100 per cent? God must have all. We hope that he takes pity on all and will have all indeed. But we cannot say that he is doing so only if we, meaning the Church, have everybody. Why should we not today alter to our use, quite humbly and dispassionately, a saying of St. Augustine's: Many whom God has, the Church does not have; and many whom the Church has, God does not have? Why, in our defeatism, which springs from a muddled feeling of pity for mankind, do we forget that it is not the truth but a heresy that there is no grace outside the Church? If we would only rid ourselves of these prejudices, grafted into us by the external Christianity of the West, we should not then feel inclined to engage in combat only if we immediately won a 100 per cent victory; we should then be justifiably proud and thankful if we won just *one* new Christian, instead of burying our ostrich-heads in the shifting sands of those who are Christians already. In short, if we demanded less of ourselves, but that less the right thing, i.e., not universal Christianity, when the *diaspora* is an inescapable "must", but a battle for new individuals, then, though immediate statistics would not look any better, the real state of our mission, in respect of its chances for the future, would surely be improved. Then we should realize in practice, not only in theory, that even in the *diaspora* the initiative can really be ours. We feel on the defensive if we get the idea (which is unfair to ourselves) that it is the Church's fault, because of her failures here and now (never mind what may be true of the Church in the past), that there are so few Christians about. We are taking the offensive if we tranquilly accept the fact of the fewness of Christians, as a fact, and set about winning new ones. We cannot simply say in despair that we are losing more than we are gaining. It all depends on what we are losing and what we are gaining. One soul apostolically won from a milieu which has already reverted to paganism is worth more than three hung on to from the remnants of traditional Christianity (one would almost like to say, folk-costume Christianity), only to be, themselves or their children, lost after all; because, not having passed through the crisis of this age in its acuteness, they are not immunized against its spirit and so will not, perhaps, stand fast in the long run. What matters in these little local offensives is not so much the statistical, demonstrable successes they may show. The courage for an approach of this kind, and just one or two new Christians to show for it, already amount to a lot, sometimes to everything. Beginnings may be disappointingly meagre; but they may amount to a victory now with unforeseeable consequences. St. Benedict did not know that he was fathering a new Western civilization when he went out with a few monks to refound monasticism on Monte Cassino.

An apostolate on the offensive, not exhausting itself in desperate efforts to save what is beyond salvage (the Church considered *as identical* with everybody in a given area), need have no fear of being fruitless in the long run. The apparent atrophy of the religious sense today is a passing phenomenon; in the period of vast upheaval in which we live, of which the past century of industralism is only the beginning, it was, *in concreto,* absolutely unavoidable and to be expected. Anti-clericalism, whether tacit, automatic and non-violent or—as it sometimes is, even today, partly through our own fault—actively provoked, will collapse, by and large, when it becomes clear everywhere that the Church desires only faith in God and love for him, and these only as the unforced decision of the human heart, not to be induced by any other means. Man's religious sense is ineradicable, nor can it, in the long run, be appeased by pseudo-objects provided by secular utopianism, economic, social or cultural. Even at the level of this world, Christianity's chances are greater than ever. And if this be doubted—I mean, the possibility of discerning such chances—well, it is precisely for the Christian to hope against all hope, knowing that God triumphs when we seem to be lost.

Of course, for all this we need faith in eternal life; a faith so strong that it is ready to purchase eternal life by the witness of earthly death. We are often lacking in this uncompromising faith. We have nothing, of course, against the possibility that after a tolerably pleasant life in this world there may be another, guaranteed better still. But the idea of directing one's life here according to this faith, in such fashion that anyone who does not share it is bound to think one mad—that's not for us. So we try by every means and with dubious zeal to demonstrate that Christianity is also the best and most reliable recipe for a happy life in this world, forgetting that the only way in which this can be so is precisely by not caring whether it is so or not. Even this hypertrophied care for the things of this world arises from the ghetto-mentality, the refusal to admit that we are living in the *diaspora*: we want to find some aspect of Christianity which will make it presentable anywhere. And the consequence of this is that there are Catholics who are Catholics by culture, by politics, by civic morals, but are not and do not want to be Catholics by faith. But in the *diaspora* situation, only he can endure to the end who truly believes in eternal life and in the promises of God.

Marie Dominique Chenu
1895-

Work is the common lot of most human beings, so common that it is difficult to think of the human condition without naturally including the fact that man is a worker. Traditionally, work is looked upon as the condemnation that befell all mankind when Adam and Eve were driven from the Garden of Eden. Some generations have dressed work up a bit by speaking of its moral virtues and its dignity, as well as of its role in accomplishing man's perfection and salvation.

Yet, in a century that has been shaped by the industrial revolutions of the past one hundred and fifty years, it is strange that no one has ever developed an adequate Christian theology of work which would be capable of guiding contemporary man.

Marie-Dominique Chenu, a French Dominican theologian, addresses this absence of such a theology in his challenging book, The Theology Of Work *(1963). Father Chenu, born in Soisy-sur-Seine, France, in 1895, is well known in his home country through his years of teaching at the University of Sorbonne and for his contribution to the study of medieval philosophy and theology. His writings include, besides the work mentioned above,* An Introduction to the Study of Saint Thomas Aquinas *(1950) and* The Theology of the Twelfth Century *(1957).*

Beginning with the observation that the role of human work is too often misunderstood, Chenu calls to Christian theologians to turn their energies toward a thorough study of the nature of work within the context of the twentieth century and to develop a sound theology of work.

In the selection below, Chenu draws attention to some of the effects of the nineteenth century's industrial revolutions, such as the creation of the proletariat, the estrangement of man and nature, the subtle process by which the machine became man's master, and the unspoken law of modern labor which does not permit the worker to be seen for who he is, or for what he thinks and feels. Chenu is convinced that the change from craft-tool to machine deeply modified the way of life of all humanity. One of his startling claims is that the working classes provide the nucleus of positive atheism, for once man was estranged from his work, he lost both God and himself.

The medieval, and particularly Thomistic, vision of Chenu is in evidence as he proposes the direction that a theology of work should take. He argues that the medieval understanding of the matter-spirit relationship can make a significant contribution to contemporary theological efforts. Chenu's insights and questions will provoke the reader to take a serious look at the phenomenon of the modern worker and to begin wondering about the nature of this human being who spends an entire lifetime at work.

THE THEOLOGY OF WORK

We shall always have workers and masters." This conservative-minded social cliché betrays a complete misconception of the rôle of work in human evolution. It was a sentiment which was fairly current in Christian thinking round about 1910, and was even enounced, somewhat ingenuously perhaps, by a highly-placed cleric of the period. The practice of zealous fraternal charity, as advocated by contemporary ecclesiastics and teachers, did little to render the platitude more acceptable or diminish its harmfulness. On the contrary, such charity tended to produce a glow of false self-righteousness in the giver which only went to camouflage its deleterious effects.

The repudiation of the class struggle which resulted, immediately revealed the ambiguity of such an attitude. On the one hand, brotherly love, as taught by the Gospel, forbids hatred, as the clash of two egotisms and the negation of human liberty. On the other hand, observation of facts, and the demands of a justice based on Gospel love, impose a true equilibrium between labour and capital, in contrast to the hypocrisy of the philanthropist and the humanitarianism of the liberal. This antagonism will not be resolved by the exercise of moral virtues to restrain envy on the one side and greed for profit on the other. A complete change in the economic structure is necessary, for this is not a question of the quarrel between rich and poor, but of the whole nature and constitution of our social and economic organisation.

The pious moralism which, in reality, devitalises the Gospel precepts and infringes the Christian condemnation of riches, still colours the thinking of many Christians; but at any rate it no longer has the sanction unwittingly provided by a short-sighted theology. Today we are far from having achieved a "theology of work," to use a recently-coined phrase; but thoughtful Christians are endeavouring to look beyond abstract morality to the study of work as a subject in its own right, of its economic functions and its historic rôle. It is no longer necessary to adorn the idea of work with a veneer of virtues which, however praiseworthy in themselves, are alien and irrelevant. In the long run, this can only confirm their inapplicability—a mistake from a theological point of view. We must understand the nature of work and its human and material origins, in order to appreciate its internal laws and its spiritual needs from a Christian standpoint. If the "civilisation of work" demands its own ethic, which up to the present no one has yet evolved, Christians can only collaborate in this evolution by considering and understanding, in the first place, what work means for the people of the twentieth century.

It is strange, and indeed depressing, to realize that Christianity, since Vittoria and Suarrez in the sixteenth century—if not since the classical Middle Ages in Western theology—possessed a theology of war. We also have a theology of commerce, even if only in the persistent condemnation (it can hardly be called an effective condemnation) of usury, which, we are told, should have stifled capitalism at birth. As well as these we have a theology of history, or rather several theologies, some of doubtful validity, such as the providentialist theology of Bossuet—but not theology of work. (By theology I do not mean an intellectual esoteric science, but an organic and rational study in the light of faith of the human values which enter, directly or indirectly, into a system of salvation.) The expression itself may be said to be quite recent; for although the phrase "morality of work" has been current since the nineteenth century, and "mystique of work" for some twenty years, the term "theology of work" appeared for the first time only five or six years ago. This is a significant point. It confirms what we have already observed, that up to the present, Christian teachers did not consider these human realities except as amorphous matter, capable of being explained only in a moral sense and sanctified under the heading of "duties of one's state of life." They commented, naturally, on the passages in Genesis dealing with the punitive aspect of work; but they gave no direct attention to its objective content. They made no attempt to discern its economic and human potentialities, or to consider its possible relationship with the divine ordering of the world.

However this absence of a theology should not trouble us overmuch, when we consider that we also lack a psychology, a sociology and a philosophy of work. Today all these are in full and simultaneous development, including the theological aspect. If they have been slow in beginning, the reason is the same in every case. Before psychology, sociology, philosophy or religion can receive the necessary impetus to advance beyond the stage of empiricism, there must be an effective awakening of consciousness. The history of nineteenth century thought records, after the technical, economical and social upheavals of the age, the first stir of this awakening which begets not only revolutions, but philosophies. Today this awareness has come of age, competent if not to solve our problems at any rate to define them. It proceeds from methodical analysis to higher theory and so, in the sense referred to above, to theology.

It is indeed true that man has always laboured and toiled in the sweat of his brow. But just as he gave no thought to analysing or defining the laws of love—although he had always experienced its emotions—until an awakening of consciousness roused his retrospective observation, so he only began to evolve a science of work when a collective awakening of consciousness enabled him and his fellow-men to observe its laws, its purposes and its historical mission. This awakening, then, was brought about during the last century when the radical transformation in the character of work confronted man, physically and spiritually, with a new reality, the conditions and structure of which profoundly effect not alone his standard of living but his whole way of life. This was a dual and unique transformation which revolutionised the relations between man and nature. The changeover from craft tool to machine not only opened up a new chapter in economic history but inaugurated a new era for mankind. The first human consequence of mechanical efficiency in this age, was unfortunately, the ill-omened creation of a proletariat. The proletariat has thus been the setting for this awakening, not only of a revolutionary but almost of a scientific awareness.

The circumstances of the birth of the proletariat are well known. Since we are engaged at the moment in studying the repercussions on Christian theology, we may note here a small but significant indication even in the terms used by theologians. Whereas Leo XIII, in his Encyclical *Rerum Novarum* (1891), speaks of "the condition of workers (opifices)," which forms the title of the document itself, Pius XI, forty years later gives as a subject-heading in his Encyclical *Quadragesimo anno*: "On the liberation of the proletariat (proletarii)." As with psychology or sociology, it was on the basis of the existence of the proletariat as a social consequence of the machine age that Christian thinkers began to evolve a theology of work. "Contrary to the divine purpose, work in these conditions tends to become degrading; inanimate matter is turned out of the factory ennobled, while the man who works on it becomes degraded." This apostolic admonition of Pius XI, re-echoing the warnings of sociologists and the revolt of the revolutionaries, contains the germ of that constructive thought which finally transcends empiricism, even the empiricism of charity to the poor.

It is thus not merely a question of broadening the scope of classic morality, or drawing from "eternal verities" marginal applications to suit the situation of the moment. We must revalue this new human terrain of work, which has become, in the machine age, a reality lacking anything in common with its previous character over thousands of years, its function and purposes as much changed as its structure. The tragic gulf between mechanisation and humanity cannot be bridged by the usual conventional phrases on the dignity of manual labour having been restored by Christianity, on the value of work as an educative discipline, or even, at the doctrinal level, on its ascetic function in a world where suffering, sin and liberation are linked together. The traditional images of potter, blacksmith and peasant with which the Bible furnished the old theologians, are not only inadequate but often encouraged a resentment against the machine and led to debatable praise of craft-working, small-scale proprietorship, the patriarchal family and the peasantry, which is both bad theology and vain romanticism. The protest of man against the idea of labour as a commodity which generates the proletariat, a protest which the Christian endorses from his own standpoint, must be reflected in a reconsideration in the domain of theology and morals. The postulates and the data for a "civilisation of work" are also, in the light of the Gospel, the postulates and the data for a "theology of work."

1. The change-over from craft tool to machine causes, over and beyond an increase in quantity, a qualitative transformation of work. Thus it ends by modifying the way of life not only of individuals but of humanity as a whole. We must therefore work out not only the extension of moral laws governing human occupations, but also define the new significance of such work in this unforeseen encounter of man and nature. For if we are to have any hope of overcoming the disasters caused by the present tyranny of the machine, or more accurately of passing from an external and necessarily forced adaptation to a real assimilation, it will be by the achievement of a rational and moral conquest of nature.

This is, in fact, the earthly destiny of man and its essential characteristic. "Let us put him in command of the fishes in the sea, and all that flies through the air, and the cattle, and the whole earth, and all the creeping things that move on earth. So God made man in his own image, made him in the image of God." (*Genesis* 1:26-27). Man is *homo sapiens*, but he can only be so, in his collective capacity at all events, by becoming *homo artifex*, which is his first definition. Man, said Mounier paradoxically, is naturally artificial.

> If man is made to become a god, naturally or supernaturally, we cannot accept that wisdom for him should consist in a prudent and monotonous conformity to a "Nature" defined once and for all . . . Man so placed is essentially *artifex*, creator of forms, maker of artifacts . . . The disciples of nature were right to remind us that the human condition is not capable of extension in every direction, and that time is necessary for man to assimilate his own transformations. But the systematic discredit which they cast on everything artificial springs from a radically false view of the nature of man. We might say, with hardly any distortion of words, that "the nature of man is artifice.

Man fulfils himself by dominating, through his discoveries, reason, strength and virtue, that Nature which is his kingdom, and out of which he creates a new world, a human world. God has appointed him lord of creation.

Man has now arrived at an important stage in this enterprise and it should also be a major stage in his self-fulfilment. The worst setbacks and the most blameworthy misdeeds cannot halt this destiny. Each victory over space and time—the two dimensions of work—reveals, even though obscured by foolish pride, its greatness and truth.

This "humanism" of work does not dismay the theologian, and the rationalisation which it involves for this technical conquest of the universe does not lessen the sense of mystery which we sometimes seem to reserve only for those realities which we have not ourselves created and to which we submit with fear. The terrible gods of the religion of Lucretius are false gods. We yield too easily to the opposition between rational and sacred, and so revert to the beliefs of our childhood. Some say that work is a profane and impious attempt to exploit nature. No; reason, the constructive reason of the technician, as well as the reason which governs our thought and contemplation, exists in ourselves. It is a unique force in the duality of its functions, the highest and most certain mark of God—more than a mark, a reflection. Its autonomy, in epistemological method, in interior liberty as in practical action, is the main point of this image, even where it runs the greatest risk of arrogantly repudiating its divine parentage. A glorious risk, which reason must meet and conquer in order to be itself. "Rationalisation," the rationalisation of time, which is the first characteristic of machine civilisation, is only the technical condition of the discovery and conquest of the "reasons" which are in things and in the universe, in which we recognise our own reason, the measure of all things, by the participation of God. The world is full of ideas, said the Ancients. Work which gives ideas birth, is a major act of adult men and should not be considered, either by right-or left-wing thinkers, as opposed to contemplation. The Christian man of wisdom—contrary to the aristocratic Greek sage or the Cartesian philosopher—finds unity in the combination of these two functions.

Marie Dominique Chenu

The civilisation of work will provide plenty of matter for the methods and mysteries of theology.

Long before the technocrats of our time, Descartes and Newton deprived the world of its divinities by making it inanimate. But theirs was an embryonic world. Without realising it (and I certainly do not forgive their ignorance), the technocrats lead us to Nature, that Nature which, as far back as the thirteenth century when techniques were first discovered in Europe, was called by the rationalist and anti-clerical Jean de Meung the "vicar of God." When we denounce the machine, we must, avoiding naive optimism, define its limits and warn against its dangers. We must also however be on our guard against biassed obscurantism. We must discover in the resources of nature the elements of the human condition. By transforming work the machine has inaugurated a new age of man in the universe.

2. Having dealt with the postulates and data for a theology of work, we must now consider its ends. They too are renewed by its changed techniques, since motives, which until recently were mainly subconscious, are implicit in its new structure, and show themselves today precisely by this awakening consciousness which has suddenly impelled them beyond their original goals. The purpose of work today is not only to enable us to earn our living. It also creates a kind of social energy, at the immediate service of humanity as a whole. The worker, in his poverty, with all his exacting demands, has a confused realisation of this admirable efficacy, as has the managing director, in his loyalty to an impersonal organisation. Production today cannot and should not be for the sole and primary motive of providing daily bread on the one side and a grossly disproportionate capitalist profit on the other. Production should extend beyond this to the human ends of individual and collective welfare in an economic system of services and needs. The "dogmas" of liberal industrialism have become bankrupt. Work is indeed a means of liberation, but in quite a different meaning.

Here the theologians have a wonderful field. For too long they have confined themselves merely to advocating moderation in profits. The sternest criticism of capitalism never went beyond these limits. Now theology can advance further than this purely moral aspect, and base itself, in a human and Christian economy, on the physical density of work as part of the fabric of the world, and, religiously speaking, of divine government. We have no hesitation in expecting the revelation of a new moral value from this new process of thought.

3. This leads us on, beyond the individual, to the evolution of society. Work is a humanising factor by becoming the pivot of a "socialisation" thanks to which humanity marks a definite stage in its collective advance.

After rationalisation, the second evil for which the machine is blamed is concentration—material, economic, financial, demographic—with all its harmful concomitants. Nothing is to be gained by further condemnation here. We must however once again seek to discover the causes and not wrongly attribute responsibility. Modern methods of production, it is true, necessitate an unprecedented physical and psychological concentration of means and forms, not only in large complexes but even in smaller organisations, which one might expect to be less demanding. Yet this overwhelming pressure generates of itself a collective consciousness which is the expression of a highly valuable communal solidarity.

Basic unit and mass assembly alike produce a phenomenon of interiorisation which, in spite of deep diversities and growing risks, slowly and painfully develops a feeling of taking part in a common effort—if it can be called common!—and of belonging to a team working for the same purpose towards the common welfare. Through this participation, even though it be compulsory, emerges a freedom born of love for a common good in which each feels himself an active member. This is the law of "community" as analysed by the sociologists. We can compare it, to some extent, with what spiritual writers of all ages, from St. Paul to St. Thérèse of the Child Jesus, observed in their subjective experience of the law by which obedience brings freedom through submission itself. Objective presentation of individuals—instead of anonymous confrontation—constitutes a spiritual presence, a feeling of brotherhood, thus creating a social atmosphere previously unrealised.

Here cold reality gives the lie to this idyllic dream. There is no worse war than that between the "communities" which, in the world of work, the classes have become. But even here we must not leave out of consideration the *nature* of things because of the evil in man. The Christian, at all events, who knows that man was driven from an earthly paradise by sin, should not be surprised. He only concludes that work, like everything else, including love, must be redeemed. This is the Christian economy of redemption. Work, according to Genesis, is the first to be affected. The *nature* of things remains, however, and with it, this social principle which releases innate spiritual forces in situations where men are joined together in common undertakings by a solidarity which long retained its primitive aggressiveness. By re-integrating man in his work, socialisation becomes a liberating force. The violent and bitter awakening of consciousness among the proletariat, has been the first effect of this law. We must not lose hope that one day, in peace and fraternity, it will come to fruition. This will necessitate, of course, the creation of these "communities" which alone can be the spiritual bond of such an interiorisation, and consequently of this enhancement of personality and freedom. It will demand the most far-reaching structural reforms. At least we know that a depersonalising collectivism is only the human perversion, in a disastrous interlude, of an operation which, when concluded, will manifest, on a plane which today is privileged, the social nature of man. Once again work reveals the significance of this nature. On this basis an authentic theology can establish the "spirituality" of work.

4. Finally, since this social progress of man, spiritual as well as economic, determines the laws of his history, we see work becoming, in man's consciousness, one of the factors of this history, through the interaction of free will and the determinism of matter. Time is effectively the field and measure of its transformations, its efficacy, its purposes. Just as in the evolution of the cosmos man is physically perfected, so in the evolution of society, man is completed socially. Here work plays a primordial rôle. The impassible gulf between matter and spirit does not destroy this historical unity, in which the Creator has made man his agent. Man is precisely the being who, indissolubly and consubstantially matter and spirit, is fitted thereby to carry into history the mystery of the spirit. Angels have no history. An old mediaeval theologian said that God, desiring to extend his love

to all, in a creative expansion, could only do so through and in an original being who, untied to matter, would carry love's destiny even into matter. This divine expansion is not only realised in carnal love, it is present wherever a community expresses itself on a basis of material work. Solidarity of work is a privileged field at a time when this solidarity effectively shapes humanity and thereby the motive force of history, since material time is the vehicle of this continuous creation. The sacred history of the Incarnation everywhere transcends this earthly history. It does not eliminate it. On the contrary, it will consummate, in a new heaven and a new earth, all temporary work as well as all unsatisfied love.

Here theology takes up one of its favourite theses. We have spoken on several occasions of "divine government." This was a current phrase—to be sternly purged of its anthropomorphism—used by the Christian teachers in the Middle Ages. Their theological works include a discussion of man's place in the universe. They observe the substantial connections of his human nature with material nature, with a view to revealing his role as *artifex*, to calculating the significance of matter not only in his body but in the fabric of the universe with which he is entrusted, and whose mechanisms he discovers in these "mutations" and "motions" which from the celestial bodies reverberate from circle to circle even into the secrets of the mind and freedom of man. These great mediaeval religious teachers go so far as to study the biological laws of nutrition and generation, since matter, as they say, "Is necessary to the truth of human nature." It is on this subject, together with the treatise on divine government, that the first part of the *Summa* of St. Thomas (*Utrum aliquid de alimento convertatur in veritatem humanae naturae*) concludes. Why have modern theologians, acquiescing in the Lutheran distinction between nature and grace, almost entirely given up this view of the world as a *natural* frame and spiritual sphere of action for man in his work? The historical perspective which we must add to it today, far from diminishing its value, increases it, just as a third dimension transfigures, without deforming, the surface of space.

Today the contemporary situation urges Christians to rediscover, in this new dimension, the forgotten vision of their forefathers, which was in fact the biblical view of nature. What is the contemporary situation—the situation which we analysed at the beginning of this study? The revolution in the character of work, enforced by the pressure of new discoveries and techniques, has released an awakening consciousness, doubtless painful, but basically founded on the inherent truths of man and of matter. The proletariat was the battleground of this awakening of consciousness. As it happened, the change-over from craft tool to machine, in transforming the nature of work, has justified this evolution. By revealing four factors—rationalisation, profit economy, concentration and the march of history—together with the new laws governing work, it has shown us the area of their temporary defeat. These factors have created a proletariat whose revolutionary awareness conceals (and might betray) a scientific realisation of the functions of work in the twentieth century. It is in this consciousness that the theology of work, like its psychology, sociology or metaphysics, can be evolved.

It is no accident, nor is it due only to the cumulation of individual defections, that the working classes provide the nucleus of positive atheism, which is so different from the middle-class atheism of free-thinkers and philosophers. This is a much deeper and more significant atheism. The reason is that man, as he grew estranged in his work, lost God in losing himself. Work no longer had any human significance and so could not have a religious one. To restore its integrity instead of invoking external moral remedies (and political remedies which are the most dubious) is, theologically speaking, to re-establish work in its cosmic and human functions, and in the design of God the Creator. It is, of course, wrong to deify work; but those who fall into this idolatry, thereby both destroying their souls and denying God, are only trying to satisfy their need to worship. This desire finds mistaken outlets because theologians failed to consider work as a subject worthy of attention in the sphere of human destiny.

A re-awakened theology will soon find inspiration and subjects for study, such as the following:

Man and the Universe. Work is at their meeting-point, and also at the conjunction of spirit and matter. Man is master of the universe: the divine purpose, the vocation of man, is revealed in Genesis. Let us see this not as an initial and pre-historic episode, in which God is purely transcendent and static, and Nature is prefabricated and unchanging, but in the cosmic unfolding of the divine plan. Let us see man as collaborator in creation and participant in his evolution by his discovering, exploiting and spiritualising Nature. This dominion over nature (work) is a divine participation, even with its possible dangers. *Homo faber* is rightfully placed in Christian, if not in "classic" humanism. The machine is the instrument of this creative enterprise.

The Nature of Man. Man is a composite of spirit and matter, body and soul are not merely in juxtaposition, nor united by an extraneous force. They are consubstantial, one through and in the other. The manifestation of the immortal soul does not lessen the unity of the *convivere*. So, too, we have a consubstantiality of (spiritual) free-will and (material, technical and economic) determinism. Work is a "human" creation by the conjunction of developing techniques and an awareness of free-will. Productive reason, in spite of differences in methods and functions, is none other, fundamentally, than contemplative reason.

The whole economy of salvation. The cosmos enters into this economy through man as a transforming force. There will be a new heaven and a new earth. Eschatological destiny will be fulfilled, in spite of the severance of death, and does not nullify man's terrestrial destiny. This, however, is enough to restrain any erroneous or naive optimism.

And finally, the *Incarnation.* God is made man; all that is human is material for grace. If work takes on human consistency, then (but only then), it becomes part of, enters into the economy of grace. This entry is twofold, first as the work of man, and secondly as the origin of a community which is itself a matter for grace. The continuing incarnation; the Mystical Body of Christ; such will be the future classic theme of a spirituality in which the world of work will find its level and its place in Christianity, and not by the acquisition of merits alone.

This spirituality is not a new phenomenon. We find it in Genesis, in St. Thomas, in St. Paul, in the first dogmas. But it speaks with a new voice, and with a fresh human approach. For too long, Christians were not conscious of these latent powers. Their spirituality—like their apostolate—retreated into the "inner life." St. Augustine, a leading example of this inner life in the West, was nevertheless deeply aware of the measure of the universe and of man, seen in space and time. In any case, the Christian heritage includes a cosmic spirituality, of which work is one of the bases. The "civilisation of work," as the twentieth century has already been called, the technical era, in his service, are fitting subjects for the grace of Christ. Today we have reached a point when the lowly and humble, by virtue of their status as workers, are clearly seen to have access to the kingdom of God.

Theology faces new concepts

We have seen how the change-over from craft tool to machine caused a revolution. This revolution, gathered force with each successive discovery in science and technique, from the steam engine to the splitting of the atom. It was based on the autonomy of motive power and had a more far-reaching effect on men's lives than any of the merely political revolutions. It permeated the very content and purpose of men's daily work. While man himself did not, of course, change his nature, his condition was changed. *Homo artifex* was affected as an individual and in his collective behaviour by this very change in the nature of work itself, a change which was extraneous to the metaphysical essence of man, but went so deep that our perception has not kept pace with its effects and we tend to under-estimate rather than over-estimate them. In a way that would formerly have been unthinkable, man now no longer lives a "natural" life, but a life which is directed and rationalised in a régime which he himself created and invented. And this work only dehumanises in the same way as it could humanise if carried out according to its own laws. How can any theologian, let alone the "moralist," not be affected by this?

Let us pass over the psychological changes, which have frequently been analysed—determinism, repetition, working to time, standardisation, fatigue, etc.—to define this radical transformation. In this encounter between man and nature work is not primarily a discipline, a perfecting of man in his work. It is first of all the making of a product. Now it is precisely by creating a product, by accommodating himself to it, by accepting the laws which govern its manufacture, that the worker achieves his completion as man. This "objectivity" which we might momentarily call dehumanising or materialist may surprise us, and does indeed disconcert a certain school of spiritual thinkers. In fact it is because—thanks to mechanisation—industrial work has demonstrated the full force of this fundamental law that it has aroused apprehension and misgivings among religious people, as well as less significant protests from the literary and philosophic aristocracy. We have here, however, as has been correctly pointed out, a perfect application to modern conditions of the theological studies carried out by the thirteenth century scholars. The worker labours for the work's sake and not for his own. This is a law of metaphysical disinterestedness governing work in action. In the continual interaction of the perfecting of the work and the perfecting of the worker, the former dominates the latter. The worker is subject to his work. The necessities of production enforce in him a degree of selflessness and objectivity which is measured not by the intention of the morality of the worker, but in his product. If in judging an actual undertaking, a piece of work or construction, we take into premature consideration the subjective purpose of the worker—his creed or his political views, his intentions or his claims—we are breaking this law, and consequently perverting an economy by a kind of irrelevance. Any theological, spiritual, or ideological theory which wholly or partly deprives work, objects, or the world of their content and their intrinsic laws, is fallacious from the beginning, since it is not based on the inherent substance of work and matter. Certain moralists who are prone to accord more importance to meritorious intentions than to the nature of things, have unwittingly succumbed to this fallacy. Such ignorance of reality, including social realities, is unforgivable today, when the whole character of work, through its technical and human evolution, stands revealed. We have doubtless had a moral philosophy of work. For some years past we have even had a mystique of work; but we have never had a theology.

Is not this a materialism which a Christian must find unacceptable? The time has now come for us to break away from certain conceptions of man and of the union of matter and spirit in man. Without going into the fundmentals of the problem, for which this is not the place, let us merely say that we must now come to a conclusion, in the latitude accorded to theologians and philosophers within Christian doctrine, as to the exact nature of man, his body and soul, matter and spirit. From the standpoint of the disciple of St. Augustine, of Descartes or of a Platonic idealist (favouring in greater or lesser degree a certain duality of the composite man whose soul is uneasily lodged in a cumbersome body), this autonomy of the worker in the perfection of his work, *perfectio operis*, is unacceptable. It is an alienation of man in his product. The theologian who, however, believes on the contrary with St. Thomas Aquinas in the substantial union of body and soul, in the ontological and psychological unity of man in the hierarchical diversity of his functions, does not consider that the superiority of mind over matter necessarily implies its independence of matter. In the first (Platonic) view the spiritual perfection of the worker would be definitely achieved apart from the perfection of the work, the latter being merely amorphous matter whose inner laws would only be a "means" towards a transcendent end. It would then make little difference what one does—the only reality is the love of God, which has nothing in common with the realities of earth. But this is not so. Work, and the "civilisation of work" has its own value, for its own integrity, for its original efficacy, for the shaping of the world, for the historic destinies of humanity. It is not, of course, an end in itself in which man finds his final achievement, as in a Marxist dictatorship of the proletariat. Work is a purpose in its rightful place, a secondary purpose. It is not a means of perfection, nor a mere collection of utilities, advantages and prosperities which pious intentions will endow with morality. The true and only victory over Marxism will lie in the correct realisation of this property of work, at the junction of mind and matter, in the civilisation of man and in the quality of that civilisation and so, eventually, in the individual and collective incarnation of the grace of Christ.

We would even go so far as to state, as Maritain does, that this new awareness of man in his work—an awareness resulting from the internal revolution in the structure of work—is a historical benefit for human society as well as the basis for a new understanding of Christianity. The spiritual aspect, naturally, remains predominant, but in a situation in which man's earthly welfare resulting from this civilisation of work—and indeed from political organisation in general—is no longer, as it was in mediaeval clericalized Christendom, a purely instrumental function. It is a scale of values which has attained maturity, with its inherent virtue and its specific efficacy. The consubstantiality of matter and spirit in man leads us to the consubstantiality of man and nature, without prejudice to the specific difference between man and nature.

We have now reached a period in history when it is no longer a question of social progress alone, of structural reforms, or even of a political revolution, but, in the light of this progress and through these reforms, of establishing a *philosophy* of man which will incorporate, explicitly and organically, the truth and value of work in the sum total of human activity. "The idea of a civilisation of work is as much philosophical as political. To use a term which is already current, we must consider the *humanism of work,* in the full meaning of the phrase. This raises the problem not only of a future educational programme which will transcend the classic and modern humanities, but will make a more profound study of the science and capacities of human work for the benefit of man in general. And here it is urgently necessary for Christian thinkers to establish a "theology of work" as defined at the beginning of this book, and of which we can now appreciate the scope and extent.

Again we could adopt another view of the human composite, a view which lays more stress on the fragility of spirit in matter, while at the same time retaining the irreducible interiority of the spirit. The uncontested master of this conception, or this spirituality, in the West, is still St. Augustine, both on account of his experiences and of his teaching. His name is enough to guarantee its orthodoxy, in spite of the eventful history of his philosophy. St. Bernard, à Kempis, Pascal, even Descartes—what a fruitful harvest, in what a variety of ages, countries, climates, experiences and philosophies! The great tradition of French moralists, clerical and lay, has handed it down so that now we find these teachings even in the cheapest manuals, catechisms and books of piety. These disciples of Augustine, Descartes and others not only denounce the risks incurred in such a confrontation of matter and the universe—and the deplorable effects of the industrialisation of this century give them ample grounds—but they even contest the principle of the substantial union of soul and body in this kind of ontological mixture which constitutes human personality, and in which work finds its justification, its truth, its historic rôle and consequently its Christian origin.

We will abstain from questioning not alone the orthodoxy, but even the Christian character of this theology. If we uncompromisingly described "man" as seen by St. Thomas Aquinas, it is because we abhor the eclecticism which sometimes leads well-meaning Christians to lose their keenness of intellect and efficacy of action. Having said this, and without any lessening of our loyalty, we welcome a fraternal discussion with the disciples of St. Augustine, confident that by understanding them we will arrive at a better understanding of ourselves. A balanced ideology must be achieved in full possession of the relevant factors and alternatives, it must be fortified against the inevitable attrition of truth, which is made worse by the exhilaration of new discoveries.

Having said this, we must admit that we have little admiration for an intelligence which is founded on a refusal of the risks which are incurred in the confrontation of objects, those very objects which are revealed to it by man and the universe. Fear is always a bad counsellor. In these circumstances, this philosophy is defeated by the violence of history. The Christian, even though he be a theologian, is consequently imprisoned in the limited confines of conservative casuistry. The determinism of these timid minds is confirmed by facts. The "spiritualism" of the nineteenth century (which no longer bore any traces of St. Augustine's teachings!), under the pretext of saving the dignity of the mind and its pure interiority, ended up in the most insipid bourgeois liberalism, which was an aristocratic perversion of liberty, a hypocrisy of interiority and a death-blow to fraternity. Historians can understand the contemptuous reaction of Marx. We must beware of this decaying theology. It was these theories which, unfortunately, prevailed over the true Augustinian philosophy in the thinking of the Christians of that time, and which are indeed still prevalent amongst some Christians today.

So it would seem, in spite of appearances to the contrary, that the spiritual solution with its austere rejection of materialism, is too facile. Such a solution too easily ignores several aspects of the problem. The Thomist position, on the other hand, implies greater difficulties, since the free exercise of mind in matter in no way lessens the inviolable and supreme destiny of the spirit, or its power of interiority, or its subtle freedom in the trammels of determinism. St. Thomas himself, in his own day and in situations which were not without parallel in ours, braved these difficulties. Without necessarily adopting his theology, we of the twentieth century can nevertheless appreciate its greatness of spirit.

Albert Dondeyne
1901-

   The twentieth century philosophy known as Existentialism has had a mixed reception in Catholic philosophical and theological circles. Perhaps the most common attitude toward it was to consider it as a passing fad which would be popular for a short time and then disappear, while the centuries old structure of Thomism would continue on unshaken and true. At times the inadequacy and the limitations of existential thought were pointed out; at times it was even shown to be downright false. Such reactions demonstrated a certain close-mindedness and suggest a poor understanding both of existential thought and of the Thomistic structure underlying the Catholic tradition for the last seven centuries.

   Happily voices have come up from Europe with a much healthier approach to the existential movement, voices of men steeped in the Thomistic tradition and aware that the basic spirit of Thomas Aquinas calls for open dialogue anchored in sincerity and fidelity. One of the most balanced of these men is Canon Albert Dondeyne, a native of Belgium (born in Lo, Belgium in 1901) and a professor of philosophy at the University of Louvain, Belgium since 1936. His brilliant teaching career as well as his excellent writings have served to provide generations of university students with the intellectual flexibility, curiosity and maturity that are essential to live out the Christian mystery in modern society. He is considered as one of Europe's outstanding intellectuals.

Dondeyne has dedicated his life to bringing about true communication between the tradition of Thomism and contemporary thought. He sees the two as compatible and mutually enriching. The Christian intellectual, he says, must be open to all the problems of the modern world, must live in continual contact with the world, must be able to see the unbeliever's point of view, must root out any tendency to be dogmatic, must pursue dialogue and be willing to learn.

The reader will find Canon Dondeyne's Faith and the World *an exciting and challenging book. Dondeyne asks whether the Christian believer exercises on today's world an influence that is sufficiently effective and whether the Christian's presence in the world has the necessary openness to produce a fruitful dialogue. These questions will quickly become the reader's as he moves through Dondeyne's reflections on the problems of faith, today's world as a turning point, truth and freedom, faith and politics, and the relevancy of Christianity to the twentieth century.*

In the extract presented below, Canon Dondeyne discusses the social problem of modern man. He perceives modern man's aspiration for a more equitable distribution of cultural goods, and for a greater and truer freedom for all, both individuals and nations, as perhaps the greatest social event of all times. Thus, the real social problem is the great longing that has risen in the hearts of millions of human beings and has transformed them into the greatest power ever known in history. Christianity, far from remaining distant to what is happening, must fully participate in shaping modern society.

FAITH AND THE WORLD

The term "social" can have more or less extensive senses. Take, for example, the expressions "social psychology," "social psychiatry," "the social nature of man"; and on the other hand, "the social problem," "social politics," and "social encyclicals." In the first three examples the term "social" points in general to man's life in community; in the three others it points to a particular and recent phenomenon in the life of the human community, namely, the striving of modern society for a more equitable distribution of cultural goods, for a greater and truer freedom for all, both individuals and nations. This social aspiration, which pervades the modern world, is one of the great events of our time and perhaps the greatest social event of all times. It will be our task in the following analysis to examine the nature of this phenomenon and lay bare its inner structure.

We are dealing here with a social event, a cultural-historical fact. This statement suffices to note that the term "problem" does not have a purely theoretical meaning here. In other words, we are not dealing with something that resembles a problem of chemistry or philosophy. What we call here a problem is rather a great longing, a gigantic purpose that has risen in the hearts of millions of human beings, workers and intellectuals, and has united them to form the greatest power history has ever known.

1. The Origin of the Social Struggle

As everybody knows, the social evolution or revolution that is at work in our present world has its source in the socio-economic evils of the last century. Some may be inclined to remark: Why go back and scrutinize the past? Why recall and rehash the evil conditions and the abuses that belonged to the liberal period, when many no longer even know that those evils existed?

It is indeed a dangerous temptation for man to allow himself to become obsessed with the past, especially when the past has been very harsh and can generate great bitterness. But this danger is not very great if those who revert to the past, have not personally suffered from its evils. Looking back to the past is even a necessity for them if they wish to understand the feelings affecting some of their contemporaries.

If at this time there are still many intellectuals who take little interest in the social problem, is not one of the reasons precisely the lack of knowledge of the past? They do not know the crying misery and want of the proletariat that prevailed during the last century, and most of them have merely read or heard vague general statements about it. They forget that many of today's laborers have been trained for the struggle by their parents and older comrades and that they still carry all these memories deep in their hearts.

Another and more compelling reason for the study of the past is this: we want to penetrate into the heart of the social problem. Now this problem is not a theoretical question but an historical fact, and a far-reaching cultural phenomenon. Like all historical events, it has a definite origin and its content cannot be separated from this origin.

The Concept of Origin

It would be useful to begin our inquiry by examining the term "origin," which plays such an important role in historical writing. A couple of observations, however, will have to suffice. The idea of "origin" contains not only the idea of the "past," but also that of "cause."

That a fact belongs to the past is not sufficient to make it the origin of what followed after it. History is not a mere succession of independent events that have no other connection than that of sequence in time. In other words, in historical writings "origin" has also a causal meaning. However, the causal bonds connecting historical events that are studied by the science of history are of a totally different order from those that belong to physics and chemistry. For man is not a lifeless thing of nature, and human conduct does not present the fixed, invariable regularity of physical events. Hydrogen molecules behaved a hundred thousand years ago just as they do now. Not so man, for man is alive, feels and thinks; he is able to appreciate values and defend them; he can either accept or reject conditions of life. In a word, he can make a project of the future, that is, as it were, "cast it before him," and gradually build what he has projected. For, as we have shown above, man is an 'historical' being, a being that makes history.

For this reason, the term "origin" has a very special sense in history. Here "origin" means the point of departure, the ground from which mankind at a certain moment leaps forward to something new. This point of departure and foundation for what is to follow later, consists mostly of three elements which are not simply juxtaposed and independent from one another but have influence on one another. They are the following.

1. There is a definite condition or, to use modern philosophical terminology, there is a *situation*, a whole of material, cultural, economic, and social conditions of existence, in which the men of a particular time live without having chosen them.

2. There is a growing consciousness of values, connected with this situation, that awakens new aspirations in man and prompts him to pursue a new line of action in order to change the existing situation and create better conditions of life.

3. There are social theories and even world views, whose aim it is to analyze and justify this growing awareness of new values, to throw light on the new aim, to devise means for its attainment, and give directives for action.

Those three elements are present at the origin of all cultural changes and of all great historical events. Let us take the French Revolution as an example. There were evil conditions in the Old Regime; the values of freedom and equality were discovered; and there were the new social theories of Jean-Jacques Rousseau and others. Taken separately, none of these three factors can sufficiently explain the French Revolution and its enormous influence on history. The three constitute one whole, and only this whole can be called the origin of the French Revolution. However, the core and the center of gravity of this whole is the growing consciousness of values. Although the conditions of the Old Regime are now a thing of the distant past and the social theory of Jean-Jacques Rousseau now appears antiquated, we cannot fail to see that the values brought to light at that time are still alive and continue to inspire our present society.

What we have said about the French Revolution applies with equal force to the social revolution that is taking place in our world. Here also we find the same three elements—namely, the social evils of the liberal period and the widespread poverty of underdeveloped countries; numerous social theories and world views; the discovery and growing awareness of new values. We will have to pay special attention here to these new values.

This digression in regard to the idea of "origin" has not been a waste of time. To our mind, it is of great importance if we wish to arrive at a correct understanding of both the origin and the object of the social problem. Origin and object are in reality inseparable. He who has a one-sided view of the origin, will also form an incorrect and one-sided picture of the object, and his attitude toward social developments will be influenced accordingly. The truth of this assertion manifests itself constantly. For instance, there are many for whom the origin of the labor struggle is to be reduced to the social evils of the last century. Since these evils have largely disappeared, these people think that the social revolution has come to an end.

Others reduce the whole social development to Marx and Marxist dialectics. What has happened and will continue to happen since Marx, they say, is and cannot be anything else than the inevitable unfolding of Marx' ideas about society and history. The film drawn by Marx, is now being unrolled. Therefore, if mankind wants to make further progress, it must put on the straitjacket of Marx's conceptual structure with its Hegelian background.

All this shows the importance of reflecting on the origin of social events.

The Emancipation of the Laboring Class

In 1886 a Belgian industrialist made the following declaration before the Belgian Labor Commission: "Industrial science consists in getting the maximum work out of a human being while paying him the lowest possible wages." This man gave expression to what was then the common concept and custom. In the socio-economic organization of industry in the second half of the nineteenth century, the laborer was reduced to a purely economic value. He was a production factor alongside the machine and a burden on the budget. In England and the U. S. A. the terms "sweating-system" and "sweat-shop" eloquently expressed this new regime of slavery.

A report of the Belgian Royal Academy of Medicine dating from the same period gives us a bleak picture of the conditions of that time: "The average working day for the industrial laborer is between thirteen and fifteen hours; here and there it is seventeen hours. The same situation exists in England, France and Belgium. Children are employed from the age of six or seven. In 1843, one third of the laborers in the Belgian weaving mills were children, and fifty per cent of these were between the ages of six and a half and ten."

The French economist Jean-Baptiste Say, who traveled to England in 1815 to study the conditions of factory workers wrote that a laborer earned only one third of what he absolutely needed to support his family even when he worked at the maximum of his physical capacity.

Today we ask ourselves how such a thing was possible. Why did the workers tolerate such inhuman conditions? Why did they not go on a strike? But the right to strike and even that to form a union did not yet exist. When the first strike took place in Lyons, police fired on the strikers and their leaders were condemned to prison.

We should not forget that, if in many countries the standard of living of the laborer has considerably improved during the last years, this has not taken place without much blood, humiliations and persecutions. Want, misery and the struggle for life, have united the workers and given them class consciousness. When Karl Marx presented his Manifesto to the world with its fiery final formula, "Workers of the world unite," his battle cry fell upon fertile soil. The social struggle arose from man's most elementary instinct: his inborn desire of self-preservation, of freedom, of a life that is worthy of man.

The Emancipation of the Underdeveloped Nations

It is still the same "struggle for life" which today spontaneously drives together the poor peoples of Asia, Africa and Latin America, and gradually unites them into a collective power. What is now taking place in the so-called "underdeveloped" continents, is a continuation on a world-wide scale of what began in Europe a century ago. It is the entrance into history of what has sometimes been called the "fourth estate," although it would be more exact to speak of the great anonymous class of the poor and the socially oppressed, who, as a famous author wrote, "plant rice to feed those who have not planted."

In fact, individual and collective *poverty and want* have not yet disappeared from our increasingly wealthier world. The theme of the misery that is predominant in underdeveloped countries has even become the favorite topic of modern economic and political literature. Father P. Lebret, the leader of the association *"Economie et Humanisme"* recently undertook a comprehensive study of that subject under the eloquent title, *Suicide or Survival of the West.*

In 1953 the Belgian statesman R. Scheyven made a report to the General Assembly of the United Nations in which he said: "59½% of the world's population is still underfed; the average life-span in India is 27 years, against 68 in Sweden; in some countries 80% are still illiterate; the average income of an Indonesian is $25 a year, in contrast to the $1,800 per capita of the American citizen. What makes the situation so hopeless and so tragic is the fact that the world's population increases by 80,000 per day, or by thirty million persons per year, and that this increase occurs mostly in the parts of the world that are plagued by poverty."

But there is more than poverty; there is also *economic slavery*, and this is even more important. For, as Hegel so realistically described it in his famous dialectics of "the master and the slave," poverty as such does not act as a revolutionary force in history, but rather the poverty that is experienced as slavery, that is, when the slave whose labor supports production and creates riches receives almost no share in this wealth. Economic slavery can easily exist with political autonomy. The nineteenth century workers in liberal Europe, by law, enjoyed the same rights and freedom as other citizens, but that freedom was more theoretical than real. It is precisely because of that tension between the ideal of liberty, equality and fraternity proposed by the law, on the one hand, and actual conditions of economic inequality and slavery, on the other, that the social revolution was born.

The same situation exists today on a world-wide level. There is no more dangerous an illusion for the Western World than to imagine that everything this side of the Iron Curtain constitutes a "free" world since the process of decolonization continues and the emancipated peoples are, one after the other, becoming members of the United Nations. Economic slavery is just as dangerous for world peace as political domination, and the yoke of this slavery still lies heavily on most of the underdeveloped countries, not because they are poor and do not own anything, but because foreign powers control and exploit their natural resources for their own advantage.

It is not so much the inequality between the poor and the rich that lies at the source of the numberless social tensions and conflicts that have afflicted the world for more than a century, but rather the inner contradiction of a situation of political freedom coupled with economic dependence.

The situation could be expressed also in this way. Since the rise of vast industrial enterprises man has become conscious of the decisive significance of the *economy* for the liberation of mankind. As Marx correctly judged, philosophy can spin the most beautiful considerations about liberating man, but it is the economy that brings about this liberation on a large scale. The important point is to lend a hand in driving economic slavery out of the world and to make the *economy* serve *all mankind.* In this way a new idea has entered the world, the idea or rather the ideal, of what is usually called *economic and social democracy,* in contrast with purely political democracy. As in every democracy, it is basically a question of an *ethical ideal,* that is, a question of bringing more truth and justice, more equality, more freedom and fraternity among men; but, in contrast with nineteenth century democracy, the accent is now placed upon the socio-economic reorganization of social life. Let us consider this social ideal more closely.

2. The Social Ideal

From the preceding pages it is evident that the social problem is more than a question of wages, and that the social struggle aims at something more than mere material improvements for the working class and the underdeveloped and retarded countries.

Yet such a "materialistic" interpretation of present day issues is still very common, even among those who are not unfavorable to social progress and like to be counted among the adherents of a spiritual philosophy of life. They readily admit that evil conditions have formerly existed. But, they add immediately, there is no need to continue to recall the past; the worker's lot has greatly improved during the last years; the economy cannot work miracles; it is high time to go in reverse; and, as was done in the good old times, we should not try to run ahead of possibilities. In other words, economic factors must be given again priority over social concerns. For otherwise the whole of society, both employers and employees, will end in ruin.

Social progress is undoubtedly conditioned by the economy and in that sense the economy has priority over the social. Even the most progressive social leaders, including Karl Marx, do not deny that. Perhaps nowhere in the world is the priority of economic production so brutally affirmed as in the countries that are dominated by Marxism. Unfortunately, it must be added that even many laborers give rise to the impression that their movement has a higher ideal than their antagonists ascribe to it. They often forget that the nearer they come to the attainment of their ideal, the heavier their own responsibility becomes, that the more rights they acquire, the greater and the more sacred their obligations will be.

It is equally true that it is very dangerous to entertain utopias in the realm of economic and social life, and we must unfortunately add once more that some workers and popular demagogues now and then give evidence of being extremely naive in their economic ideas. They seem to believe that a country's wealth is inexhaustible and that prosperity for all would come about at once if the so-called "huge" gains of the capitalists and managers of factories were taken away from them and distributed among the people. However great and exaggerated those gains sometimes may be, they represent but a small portion of the total economic earnings in comparison with the sums that are paid to the mass of workers in the form of wages and social security.

It goes without saying that the economy constitutes the basic condition for social progress, but a condition is but a prerequisite and not an ultimate goal. In other words, the social struggle is not merely a struggle for higher and more just wages, and the social problem is not a mere "problem of justice," in the ancient sense of the term. The medieval lord was also obliged to observe law and justice in regard to his subjects. The aim of today's social struggle is not so much to obtain higher wages within the frame of an existing socio-economic system, but to cause the renewal and reorganization of this system itself and, in general, of interhuman relationships. Mankind, at the present, is perhaps going through the most profound revolution of all times; a new socio-economic order is being born, civilization enters into a new phrase.

A New Phase of Civilization

The mighty development of the positive sciences and the huge progress of industrial technology are no doubt the most characteristic and influential factors of present-day Western civilization. They make the West stand out greatly in contrast with the Middle Ages and with the East of today. The soaring flight of science and technology are the reason why, in popular language, "Western" and "modern" have become synonymous. When it is said that China, India or Africa are on the way to modernization, this means in the first place that they are taking over the scientific and industrial progress of the West together with the limitless possibilities of production therein contained. It is almost impossible to calculate the influence of technological progress on the material, cultural, social, national and international appearance of the world. Only in the light of this fundamental fact, can we understand our time and fully realize the significance of the contemporary social development.

The development of industry inevitably brings with it a parallel rise of the intellectual and cultural level of the common man. It could not be otherwise. A great capacity of production presupposes an equal capacity of consumption of the produced goods, otherwise it could not be maintained. For example, there would be no use for a well-organized press if the mass of the people were unable to read. Technological progress goes hand in hand with the development of man's awareness, the more so because technology makes distance meaningless and fosters the unification of the world. The whole world, as it were, belongs to him, and he cannot see why there should exist privileged classes or peoples in the world.

For this reason the working class has become aware, on the one hand, of the enormous possibilities technology offers for the material and cultural betterment of the masses, and on the other hand, of the important role the worker plays in modern society and the power he wields. The steelworker or teamster knows very well that when his union calls a strike, the whole economic life of the union is paralyzed.

This, then, is the greatest event of our time: because industrial development has opened up almost limitless possibilities, because also the working class has become aware of its role and place in society, there has arisen for the first time in history the idea that it is possible for the masses to share in the achievements of modern culture. The concept of a strictly limited class of privileged owners and, on the other hand, the great masses of non-owners no longer belongs to our time. This concept will gradually have to yield before the ideal of greater equality in regard to opportunities of life, a more equitable distribution of property and the participation of all in the fruits of civilization. This ideal is no longer considered utopian, but it is thought of as a possibility, a goal that can be attained, a program for the future. The idea of "common good," of social welfare thus acquires a new content and structure. It is evident that a realization of this new "common good" necessitates a greater participation of all in the administration and control of economic, social and political life, as well as a greater mutual solidarity and cooperation of all peoples. All this we find re-expressed in today's slogans: freedom, equality, emancipation, and democracy.

Albert Dondeyne

A Renewed Democratic Ideal

It is quite possible, of course, that the above-mentioned slogans are sometimes improperly used. Nevertheless, they indicate the heart beat of our own time. This is not the heart beat of an anemic, exhausted world, as is sometimes maintained, but rather the heart beat of a humanity that has become aware of the opportunities and possibilities offered to men through the high development of technology.

Freedom and Democracy! Of course, the issue is not the philosophical or psychological question of free will, whether man has genuine freedom of choice. Neither is it a question of purely political democracy or equality before the law. What is at stake is the whole of material, economic and social conditions of life that are necessary for the free unfolding of man's powers, for the liberation of his mind and his whole personality. A few examples will serve to explain this more fully.

When we are ill, we are less free, we are handicapped in the full exercise of many of our activities. If we are wealthy we can obtain relief by means of an expensive operation or take a long rest, all this with the hope of regaining our freedom. In many countries those means are not at the disposal of the ordinary worker. When sickness enters his home, it is a catastrophe for himself and his family, a sort of enslavement from which he is unable to free himself. In view of the progress of medicine, such a situation of inequality in regard to the most elementary of all values, health, is no longer tolerable. Another example. How often does it not happen that a promising boy, the first in his class, is the child of a worker. His companion, less clever and less proficient, is the son of a physician. Nevertheless, in many countries the son of the worker has to go to the factory at sixteen, while the other, though less gifted, can continue his studies through college and perhaps the university. The first does not have the opportunity to make his talents bear fruit, but the other does.

It is this excessive inequality in *actual freedom* that the modern world has in mind when it advocates liberty, equality and democracy. Unlike the time of the French Revolution, the question is not now so much one of equality before the law or

301

of fundamental liberties, for these are guaranteed by all modern constitutions. But it is rather a matter of greater social equality, more social freedom. Since all this is to a great extent conditioned by the economy, it implies a more effective participation of the whole community in economic, social and political life. In short, it is a matter of *economic and social democracy*. But what, one may ask, is the difference between political and socio-economic democracy?

Political democracy refers to the political regime that was born of the French Revolution and is characterized by the equality of the citizens before the law and the great individual freedoms which have been written down in every modern constitution, such as freedom of the person in regard to the judiciary power (no one can be punished except in virtue of law), freedom in regard to property and dwelling, freedom of worship, opinion and the press, of education and political assembly.

Socio-economic democracy, on the other hand, refers to a socio-economic regime which guarantees more *actual freedom and equality of opportunities of life,* and this, of course, is not possible without a more equitable distribution of wealth and a more effective voice of the whole community in the control of the economy.

It would be wrong and dangerous to consider these two forms of democracy as opposite terms. Yet this is done implicitly when it is said, as actually happens in some circles, that the socio-economic democracy should be honored as the *true* democracy, whereas the other is a *purely formal* one. The opposition of "true" to "formal" can give the impression that political democracy is a lie, that it does not contain any truly liberating value. This is most certainly incorrect. It will always be necessary to have political freedoms in order to prevent the socio-economic democracy from becoming a political dictatorship, as is certainly the case of most of the "popular" democracies behind the Iron Curtain. Both forms of democracy should be considered to be essential and complementary elements of integral democracy, that is, of the democracy that is fully worthy of man.

Taking all that into consideration, we can now draw this conclusion: the social problem is more than a question of wages; it is a struggle of individuals and peoples for a life that is more worthy of man. What is happening in our present society is a cultural development, a slow birth of a new phase of civilization; it is the gradual formation of a new socio-economic order, which will be characterized by the primacy of labor in its manifold forms, by a more balanced distribution and a more social owner-ship and administration of the goods of this world, by a greater equality for all in regard to the development of personality, by truer solidarity among peoples and an increasing economic unification of the world. In short, the present social struggle wants to bring more truth and justice to men at a moment when the world is becoming one as a result of technical progress. In this sense the social struggle is, in its deepest essence, a struggle for an *ethical ideal,* in which the *whole of mankind,* employees and employers, individuals and governments, poor and rich continents, are all involved, over and above any philosophical and religious differences that might separate them.

The first and most important task of our time, is to enlist, around this ethical ideal, the great masses of men of good will. On its success or failure will depend whether the social question will be solved in a human or in an inhuman way. Of course, great difficulties will be encountered, especially if one is dissatisfied with vague purposes and determined to use effective means for the attainment of the goal. Great differences of opinions will always arise when it is a question of choosing and organizing the particular socio-economic system that will best serve the social ideal. But this is not so bad, provided the aim itself is not sacrificed and the divergences do not lead to fanaticism. One and the same goal can be served in many ways and the cooperation of men of good will can assume many forms. Let us consider this question now.

3. Co-ordination of the Social Forces

There are divergences that are in principle unbridgeable. Communism and Christianity, for instance, will continue to consider each other as irreconcilable powers as long as Communism continues to consider its atheistic view of life to be inseparable from its socio-economic ideas. But not all divergencies are of this kind. It happens only too often that a cooperation which in principle would be possible and fruitful, is made difficult because of a confusion of ideas. Some think in too "monolithic" a fashion and neglect the multi-dimensional character of social reality. Everything we have said above about the structure of the world of human truths and of human values can be applied here also.

One of the dangers that threatens every form of human cooperation, is the dogmatizing one-sidedness that attempts to reduce the complexity and mobility of life to a rigid theoretical structure of concepts or an ideology. We must, therefore, examine the importance of social theories in the social struggle.

Social Ideologies and Social Study

It is certainly not our intention to deny the importance of theoretical study and reflection, for the sole liberating activity is one built on truth. However, a distinction must be made between diligent study, the perpetual search for truth and insight, and grandiose theoretical constructions, so-called ideologies. Study and reflection are never complete, for they are life and movement. Ideologies, on the other hand, always resemble a finished product; they usually present themselves as aprioristic constructions and closed systems to which nothing more ought to be added. Study searches for a solution; an ideology claims that it is a solution. When ideologies are not carefully handled, they often result in dogmatism, misunderstanding and intolerance. They become the aim of the struggle and at the same time, its principal weapon.

If this happens, the question that should guide every purposeful social action: "What, in particular concrete circumstances, is the best plan, from the standpoint of short range and long range, to promote the people's welfare?" is then replaced by this: "How can we secure the quickest victory for our theory about the organization of enterprises, the planning of production, etc.?" Much misunderstanding would be removed and a great step in the direction of a better relationship would be made if we simply asked ourselves what exactly we want to attain, instead of making comparisons between ideologies. It may, therefore, be useful to pause for a moment and consider the significance of theory in regard to social developments.

Two things must be kept in mind here. First, it would be erroneous to reduce present-day social developments to the two factors of theory and practice. There is a third factor, that of a growing awareness of value and concern for value. We have already called attention to this factor. What lies at the origin of the French Revolution and the democratic movement which it caused throughout the world, is not so much the theory of Jean-Jacques Rousseau concerning man and society, but rather the discovery of political equality and freedom as indispensable means for the emancipation of man. The same is true of modern social developments. There are innumerable social theories. All say worthwhile things but none have said the last word. More important than these theories themselves are the values which they desire to foster. The theories are less values in themselves than attempts to throw light on man's growing value-consciousness, attempts to analyze these values and seek their foundations, to guide man in his leap toward new goals and devise means for their attainment. A theory can change; it may be based even on false metaphysical grounds; yet the value with which it is concerned may continue to operate and attract man.

Secondly, within any theory a distinction must be made between its economic, social and political content and its metaphysical infrastructure or superstructure. The fact that this distinction is often forgotten undoubtedly makes it very difficult, even for men of good will, to enter into a fruitful dialogue.

Although, as we have seen, man's world of truth is one, yet it is not undivided. Thus it is not necessary to first solve the ultimate metaphysical questions regarding the mystery of human existence, e.g., that there is a God and that the soul is immortal, before one is able to distinguish a precious work of art from a worthless canvas, an economy that leads to prosperity from another that will end in disaster, a social and political regime that is not worthy of man from one that safeguards freedom, peace and justice.

Even an unbeliever can realize that freedom of worship belongs to the most elementary rights of man and that a true democracy must not only respect this freedom but should positively make it possible. In short, it is possible to foster spiritual, personalistic politics while adhering to a non-spiritual metaphysics in the realm of philosophy.

Personalism and spiritualism are terms that have a twofold meaning. A first meaning is related to the level of *the immediate experience of existence and description of existence*. We experience in ourselves a manifold spiritual life that constitutes our being-men, for "not of bread alone does man live." All values, both spiritual and material, are thus also experienced as being of and for man, as means that are in the service of the human person, for the human person is an end-in-itself. All this can be recognized as well by the unbeliever as by the believer. But another question may come up: What happens to man after death? Is man immortal or not? This is a metaphysical question which is not solved by means of a mere description of the experience of existence. He who replies in the affirmative gives a higher and richer content to the terms "spirit," and "person"; we are then dealing with a "spiritualism" in the *metaphysical and religious* sense of the word.

It seems to be characteristic of the old European continent to approach economic, social and political questions from the highest metaphysical viewpoint, whereas the Anglo-Saxon countries prefer to consider experience as *the* great teacher, and let it give guidance to action. In this way, Continental thinkers easily identify the strictly social and political content of a theory with its metaphysical infrastructures and superstructure. They find it difficult to understand that a materialistic metaphysics can be coupled with a spiritual ethics, and also the reverse, viz., that a spiritual and theocentric metaphysics can possess a genuine sense of temporal and material values. Clearly, such an attitude is the source of much misunderstanding and dogmatism. The confusion of religion and politics is also closely connected with it.

Let this be properly understood. We do not hold that a conviction regarding the meaning of life is not important for the proper course of social and political life. A spiritual metaphysics is no doubt a great safeguard for the spiritual values of society. Unbelieving materialism, on the other hand, can constitute a danger for social life, as we have already shown. When one sees man ultimately as nothing but a cluster of atoms which disintegrates after death, one can easily be led to deal with man as a mere handful of atoms. That is why Nietzsche, the great atheist, was so concerned about the growth of unbelief. He was convinced that mankind would have to pass through a severe crisis before it would be able to live, without God, a life worthy of man. What we mean, then, is only this: an unbeliever, who calls himself a materialist in the realm of metaphysics, can be very sensitive to, and have a great interest in the things of the spirit and therefore work for an economic and social system of politics that fosters the things of the spirit. Divergences in the realm of philosophy and religion in regard to the meaning of the world are not necessarily obstacles in the way of sincere and fruitful cooperation. Moreover, this kind of cooperation exists in most Anglo-Saxon countries. Why could it not be possible elsewhere too? But this presupposes that we take account of still another distinction which we have frequently met in our previous considerations, the distinction between the objective side and the subjective-ethical side of every human undertaking.

Social Structures and Social Ethics

As we have said, the social struggle is basically a struggle for an ethical ideal. This, however, does not mean that it has no other aim than to spread better feelings toward our fellow-men in the world. Feelings of good will alone are not sufficient to liberate mankind. Human freedom is bound up with matter and with the world, and it could never reach maturity and autonomy without appropriate *objective* conditions of life.

It goes without saying that the *first* and *immediate* purpose of the social struggle lies in the realm of objective and social structures and achievements. This follows from the very concept of the social struggle. The immediate effect of a co-ordination of all socially-minded forces, is not the inner liberation of man—for this is the task of education and personal effort—but the humanization of man's objective conditions of life; for instance, the improvment of working conditions and of human relations in great industrial enterprises, a more carefully planned organization of the economy, the democratization of education, better laws in the realms of public health, housing, and pensions.

However, as we have repeatedly said, the objective conditions of life are only means, they are not the ultimate goal. The final goal is man himself considered individually and collectively, that is, the rising of man toward a better, more ample life that is worthy of man, with more justice and fraternity among men. What would be the use of constantly stressing the primacy of work if the laborer himself no longer highly esteems and loves his work, has no longer any pride in his work? A more equitable social legislation can raise everyone's opportunities for a better life, but even then it remains necessary that individuals will use these opportunities. This no law can guarantee. The abolition of class differences can bring about more solidarity among men, but it can also harden interhuman relations, foster jealousy, ambition and egotistic individualism. To constantly improve social *legislation* and to *educate men in a better social spirit* are two different things.

We should never forget that the socio-economic reorganization of society presupposes a parallel cultural and ethical re-education of its members. Or again, a renewal of the economic and social system must go hand in hand with a renewal of man himself. The ancient saying, "what value have laws without morals?" (*quid leges sine moribus?*) is perhaps more to the point than ever before, now that "laws" increase constantly in complexity and demand more and more of us.

Our next question, therefore, is: In connection with the distinction between the objective and the ethical side of the social struggle, how should the cooperation of men of good will be planned and fostered? Particularly in our Christian organizations, it is considered almost self-evident that cooperation with men who hold divergent views is possible only on the level of objective achievements, but that such cooperation is completely out of the question as soon as it becomes a matter of the cultural and ethical formation of men, e.g., of the workers and especially youth.

I ask myself whether this viewpoint is really so "self-evident" and whether a milder attitude would not possess a greater educational value, provided everything is done with care, the autonomy of the respective organizations is not endangered, and the differences in the philosophy of life are not buried under the bushel. A genuine social education is, after all, hardly thinkable without an understanding of those who think differently. Moreover, no mutual understanding is possible without effective and sincere contacts, even though at the beginning this contact might exist only between the heads of the educational institutions concerned. Moreover, the great problems encountered by young workers in their daily lives are almost the same whether they belong to a Catholic trade union, a neutral or socialist organization or none at all. Many of those problems are crucial for the spiritual health of the people and are so complicated that they can be solved only through the cooperation of all who are competent in the matter and of all men of good will. Such men are found wherever work is done for the education of youth and not only in one's own group.

The International Dimension of the Social Problem

We can never sufficiently insist upon the fact that at this time the social problem has taken on an international character and that the struggle's center of gravity lies no longer in Europe but in Asia, Africa and South America. Awareness of this international character of the social struggle could be a powerful incentive toward a better understanding among socially-minded men. Divisions within one's own country should not prevent cooperation on the international plane.

The question may be asked whether small countries like Belgium, Holland or Switzerland are able to exercise influence upon world events. Although one may be inclined to belittle their influence, it must not be underestimated. Several possibilities of action present themselves.

Firstly, there is the country's own foreign policy and the possibility of assistance given to underdeveloped countries. It often happens that progressive social politics for the interior of a country are coupled with a very conservative and unsocial attitude in the matter of foreign policy. Here lies a field of social action even for small countries.

Secondly, there is the possibility of promoting the unity of Western Europe. The social attitude that will be adopted by a unified Europe could have great significance for the future of the world.

Finally there is the formation of public opinion. In this field there are such works as *Pax Christi*, assistance to Latin America, the action of Father Pire, winner of the Nobel Prize, the World organization of Catholic Young Workers, the "Building Order," the Review *World Justice* of Louvain, the study center *Economie et Humanisme* of Father Lebret, O.P., to mention only a few of the works inspired by Christian thought. All these are very important and deserve powerful support. Their influence on world opinion and, via world opinion, on politics of the United States, could prove greater than one might suspect. Among other things, they can aid in enlisting the great international community of the Christian faithful—which certainly is not a force that should be underestimated—and mobilize it for the service of the social ideal. This in turn brings us a new series of problems which are related to the significance of Christianity in today's social development.

4. Christianity and the Social Development of the World

"Religion," Karl Marx said, "is the opium of the people." Christianity, on the contrary claims to be the most solid foundation and the strongest guarantee of a renewal of the temporal order that will be worthy of man.

However, the great significance of Christianity for today's world is almost completely obscured when, as often happens, Christianity is presented as a socio-economic ideology alongside many others, or as the strongest antagonist of the Marxist concept of society. Marxism, to the extent that it identifies itself with godlessness, cannot have a more powerful enemy than Christianity; but as a defender of a specific economy, of the extreme form of planned economy, its antagonist is not Christianity but capitalistic liberalism. For Christianity is not an economic theory but a religion and an ethics of religious inspiration. It is not impossible that in particular circumstances, a far-reaching planning and "collectivization" of economic life might not be almost the only way to make underdeveloped countries attain a relatively high degree of prosperity in a fairly short time. In any case, the question is not a religious but an economic problem and is to be solved not by theologians but by economists. The only thing faith demands is that whatever economic policy a country may choose, it must respect man and recognize the inalienable rights and values of the human person.

The widespread representation of Christianity as the antagonist of the communist social system or even of the socialist organization of society, is very dangerous. It creates the impression that the Christian faith is primarily a negative and conservative force in social matters, that it is the strongest bulwark of the capitalist concept of society and the distribution of wealth. Christianity thereby loses much of its creative value for the proper solution of the social world crisis.

This loss is very unfortunate, especially when one reflects upon the enormous positive power that Christianity could wield for the improvement and reorganization of our profoundly shaken world. Yet this force can be effectively applied only when Christianity pays heed to the true causes of the social disease and fights the evil in its roots. Not communism in the ultimate source of today's crisis but the crying economic inequality and enslavement of which we have already spoken, and for which communism claims to have an answer. So long as these conditions continue to exist, peace will be impossible in the world and we must expect the worst. The question therefore is: How can Christianity foster social justice in the world of today? What are the conditions that are required for this purpose?

Christianity as a Moral Force

The social struggle is fundamentally a struggle for an ethical ideal. Its ultimate end is to bring more truth and justice in the world, to put the riches of nature at the disposal of all mankind, to humanize the relations among men, to bring about a more just distribution of wealth; in short, to construct a world that is not governed by money but by a truer recognition of man by man.

Now, as we have seen, Christianity is essentially a message of love, whose first task is to reveal *God's love to the world in the concrete form of effective brotherly love*: "Beloved, let us love one another, for love is from God. And everyone who loves is born of God, and knows God" (John 4, 7). Hence love of God and concern for mankind are inseparably united: "For how can he who does not love his brother, whom he sees, love God whom he does not see?" (I John 4, 20). And Our Lord tells us in the Gospel that "You will know the tree by its fruits." Now, the fruits of God's Word and God's Spirit are: "love, joy, peace" (Gal. 5, 22). There is no peace, however, without justice.

All this means that perhaps Christianity has never had such great opportunities as in our own day. But it also means that the Christians will never have committed a greater treason than now if they remain aloof from the struggle at this decisive turning point of history, if they act merely as neutral onlookers who prudently wait for further developments of the struggle, or, what is still worse, if they play the conservatives through clever sophistry help to maintain falsehood and injustice in the world.

We have already quoted Cardinal Suhard's words: "The greatest fault that Christians of the twentieth century could commit would be to let the world organize and unify itself without them." This unification of our world means more than a geographical unification by the narrowing of geographic distances; it means, first of all, a social unification, a gradual elimination of the enormous social and economic inequalities which still continue to divide mankind into two groups: the small group of the rich and the large group of the poor. Nothing worse could happen than that the moral sensitivity for values of today's Christian community should not be in harmony with the sensitivity for values of the present world. The most striking characteristics of this sensitivity have been described in the foregoing chapters: they are the sense of solidarity, of equality, of historicity; in a word, sensibility for *social* justice, for *creative* justice.

It is, therefore, of the highest importance for our time that we become more conscious of, and give greater emphasis to the *positive dynamic character* of Christian morals. A Christianity that is understood properly cannot adopt a petrified attitude of life, which is the enemy of progress, adaptation and creation. Is there any power on earth more dynamic than loving, watchful concern for man? Of course, Christian ethics, like any other ethics, contains prohibitive commandments, as "Thou shalt not steal," "Thou shalt not kill." But these negative norms themselves are in the service of a positive sense of values and practice of virtues: "Thou shalt love thy neighbor as thyself," and do for him what you would want him to do for yourself. Hence, Christian ethics contains the positive obligation of rethinking our attitudes in regard to property, the care of health, the dissemination of education, and, in general, of the objective social structures in line with economic development and in view of a more equitable distribution of wealth and a greater equality of opportunities for all.

Characteristics of Christian Social Action. The fact that Christian ethics always and everywhere aims at man and subordinates everything to man and to the fundamental values and rights of man, endows the social action of the Christian with a number of characteristics which by that fact offer great safeguards for our time.

First, the Christian does not go to work in an aprioristic and dogmatizing way. He accents the distinction between ends and means. He knows very well that a more genuine recognition of man by man pre-supposes, in the order of means, many and profound reforms affecting the economic and social structure of the world. But he does not believe that there exists an *a priori* for all these problems; experience and expertness must remain the principal teachers in all those matters. This distinction between end and means is of great importance for mankind. The confusion of end and means is the sign of a petrified and dogmatizing spirit and the source of fanaticism.

Secondly, because Christian ethics starts from a great respect for man, it spontaneously prefers order to disorder, law-abiding evolution to revolution and terror. Moderation, understanding, patience, and respect for the law are very important ethical values. To sacrifice whole generations in order to establish a new world in the shortest possible time, is inhuman and dangerous, for terror calls forth more terror and lowers man to the level of the brute. There is then great danger that the long awaited new world will ultimately lead to worse evils than the old order ever knew.

Thirdly, since the Christian believer attributes a religious dimension to human existence, he puts certain moral values in the foreground and pays special attention to them. For example, his social action will quite naturally be explicitly personalistic; it will stress the rights, values and freedoms of the human person, because in the Christian perspective man is an object of divine love and, therefore, has a limitless value and truth. Another consequence is the fact that Christian ethics is more demanding than many other ethical systems in regard to the morals of marriage and the family, for it sees a religious and sacramental meaning in the marriage bond: "this is a great mystery in Christ and in the Church." For the Christian, the consent by which man and woman bind themselves is a great and holy mystery because it is confirmed by God, symbolizes Christ's love for His Church, and inaugurates their mission in that same Church. Sickness and death have also a sacred significance in Christianity and are therefore treated with a holy respect. This the Christian believer cannot keep out of his mind when he enters the field of social health and the nursing of the sick. Finally, because the Christian believer recognizes an ecclesiastical community of faith alongside the community of the State, he wants a social order in which there is sufficient freedom for the proclamation of God's Word, the exercise of worship, the practice of charity, and the Church's spiritual task of education.

In short, the Christian views of life and of the world have their repercussions on the Christian believer's ideal of the human society, and on his endeavors to realize it. For this reason there exists a "Christian social doctrine."

The Christian Social Doctrine

It is customary to call "Christian social doctrine" the expression of Christian ethics in the realm of social life, social action, and organization of society. It is not easy, however, to determine its exact meaning. Moreover, when this meaning is not stated with precision and prudently handled, it can easily lead to conservatism.

What do we understand by "Christian social doctrine?" It means a theory about society that is inspired by Christian ethics. In other words, it is a unified whole of principles, designed to indicate the *conditions that a temporal society must necessarily fulfill,* in regard to both man's sense for subjective and ethical values and the objective structures of society, to make this society be in harmony with the ideas sanctioned by Christianity concerning the human person, his fundamental rights, freedoms, and values. Just as Christian ethics itself, the social doctrine of Christianity is an *open and dynamic* doctrine, or more exactly, it is a *whole of imperatives* regarding the ordering of society; but it is not one of the many economic and social systems in the technical sense of the word, such as the liberal, neoliberal, socialist and communist systems.

For example, Christianity does not honor any definite regulation of property, but could live in harmony with many different regulations, on condition that they respect certain fundamental principles. The same can be said in regard to the policy of employment, the structure of enterprises, social security, the organization of medicine, and public health. In all these fields, two ways are usually open, one more individualistic and liberal, the other more collectivistic and planned. In between, there are many different mixtures of the two. Faith does not indicate which form is best for specific circumstances. Nor can it be said *a priori* of any purely economic and social regime that it is specifically Christian, but every regime must observe certain requirements to be in harmony with the Christian concept of man and society. Thus we can understand that in some countries, like England, most Catholics favor a socialistic organization of society; whereas in others they prefer a more liberal or neoliberal organization.

Evidently our intention is not to develop here a Christian social doctrine. We merely wish to call attention to a few ideas which readily give rise to misunderstandings and sophistical arguments.

The Concept of "Social Principle." Christian social doctrine, like any doctrine about society, starts from general and abstract principles. Social principles, however, are not like mathematical axioms whose universality and perpetual validity suffer no exceptions; such as, two plus two is always and everywhere four. Social principles are mostly *affirmations of value* that are generally valid, and like any accepted value, lead to a *universal norm of conduct.* This norm of conduct indicates how man ought to behave generally in order to give practical recognition to some definite value and foster its application in the world. Now, even when we are in the presence of a value that must be universally accepted and is inviolable, that is, a value that must be respected and fostered in all times and places, this does mean that the corresponding *norm of conduct* must likewise be universal and inviolable. The reason for it is very simple: no concrete human action can simultaneously

315

serve and foster all values. Every human action and under-taking is limited and even ambiguous; that is, it favors one value and is harmful to another. Moreover, a hierarchy exists among values, and this implies that sometimes one value must temporarily give way before another. A couple of examples will clarify this matter.

Life and health must, no doubt, be reckoned among the most fundamental and universally accepted values of life, to which every man has a right. This is expressed in a well-known norm of conduct, which forbids us to kill or to injure the health of another person. This rule of conduct is universal and yet exceptions can be thought of, as for example, in case of lawful self-defense.

In the matter of medical care, "free choice" is rightly considered a universally and inviolable value; it, therefore, must be taken into account in the organization of social medicine. By "free choice" is understood the patient's liberty to choose the physician and the medical institution of his preference, and on the other hand, the liberty of the physician to exercise his medical art according to his own judgment. Free choice, like any other value that man desires, is a sort of ideal; hence man can come more or less near to it but, because of his limita-tions, man can never completely achieve it. The ideal form of free choice, when we consider it from the standpoint of the patient, would exist if *every* man, in *all* circumstances, were able to make a *completely* motivated choice from among *all* physicians, and choose the one whom he considers *the best*. But this is evidently impossible except perhaps for a multi-millionaire. The free choice is rather extensive for some; for others it is very limited, and there are still plenty of people in the world who because of their financial condition have no choice whatsoever.

Hence the question: How can we give a maximum of choice to everyone? This will require organization and regu-lation. Regulation means that the freedom of some will be curtailed in order to give greater liberty to others. For instance, travelling on the left hand side of the road is forbidden to keep the road free for all. In a similar way it could happen that unlimited freedom of choice in regard to social medicine is financially impossible or leads to countless abuses. Regulation thus becomes inevitable and the question then is: How should the care of health be organized in order that in these specific circumstances and with these available means the best care possible will be put at the disposal of all, while at the same time a maximum of freedom of choice will be guaranteed?

To summarize, we can say that social principles are in the first place *affirmations of values*. But all values cannot be simultaneously and equally fostered by every social action and regulation. The precise task of the social worker and the politician is to construct a social order which 1) takes into account, in these specific circumstances, the hierarchy of values, especially those that are essential and indispensable conditions of life and to which every man has a right; 2) gives as much liberty and opportunity as possible to everybody; 3) and for this purpose introduces as much restriction as is required.

Catholic Doctrine of Property. Another important point in the Church's social doctrine is that which concerns property. If the Catholic teaching regarding property is not properly explained, it may give the impression that the Church desires especially to protect the existing wealth of the rich, whereas on the contrary she desires a wider distribution of ownership and a more equitable division of wealth, so that "all may be able to enjoy the benefits of ownership" (Pius XII). On the other hand, this does not mean that the Church condemns the powerful concentration of capital without which a modern economy is impossible. However, the formation of capital can come about in many ways and can go together with a widespread distribution of wealth.

The Catholic doctrine regarding property is very simple and comes down to the following:

The riches of the earth are for man, and not vice versa. Originally, says St. Thomas, and as they have come from the hands of the Creator, the goods of this world belong to no one in particular, but they exist for mankind. And Jacques Leclercq writes that "the whole of the goods of the earth is destined for the whole of men."

However, this final destiny of earthly goods would remain meaningless if ownership were not regulated in any way. In this regulation we always find a sphere of *private property,* in the strict sense of the term, alongside the sphere of *collective ownership.* If anyone for any reason were allowed to seize anything he wished, a free, peaceful and prosperous social existence of men and nations would be impossible. We must add that exclusively collective ownership would not suffice. Man cannot fulfill his task in the world if there is no sphere of goods that he can consider his own, as something which he can dispose of at will and freely. Otherwise, not only is the incentive for labor removed but it is even impossible for him to construct his future freely and autonomously, to exercise his duties as a father of a family, to assume responsibility for his functions, and to play his role in society. A definite sphere of private ownership is therefore required by nature and should be guaranteed in any system of property; this, in fact, is what generally happens. Stealing is forbidden, even in communist regimes.

Hence, the principle of law, "to every man his due," the distinction between "mine and thine," between "ours and theirs," have a permanent ethical significance. This is expressed negatively in the commandment, "Thou shalt not steal." But the doctrine of property also has a positive side, which flows from the fundamental destiny of earthly riches. It is nothing else than the demand that, as civilization advances, the system of ownership be adjusted to new possibilities, that the socio-economic regime be constantly improved, and that man come ever nearer to the ideal of justice and fraternity, viz., to distribute property as widely and as effectively as possible.

Evidently, this doctrine represents an open and dynamic conception of property. It goes without saying that the positive significance of the Christian doctrine of property is not brought to light by emphasizing only the negative aspect; "Thou shalt not steal."

There is, however, a second way of being one-sided and presenting a false picture of the Catholic concept of ownership. This happens when one gives so much priority to private property that collective ownership is considered almost a necessary evil, a sort of invasion of private ownership; and it is then considered to be permissible only when there is no other way, or, as is expressed in the traditional formula, when "the general welfare absolutely requires it."

Yet, since man is by nature a social being who can live only in society, private property and collective property are equally *primary*. We may add that these two formulae concerning ownership have always existed together in history as two complementary elements of every system of ownership that is worthy of man, although the relation between the two has not always been the same.

In a primitive society, in which the economy is still very archaic and the individual does not enjoy any security at all outside the group, the regime is principally collective. To the extent that the economy gives increasing autonomy and freedom of movement to the individual, collective ownership decreases without, however, disappearing entirely. Even when liberalism reached its apex, collective ownership continued to play a great role and the distinction between "ours" and "theirs" was as absolute as between "mine" and "thine."

The relation and interconnection between private and collective property can take on innumerable forms, but one thing remains certain throughout, namely, that both types of ownership are "primary" and that it is erroneous to consider collective ownership as an infringement upon private ownership that is sometimes demanded by the circumstances. On the contrary, collective ownership can also be a means of insuring a greater and more just distribution of private ownership.

The Concept of "Common Good." A third point of Christian social doctrine deserves our attention—namely, the idea of "common good." Christian social doctrine insists upon the fundamental principle of political wisdom that all economic, social and political action must be governed by the common good and that it must be the decisive standard and criterion for all changes in the structure of society.

The expression "common good" (*bonum commune*) designates that maximum of general welfare that is thought to be attainable by a human society in specific circumstances.

This common welfare comprises not only economic well-being but also the intellectual, cultural, spiritual, and moral growth of the members of the community, the recognition of one another's liberties, the constant improvement of inter-human relations, the protection and promotion of the fundamental values of the person and, finally, the stability of the social order which we call "peace" and without which no vigorous society worthy of man can exist.

It is important to note, however, that it would be a mistake to conceive this "common welfare" as a static, immovable and closed reality; on the contrary, it must remain open to constant adjustment, improvement and growth. When welfare is at a stand-still, it is in reality going backwards. A nation fares well only when it is directed to the future and remains eager to improve the common welfare of all.

This must be kept in mind when we take the primacy of the common welfare as our standard of economic, social and political action. For this common welfare can be conceived in two ways: either we speak of the actual situation of welfare as it has existed until now and of what is needed for its preservation, or we have in mind the welfare considered attainable in the foreseeable future and the means required for its achievement. A conservative is actually the man who rivets his attention on the welfare that has been, and who wishes perhaps some improvement of conditions, but lacks the imagination and daring to make a project of a better future and create the necessary organisms that will make this project possible. Hence the expression "that which is *necessary* for the common welfare" is rather ambiguous; it can easily be misused in favor of a conservative attitude and serve to put obstacles in the way of the free creation of a better world; for it is true that this better world is not absolutely "necessary."

Common welfare constantly develops further; consequently there is also an evolution of the social and economic organization required by this common welfare. In other words, laws and rights are subject to development. This brings us to the fourth point: the concept of law and right and, especially of natural law.

The Concepts "Law" and "Right." The social doctrine of the Church rejects a purely positivistic concept of rights. In other words, the fact that a certain law exists does not mean that the right in question is a genuine right. A law is good, creates a genuine right only when it conforms to the natural law on the one hand, and fosters the common welfare on the other.

The idea of "natural law" is a delicate one. It is also an open and dynamic idea. Usually we understand by *natural law* the whole of fundamental, very general and inalienable rights that flow immediately from the dignity and autonomy of the human person himself and thus have to be recognized by positive legislation which respects the dignity of man. For instance, man has a natural right to life and health, to freedom of conscience and religion, to work and a form of private property, to strive for an order of society that is more in harmony with man's dignity. The natural law does not indicate concretely how these fundamental rights are to be safeguarded and fostered in the course of historical contingencies; this is regulated only by the law of custom and by positive legislation. Nature demands that society be ordered, but the precise form of this order is determined by positive legislation, of which the law of custom is a part.

Positive law comprises both the law of custom and the law resulting from positive legislation. Since natural welfare is constantly developing, the task of sound statemanship is to adjust legislation constantly to new needs and to the new possibilities that arise in accordance with the evolution of civilization. As we stated above, all legislation, to be good and sound, must take into account the natural law, on the one hand, and the welfare of the whole people, on the other.

Man is a historical being. He experiences his nature as a potentiality and a never completed task rather than as something perfectly fixed. Hence new demands for rights may arise which formerly had no meaning, but which can be considered to be demands of nature when man reaches a certain level of development. In this way we arrive at the meaning that is commonly given to "right" in our modern so-called "declarations of the rights of man." By "right" here is usually understood a whole of demands or quasi-demands which, in view of the progress of civilization, must be accepted as the norm of positive legislation. For instance, it will be maintained that every child has a right to education until its fourteenth or sixteenth year, or even to a higher education if one has the necessary capacity for it. Here, of course, we are not speaking of a universal "natural right" in the sense attached to the term in the seventeenth or eighteenth centuries, that is, of a right that belongs to men of all times and all places. What it means here is that, in view of the present development of civilization, education and instruction must henceforth be considered *fundamental values of life to which every man has a right* since they have become a possibility for everyone. Therefore, the state has the duty to adjust its laws to the new possibilities in the matter of instruction and education for the purpose of securing a more equitable distribution of wealth. The same can be said of the numerous reforms of economic and social structures, such as more universal medical care, social security, and the right to work.

It is most important that we do not underestimate this new meaning of the term "right," if we do not wish to engage in endless discussions about the scope of the natural law, and especially if we want to avoid fostering conservatism through too rigid a concept of natural law.

The Concept "Social Pluralism." A last point deserves our attention but we shall consider it again in the chapter concerning *Denominational Political Parties.* I mean the problem of so-called social pluralism. The Church has always encouraged the organization of Christian social works and institutes. She sees in them a guarantee not only for the free exercise of her spiritual mission, but also a safeguard for the proper progress of temporal society. In fact, a certain type of pluralism can foster the spirit of enterprise and a wholesome competition in social life.

However, there exists at the present time, especially among intellectuals, a tendency of calling into doubt the usefulness and timeliness of this social pluralism. It is feared, and not without reasons, that separate Christian organizations lead to a kind of "apartheid," an aloofness; with the result that Christian believers then live quasi-isolated from the present world, compromise the Church in temporal affairs, and prevent the unification of all progressive social forces.

Much truth is present in these apprehensions. Yet this should not be considered a sufficient motive for condemning Christian cultural and social organizations. First of all, if Christians organize themselves separately, this happens mainly because they do not feel at home in neutral organizations since the views of life and the world that often prevail in them are anything but neutral. Secondly, it is an exaggeration to maintain that the establishment of Christian works necessarily isolates the faithful from the world.

A Catholic University, for instance, which is faithful to its own mission as a university, is not foreign to university life; it is rather a contribution made by Catholics to the international world of learning. The same applies to the Christian labor movement; it does not create a separate social world and should never consider itself such. Its task is to cooperate in the construction of a world that is more worthy of man and serves the benefit of all.

In regard to the danger that the Church may be compromised by getting involved in temporal affairs, this also should not be exaggerated. Christian socialworks, such as polyclinics, labor unions, cooperatives, mutual benefit societies, are not Church institutions, whose administration and responsibility should rest with ecclesiastical authorities. They are works of Christian laymen, administered by laymen who assume responsibility for them. In a democratic society, the faithful have the same right as anybody else to organize themselves freely and to strive together toward certain purposes.

This separate organization, of course, should not lead to "apartheid," to "separatism." As we have remarked, such aloofness is harmful not only for the message of faith because contact with those who think differently is then gradually lost, but also for the general welfare because a strongly organized Catholic community can easily become a state within a state. It is important, therefore, to keep constantly in mind the danger that is undeniably connected with separate organizations, and to do everything possible to eliminate it. Three points are most important in this respect.

First, the creation of separate organizations must never become an end in itself which then will go beyond all bounds; it must be done with moderation, that is, keeping in mind the welfare of the entire population and in subordination to this common welfare, for the general welfare must always remain the criterion for the separate activity of the respective population groups. For example, when Catholics establish their own schools, they must not forget the others and always keep in mind the welfare of the entire school system. Secondly, within the separate organizations themselves a spirit of openness for the preservation of a dialogue with others must exist. Thirdly, it is especially important that the Church and the temporal organization of the faithful should not be so interwoven and interconnected that they become practically indistinguishable.

A flourishing Catholic university, for example, is a blessing for the Church as well as for the world of learning, but that blessing would lose much of its significance for both the Church and the temporal society if the university world were divided into two camps: on the one side, the world of Catholic universities, where only Catholics teach and study and, on the other, a world of neutral universities which are open only to non-Catholic professors and students. The same can be said of all organizations that have secular purposes. If this is admitted, then one must draw the inevitable practical conclusion: a Catholic who does not feel at home in Catholic organizations and sincerely believes that he can serve his Church and his country better in neutral institutions—by which, of course, we mean those that are really neutral—should not be looked upon as a second-rate Catholic and be treated as such.

In short, a sociological pluralism can be healthy and sound on condition that it is a moderate and open pluralism.

Thomas Merton
1915-1968

When Thomas Merton died suddenly in Bangkok in 1968, the American Catholic church lost one of her most challenging and stimulating personalities. For more than two decades, through his writing, he had generously served post World War II Catholicism in its search for meaning and relevancy in modern America. Though perhaps best known for The Seven Storey Mountain, *his autobiography up to the age of 33, he was the author of more than 50 published books, dozens of articles and poems, and writings circulated only at the Trappist Monastery of Gethsemani, Kentucky and among fellow Cistercians.*

Merton was born in France in 1915. His mother was American, his father a New Zealander. At age one he was brought to America, lost his mother when he was six, and returned to Europe when he was ten years old. He went to schools in France and England. In 1934, he returned to the United States and attended Columbia University. There he earned his baccalaureate and masters degrees in English. Merton was converted to Catholicism in 1938 and entered Gethsemani on December 10, 1941. The life of solitude and prayer for which he yearned was counterbalanced by an apostolate of the written word throughout his 27 years as a Trappist monk. He received permission from his superiors in 1965 to live a short distance from the monastery as a hermit. Rarely did he travel beyond Gethsemani. Acceding to the request of various Trappist abbots in 1968, he journeyed to the Far East to attend a conference on monasticism in Bangkok and to visit several Trappist monasteries in the Orient. He died in Bangkok, apparently accidentally electrocuted by a faulty electric fan. The day was December 10, the anniversary date of his entry into Gethsemani.

It is difficult to evaluate a man of Merton's stature with a distance scarcely more than ten years separating us from his life. Clearly he is a major religious personality of twentieth century America. Perhaps his lasting value will be due more to what he tried to do with his life than to his writings. Yet, in some way, we have access to his life only through his writings.

Merton's reflective writing on the situation of contemporary America and the western culture is disconcerting. In turning his attentive intellect toward the question of social justice in our day, he seeks to push beyond the surface level of activity and get to the why of things. Conjectures of a Guilty Bystander, *which he describes as a personal version of the world in the 1960s, is a forceful statement of why our present society is torn apart by racism, poverty, fraud, and violence. His is a meditative why, the kind that will disturb the reader and pull him into the meditation: we have ceased to think; there is no time to reason; we have filled our minds and emotions with rubbish. Though well intended, gestures to correct the present situation are almost totally ineffective. The hope of the future lies in the liberal minority of thinking, questioning, truth-seeking people but, for Merton, we must now begin "slowly and laboriously to divest ourselves one by one of all our coverings of fiction and delusion." The western civilization must learn to accept the fact that it developed out of the revelation of God in Man. And the Christian must take the risk of coming to see, by way of an intolerable purification, the true meaning of Christianity in social life.*

The following reading is from Part II of Conjectures, *and is entitled, "Truth and Violence: An Interesting Era."*

CONJECTURES OF
A GUILTY BYSTANDER

PART TWO

TRUTH AND VIOLENCE: AN INTERESTING ERA

T his is no longer a time of systematic ethical speculation, for such speculation implies time to reason, and the power to bring social and individual action under the concerted control of reasoned principles upon which most men agree.

There is no time to reason out, calmly and objectively, the moral implications of technical developments which are perhaps already superseded by the time one knows enough to reason about them.

Action is not governed by moral reason but by political expediency and the demands of technology—translated into the simple abstract formulas of propaganda. These formulas have nothing to do with reasoned moral action, even though they may appeal to apparent moral values—they simply condition the mass of men to react in a desired way to certain stimuli.

Men do not agree in moral reasoning. They concur in the emotional use of slogans and political formulas. There is no persuasion but that of power, of quantity, of pressure, of fear, of desire. Such is our present condition—and it is critical!

Bonhoeffer wrote, shortly before his death at the hands of the Nazis, that moral theorizing was outdated in such a time of crisis—a time of villains and saints, and of Shakespearian characters. "The villain and the saint have little to do with systematic ethical studies. They emerge from the primeval depths and by their appearance they tear open the infernal or the divine abyss from which they come and enable us to see for a moment into mysteries of which they had never dreamed."

And the peculiar evil of our time, Bonhoeffer continues, is to be sought not in the sins of the good, but in apparent virtues of the evil. A time of confirmed liars who tell the truth in the interest of what they themselves are—liars. A hive of murderers who love their children and are kind to their pets. A hive of cheats and gangsters who are loyal in pacts to do evil. Ours is a time of evil which is so evil that it can do good without prejudice to its own iniquity—it is no longer threatened by goodness. Such is Bonhoeffer's judgment of a world in which evil appears in the form of probity and righteousness. In such a time the moral theorist proves himself a perfect fool by taking the "light" at its face value and ignoring the abyss of evil underneath it. For him, as long as evil takes a form that is theoretically "permitted," it is good. He responds mentally to the abstract moral equation. His heart does not detect the ominous existential stink of moral death.

"It is not by astuteness, by knowing the tricks, but by simple steadfastness in the truth of God, by training the eye upon this truth until it is simple and wise, that there comes the experience and knowledge of the ethical reality."

—Bonhoeffer, *Ethics*

* * *

We live in crisis, and perhaps we find it interesting to do so. Yet we also feel guilty about it, as if we *ought not to be* in crisis. As if we were so wise, so able, so kind, so reasonable, that crisis ought at all times to be unthinkable. It is doubtless this "ought," this "should" that makes our era so interesting that it cannot possibly be a time of wisdom, or even of reason. We think we know what we ought to be doing, and we see ourselves move, with the inexorable deliberation of a machine that has gone wrong, to do the opposite. A most absorbing phenomenon which we cannot stop watching, measuring, discussing, analyzing, and perhaps deploring! But it goes on. And, as Christ said over Jerusalem, we do not know the things that are for our peace.

* * *

We are living in the greatest revolution in history—a huge spontaneous upheaval of the entire human race: not the revolution planned and carried out by any particular party, race, or nation, but a deep elemental boiling over of all the inner contradictions that have ever been in man, a revelation of the chaotic forces inside everybody. This is not something we have chosen, nor is it something we are free to avoid.

This revolution is a profound spiritual crisis of the whole world, manifested largely in desperation, cynicism, violence, conflict, self-contradiction, ambivalence, fear and hope, doubt and belief, creation and destructiveness, progress and programs that only dull the general anguish for a moment until it bursts out everywhere in a still more acute and terrifying form. We do not know if we are building a fabulously wonderful world or destroying all that we have ever had, all that we have achieved!

All the inner force of man is boiling and bursting out, the good together with the evil, the good poisoned by evil and fighting it, the evil pretending to be good and revealing itself in the most dreadful crimes, justified and rationalized by the purest and most innocent intentions.

Man is all ready to become a god, and instead he appears at times to be a zombie. And so we fear to recognize our *kairos* and accept it.

* * *

Our times manifest in us a basic distortion, a deep-rooted moral disharmony against which laws, sermons, philosophies, authority, inspiration, creativity, and apparently even love itself would seem to have no power. On the contrary, if man turns in desperate hope to all these things, they seem to leave him more empty, more frustrated, and more anguished than before. Our sickness is the sickness of disordered love, of the self-love that realizes itself simultaneously to be self-hate and instantly becomes a source of universal, indiscriminate destructiveness. This is the other side of the coin that was current in the nineteenth century: the belief in indefinite progress, in the supreme goodness of man and of all his appetites. What passes for optimism, even Christian optimism, is the indefectible hope that eighteenth- and nineteenth- century attitudes can continue valid, can be *kept* valid just by the determination to smile, even though the whole world may fall to pieces. Our smiles are symptoms of the sickness.

* * *

We are living under a tyranny of untruth which confirms itself in power and establishes a more and more total control over men in proportion as they convince themselves they are resisting error.

Our submission to plausible and useful lies involves us in greater and more obvious contradictions, and to hide these from ourselves we need greater and ever less plausible lies. The basic falsehood is the lie that we are totally dedicated to truth, and that we can remain dedicated to truth in a manner that is at the same time honest and exclusive: that we have the monopoly of all truth, just as our adversary of the moment has the monopoly of all error.

We then convince ourselves that we cannot preserve our purity of vision and our inner sincerity if we enter into dialogue with the enemy, for he will corrupt us with his error. We believe, finally, that truth cannot be preserved except by the destruction of the enemy—for, since we have identified him with error, to destroy him is to destroy error. The adversary, of course, has exactly the same thoughts about us and exactly the same basic policy by which he defends the "truth." He has identified us with dishonesty, insincerity, and untruth. He believes that, if we are destroyed, nothing will be left but truth.

* * *

If we really sought truth we would begin slowly and laboriously to divest ourselves one by one of all our coverings of fiction and delusion: or at least we would desire to do so, for mere willing cannot enable us to effect it. On the contrary, the one who can best point out our error, and help us to see it, is the adversary whom we wish to destroy. This is perhaps why we wish to destroy him. So, too, we can help him to see his error, and that is why he wants to destroy us.

In the long run, no one can show another the error that is within him, unless the other is convinced that his critic first sees and loves the good that is within him. So while we are perfectly willing to tell our adversary he is wrong, we will never be able to do so effectively until we can ourselves appreciate where he is right. And we can never accept his judgment on our errors until he gives evidence that he really appreciates our own peculiar truth. Love, love only, love of our deluded fellow man as he actually is, in his delusion and in his sin: this alone can open the door to truth. As long as we do not have this love, as long as this love is not active and effective in our lives (for words and good wishes will never suffice) we have no real access to the truth. At least not to moral truth.

* * *

There are religious people who fear socialism, because they fear the revelation of their own injustice, egoism, and inertia. Socialists who fear religion, because they fear the unmasking of their own complacent sophistries, the puerile, pragmatic games they have played with truth, their own pseudoreligion, which is far more foolish and superstitious than the spiritual religions they claim to have exploded.

* * *

The crisis of the present moment in history is the crisis of Western civilization: more precisely of European civilization, the civilization that was founded on the Greco-Roman culture of the Mediterranean, and built up by the gradual incorporation of the barbarian invaders into the Judeo-Roman-Christian religious culture of the fallen Roman Empire. Into this crisis I was born. By this crisis my whole life has been shaped. In this crisis my life will be consumed—but not, I hope, meaninglessly!

* * *

We have hated our need for compassion and have suppressed it as a "weakness," and our cruelty has far outstripped our sense of mercy. Our humanity is sinking under the waves of hatred and desperation, and we are carried away by a storm that would never have been so terrible if we were not capable of such feelings of guilt about it! That is why the intellectuals of the nineteenth and twentieth centuries have willed at any price to throw off the Nessus shirt of Christianity with its burning remorse of conscience. And that is why I sought refuge in compunction and in conscience, even though this has meant living in anguish, in hesitation, and in frequent questioning. Europe indeed stands for independence precisely because it stands for questioning, free inquiry. Europe learned long ago to be free from the fore-gone conclusion. This is by no means un-Christian. For the first Europeans who became Christians had to doubt the old, dead, cosmic religions, the nature philosophies, the saving power of the mysteries, or the sanctifying force of the Jewish Law before they could have faith in Christ. This is why they seemed to be "atheists" to the Romans.

We too often forget that Christian faith is a principle of questioning and struggle before it becomes a principle of cer-titude and of peace. One has to doubt and reject everything else in order to believe firmly in Christ, and after one has begun to believe, one's faith itself must be tested and purified. Christian-ity is not merely a set of foregone conclusions. The Christian mind is a mind that risks intolerable purifications, and some-times, indeed very often, the risk turns out to be too great to be tolerated. Faith tends to be defeated by the burning presence of God in mystery, and seeks refuge from him, flying to comfort-able social forms and safe conventions in which purification is no longer an inner battle but a matter of outward gesture.

* * *

Europe stands for freedom, diversity, self-knowledge, so-phistication, personalism, creativity. The European mind is active, subtle, critical, proud, resourceful, adventurous. It is at the same time romantic and cynical, wild and disciplined, tender and unscrupulous.

And in the end the European, with all his love of certainty, free investigation, and liberal truth, becomes a first-class liar lying to all others after having first lied to himself. Yet he is per-haps readier than any other to admit his own lie when the time comes to do so. At least he is ready to do this if he is English, because all that is best in Europe remains alive in England—along with some of the worst.

* * *

There remains, however, one most embarrassing truth about Western civilization that must be recognized, at least by the Christian, in spite of the confusion and guilt which this recogni-tion must inevitably bring with it: the world of Christendom, that is to say the world of the West, Europe, Russia, America, is the world into whose history the revelation of God as man broke through, profoundly modifying all human structures and cultural developments. This does not mean that all other cultures are, as regards this revelation, completely insignificant—quite the contrary. They all point to it in their own way. But it was into *our* history that God came, revealing Himself as man, and it was to *us* that was entrusted the task of bearing His revelation of Himself to other cultures. It may be said at once that, in so far as this meant more than a unilateral imposition of our interpretation of God's message upon others, in so far as it demanded a close, attentive, and humble awareness of the way those other traditions were already open to the possibility of God in Man, the Western mission to the rest of the world has largely failed.

The point is not to praise Western culture as perfectly Christian (which it obviously is not, and has never really been) or to blame it as a betrayal of Christianity. More important, and far more difficult, is the actual Christian task, the disconcerting task, of accepting ourselves as we are, in our confusion, infidelity, disruption, ferment and even desperation, as the civilization that developed out of the revelation of God in Man.

As Bonhoeffer says: our history has a special seriousness and our heritage is not like that of other peoples because, whether we like it or not, admit it or not, "our forefathers are the witnesses of the entry of God into history." And we may add, others of our forefathers have been unfaithful to this revelation, so unfaithful that we are now involved in a situation that would be utterly tragic but for the fact that the promises of God do not change, and the humanity He accepted was, and remains, in all truth, *our* humanity.

In one word: the only way in which I can make sense in the unparalleled confusion and absurdity of the breakdown of Western culture is to recognize myself as part of a society both sentenced and redeemed: a society which, if it can accept sentence and redemption, will live. A society which has received the mercy of Christ and been unfaithful to Him. And if my society cannot face this truth, it will destroy itself and perhaps everyone else besides.

* * *

Once again, let me be clear about this word "breakdown." It is bound to be taken as an incomprehensible affront by all those who are firmly convinced that the technological power of our society represents the highest development of man, the beginning of the golden age of plenty and of perfect freedom. I am as ready as the next man to admire the astonishing achievements of technology. Taken by themselves, they are magnificent. But taken in the context of *unbalance* with the other aspects of human existence in the world, the very splendor and rapidity of technological development is a factor of disintegration.

The Greeks believed that when a man had too much power for his own good the gods ruined him by helping him increase his power at the expense of wisdom, prudence, temperance, and humanity until it led automatically to his own destruction.

Suppose a hundred men who in a former age would have died of typhoid fever today crashed to their deaths in a supersonic jet plane. Does the fact that typhus is controllable and that supersonic flight is possible make any difference in their deaths? Or, if technology means safety, and if life is easily and surely prolonged, travel safer, and so on: what difference does this make if, in the congested, irrational, frustrated and bored society that results, everyone nurses an acute and pathological death wish, and if weapons are at hand that might conceivably implement that wish in drastic fashion?

What I am saying is, then, that it does us no good to make fantastic progress if we do not know how to live with it, if we cannot make good use of it, and if, in fact, our technology becomes nothing more than an expensive and complicated way of cultural disintegration. It is bad form to say such things, to recognize such possibilities. But they are possibilities, and they are not often intelligently taken into account. People get emotional about them from time to time, and then try to sweep them aside into forgetfulness. The fact remains that we have created for ourselves a culture which is not yet livable for mankind as a whole.

Never before has there been such a distance between the abject misery of the poor (still the great majority of mankind) and the absurd affluence of the rich. Our gestures at remedying this situation are well meant but *almost totally* ineffective. In many ways they only make matters worse (when for instance those who are supposed to be receiving aid realize that in fact most of it goes into the pockets of corrupt politicians who maintain the *status quo*, of which the misery of the poor is an essential part).

The problem of racism—by no means confined to the southern United States, South Africa, or Nazi Germany—is becoming a universal symptom of homicidal paranoia. The desperation of man who finds existence incomprehensible and intolerable, and who is only maddened by the insignificance of the means taken to alleviate his condition.

The fact that most men believe, as an article of faith, that we are now in a position to solve all our problems does not prove that this is so. On the contrary, this belief is so unfounded that it is itself one of our greatest problems.

* * *

Bonhoeffer was so convinced that the *historical* unity of the West is based on Christ that he even went so far as to assert that for this reason no European war could be a total war. Doubtless he wrote that before the beginning of World War II. Doubtless, also, this passage is not perfectly clear, because in other places, focusing on the apostasy of the West from Christ as the apocalyptic problem of our time, he implies that this infidelity does open the way infallibly to total war. In any event he lived to see that total war was not impossible in the West! In fact the history of the West in the twentieth century hinges entirely on the ever-present possibility of total war between nations that have a Christian heritage. Not only that, but an appeal is even made to Christianity itself to justify total war against total evil. And Communist eschatology—which justifies the Russian view of total war—is itself rooted in hidden Christian assumptions. What has happened is not that the bond of *historical* unity holds the formerly Christian West together, but that new forms of irrationality and fanaticism, making use of distorted notions borrowed from their common Christian heritage, appeal to the final and total use of force as the way to definitive unity—by the elimination of the one adversary who is the source of all division and disruption. For the West, this one Antichrist is

Communism. For the Communists it is capitalist imperialism. Not even the obvious divisions within the two camps can persuade men to drop this paranoid obsession with *one* presumed source of all evil.

* * *

Certainly America seems to have lost much in World War II. It has come out a bloated, suspicious, truculent militarist and one who is not without paranoid tendencies: yet there are in America also, fully alive and fully creative, some of the best tendencies of European independence and liberal thought. No matter how we may criticize Europe and America, they are still in full strength, and in their liberal minority the hope of the future still lies.

Our ability to see ourselves objectively and to criticize our own actions, our own failings, is the source of a very real strength. But to those who fear truth, who have begun to forget the genuine Western heritage and to become immersed in crude materialism without spirit, this critical tendency presents the greatest danger. Indeed it must seem perilous to those who cultivate a simultaneous complacent certitude of might and right in order to destroy without hesitation the ideological enemy. Wait until we have completely lost our European humor (from which American humor is derived) and we will be in a posture to blast Russia or China quite seriously off the face of the earth, unable to see the grim joke that in so doing we are also destroying ourselves and anything good that was left for us to "save" by war. It is precisely the dogmatic *humorlessness* of the self-designated realists that is the greatest danger. They are the ones who have shrugged off practically all that was left of Europe in our society. I for one mean to preserve all the Europe that is in me as long as I live, and above all I will keep laughing until they close my mouth with fallout.

* * *

The central problem of the modern world is the complete emancipation and autonomy of the technological mind at a time when unlimited possibilities lie open to it and all the resources seem to be at hand. Indeed, the mere fact of questioning this emancipation, this autonomy, is the number-one blasphemy, the unforgivable sin in the eyes of modern man, whose faith begins with this: science can do everything, science must be permitted to do everything it likes, science is infallible and impeccable, all that is done by science is right. No matter how monstrous, no matter how criminal an act may be, if it is justified by science it is unassailable.

The consequence of this is that technology and science are now responsible to no power and submit to no control other than their own. Needless to say, the demands of ethics no longer have any meaning if they come in conflict with these autonomous powers. Technology has its own ethic of expediency and efficiency. What *can* be done efficiently *must* be done in the most efficient way—even if what is done happens, for example, to be genocide or the devastation of a country by total war. Even the long-term economic interests of society, or the basic needs of man himself, are not considered when they get in the way of technology. We waste our natural resources, as well as those of undeveloped countries, iron, oil, etc., in order to fill our cities and roads with a congestion of traffic that is in fact largely useless, and is a symptom of the meaningless and futile agitation of our own minds.

The attachment of the modern American to his automobile, and the *symbolic* role played by his car, with its aggressive and lubric design, its useless power, its otiose gadgetry, its consumption of fuel, which is advertised as having almost supernatural power ... this is where the study of American mythology should begin.

Meditation on the automobile, what it is used for, what it stands for—the automobile as weapon, as self-advertisement, as brothel, as a means of suicide, etc.—might lead us at once right into the heart of all contemporary American problems: race, war, the crisis of marriage, the flight from reality into myth and fanaticism, the growing brutality and irrationality of American mores.

I thoroughly agree with Bonhoeffer when he says:

> The demand for absolute liberty brings men to the depths of slavery. The master of the machine becomes its slave. The machine becomes the enemy of

men. The creature turns against its creator in a strange reenactment of the Fall. The emancipation of the masses leads to the reign of terror of the guillotine. Nationalism leads inevitably to war. The liberation of man as an absolute ideal leads only to man's self-destruction.   —*Ethics*

If technology really represented the rule of reason, there would be much less to regret about our present situation. Actually, technology represents the rule of *quantity,* not the rule of reason (quality=value=relation of means to authentic human ends). It is by means of technology that man the person, the subject of qualified and perfectible freedom, becomes *quantified,* that is, becomes part of a mass—mass man—whose only function is to enter anonymously into the process of production and consumption. He becomes on one side an implement, a "hand," or better, a "bio-physical link" between machines: on the other side he is a mouth, a digestive system and an anus, something *through which* pass the products of his technological world, leaving a transient and meaningless sense of enjoyment. The effect of a totally emancipated technology is the regression of man to a climate of moral infancy, in total dependence not on "mother nature" (such a dependence would be partly tolerable and human) but on the pseudonature of technology, which has replaced nature by a closed system of mechanisms with no purpose but that of keeping themselves going.

If technology remained in the service of what is higher than itself—reason, man, God—it might indeed fulfill some of the functions that are now mythically attributed to it. But becoming autonomous, existing only for itself, it imposes upon man its own irrational demands, and threatens to destroy him. Let us hope it is not too late for man to regain control.

* * *

The greatest need of our time is to clean out the enormous mass of mental and emotional rubbish that clutters our minds and makes of all political and social life a mass illness. Without this housecleaning we cannot begin to *see.* Unless we *see* we cannot think. The purification must begin with the mass media. How?

Thomas Merton

* * *

A pharisee is a righteous man whose righteousness is nourished by the blood of sinners.

How to be a pharisee in politics: At every moment display righteous indignation over the means (whether good or evil) which your opponent has used to attain the same corrupt end which you are trying to achieve. Point to the means he is using as evidence that your own purposes are righteous—even though they are the same as his. If the means he makes use of are successful, then show that his success itself is proof that he has used corrupt methods. But in your own case, success is proof of righteousness.

In politics, as in everything else, pharisaism is not self-righteousness only, but the conviction that, in order to be right, it is sufficient to prove that somebody else is wrong. As long as there is one sinner left for you to condemn, then you are justified! Once you can point to a wrongdoer, you become justified in doing anything you like, however dishonest, however cruel, however evil!

* * *

We are all convinced that we desire the truth above all. Nothing strange about this. It is natural to man, an intelligent being, to desire the truth. (I still dare to speak of man as "an intelligent being"!) But actually, what we desire is not "the truth" so much as "to be in the right." To seek the pure truth for its own sake may be natural to us, but we are not able to act always in this respect according to our nature. What we seek is not the pure truth, but the partial truth that justifies our prejudices, our limitations, our selfishness. This is not "the truth." It is only an argument strong enough to prove us "right." And usually our desire to be right is correlative to our conviction that somebody else (perhaps everybody else) is wrong.

Why do we want to prove them wrong? Because we need them to be wrong. For if they are wrong, and we are right, then our untruth becomes truth: our selfishness becomes justice and virtue: our cruelty and lust cannot be fairly condemned. We can rest secure in the fiction that we have determined to embrace as "truth." What we desire is not the truth, but rather that our lie should be proved "right," and our iniquity be vindicated as "just." This is what we have done to pervert our natural, instinctive appetite for truth.

No wonder we hate. No wonder we are violent. No wonder we exhaust ourselves in preparing for war! And in doing so, of course, we offer the enemy another reason to believe that *he* is right, that he must arm, that he must get ready to destroy us. Our own lie provides the foundation of truth on which he erects his own lie, and the two lies together react to produce hatred, murder, disaster.

* * *

Is there any vestige of truth left in our declaration that we think for ourselves? Or do we even trouble to declare this any more? Perhaps the man who says he "thinks for himself" is simply one who does not think at all. Because he has no fully articulate thoughts, he thinks he has his own incommunicable ideas. Or thinks that, if he once set his mind to it, he could have his own thoughts. But he just has not got around to doing this. I wonder if "democracies" are made up entirely of people who "think for themselves" in the sense of going around with blank minds which they imagine they *could* fill with their own thoughts if need be.

Well, the need has been desperately urgent, not for one year or ten, but for fifty, sixty, seventy, a hundred years. If, when thought is needed, nobody does any thinking, if everyone assumes that someone else is thinking, then it is clear that no one is thinking either for himself or for anybody else. Instead of thought, there is a vast, inhuman void full of words, formulas, slogans, declarations, echoes—ideologies! You can always reach out and help yourself to some of them. You don't even have to reach at all. Appropriate echoes already rise up in your mind— they are "yours." You realize of course that these are not yet "thoughts." Yet we "think" these formulas, with which the void in our hearts is provisionally entertained, can for the time being "take the place of thoughts"—while the computers make decisions for us.

Nothing can take the place of thoughts. If we do not think, we cannot act freely. If we do not act freely, we are at the mercy of forces which we never understand, forces which are arbitrary, destructive, blind, fatal to us and to our world. If we do not use our minds to think with, we are heading for extinction, like the dinosaur: for the massive physical strength of the dinosaur became useless, purposeless. It led to his destruction. Our intellectual power can likewise become useless, purposeless. When it does, it will serve only to destroy us. It will devise instruments for our destruction, and will inexorably proceed to use them. . . . It has already devised them.

* * *

Thinking men. Better still, *right-thinking* men! Who are they? The right-thinking man has an instinctive flair for the words and formulas that are most acceptable to his group: and in fact he is partly responsible for making them acceptable. He is indeed a man of timely ideas, opportune ideas.

He is the man whose formulas are replacing the outworn formulas of the year before. And no doubt the formulas of the year before were his also: they were the ones with which he supplanted the formulas of two years ago, which perhaps were his too. The right-thinking man has a knack of expressing, and indeed of discovering, the attitudes that everyone else is unconsciously beginning to adopt. He is the first one to become conscious of the new attitude, and he helps others to become aware of it in themselves. They are grateful to him. They respect him. They listen to his utterances. He is their prophet, their medicine man, their shaman. They talk like him, they act like him, they dress like him, they look like him. And all this brings them good luck. They despise and secretly fear others who have different formulas, dress differently, act differently, speak differently.

Fortunately, though, all right-thinking men think the same these days. At least all who belong to the same tribal society. Even those who do not conform are in their own way a justification of the right-thinking man: the beatnik is necessary to make the square unimpeachably respectable.

The right-thinking men are managers, leaders, but not egg-heads. Hence they can be believed. They can justify any wrong road, and make it seem the *only* road. They can justify everything, even the destruction of the world.

* * *

Gandhi saw that Western democracy was *on trial.* On trial for what? On trial to be judged by its own claims to be the rule of the people by themselves. Not realizing itself to be on trial, assuming its own infallibility and perfection, Western democracy has resented every attempt to question these things. The mere idea that it might come under judgment has seemed absurd, unjust, diabolical. Our democracy is now being judged, not by man but by God. It is not simply being judged by the enemies of the West and of "democracy." When anyone is judged by God, he receives, in the very hour of judgment, a gift from God. The gift that is offered him, in his judgment, is *truth.* He can receive the truth or reject it; but in any case truth is being offered silently, mercifully, in the very crisis by which democracy is put to the test. For instance, the problem of integration.

When one is on trial in this life, he is at the same time receiving mercy: the merciful opportunity to anticipate God's decision by receiving the light of truth, judging himself, changing his life. Democracy has been on trial in Berlin, in Alabama, in Hiroshima. In World War II. In World War I. In the Boer War. In the American Civil War. In the Opium War. What have we learned about ourselves? What have we seen? What have we admitted? What is the truth about us? Perhaps we still have time, still have a little light to see by. But the judgment is getting very dark. . . . The truth is too enormous, too ominous, to be seen in comfort. Yet it is a great mercy of God that so many of us can recognize this fact, and that we are still allowed to *say* it.

* * *

We have got ourselves into a position where, because of our misunderstanding of theoretical distinctions between the "natural and the supernatural," we tend to think that nothing in man's ordinary life is really supernatural except saying prayers and performing pious acts of one sort or another, pious acts which derive their value precisely from the fact that they rescue us, momentarily, from the ordinary routine of life. And therefore we imagine that Christian social action is not Christian *in itself*, but only because it is a kind of escalator to unworldliness and devotion. This is because we apparently cannot conceive material and worldly things seriously as having any capacity to be "spiritual." But Christian social action, on the contrary, conceives man's work itself as a *spiritual* reality, or rather it envisages those conditions under which man's work can *recover* a certain spiritual and holy quality, so that it becomes for man a source of spiritual renewal, as well as of material livelihood.

Christian social action is first of all action that discovers religion in politics, religion in work, religion in social programs for better wages, Social Security, etc., not at all to "win the worker for the Church," but because God became man, because every man is potentially Christ, because Christ is our brother, and because we have no right to let our brother live in want, or in degradation, or in any form of squalor whether physical or spiritual. In a word, if we really understood the meaning of Christianity in social life we would see it as part of the redemptive work of Christ, liberating man from misery, squalor, subhuman living conditions, economic or political slavery, ignorance, alienation.

* * *

Once this has been said, we understand what it might mean to transform the world by political principles spiritualized by the Gospel. It is an attempt to *elevate man*, whether professedly Christian or not, to a level consonant with his dignity as a son of God, redeemed by Christ, liberated from the powers that keep him in subjection, the old dark gods of war, lust, power, and greed. In such a context, political action itself is a kind of spiritual action, an expression of spiritual responsibility, and a witness to Christ. But never merely by the insertion of religious clichés into political programs.

Such social action implies three great emphases. First, emphasis on the *human* as distinct from the merely collective, the technological. Affirmation of *man* and not of the process of production. Saving man from becoming a cog in an enormous machine, a mere utensil for production. Liberation of man from the tyranny of the faceless mass in which he is submerged without thoughts, desires, or judgments of his own, a creature without will or without light, the instrument of the power politician.

Second, emphasis on the *personal*—for if we merely respect man's nature, and *we must respect that nature*, we still do not go far enough. The personal values are those that are spiritual and incommunicable, and hence they evade analysis.

To respect the personal aspect in man is to respect his solitude, his right to think for himself, his need to learn this, his need for love and acceptance by other persons like himself. Here we are in the realm of freedom and of friendship, of creativity and of love. And it is here that religion begins to have a meaning: for a mass religion of faceless ones delivers men over to the demons.

Third, emphasis on *wisdom* and *love*—a sapiential view of society is less activistic, more contemplative; it enables men and institutions to see life in its wholeness, with stability and purpose, though not necessarily in a politically conservative sense. This is the view which prevailed in the ancient traditional cultures that lasted for centuries because they were rooted in the patterns of the cosmos itself, and enabled man to live according to the light of wisdom immanent in the world and in the society of which he formed a part.

* * *

Christian social action must liberate man from all forms of servitude, whether economical, political, or psychological. The words are easily said. Anyone can say them, and everyone does in some way or other. And yet in the name of liberty, man is enslaved. He frees himself from one kind of servitude and enters into another. This is because freedom is bought by obligations, and obligations are bonds. We do not sufficiently distinguish the nature of the bonds we take upon ourselves in order to be free.

If I obligate myself spiritually in order to be free economically, then I buy a lower freedom at the price of a higher one, and in fact I enslave myself. (In ordinary words, this is called selling my soul for the sake of money, and what money can buy.)

Today, as a matter of fact, there is very little real freedom anywhere because everyone is willing to sacrifice his spiritual liberty for some lower kind. He will compromise his personal integrity (spiritual liberty) for the sake of security, or ambition, or pleasure, or just to be left in peace.

* * *

The signals have been changed. The United States has become a great power in the world precisely at the moment when a wholly new political language has been instituted. And our statesmen have not learned the new language. They are generally unable to interpret the new signals. They have eyes and see not, ears and hear not. What they say no longer really makes sense. There have been new words coined, new kinds of meaning, new ways of doing things. Opportunistic, mysterious signs and symbols for action different from our kind of action. When will we learn the signals?

Instead of learning them, we devise our own concept of political realities and try to make international conflicts fit our *a priori* dogmatic declarations. We decide that Cuba is all ready to throw off the yoke of Castro, and this brings on the fiasco of the Bay of Pigs. After we have made fools of ourselves we discover that the men providing us with information have, instead, fed us our own propaganda! Let us at least learn that even the best and most starry-eyed of ideologies is no substitute for a humble attention to concrete and unacceptable *fact*.

* * *

Here is a statement of Gandhi that sums up clearly and concisely the whole doctrine of nonviolence: "The way of peace is the way of truth." "Truthfulness is even more important than peacefulness. Indeed, *lying is the mother of violence*. A truthful man cannot long remain violent. He will perceive in the course of his research that he has no need to be violent, and he will further discover that so long as there is the slightest trace of violence in him, he will fail to find the truth he is searching." Why can we not believe this immediately? Why do we doubt it? Why does it seem impossible? Simply because we are all, to some extent, liars.

345

* * *

The mother of all other lies is the lie we persist in telling ourselves about ourselves. And since we are not brazen enough liars to make ourselves believe our own lie individually, we pool all our lies together and believe them because they have become the big lie uttered by the *vox populi*, and this kind of lie we accept as ultimate truth. "A truthful man cannot long remain violent." But a violent man cannot begin to look for the truth. To start with, he wants to rest assured that his enemy is violent, and that he himself is peaceful. For then his violence is justified. How can he face the desperate labor of coming to recognize the great evil that needs to be healed in himself? It is much easier to set things right by seeing one's own evil incarnate in a scapegoat, and to destroy both the goat and the evil together.

* * *

Gandhi does not mean that everyone may expect to become nonviolent by wishing to do so. But that all who dimly realize their need for truth should seek it by the way of nonviolence, since there is really no other way. They may not fully succeed. Their success may be in fact very slight. But for a small measure of good will they will at least *begin* to attain the truth. Because of them there will be at least a little truth in the darkness of a violent world. This idea of Gandhi cannot, however, be understood unless we remember his basic optimism about human nature. He believed that in the hidden depths of our being, depths which are too often completely sealed off from our conscious and immoral way of life, we are more truly nonviolent than violent. He believed that love is more natural to us than hatred. That "truth is the law of our being."

If this were not so, then "lying" would not be the "mother of violence." The lie brings violence and disorder into our nature itself. It divides us against ourselves, alienates us from ourselves, makes us enemies of ourselves, and of the truth that is in us. From this division hatred and violence arise. We hate others because we cannot stand the disorder, the intolerable division in ourselves. We are violent to others because we are already divided by the inner violence of our infidelity to our own truth. Hatred projects this division outside ourselves into society.

This is not so far from the traditional doctrine of the Fathers of the Church concerning original sin! Note of course that the doctrine of original sin, properly understood, is *optimistic*. It does not teach that man is by nature evil, but that evil in him is unnatural, a disorder, a sin. If evil, lying, and hatred were natural to man, all men would be perfectly at home, perfectly happy in evil. Perhaps a few seem to find contentment in an unnatural state of falsity, hatred, and greed. They are not happy. Or if they are, they are unnatural.

* * *

Berdyaev pointed out that in the old days we used to read of utopias and lament the fact that they could not be actualized. Now we have awakened to the far greater problem: how to prevent utopias from being actualized.

* * *

Douglas Steere remarks very perceptively that there is a pervasive form of contemporary violence to which the idealist fighting for peace by nonviolent methods most easily succumbs: activism and overwork. The rush and pressure of modern life are a form, perhaps the most common form, of its innate violence. To allow oneself to be carried away by a multitude of conflicting concerns, to surrender to too many demands, to commit oneself to too many projects, to want to help everyone in everything is to succumb to violence. More than that, it is cooperation in violence. The frenzy of the activist neutralizes his work for peace. It destroys his own inner capacity for peace. It destroys the fruitfulness of his own work, because it kills the root of inner wisdom which makes work fruitful.

* * *

The tactic of nonviolence is a tactic of love that seeks the salvation and redemption of the opponent, not his castigation, humiliation, and defeat. A pretended nonviolence that seeks to defeat and humiliate the adversary by spiritual instead of physical attack is little more than a confession of weakness. True nonviolence is totally different from this, and much more difficult. It strives to operate without hatred, without hostility, and without resentment. It works without aggression, taking the side of the good that it is able to find already present in the adversary. This may be easy to talk about in theory. It is not easy in practice, especially when the adversary is aroused to a bitter and violent defense of an injustice which he believes to be just. We must therefore be careful how we talk about our opponents, and still more careful how we regulate our differences with our collaborators. It is possible for the most bitter arguments, the most virulent hatreds, to arise among those who are supposed to be working together for the noblest of causes. Nothing is better calculated to ruin and discredit a holy ideal than a fratricidal war among "saints."

* * *

American Catholics pray, no doubt sincerely, for the "conversion of Russia." Is this simply a desire that the Russians will stop menacing us, will stop being different from us, will stop challenging us, will stop trying to get ahead of us? Is it for this that we pray and do penance? That the Russians may all suddenly embrace the very same kind of Catholicism that is prevalent in the United States, along with all the social attitudes of American Catholics, all their customs, their religious clichés, and even their prejudices? This is a dream, and not even a very good one. It would indeed harm us greatly if all the rest of the world suddenly enclosed itself within our own limitations. Who would then challenge and complete us?

Until we recognize the right of other nations, races, and societies to be different from us and to stay different, to have different ideas and to open up new horizons, our prayer for their conversion will be meaningless. It will be no better and no worse, perhaps, than the Russian Communist's idea that we will someday become *exactly like him*. And if we are not prepared to do so . . . he will destroy us. For he wants us to have all his attitudes, his prejudices, and his limitations. Until we feel in our own hearts the sufferings, the desires, the needs, the fears of the Russians and Chinese as if they were our own, in spite of political differences, until we *want* their problems to be solved in much the same way as we want our own to be solved: until then it is useless to talk about "conversion"—it is a word without significance.

* * *

The realm of politics is the realm of waste. The Pharaohs at least built pyramids. With the labor of hundreds and thousands of slaves, they built temples, and they built pyramids. Perhaps in a certain sense this labor was wasted: yet it has meaning, and its meaning remains powerful and eloquent, if mysterious, after centuries. The work of the slaves was forced, it was cruel, but it was work. It still had a kind of human dimension. There was something of grandeur about it. The slaves lived, and saw "their" pyramids grow. Our century is not a century of pyramids, but of extermination camps: in which man himself is purely and deliberately wasted, and the sardonic gesture, saving the hair, the teeth, and the clothes of the victims, is simply a way of pointing to the *wasting of humanity*.

It was a way of saying: "These people, whom you think to be persons, whom you are tempted to value as having souls, as being spiritual, these are nothing, less than nothing. The detritus, the facts and chemicals that can be derived from them, the gold fillings in their teeth, their hair and skin, are more important than they. We are so much better and more human than they that we can afford to destroy a whole man in order to make a lampshade out of his skin. He is nothing!"

* * *

Religious belief, on the deepest level, is inevitably also a principle of freedom. To defend one's faith is to defend one's own freedom, and at least implicitly the freedom of everyone else. Freedom from what, and for what? Freedom from control that is not in some way immanent and personal, a power of love. Religious belief in this higher sense is then always a liberation from control by what is less than man, or entirely exterior to man. He who receives the grace of this kind of religious illumination is given a freedom and an experience which leave him no longer fully and completely subject to the forces of nature, to his own bodily and emotional needs, to the merely external and human dictates of society, the tyranny of dictatorships. This is to say that his attitude to life is independent of the power inevitably exercised over him, exteriorly, by natural forces, by the trials and accidents of life, by the pressures of a not always rational collectivity.

* * *

Since I am a Catholic, I believe, of course, that my Church guarantees for me the highest spiritual freedom. I would not be a Catholic if I did not believe this. I would not be a Catholic if the Church were merely an organization, a collective institution, with rules and laws demanding external conformity from its members. I see the laws of the Church, and all the various ways in which she exercises her teaching authority and her jurisdiction, as subordinate to the Holy Spirit and to the law of love. I know that my Church does not look like this to those who are outside her; to them the Church acts on a principle of authority but not of freedom. They are mistaken. It is in Christ and in His Spirit that true freedom is found, and the Church is His Body, living by His Spirit.

At the same time, this aspiration to spiritual, interior, and personal freedom is not foreign to the other branches of Christianity and to the other great religions of the world. It is one thing that all the higher religions have in common (though doubtless on different levels), and it would be no advantage to a Catholic to try to deny this: for what brings out the dignity and grandeur of all religion is by that very fact a point in favor of Catholicism also. It is true that in the Catholic Church we believe that we have truly received the Spirit of God, the Spirit of Sonship which makes us free with the freedom of the sons of God. It is true that Protestants make this claim no less firmly, and perhaps indeed it is characteristic of them to make it with great emphasis. I am not the one to judge each individual and sincere Protestant as wrong when he says this of himself. How do I know what grace God can and does give to the sincere evangelical Christian who obeys the light of his conscience and follows Christ according to the faith and love he has received? I am persuaded that he would have greater security and clearer light if he were in my Church, but he does not see this as I do, and for this there are deeper and more complex reasons than either he or I can understand. Let us try to understand them, but meanwhile let us continue each in his own way, seeking the light with all sincerity.

The Jews, too: the promise to Abraham is a promise of freedom, of independence under God, and the passage through the Red Sea was the passage out of Egyptian slavery into the liberty of the people God had formed and chosen for Himself, to be His own people, to live in fidelity to a covenant, which is a free agreement and a bond of liberty and love.

The fidelity of Israel to the covenant meant refusing to be enslaved by the fascination and lure of the cosmic nature cults, refusing to surrender to the blind cycle of nature and to the domination of the forces of the earth. What did the prophets protest against more than the infidelity by which Israel forfeited her freedom and her espousal to Yahweh in liberty and in love?

This same intransigeance is found in Islam: a freedom which lifts the believer above the limitations dictated by nature, by race, by society: incorporation in a higher community, delivered from the fascination of idols, even idols of the mind, and set free to travel in a realm of white-hot faith as bare and grand as the desert itself, faith in the One God, the compassionate and the merciful. What are compassion and mercy but the gifts of freedom to freedom? What are they but deliverance from limitation, slavery, doubt, subservience to passion and to prejudice?

Whatever may be said of the great Oriental religions and their "cosmic" character, they aim ultimately at liberation from the unending natural round, at freedom of spirit, at emptiness, and they all give man a principle of liberty by which he can rise above domination by necessity and process, study and judge the world around him, study and judge the forces of passion and delusion that go into operation when he confronts the world in his own isolated ego.

* * *

Freedom from domination, freedom to live one's own spiritual life, freedom to seek the highest truth, unabashed by any human pressure or any collective demand, the ability to say one's own "yes" and one's own "no" and not merely to echo the "yes" and the "no" of state, party, corporation, army, or system. This is inseparable from authentic religion. It is one of the deepest and most fundamental needs of man, perhaps the deepest and most crucial need of the human person as such: for without recognizing the challenge of this need no man can truly be a person, and therefore without it he cannot fully be a man either. The frustration of this deep need by irreligion, by secular and political pseudoreligion, by the mystiques and superstitions of totalitarianism, have made man morally sick in the very depths of his being. They have wounded and corrupted his freedom, they have filled his love with rottenness, decayed it into hatred. They have made man a machine geared for his own destruction.

* * *

It is because religion is a principle and source of the deepest freedom that all totalitarian systems, whether overt or implicit, must necessarily attack it. Yet at the same time the situation is very complex, because those who attack religion rarely do so except in the name of the same values which religion itself protects. All attacks on religious belief are to some extent to be seen as partial judgments passed by history on organized religion. The slightest failure in fidelity, in inner freedom, in integrity, in truth warrants an instant criticism and attack by those who wish to destroy religion by proving that it is not and has never been what it claims to be. The cult of the Absolute is attacked in the name of the Absolute. Truth is destroyed in the name of truth. But the fact that these attacks on religion generally lack understanding, and lack it because they lack compassion, and lack compassion because they do not know man, means that even the most sincere attack on religion always has in it some culpable blindness. This I do not say blaming men who, in attacking religion, have perhaps had more integrity than I have had in practicing it. But it is essential above all to understand that the basic principle of all spiritual freedom, all freedom from what is less than man, means first of all submission to what is more than man. And this submission begins with the recognition of our own limitation.

Hence, to attack religion because human beings have human limitations, and seek to be liberated from them, is a kind of pharisaism. But this pharisaism in turn is perhaps due in large measure to the pharisaism of religious people themselves who, once they have embraced a spiritual ideal as credible and worthy of admiration, at once begin to speak and act as if they had attained it.

* * *

We are afflicted, hesitant, dubious in our speech, above all where we know we are *obliged* to speak. Language has been so misused that we fear and mistrust it. We do not mind playing with words, manipulating them, but when the game gets serious we lose courage. And we lose courage for the silliest possible reason: our inborn natural sense of the *logos*, our love for reasonable expression, our healthy delight in it, shames us with a false sense of guilt. We are drawn to the logos with a strong and noble attraction, but at the same time held back by unnatural fear. The more earnestly we hope to tell the truth, the more secretly we are convinced that we will only add another lie to all the others told by our contemporaries. We doubt our words because we doubt our very selves—and woe to us if we do not doubt our words and ourselves!

There have been so many words uttered in contempt of truth, in despite of love, honor, justice, and of all that is good. Even these concepts themselves (truth, honor, goodness) have become sick and rotten to us, not because they are defiled, but because we are. Nevertheless, we must risk falsity, we must take courage and speak, we must use noble instruments of which we have become ashamed because we no longer trust ourselves to use them worthily. We must dare to think what we mean, and simply make clear statements of what we intend. This is our only serious protection against repeated spiritual defilement by the slogans and programs of the unscrupulous.

Clement of Alexandria remarks that Christ our Lord, taking bread, first spoke, blessing the bread, then broke it and gave it to His disciples, for He willed them to know what it was that He was giving them. The word, therefore, was as important as the act, and in both the Lord, Himself the Word of God, gave Himself to us.

Clement says: "Reasonable speech, logos, regenerates the soul and orients it towards the noble and beautiful act [Kalokagathia]. Blessed is he who is adept in both word and work. . . . That which the act presents to our sight, is made intelligible by the word. The word prepares the way for action and disposes the hearers to the practice of virtue. There is a saving word just as there is a saving work. And justice does not take shape without *logos*."

—*Stromateis I*, 10, n.46

* * *

Shall I say that we are confronted with a choice: either to live by the truth or be destroyed? (Pilate said: "What is truth?")

Shall I say that we are being given one last chance to be Christians, and that if we do not accept it, then we are done for? And not only we the "Christians," but also everybody in our society, the society once based on Christian principles?

Shall I say that we are offered one last opportunity to work out in practice the social implications of the Gospel, and that if we fail we shall have an earthly hell, and either be completely wiped out or doomed to a future of psychopathic horror in the new barbarism that must emerge from the ruins we have brought down upon our own heads?

Why should I use tired expressions like these: "The social implications of the Gospel?" Such words arouse no response. They no longer penetrate the mind of the hearer. But you see, we must begin at last to take to heart the words that mean something, and not simply those that awaken a reflex of some sort, a jolt, a shudder, a twitching of the head in the people who hear us.

Is it possible to transform the world on Christian principles? (And some people will wonder if it is even possible to ask this question with a straight face.)

What do you mean "Christian principles?"

Certainly *Mater et Magistra* and *Pacem in Terris* are clear enough statements of them. A society built on Christian principles is one in which every man has the right and opportunity to live in peace, to support himself by meaningful, decent, and productive work, work in which he has a considerable share of responsibility, work which is his contribution to the balance and order of a society in which a reasonable happiness is not impossible.

A Christian society? Such a society is not one that is run by priests, not even necessarily one in which everybody has to go to Church: it is one in which work is for production and not for profit, and production is not for its own sake, not merely for the sake of those who own the means of production, but for all who contribute in a constructive way to the process of production. A Christian society is one in which men give their share of labor and intelligence and receive their share of the fruits of the labor of all, and in which all this is seen in relation to a transcendental purpose, the "history of salvation," the Kingdom of God, a society centered upon the divine truth and the divine mercy.

Sometimes there may be a little truth in the suspicion that Christian social action lacks seriousness because it may be exploited for the sake of *something else* of an entirely different essence, something otherworldly that has nothing at all to do with things like wages and work, or with politics, war, and peace.

That is the trouble. We have got ourselves into a position where, because of our misunderstanding of theoretical distinctions between the "natural and the supernatural" we tend to think that nothing in man's ordinary life is really supernatural except saying prayers and performing pious acts of one sort or another, pious acts which derive their value precisely from the fact that they rescue us, momentarily, from the ordinary routine of life.

* * *

Since I am a man, my destiny depends on my human behavior: that is to say upon my decisions. I must first of all appreciate this fact, and weigh the risks and difficulties it entails. I must therefore know myself, and know both the good and the evil that are in me. It will not do to know only one and not the other: only the good, or only the evil. I must then be able to love the life God has given me, living it fully and fruitfully, and making good use even of the evil that is in it. Why should I love an ideal good in such a way that my life becomes more deeply embedded in misery and evil?

To live well myself is my first and essential contribution to the well-being of all mankind and to the fulfillment of man's collective destiny. If I do not live happily myself how can I help anyone else to be happy, or free, or wise? Yet to seek happiness is not to live happily. Perhaps it is more true to say that one finds happiness by not seeking it. The wisdom that teaches us deliberately to restrain our desire for happiness enables us to discover that we are already happy without realizing the fact.

To live well myself means for me to know and appreciate something of the secret, the mystery in myself: that which is incommunicable, which is at once myself and not myself, at once in me and above me. From this sanctuary I must seek humbly and patiently to ward off all the intrusions of violence and self-assertion. These intrusions cannot really penetrate the sanctuary, but they can draw me forth from it and slay me before the secret doorway.

If I can understand something of myself and something of others, I can begin to share with them the work of building the foundations for spiritual unity. But first we must work together at dissipating the more absurd fictions which make unity impossible.

* * *

How glad, how grateful men are when they can learn from another what they have already determined, in their hearts, to believe for themselves.

They do not realize that they have already promised their assent to this or that proposition: that they are committed to it in advance. When it comes to them from another they think they have made a discovery. They enjoy something of the excitement of discovery. They have, indeed, discovered a little of what was hidden in themselves: a legitimate joy.

Yet perhaps the other one only told them this because he, in turn, *sensed that it was what they wanted to hear from him.* He himself divined it in them: though of course it was also in himself. This, too, seemed a "discovery" to him.

Thus we encourage one another to cling firmly and blindly to prejudice.

* * *

The terrible thing about our time is precisely the ease with which theories can be put into practice. The more perfect, the more idealistic the theories, the more dreadful is their realization. We are at last beginning to rediscover what perhaps men knew better in very ancient times, in primitive times before utopias were thought of: that liberty is bound up with imperfection, and that limitations, imperfections, errors are not only unavoidable but also salutary.

The best is not the ideal. Where what is theoretically best is imposed on everyone as the *norm*, then there is no longer any room even to be good. The best, imposed as a norm, becomes evil.

One might argue that the best, the highest, is imposed on all in monasteries. Far from it: St. Benedict's principle is that the Rule should be moderate, so that the strong may desire to do more and the weak may not be overwhelmed and driven out of the cloister.

You must be free, and not involved. Solitude is to be preserved, not as a luxury but as a necessity: not for "perfection" so much as for simple "survival" in the life God has given you.

Hence, you must know when, how, and to whom you must say "no." This involves considerable difficulty at times. You must not hurt people, or want to hurt them, yet you must not placate them at the price of infidelity to higher and more essential values.

People are constantly trying to use you to help them create the particular illusions by which they live. This is particularly true of the collective illusions which sometimes are accepted as ideologies. You must renounce and sacrifice the approval that is only a bribe enlisting your support of a collective illusion. You must not allow yourself to be represented as someone in whom a few of the favorite daydreams of the public have come true. You must be willing, if necessary, to become a disturbing and therefore an undesired person, one who is not wanted because he upsets the general dream. But be careful that you do not do this in the service of some other dream that is only a little less general and therefore seems to you to be more real because it is more exclusive!

* * *

A distinction: to be "thought of" kindly by many and to "think of" them kindly is only a diluted benevolence, a collective illusion of friendship. Its function is not the sharing of love but complicity in a mutual reassurance that is based on nothing. Instead of cultivating this diffuse aura of benevolence, you should enter with trepidation into the deep and genuine concern for those few persons God has committed to your care—your family, your students, your employees, your parishioners. This concern is an involvement, a distraction, and it is vitally urgent. You are not allowed to evade it even though it may often disturb your "peace of mind." It is good and right that your peace should be thus disturbed, that you should suffer and bear the small burden of these cares that cannot usually be told to anyone. There is no special glory in this, it is only duty. But in the long run it brings with it the best of all gifts: it gives life.

Unlike the great benevolent and public movements, full of noisy and shared concern, it is not foggy, diffuse, devouring, and absurd. Only a personal concern of this kind leads to love.

* * *

There are various ways of being happy, and every man has the capacity to make his life what it needs to be for him to have a reasonable amount of peace in it. Why then do we persecute ourselves with illusory demands, never content until we feel we have conformed to some standard of happiness that is not good for us only, but for *everyone*? Why can we not be content with the secret gift of the happiness that God offers us, without consulting the rest of the world? Why do we insist, rather, on a happiness that is approved by the magazines and tv? Perhaps because we do not believe in a happiness that is given to us for nothing. We do not think we can be happy with a happiness that has no price tag on it.

If we are fools enough to remain at the mercy of the people who want to sell us happiness, it will be impossible for us ever to be content with anything. How would they profit if we became content? We would no longer need their new product.

The last thing the salesman wants is for the buyer to become content. You are of no use in our affluent society unless you are always just about to grasp what you never have.

The Greeks were not as smart as we are. In their primitive way they put Tantalus in hell. Madison Avenue, on the contrary, would convince us that Tantalus is in heaven.

God gives us freedom to make our own lives within the situation which is the gift of His love to us, and by means of the power His love grants us. But we feel guilty about it. We are quite capable of being happy in the life He has provided for us, in which we can contentedly make our own way, helped by His grace. We are ashamed to do so. For we need one thing more than happiness: we need approval. And the need for approval destroys our capacity for happiness. "How can you believe, who seek glory one from another?"

For in the United States, approval has to be bought—not once, not ten times, but a thousand times over every day.

Leon Bloy remarked on this characteristic of our society: A businessman will say of someone that he *knows* him if he *knows he has money.*

To say of someone "I do not know him" means, in business, "I am not so sure that he will pay."

But if he has money, and proves it, then "I know him."

So we have to get money and keep spending it in order to be known, recognized as human. Otherwise we are excommunicated.

* * *

Einstein was a great prophet of the now dead age of liberalism. He emerged with the disconcerting kindness and innocence of the liberal, came forth from the confusions of his day to produce for us all a little moment of clarity, and also, as an afterthought, he left us the atomic bomb. But we cannot take the bomb as a pretext for looking down on his liberalism, or doubting his benevolence.

* * *

Our thought should not merely be an answer to what some-one else has just said. Or what someone else might have said. Our interior word must be more than an echo of the words of someone else. There is no point in being a moon to somebody else's sun, still less is there any justification for our being moons of one another, and hence darkness to one another, not one of us being a true sun.

It may seem that a child begins by *answering* his parents. This is not true. What is important in the child is his primal ut-terance, his response to *being*, his own free cries and signs, his admiration.

It is true that he has to learn language. Unfortunately in learning to speak, he also learns to answer *as expected*. Thus he learns more than language: he acquires, with words themselves, a kind of servitude. He gives out the words that are asked of him, that evoke a pleasant or approving response. He ceases to acclaim reality and responds to demands, or evades punishment, or engineers consent. He does not merely answer: he conforms, or he resists. He is already involved in public relations.

Would that we could remember how to answer or to keep silence. To learn this, we must learn even to go without answer-ing. One may say: "But to answer is to love." Certainly there is no love without response. But merely to submit one's intelli-gence, to make a deal, to conciliate, to compromise with error or injustice is not love. Silence, too, is a response. It can at times be the response of a greater love, and of a love that does not endanger truth or sacrifice reason in order to placate a too de-manding or too needy lover.

St. Alphonsus Rodriguez said: "Answer nothing, nothing, nothing."

Johannes Baptist Metz
1928-

Fresh interpretations of the world and of the human being who rises up as world-builder are the stuff of which vibrant Christianity is made. The temptation to accept a set of dogmatic sounding statements as an accurate summary of existence and to cease questioning and searching is always an attractive one. Fortunately, theologians continue to appear who remind the Christian that he must push on in the effort to comprehend the mystery of the world and must seek new ways to interpret the situation in which Christianity finds itself.

Theology of the World *provides the serious Christian with insights that make it possible to shatter rigid intellectual frameworks and to construct a new approach to the problems that are pressing in upon modern man. As a fact, warfare, politics, terrorism, the nuclear age, international poverty and hunger, limited resources, population, and a host of other problems must be adequately resolved. The role that the Christian theology plays in resolving them depends on how relevant that theology is to modern life. Johannes B. Metz, professor of theology in Münster and author of* Theology of the World, *offers a thesis that is almost startling. Yet, when carefully thought through, it suggests a vision that may be broad enough to encompass the whole of modern man's problematic condition.*

As the title of the book indicates, Metz is concerned with the world, the secular, and the way it is interpreted by the Christian. He recognizes that Christians can simply ignore the world and go through their acts of piety behind locked doors as though there had never been a Pentecost, and they can move through time without noting the process of change. But such an attitude will render them irrelevant to the only world in which they dwell and reveal their fundamental rejection of the secularization of the world.

To counter this tendency, Metz proposes that the modern process of secularization has arisen not against Christianity but through it. "It is originally a Christian event and hence testifies in our world situation to the power of the 'hour of Christ' at work within history." The Incarnation marked the beginning of the secularization of the world. The birth of Christ released the world to find its own worldliness, a process which more than ever before brings world and God into union. Man appears as the mediator between God and world, and as Christian takes on responsibility for leaving the world its secularity. To Christianize the world means to secularize it, to bring it into its own, bestowing on it the scarcely conceived heights and depths of its own worldly being.

The passage below addresses the Christian's responsibility for planning the future in a secular world. Metz presents several characteristics of the world with which the Christian should be familiar and then explores the possible ways that the Christian can be involved in planning the world's future. He concludes that the much-vaunted progress of the technological era will be rather empty if not enriched by the Christian tradition of hope and love.

THEOLOGY OF THE WORLD

I should like to make two points concerning the particular responsibility of Christians in our planned technological society: one concerns the starting point of this responsibility, and the second the indirect, that is, socially critical forms of this responsibility.

1

Christian responsibility must take clear account of the situation in which and for which it seeks to present faith as hope. It must—briefly—begin by establishing the situation and giving an account of it. This account should at the same time show to what extent the "future" and, more specifically, a "planned or plannable future" is not today an arbitary, but a central theme and problem of the Christian's responsibility.

I should like to provide this résumé by first listing some characteristics of the world to which our Christian responsibility today must apply and from which it must start, and then by trying to gather these individual definitions to give a sense of that world and reality that governs our technological and plan-orientated attitude to the future.

(1) The place where the responsibility of the Christian community starts is *the world in its permanent and growing worldliness.* I am aware that this proposition, which I endeavored to develop some years ago, is not unproblematical and also not unambiguous. It was, moreover, questioned at the time. Nevertheless, I should like to retain this formula for this account, which is more in the nature of a preliminary reconnaissance.

A worldly world—this is not a metaphysical definition of the world, which would ultimately prove to be an empty pleonasm. It is, rather, an historical definition of the world in its present nature. And if it is described further as a world that remains and grows in its worldliness, then this means that worldliness does not have merely a transitional character, but that of an epoch, which helps to determine the world situation for the foreseeable future.

A worldly world—this is the result of an historical process that began in the West and today, as the world becomes increasingly unified, is rapidly becoming the situation of all people and all cultures. Let us briefly consider here its chief features in order to understand the situation from which Christian responsibility for the future begins.

(a) In Western history this process of the world becoming worldly has the form of "secularization." Since the late Middle Ages, slowly, but all the more definitely and irreversibly, man, his society, his science, his culture, his economy, have moved out of the great all-inclusive edifice that was medieval Christendom and its theopolitical structure, in which the theology and the Church possessed the key to every sphere of life. The political exodus begins early on: the national states emerge, press for autonomy, and create independent social and cultural centers. Since the time of Columbus men no longer go out to win back the Holy Land, but to discover the world. Philosophy throws off the tutelage of theology. As Kant was to put it later, it no longer wants to be a maidservant carrying the train of theology, but to carry the torch of reason in front of it. The Galileo affair was symptomatic of the momentous rejection by the natural sciences of the authority of the Christian understanding of the world. The age of the Enlightenment, on the one hand, and the political, social, scientific, and technological revolutions that began in it on the other, show that the world now to a special degree and in a hitherto unknown way becomes the business of man, that he, man, now orders his affairs himself and takes them under the protection of his freedom and his political responsibility. In a sense, the world determines itself. It sets itself its own goals, which emerge automatically from within itself. The social structure of this world is no longer given directly "by the grace of God," but its organization now depends on human conventions and goals. For a long time the

Church has observed this process only with resentment—to some extent even up to the recent council—regarding it exclusively as a falling away and a false emancipation and only very slowly finding the courage to let the world become secular in this sense and see this process not just as an event which is against the historical intentions of Christianity, but also as something that is partly determined by the innermost historical impulses of Christianity itself and its message.

(b) Moreover, this secularizing process—and this is of particular importance in this context—finds its form in the technological hominization and manipulation of the world. With the rise and development of the natural sciences, the world changed from being the environment enfolding man to being the object and material of transformation by man. "Whereas man in the pre-technological age knew only realizable aims set up by himself, inasmuch as they were pre-given by the structure of his own physical being and the reality surrounding it—whereas, in other words, he lived previously out of concrete "nature," pre-given to him and supporting him biologically and as a human being, he can now set himself aims (though not without limits) that he chooses arbitrarily, and in relation to them construct a . . . world that did not previously exist in order to reach them. He not only interprets the world about him and its effects in terms of his human life, but he creates this world himself." From being an observer man becomes the transformer of his world reality; from being *homo sapiens* he again becomes *homo faber*—"but this time the overseer of a world and through that more than ever the overseer of himself. No longer an animal that has to work, but a creator": *homo creator*, or, to put it more carefully, *homo manipulator*. And the world seems a world delivered up to him and his manipulation, a world hominized to an extreme degree. But this hominization is not limited to the pure world of natural objects; it is extended increasingly to *all* the spheres of man's life. It seems also to hand over the future of the world and of man more and more to rationalized planning. "Modern medicine and social medicine, modern sociology and similar branches of scientific anthropology testify to [such planning]. Modern biochemistry and genetics open up to man the first states in methods to manipulate the biological origin of his life. He does not just passively experience his social and political fate, but plans long-term social and political systems; he discovers and learns to use methods to manipulate ideologically both the individual and human collectives—methods which, even consciously, are no longer the simple communication of knowledge to the other and the appeal to his free decision, but which by means of scientific and psychological techniques are able to change the mentality of both the individual and human collectives. . . . Man manipulates man through all the newly created social networks provided by mass communications, by the consumer-goods system, by political education under authoritarian systems, and in many similar ways. For all these new social networks—and they do not just simply come into being, but are planned and carried out with full calculation of their effect on humanity—are just so many self-manipulations of man."

(c) The secularization process extends also to the radical *pluralization* of secular areas and to corresponding attitudes towards the secular. This state of affairs is familiar to us on all sides. The pluralization of our life, requiring as it does that we constantly change roles, often leads to a spiritual and intellectual "overburdening" which arouses in the inhabitants of this secular world quite new ways of seeking relief. The tendency grows to flee into an artificial world outside this one, there is a readiness to hand oneself over to an ideology which does away violently with these pluralist areas of life and experience and promises security. In his novel *The Man Without Qualities* Robert Musil describes this pluralistic situation and the consequences that follow from it: As "an inhabitant of Cacania," man in this pluralistic situation has at least nine characteristics, namely, "professional, national, state, class, geographical, sexual, conscious, unconscious, and perhaps also private. He unites them within himself, but they dissolve him, and he is really nothing but a small hollow in the ground that has been washed out by all these streams. . . . That is why every man has another, tenth character, namely, the passive fantasy of unfilled rooms. It allows man everything, but not the one thing of taking seriously what his at least nine other characters are doing and what happens to them; that is, in other words, precisely the one thing that should fill him."

(d) The process of the secularization of the world has, finally, from a religious point of view, the quality of *de-numinization,* or, as Max Weber expressed it, of "dispelling the magic" of the world. However much today it might have become fashionable theological jargon to speak of a de-numinized, de-divinized, God-less world, there is concealed behind this work an inescapable, stinging truth. A secularized world is the world that experiences itself in its non-divinity; a world whose frontiers do not shade off into the infinity of God; a world that is not itself directly diaphanous, as it were transparent towards God, that is a world in which God does not "appear"; a world that does not present itself to man as God's majestic and untouchable representative, but as the building-site and laboratory of man and his planning; a world that seems, therefore, to have come down from its high dignity as the creation of God; a world which does not *exist* in pre-established order and from which an "eternal order of things" could be read, but which is coming into being as a result of human action, in the process of directed scientific and technological planning or social and political revolutions. This is a world where man discovers not *vestigia Dei* in nature and history, but the marks of his own activity. It is a world where at the same time man comes upon himself everywhere and is constantly in danger of regarding himself in Promethean style as the creator of this world and its history *or* of despairing at its stony facelessness, its lack of promise, at the process of radical objectivization which he himself has "taken on"—with both extremes seeming finally to come together.

(2) In order to grasp this secular world in its full weight and definition before taking it as the starting point of our Christian responsibility for the future and above all to ask the specific question about our responsibility for the future, we must enquire into the unified and comprehensive world view that governs this manifold secularization process in which the pre-eminence of man and of human action is founded in the shaping and realization of the world. We may formulate this second step in our attempted résumé of our situation in the following propo-

sition: The process of the growing secularization of the world is governed by a world view that is coming into being in history beneath the primacy of the future.

The so-called "new age" in which the process of secularization is taking place is marked by a constant will towards the "new." This will towards the new operates on the basis of the social, political, and technological revolutions. Mankind in this new age seems to be fascinated by only one thing: the future as something that has not yet existed. The future is essentially reality that does not yet exist, that has never existed, that is truly "new." Our relation to this kind of future cannot therefore be purely contemplative or purely imaginative, since pure contemplation and pure imagination refer only to reality that already exists. Our relation to this future is markedly operative in character, and any theory of this relationship is therefore a theory that is related to action: it is characterized by a new relationship between theory and practice.

In this orientation towards the future man no longer experiences his world as something imposed on him by fate, as sovereign and untouchable nature surrounding him. The world appears rather as coming into being through him and his technological activity and hence becoming "worldly". The process of so-called "secularization," as we have endeavored to outline it above, and the primacy of the future in the modern view of the world are inwardly connected.

The categorical pre-eminence of the future in modern man's attitude to life and the world has been increasingly responsible for a crisis in the familiar religious concepts of the Christian faith. And the whole of the modern critique of religion, especially Marxist, could be summed up by saying that Christianity, like religion in general, is helpless against this primacy of the future in our understanding of the world. Thus this new world-awareness often regards itself as the liquidation of religious awareness, as the beginning of a poor-religious age, in which any orientation towards the beyond is seen to be purely speculative and must be replaced by an orientation towards a future conceived of purely in terms of planning and action.

This may, for all its brevity, serve to characterize the present situation from which Christian responsibility for the future has to start. I hope, at any rate, to have succeeded in showing that the question of responsibility for the future is not an arbitrary one, but central to the relationship between faith and the world today.

2

What form does the responsibility of the Christian community take and what possibilities are open to it in this situation? Is such responsibility still possible? And is it still necessary? How could it still be in any way a yardstick? How and where are there here today still points at which they intersect and therefore the beginnings of a fruitful conflict between the world process described and the Christian Gospel?

(1) Here we might consider, in a general theological way, the Christian responsibility for the one future of the world.

First, it could be shown that there is an inner causal connection between a view of the world governed by the primacy of reason—as an historical world actively coming into existence, and the Jewish-Christian view of the world found in scripture. This demonstration would not necessarily have anything to do with a subsequent adaptation of scriptural faith to the world situation described. This demonstration would not need to use intellectually dishonest tricks to make its point. It could serve chiefly to ask something more of faith and of the Christian community, namely, a readiness to share in the critical responsibility for the present world, not to seek the image of one's own future beside or above it, but in it, because faith itself is partly responsible historically for this world situation.

Second, the peculiar nature of the Christian conscience for the future could be explained, the specific form of Christian hope, and it could be clearly stated that this hope itself liberates the element of active shaping of the world, and that therefore the familiar alternative between orientation towards transcendence and orientation towards the future, between the promise and the historical demand, between expectation and fighting, between the eschatological hope of the Christian and the active shaping of the world, is fundamentally false. In this connection it would need to be shown that the hope which Christian faith has in regard to the future cannot be realized independently of

369

the world and its future, that this hope must answer, must be responsible for, the one promised future and hence also for the future of the world.

Neither of these general points can be pursued here. Moreover, as far as our subject is concerned, they are in constant danger of seeking to solve the particular problem by a mighty abstraction. The statement that Christian hope is not a sedative but a stimulator of active shaping of the world is correct, but it is still too general to suffice for the definition of the relationship between hoping and planning, between eschatological faith in the promise and technological planning for the future. When one talks in these generalities everything can be combined harmoniously. But what is the relation of Christian hope to *planning* for the future? And what is the relation between this technologically planned future and the expected future of the kingdom of God? This is a question we must face. We cannot get rid of it by ready distinctions, such as differentiating between a planned future of the world and a transcendental future of hope. It is precisely our problem that this planned future of the world seems more and more to take all the future from hope. "We must resolutely turn our backs on the easy distinctions that we always have to hand when we speak of the future in a Christian way; the distinction, for example, when we say that politics is concerned with the future of this world, whereas the Church is concerned with the transcendental future. Technology and economics plan the future of things, whereas faith keeps guard over the personal future. In practice we know what is coming, but not who is coming, whereas faith does not know what is coming, but rather who is coming." These distinctions do not help us. They do not solve and liberate, but only veil the truth. And the question remains: what is the particular nature of the Christian's responsibility for planning the future in our technological society?

(2) If I am right, this responsibility is of an *indirect* nature. This is that the Christian understanding of faith cannot interfere directly in the technological planning process. This planning process has its own laws and ways of proceeding. These laws are part of its nature. But is any other responsibility possible

towards this planning for the future except that of the immanent expert coping with things themselves?

Planning tasks, precisely when they are pursued in a comprehensive way and on a long-term basis, are always tasks involving government. Planning for the future is not only a technological and scientific, but also always a *political* problem. And the idea of a technocratic society in which, in place of politics, there is only technology, in which, then, all political problems of government are transformed into purely technological problems of planning, is an ideology, though perhaps a very modern one. "It is the case that pragmatic planning is dictated by the thing itself. But this compulsion does not work directly, but through the subjectivity of individuals and groups, in whose consciousness there are always those interests and needs from which alone the compulsion of the thing can be recognized. It is seldom enough that what the thing requires is obvious to everyone, and that it is, accordingly, at once possible to fulfill this demand. The usual situation is that of the clash of interests, the divergence of needs, of the complicated mutual interference and overlapping of these needs and interests. And the question of priority and of greater urgency is rarely settled by pure irresistible argument. It is also necessary to have influence. The social "pluralism" of organized interests is not made unpolitical by planning, but, on the contrary, is made political in the extreme. All planning of any dimension involves many different interests in many different ways, calling them forth and furthering their organization. Whoever wants to carry through planning must, therefore, in the classical sense, act "politically" and advance his plan, or himself, to those places where the decisions are made. This is the reason for the fact that, against the expectations nourished by the idea of technocracy, technicians and planning experts are increasingly involved in politics, instead of living in the certain expectation of the euthanasia of politics." The irremovable gap between planning and political domination is also confirmed by modern scientific theories of decisions, which work with cybernetic and mathematical, sociological, economic, and other models. For these theories can certainly rationalize social and political practice *within* a particular nexus of ends and means, but with its methods it cannot decide the priorities of the purpose to be pursued. Here decision—despite this scientific rationalization—becomes again a political problem.

It is at this point of the social and political dimension of planning for the future that the responsibility of the Christian indirectly begins: not by the Christian community itself again pressing towards political domination, but by its speaking from out of its Christian conscience on behalf of the future and making a liberating critique of the social and political reality in which these planning arrangements are set up. This requires, of course, that the Christian community mobilizes in a quite new way the socially critical and, as it were, "political" potentiality of its faith and its hope and love.

The Christian community finds the theological basis of its socially critical task in the eschatological dimension of its self-understanding, which is at the same time a dimension of universal humanization. And these eschatological promises of the scriptural tradition—freedom, peace, justice, reconciliation—cannot be made private. They force one ever anew into social responsibility. It is true that these promises cannot be identified with any social situation that has been achieved. In these identifications, of which the history of Christianity is full, that "eschatological proviso" which reveals the provisional nature of every stage that society has attained is abandoned. In its provisionless, be it noted, not in its arbitrariness. For this "eschatological proviso" does not create in us a negative, but a dialectical and critical attitude to the society we are faced with. The promises to which it refers are not an empty horizon of vague religious expectations, but a critical and liberating imperative for our own present time. They are a spur and a task to make them effective in the historical conditions of our time and thus to "make them true." Our orientations towards these promises therefore, constantly changes anew our present historical awareness. It brings and forces us constantly into a critical and liberating position towards the social circumstances about us.

We cannot here elaborate on the socially critical task of Christian faith and the Christian community. Precisely in regard to its responsibility for the planning process in our technological society the Christian community must discover its "public" responsibility anew, that is, in a second act of self-understanding—not in order to develop its own social and political conception separate from others, in a kind of "ideological self-authorization," but in order to bring out the socially critical elements that are contained in the eschatological Gospel. Its "public" responsibility, therefore, is a responsibility that is critically liberating. As a socially separate institution the Christian community can formulate its universal claim in a pluralistic society without ideology only if it presents it *as criticism*. In conclusion I should like to mention some of these critical elements in regard to our planned technological society:

(a) The Christian community must mobilize its socially critical potentiality, in the sense that it must protest against every attempt to regard the individual living at the moment simply as the material and the means for building up a technologically rationalized future, seeing individuality only as a function of a technologically governed social process. Here more than ever it must become the advocate of the poor and oppressed, who are "poor" precisely because they cannot be defined by the value of their position in the so-called progress of mankind.

(b) The Christian community will constantly assert in the public awareness of our social and political reality the gap between hope and planning: the gap that exists between what is sought in every movement towards the future and what has already been achieved. "What is really disappointing is experienced or predicted human life as it emerges or will emerge out of industrial society . . . As long as socialism is being built up, it can preserve the magic of genuine transcendence. In the degree to which it is built up it loses this magic . . . But can man live without any transcendence, after the transcendence of the future which follows the transcendence of God has been eliminated?" Hence the Christian community, for whom history *as a whole* stands beneath the "eschatological promise" of God, will not object to any attempt to make the future *as a whole* the content of technological planning and hence secretly—in a suspect ideological way—making science and technology the subjective content of the whole of history.

(c) As we have remarked earlier, the technological planning process has priorities and preferences in its programming which are not purely technological and rational, but social and political. Here the Christian community, with its testimony of love, will work so that in this social and political reality an awareness of solidarity grows up which does not shut its eyes to the needs of others and hence of the men to come, and which therefore concentrates the technological process of planning more than before on those troubles that threaten in our own time and, above all, in the foreseeable future as well: famine due to over-population, extreme contrast in economic conditions, educational opportunities, epidemic illnesses, and so forth. Thus the indirect form of the responsibility of the Christian community for planning for the future requires the "publication," the socially critical mobilization of its original heritage: hope and love. The Christian community must bring this "tradition" of hope and love into our planned society, which is more and more losing its memory and therefore losing its history. Without it our much-vaunted progress will lack that creative and liberating resistance through which alone it has a chance of truly being called "progress."

Gustavo Gutiérrez
1928-

To most North American Catholics, Latin America is a
general term used to describe all those countries south of the
United States that need the help of missionaries in order to be
saved. It is only in recent years that people in the United States
have become aware of the rich cultures that once existed in Latin
America and have learned something of the way that the countries of Latin America have been exploited and oppressed. The
peoples of Latin America have begun to speak out to the rest of
the world, demanding that social justice be administered in their
behalf. The dehumanizing situation in which they have been
forced to dwell is almost beyond comprehension. Increased
knowledge of it can only make the North American Christian
uncomfortable and raise serious questions: In the light of this
situation, how should Christianity respond? At what point does
fidelity to the gospel message call for revolution? Within the
context of exploitation and oppression, what is the meaning of
basic Christian terms, such as community, faith, love, commitment, salvation, Jesus Christ?

Central to the Latin American experience, from the Christian perspective, is a style of theological reflection that is
anchored in the traditions and tragedies of the people of these
countries. It is referred to as "liberation theology." In an age in
which international relationships are becoming more common,

it is essential that the Christian be aware of this theology and make use of it in constructing an adequate contemporary world view.

We have chosen portions of A Theology of Liberation, *by Gustavo Gutiérrez, to introduce the North American reader to the theological reflection that has been developing for several years in Latin America. Father Gutiérrez is considered to be one of the outstanding proponents of liberation theology and perhaps one of the most important Christian theorists in the world today.*

His starting point is the experience of shared efforts to abolish the current unjust situation in Latin America and to build a different society, freer and more human. His goal is to think through the Christian faith, strengthen Christian love, and give reason to Christian hope from within a commitment which seeks to become more radical, total, and efficacious. Given the conditions of life now existing in Latin America, he questions the very meaning of Christianity and the mission of the Church.

After exploring the concepts of theology and liberation, Father Gutiérrez attempts to clarify the fundamental problem confronting Christianity in Latin America today. He evaluates the options that lie before the Latin American Church and proposes a perspective into which the problems of the Church can be incorporated. While cautioning the Church not to fall into intellectual self-satisfaction and triumphalism, he calls for a day by day acceptance of the gift of the spirit. The test of the Church's authenticity in Latin America will be the degree to which she lives genuine solidarity with the exploited masses and participates in liberating man from everything that dehumanizes him.

A THEOLOGY OF LIBERATION

The world today is experiencing a profound and rapid socio-cultural transformation. But the changes do not occur at a uniform pace, and the discrepancies in the change process have differentiated the various countries and regions of our planet.

Contemporary man has become clearly aware of this unequal process of transformation, of its economic causes, and of the basic relationships which combine to determine conditions and approaches. He examines his own circumstances and compares them to those of others; since he lives in a world where communication is fast and efficient, the conditions in which others live are no longer distant and unknown. But man goes beyond the limited expectations which such a comparison might create. He sees the process of transformation as a quest to satisfy the most fundamental human aspirations—liberty, dignity, the possibility of personal fulfillment for all. Or at least he would like the process to be moving toward these goals. He feels that the satisfaction of these aspirations should be the purpose of all organization and social activity. He knows also that all his plans are possible, able to be at least partially implemented.

Finally, history demonstrates that the achievements of humanity are cumulative; their effects and the collective experience of the generations open new perspectives and allow for even greater achievements in the generations yet to come.

The phenomenon of the awareness of differences among countries characterizes our era, due to the bourgeoning of communications media; it is particularly acute in those countries less favored by the evolution of the world economy—the poor countries where the vast majority of people live. The inhabitants of these countries are aware of the unacceptable living conditions of most of their countrymen. They confirm the explanation that these inequalities are caused by a type of relationship which often has been imposed upon them. For these reasons, the efforts for social change in these areas are characterized both by a great urgency and by conflicts stemming from differences of expectations, degrees of pressure, and existing systems of relationships and power. It is well to clarify, on the one hand, that the current (and very recent) level of expectations of the poor countries goes far beyond a mere imitation of the rich countries and is of necessity somewhat indistinct and imprecise. On the other hand, both the internal heterogeneity and the presence of external determinants in these societies contribute to defining different needs in different groups. All of this causes a dynamics of action which is inevitably conflictual.

The poor countries are not interested in modeling themselves after the rich countries, among other reasons because they are increasingly more convinced that·the status of the latter is the fruit of injustice and coercion. It is true that the poor countries are attempting to overcome material insufficiency and misery, but it is in order to achieve a more human society.

THE CONCEPT OF DEVELOPMENT

The term *development* seems tentatively to have synthesized the aspirations of people today for more human living conditions. The term itself is not new, but its current usage in the social sciences is new, for it responds to a different set of issues which has emerged only recently. Indeed, the old wealth-poverty antinomy no longer expresses all the problems and contemporary aspirations of mankind.

Origin

For some, the origin of the term *development* is, in a sense, negative. They consider it to have appeared in opposition to the term *underdevelopment,* which expressed the situation—and anguish—of the poor countries compared with the rich countries.

It would perhaps be helpful to recall some of the more important trends which helped clarify the concept of development.

First of all, there is the work of Joseph A. Schumpeter, the first economist after the English classics and Marx to concern himself with long-term processes. Schumpeter studied a capitalism characterized by a "circular flow," that is, a system which repeats itself from one period to the next and does not suffer appreciable structural change. The element which breaks this equilibrium and introduces a new dynamism is an *innovation*. Innovations are on the one hand technico-economic, since they are supposed to have originated in these areas; but they are simultaneously politico-social, because they imply contradicting and overcoming the prevailing system. Schumpeter calls this process *Entwicklung*, which today is translated as "development," although earlier renderings were "evolution" or "unfolding."

The work of the Australian economist Colin Clark represents another important contribution. Clark affirms that the objective of economic activity is not wealth, but well-being, a term understood to mean the satisfaction derived from the resources at one's disposal. He proposes to measure well-being by making comparisons in time and space. The differences among countries are shown by various indicators. His calculations show that the highest levels of well-being are found in the industrialized countries. Clark designated the road toward industrialization which poor countries are to follow as "progress" (not development).

The Bandung Conference of 1955 also played an important role in the evolution of the term, although on a different level. A large number of countries met there, especially Asian and African countries. They recognized their common membership in a Third World—underdeveloped and facing two developed worlds, the capitalist and the socialist. This conference marked the beginning of a policy which was supposed to lead out of this state of affairs. Although the deeds that followed did not always correspond to the expectations aroused, Bandung nevertheless signalled a deepened awareness of the fact of underdevelopment and a proclamation of its unacceptability.

Approaches

The concept of development has no clear definition; there are a variety of ways to regard it. Rather then reviewing them all at length, we will recall briefly the general areas involved.

Development can be regarded as purely economic, and in that sense it would be synonymous with *economic growth.*

The degree of development of a country could be measured, for example, by comparing its gross national product or its per capita income with those of a country regarded as highly developed. It is also possible to refine this gauge and make it more complex, but the presuppositions would still be the same: development consists above all in increased wealth or, at most, a higher level of well-being.

Historically, this is the meaning which appears first. What led to this point of view was perhaps the consideration of the process in England, the first country to develop and, understandably enough, the first to be studied by economists. This viewpoint was later reinforced by the mirage which the well-being of the rich nations produced.

Those who champion this view today, at least explicitly, are few in number. Currently its value lies in serving as a yardstick to measure more integral notions. However, this focus continues to exist in a more or less subtle form in the capitalistic view of development.

The deficiencies of the above-mentioned view have led to another more important and more frequently held one. According to it, development is a *total social process,* which includes economic, social, political, and cultural aspects. This notion stresses the interdependence of the different factors. Advances in one area imply advances in all of them and, conversely, the stagnation of one retards the growth of the rest.

A consideration of development as a total process leads one to consider also all the external and internal factors which affect the economic evolution of a nation as well as to evaluate the distribution of goods and services and the system of relationships among the agents of its economic life. This has been carefully worked out by social scientists concerned with so-called Third World countries. They have reached the conclusion that the dynamics of world economics leads simultaneously to the creation of greater wealth for the few and greater poverty for the many.

From all this flows a strategy of development which, taking into account the different factors, will allow a country to advance both totally and harmoniously and to avoid dangerous setbacks.

To view development as a total social process necessarily implies for some an ethical dimension, which presupposes a concern for human values. The step toward an elaboration of a *humanistic perspective* of development is thus taken unconsciously, and it prolongs the former point of view without contradicting it.

Francois Perroux worked consistently along these lines. Development for him means "the combination of mental and social changes of a people which enable them to increase, cumulatively and permanently, their total real production." Going even further, he says, "Development is achieved fully in the measure that, by reciprocity of services, it prepares the way for reciprocity of consciousness."

It would be a mistake to think that this point of view, which is concerned with human values, is the exclusive preserve of scholars of a Christian inspiration. Converging viewpoints are found in Marxist-inspired positions.

This humanistic approach attempts to place the notion of development in a wider context: a historical vision in which mankind assumes control of its own destiny. But this leads precisely to a change of perspective which—after certain additions and corrections—we would prefer to call liberation. We shall attempt to clarify this below.

THE PROCESS OF LIBERATION

From the Critique of Developmentalism to Social Revolution

The term *development* has synthesized the aspirations of poor peoples during the last few decades. Recently, however, it has become the object of severe criticism due both to the deficiencies of the development policies proposed to the poor countries to lead them out of their underdevelopment and also

381

to the lack of concrete achievements of the interested governments. This is the reason why *developmentalism (desarrollismo)*, a term derived from *development (desarrollo)*, is now used in a pejorative sense, especially in Latin America.

Much has been said in recent times about development. Poor countries competed for the help of the rich countries. There were even attempts to create a certain development mystique. Support for development was intense in Latin America in the '50s, producing high expectations. But since the supporters of development did not attack the roots of the evil, they failed and caused instead confusion and frustration.

One of the most important reasons for this turn of events is that development—approached from an economic and modernizing point of view—has been frequently promoted by international organizations closely linked to groups and governments which control the world economy. The changes encouraged were to be achieved within the formal structure of the existing institutions without challenging them. Great care was exercised, therefore, not to attack the interests of large international economic powers nor those of their natural allies, the ruling domestic interest groups. Furthermore, the so-called changes were often nothing more than new and underhanded ways of increasing the power of strong economic groups.

Developmentalism thus came to be synonymous with *reformism* and modernization, that is to say, synonymous with timid measures, really ineffective in the long run and counterproductive to achieving a real transformation. The poor countries are becoming ever more clearly aware that their underdevelopment is only the by-product of the development of other countries, because of the kind of relationship which exists between the rich and the poor countries. Moreover, they are realizing that their own development will come about only with a struggle to break the domination of the rich countries.

This perception sees the conflict implicit in the process. Development must attack the root causes of the problems and among them the deepest is economic, social, political and cultural dependence of some countries upon others—an expression of the domination of some social classes over others. Attempts to bring about changes within the existing order have proven futile. This analysis of the situation is at the level of scientific rationality. Only a radical break from the status quo, that is, a profound transformation of the private property system, access to power of the exploited class, and a social revolution that would break this dependence would allow for the change to a new society, a socialist society—or at least allow that such a society might be possible.

In this light, to speak about the process of *liberation* begins to appear more appropriate and richer in human content. Liberation in fact expresses the inescapable moment of radical change which is foreign to the ordinary use of the term *development*. Only in the context of such a process can a policy of development be effectively implemented, have any real meaning, and avoid misleading formulations.

Man, the Master of his Own Destiny

To characterize the situation of the poor countries as dominated and oppressed leads one to speak of economic, social, and political liberation. But we are dealing here with a much more integral and profound understanding of human existence and its historical future.

A broad and deep aspiration for liberation inflames the history of mankind in our day, liberation from all that limits or keeps man from self-fulfillment, liberation from all impediments to the exercise of his freedom. Proof of this is the awareness of new and subtle forms of oppression in the heart of advanced industrial societies, which often offer themselves as models to the underdeveloped countries. In them subversion does not appear as a protest against poverty, but rather against wealth. The context in the rich countries, however, is quite different from that of the poor countries: we must beware of all kinds of imitations as well as new forms if imperialism—revolutionary this time—of the rich countries, which consider themselves central to the history of mankind. Such mimicry would only lead the revolutionary groups of the Third World to a new deception regarding their own reality. They would be led to fight against windmills.

But, having acknowledged this danger, it is important to remember also that the poor countries would err in not following these events closely since their future depends at least partially upon what happens on the domestic scene in the dominant countries. Their own efforts at liberation cannot be indifferent to that proclaimed by growing minorities in rich nations. There are, moreover, valuable lessons to be learned by the revolutionaries of the countries on the periphery, who could in turn use them as corrective measures in the difficult task of building a new society.

What is at stake in the South as well as in the North, in the West as well as the East, on the periphery and in the center is the possibility of enjoying a truly human existence, a free life, a dynamic liberty which is related to history as a conquest. We have today an ever-clearer vision of this dynamism and this conquest, but their roots stretch into the past.

The fifteenth and sixteenth centuries are important milestones in man's understanding of himself. His relationship with nature changed substantially with the emergence of experimental science and the techniques of manipulation derived from it. Relying on these achievements, man abandoned his former image of the world and himself. Gilson expresses this idea in a well-known phrase: "It is because of its physics that metaphysics grows old." Because of science man took a step forward and began to regard himself in a different way. This process indicates why the best philosophical tradition is not merely an armchair product; it is rather the reflective and thematic awareness of man's experience of his relationships with nature and with other men. And these relationships are interpreted and at the same time modified by advances in technological and scientific knowledge.

Descartes is one of the great names of the new physics which altered man's relationship to nature. He laid the cornerstone of a philosophical reflection which stressed the primacy of thought and of "clear and distinct ideas," and so highlighted the creative aspects of human subjectivity. Kant's "Copernican Revolution" strengthened and systematized this point of view. For him our concept ought not to conform to the objects, but rather "the objects, or, in which is the same thing, that experience, which alone as given objects they are *cognized,* must conform to my conceptions." The reason is that "we only cognize in things *a priori* that which we ourselves place in them." Kant was aware that this leads to a "new method" of thought, to a knowledge which is critical of its foundations and thus abandons its naiveté and enters an adult stage.

Hegel followed this approach, introducing with vitality and urgency the theme of history. To a great extent his philosophy is a reflection on the French Revolution. This historical event had vast repercussions, for it proclaimed the right of every man to participate in the direction of the society to which he belongs. For Hegel man is aware of himself "only by being acknowledged or 'recognized' " by another consciousness. But this being recognized by another presupposes an initial conflict, "a life-and-death struggle," because it is "solely by risking life that freedom is obtained."

Through the lord-bondsman dialectic (resulting from this original confrontation), the historical process will then appear as the genesis of consciousness and therefore of the gradual liberation of man. Through the dialectical process man constructs himself and attains a real awareness of his own being; he liberates himself in the acquisition of genuine freedom which through work transforms the world and educates man. For Hegel "world history is the progression of the awareness of freedom." Moreover, the driving force of history is the difficult conquest of freedom, hardly perceptible in its initial stages. It is the passage from awareness of freedom to real freedom. "It is Freedom in itself that comprises within itself the infinite necessity of bringing itself to consciousness and thereby, since knowledge about itself is its very nature, to reality." Thus man gradually takes hold of the reins of his own destiny. He looks ahead and turns towards a society in which he will be free of all alienation and servitude. This focus will initiate a new dimension in philosophy: social criticism.

Marx deepened and renewed this line of thought in his unique way. But this required what has been called an "epistemological break" (a notion taken from Gaston Bachelard) with previous thought. The new attitude was expressed clearly in the famous *Theses on Feuerbach,* in which Marx presented concisely but penetratingly the essential elements of his approach. In them, especially in the First Thesis, Marx situated himself equidistant between the old materialism and idealism; more precisely, he presented his position as the dialectical transcendence of both. Of the first he retained the affirmation of the objectivity of the external world; of the second he kept man's transforming capacity. For Marx, to know was something indissolubly linked to the transformation of the world through work. Basing his thought on these first intuitions, he went on to construct a scientific understanding of historical reality. He analyzed capitalistic society, in which were found concrete instances of the exploitation of man by his fellows and of one social class by another. Pointing the way towards an era in history when man can live humanly, Marx created categories which allowed for the elaboration of a science of history.

The door was opened for science to help man take one more step on the road of critical thinking. It made him more aware of the socio-economic determinants of his ideological creations and therefore freer and more lucid in relation to them. But at the same time these new insights enabled man to have greater control and rational grasp of his historical initiatives. (This interpretation is valid unless of course one holds a dogmatic and mechanistic interpretation of history.) These initiatives ought to assure the change from the capitalistic mode of production to the socialistic mode, that is to say, to one oriented towards a society in which man can begin to live freely and humanly. He will have controlled nature, created the conditions for a socialized production of wealth, done away with private acquisition of excessive wealth, and established socialism.

But modern man's aspirations include not only liberation from *exterior* pressures which prevent his fulfillment as a member of a certain social class, country, or society. He seeks likewise an *interior* liberation, in an individual and intimate dimension; he seeks liberation not only on a social plane but also on a psychological. He seeks an interior freedom understood however not as an ideological evasion from social confrontation or as the internalization of a situation of dependency. Rather it must be in relation to the real world of the human psyche as understood since Freud.

A new frontier was in effect opened up when Freud highlighted the unconscious determinants of human behavior, with repression as the central element of man's psychic make-up. Repression is the result of the conflict between instinctive drives and the cultural and ethical demands of the social environment. For Freud, unconscious motivations exercise a tyrannical power and can produce aberrant behavior. This behavior is controllable only if the subject becomes aware of these motivations through an accurate reading of the new language of meanings created by the unconscious. Since Hegel we have seen *conflict* used as a germinal explanatory category and *awareness* as a step in the conquest of freedom. In Freud however they appear in a psychological process which ought also to lead to a fuller liberation of man.

The scope of liberation on the collective and historical level does not always and satisfactorily include psychological liberation. Psychological liberation includes dimensions which do not exist in or are not sufficiently integrated with collective, historical liberation. We are not speaking here, however, of facilely separating them or putting them in opposition to one another. "It seems to me," writes David Cooper, "that a cardinal failure of all past revolutions has been the dissociation of liberation on the mass social level, i.e. liberation of whole classes in economic and political terms, and liberation on the level of the individual and the concrete groups in which he is directly engaged. If we are to talk of revolution today our talk will be meaningless unless we effect some union between the macro-social and micro-social, and between 'inner reality' and 'outer reality.' " Moreover, alienation and exploitation as well as the very struggle for liberation from them have ramifications on the personal and psychological planes which it would be dangerous to overlook in the process of constructing a new society and a new man. These personal aspects—considered not as excessively privatized but rather as encompassing all human dimensions—are also under consideration in the contemporary debate concerning greater participation of all in political activity. This is so even in a socialist society.

In this area, Marcuse's attempt, under the influence of Hegel and Marx, to use the psychoanalytical categories for social criticism is important. Basing his observations on a work which Freud himself did not hold in high regard, *Civilization and its Discontents,* Marcuse analyzes the *over-repressive* character of the affluent society and envisions the possibility of a non-repressive society, a possibility skeptically denied by Freud. Marcuse's analyses of advanced industrial society, capitalistic or socialistic, lead him to denounce the emergence of a one-dimensional and oppressive society. In order to achieve this non-repressive society, however, it will be necessary to challenge the values espoused by the society which denies man the possibility of living freely. Marcuse labels this the Great Refusal: "the specter of a revolution which subordinates the development of the productive forces and higher standards of living to the requirements of creating solidarity for the human species, for abolishing poverty and misery beyond all national frontiers and spheres of interest, for the attainment of peace."

We are not suggesting, of course, that we should endorse without question every aspect of this development of ideas. There are ambiguities, critical observations to be made, and points to be clarified. Many ideas must be reconsidered in the light of a history that advances inexorably, simultaneously confirming and rejecting previous assertions. Ideas must be reconsidered too in light of praxis, which is the proving ground of all theory, and in light of socio-cultural realities very different from those from which the ideas emerged. But all this should not lead us to an attitude of distrustful reserve toward these ideas; rather it should suggest that the task to be undertaken is formidable. And the task is all the more urgent because these reflections are attempts to express a deeply-rooted sentiment in today's masses: the aspiration to liberation. This aspiration is still confusedly perceived, but there is an ever greater awareness of it. Furthermore, for many people in various ways this aspiration—in Vietnam or Brazil, New York or Prague—has become a norm for their behavior and a sufficient reason to lead lives of dedication. Their commitment is the backbone which validates and gives historical viability to the development of the ideas outlined above.

To conceive of history as a process of the liberation of man is to consider freedom as a historical conquest; it is to understand that the step from an abstract to a real freedom is not taken without a struggle against all the forces that oppress man, a struggle full of pitfalls, detours, and temptations to run away. The goal is not only better living conditions, a radical change of structures, a social revolution; it is much more: the continuous creation, never ending, of a new way to be a man, a *permanent cultural revolution.*

In other words, what is at stake above all is a dynamic and historical conception of man, oriented definitively and creatively toward his future, acting in the present for the sake of tomorrow. Teilhard de Chardin has remarked that man has taken hold of the reins of evolution. History, contrary to essentialist and static thinking, is not the development of potentialities preexistent in man; it is rather the conquest of new, qualitatively different ways of being a man in order to achieve an ever more total and complete fulfillment of the individual in solidarity with all mankind.

The Concept of Liberation Theologically Considered

Although we will consider liberation from a theological perspective more extensively later, it is important at this time to attempt an initial treatment in the light of what we have just discussed.

The term *development* is relatively new in the texts of the ecclesiastical magisterium. Except for a brief reference by Pius XII, the subject is broached for the first time by John XXIII in the encyclical letter *Mater et Magistra. Pacem in terris* gives the term special attention. *Gaudium et spes* dedicates a whole section to it, though the treatment is not original. All these documents stress the urgency of eliminating the existing injustices and the need for an economic development geared to the service of man. Finally, *Populorum progressio* discusses development as its central theme. Here the language and ideas are clearer, the adjective *integral* is added to development, putting things in a different context and opening new perspectives.

These new viewpoints were already hinted at in the sketchy discussion of Vatican Council II on dependence and liberation. *Gaudium et spes* points out that "nations on the road to progress . . . continually fall behind while very often their *dependence* on wealthier nations deepens more rapidly, even in the economic sphere" (no. 9). Later it acknowledges that "although nearly all peoples have gained their independence, it is still far from true that they are free from excessive inequalities and from every form of *undue dependence*" (no. 85).

These assertions should lead to a discernment of the need to be free from the dependence, to be liberated from it. The same *Gaudium et spes* on two occasions touches on liberation and laments the fact that it is seen exclusively as the fruit of human effort: "Many look forward to a genuine and total *emancipation* of humanity wrought solely by human effort. They are convinced that the future rule of man over the earth will satisfy every desire of his heart" (no. 10). Or it is concerned that liberation be reduced to a purely economic and social level: "Among the forms of modern atheism is that which anticipates the *liberation* of man especially through his economic and social emancipation" (no. 20). These assertions presuppose, negatively speaking, that liberation must be placed in a wider context; they criticize a narrow vision. They allow, therefore, for the possibility of a "genuine and total" liberation.

Unfortunately, this wider perspective is not elaborated. We find some indications, however, in the texts in which *Gaudium et spes* speaks of the birth of a "new humanism, one in which man is defined first of all by his responsibility toward his brothers and toward history" (no. 55). There is a need for men who are makers of history, "men who are truly new and artisans of a new humanity" (no. 30), men moved by the desire to build a really new society. Indeed, the conciliar document asserts that beneath economic and political demands "lies a deeper and more widespread longing. Persons and societies thirst for a full and free life worthy of man—one in which they can subject to their own welfare all that the modern world can offer them so abundantly" (no. 9).

All this is but a beginning. It is an oft-noted fact that *Gaudium et spes* in general offers a rather irenic description of the human situation; it touches up the uneven spots, smoothes the rough edges, avoids the more conflictual aspects, and stays away from the sharper confrontations among social classes and countries.

The encyclical *Populorum progressio* goes a step further. In a somewhat isolated text it speaks clearly of "building a world where every man, no matter what his race, religion or nationality, can live a fully human life, freed from servitude imposed on him by other men or by natural forces over which he has not sufficient control" (no. 47). It is unfortunate, however, that this idea was not expanded in the encyclical. From this point of view, *Populorum progressio* is a transitional document. Although it energetically denounces the "international imperialism of money," "situations whose injustice cries to heaven," and the growing gap between rich and poor countries, ultimately it addresses itself to the great ones of this world urging them to carry out the necessary changes. The outright use of the language of liberation, instead of its mere suggestion, would have given a more decided and direct thrust in favor of the oppressed, encouraging them to break with their present situation and take control of their own destiny.

The theme of liberation appears more completely discussed in the message from eighteen bishops of the Third World, published as a specific response to the call made by *Populorum progressio*. It is also treated frequently—almost to the point of being a synthesis of its message—in the conclusions of the Second General Conference of Latin American Bishops held in Medellín, Colombia, in 1968, which have more doctrinal authority than the eighteen bishops' message. In both these documents the focus has changed. The situation is not judged from the point of view of the countries at the center, but rather of those on the periphery, providing insiders' experience of their anguish and aspirations.

The product of a profound historical movement, this aspiration to liberation is beginning to be accepted by the Christian community as a sign of the times, as a call to commitment and interpretation. The Biblical message, which presents the work of Christ as a liberation, provides the framework for this interpretation. Theology seems to have avoided for a long time reflecting on the conflictual character of human history, the confrontations among men, social classes, and countries. St. Paul continuously reminds us, however, of the paschal core of Christian existence and of all of human life: the passage from the old man to the new, from sin to grace, from slavery to freedom.

"For freedom Christ has set us free" (Gal. 5:1), St. Paul tells us. He refers here to liberation from sin insofar as it represents a selfish turning in upon oneself. To sin is to refuse to love one's neighbors and, therefore, the Lord himself. Sin—a breach of friendship with God and others—is according to the Bible the ultimate cause of poverty, injustice, and the oppression in which men live. In describing sin as the ultimate cause we do not in any way negate the structural reasons and the objective determinants leading to these situations. It does, however, emphasize the fact that things do not happen by chance and that behind an unjust structure there is a personal or collective will responsible—a willingness to reject God and neighbor. It suggests, likewise, that a social transformation, no matter how radical it may be, does not automatically achieve the suppression of all evils.

But St. Paul asserts not only that Christ liberated us; he also tells us that he did it in order that we might be free. Free for what? Free to love. "In the language of the Bible," writes Bonhoeffer, "freedom is not something man has for himself but something he has for others . . . It is not a possession, a presence, an object, . . . but a relationship and nothing else. In truth, freedom is a relationship between two persons. Being free means 'being free for the other,' because the other has bond me to him. Only in relationship with the other am I free." The freedom to which we are called presupposes the going out of oneself, the breaking down of our selfishness and of all the structures that support our selfishness; the foundation of this freedom is openness to others. The fullness of liberation—a free gift from Christ—is communion with God and with other men.

CONCLUSION

Summarizing what has been said above, we can distinguish three reciprocally interpenetrating levels of meaning of the term *liberation,* or in other words, three approaches to the process of liberation.

In the first place, *liberation* expresses the aspirations of oppressed peoples and social classes, emphasizing the conflictual aspect of the economic, social, and political process which puts them at odds with wealthy nations and oppressive classes. In contrast, the word *development,* and above all the policies characterized as developmentalist [*desarrollista*], appear somewhat aseptic, giving a false picture of a tragic and conflictual reality. The issue of development does in fact find its true place in the more universal, profound, and radical perspective of liberation. It is only within this framework that *development* finds its true meaning and possibilities of accomplishing something worthwhile.

At a deeper level, *liberation* can be applied to an understanding of history. Man is seen as assuming conscious responsibility for his own destiny. This understanding provides a dynamic context and broadens the horizons of the desired social changes. In this perspective the unfolding of all of man's dimensions is demanded—a man who makes himself throughout his life and throughout history. The gradual conquest of true freedom leads to the creation of a new man and a qualitatively different society. This vision provides, therefore, a better understanding of what in fact is at stake in our times.

Finally, the world *development* to a certain extent limits and obscures the theological problems implied in the process designated by this term. On the contrary the word *liberation* allows for another approach leading to the Biblical sources which inspire the presence and action of man in history. In the Bible, Christ is presented as the one who brings us liberations. Christ the Savior liberates man from sin, which is the ultimate root of all disruption of friendship and of all injustice and oppression. Christ makes man truly free, that is to say, he enables man to live in communion with him; and this is the basis for all human brotherhood.

This is not a matter of three parallel or chronologically successive processes, however. There are three levels of meaning of a single, complex process, which finds its deepest sense and its full realization in the saving work of Christ. These levels of meaning, therefore, are interdependent. A comprehensive view of the matter presupposes that all three aspects can be considered together. In this way two pitfalls will be avoided: first, *idealist* or *spiritualist* approaches, which are nothing but ways of evading a harsh and demanding reality, and second, shallow analyses and programs of short-term effect initiated under the pretext of meeting immediate needs.

CHAPTER THIRTEEN

POVERTY: SOLIDARITY AND PROTEST

For some years now we have seen in the Church a recovery of a more authentic and radical witness of poverty. At first this occurred within various recently founded religious communities. It quickly went beyond the narrow limits of "religious poverty," however, raising challenges and questions in other sectors of the Church. Poverty has become one of the central themes of contemporary Christian spirituality and indeed has become a controversial question. From the concern to imitate more faithfully the poor Christ, there has spontaneously emerged a critical and militant attitude regarding the counter-sign that the Church as a whole presents in the matter of poverty.

Those who showed this concern—with John XXIII at the head—knocked insistently at the doors of Vatican II. In an important message in preparation for the opening of the Council, John opened up a fertile perspective saying, "In dealing with the underdeveloped countries, the Church presents herself as she is and as she wants to be—as the Church of all men and especially the Church of the poor." Indeed, from the first session of the Council the theme of poverty was very much in the air. Later there was even a "Schema 14," which on the issue of poverty went beyond "Schema 13" (the draft for *Gaudium et spes*). The final results of the Council, however, did not correspond to the expectations. The documents allude several times to poverty, but it is not one of the major thrusts. Later, *Populorum progressio* is somewhat more concrete and clear with regard to various questions related to poverty. But it will remain for the Church on a continent of misery and injustice to give the theme of poverty its proper importance: *the authenticity of the preaching of the Gospel message depends on this witness.*

Gustavo Gutiérrez

The theme of poverty has been dealt with in recent years, especially in the field of spirituality. In the contemporary world, fascinated by a wealth and power established upon the plunder and exploitation of the great majorities, poverty appeared as an inescapable precondition to sanctity. Therefore the greatest efforts were to meditate on the Biblical texts which recall the poverty of Christ and thus to identify with Christ in this witness.

More recently a properly theological reflection on poverty has been undertaken, based on ever richer and more precise exegetical studies. From these first attempts there stands out clearly one rather surprising result: poverty is a notion which has received very little theological treatment and in spite of everything is still quite unclear. Lines of interpretation overlap; various exegeses still carry weight today, even though they were developed in very different contexts which no longer exist; certain aspects of the theme function as static compartments which prevent a grasp of its overall meaning. All this has led us onto slippery terrain on which we have tried to maneuver more by intuition than by clear and well-formulated ideas.

AMBIGUITIES IN THE TERM "POVERTY"

Poverty is an equivocal term. But the ambiguity of the term does nothing more than express the ambiguity of the notions themselves which are involved. To try to clarify what we understand by *poverty,* we must clear the part and examine some of the sources of the ambiguity. This will also permit us to indicate the meaning we will give to various expressions which we will use later.

The term *poverty* designates in the first place *material poverty,* that is, the lack of economic goods necessary for a human life worthy of the name. In this sense poverty is considered degrading and is rejected by the conscience of contemporary man. Even those who are not—or do not wish to be—aware of the root causes of this poverty believe that it should be struggled against. Christians, however, often have a tendency to give material poverty a positive value, considering it almost a human and religious ideal. It is seen as austerity and indifference to the things of this world and a precondition for a life in conformity with the Gospel. This interpretation would mean that the demands of Christianity are at cross purposes to the great aspirations of people today, who want to free themselves from subjection to nature, to eliminate the exploitation of some people by others, and to create prosperity for everyone. The double and contradictory meaning of *poverty* implied here gives rise to the imposition of one language on another and is a frequent source of ambiguities. The matter becomes even more complex if we take into consideration that the concept of material poverty is in constant evolution. Not having access to certain cultural, social, and political values, for example, is today part of the poverty that people hope to abolish. Would material poverty as an "ideal" of Christian life also include lacking these things?

On the other hand, poverty has often been thought of and experienced by Christians as part of the condition—seen with a certain fatalism—of marginated peoples, "the poor," who are an object of our mercy. But things are no longer like this. Social classes, nations, and entire continents are becoming aware of their poverty, and when they see its root causes, they rebel against it. The contemporary phenomenon is a collective poverty that leads those who suffer from it to forge bonds of solidarity among themselves and to organize in the struggle against the conditions they are in and against those who benefit from these conditions.

What we mean by material poverty is a subhuman situation. As we shall see later, the Bible also considers it this way. Concretely, to be poor means to die of hunger, to be illiterate, to be exploited by others, not to know that you are being exploited, not to know that you are a person. It is in relation to this poverty—material and cultural, collective and militant—that evangelical poverty will have to define itself.

The notion of *spiritual poverty* is even less clear. Often it is seen simply as an interior attitude of unattachment to the goods of this world. The poor person, therefore, is not so much the one who has no material goods; rather it is he who is not attached to them—even if he does possess them. This point of view allows for the case of the rich man who is spiritually poor as well as for the poor man who is rich at heart. These are extreme cases that distract attention toward the exceptional and the accessory. Claiming to be based on the Beatitude of Matthew concerning "the poor in spirit," this approach in the long run leads to comforting and tranquilizing conclusions.

This spiritualistic perspective rapidly leads to dead ends and to affirmations that the interior attitude must necessarily be incarnated in a testimony of material poverty. But if this is so, questions arise: What poverty is being spoken of? The poverty that the contemporary conscience considers subhuman? Is it in this way that spiritual poverty should be incarnated? Some answer that it is not necessary to go to such extremes, and they attempt to distinguish between destitution and poverty. The witness involves living poverty, not destitution. But then, as we have said, we are not referring to poverty as it is lived and perceived by people today, but rather to a different kind of poverty, abstract and made according to the specifications of our spiritual poverty. This is to play with words—and with people.

The distinction between evangelical counsels and precepts creates other ambiguities. According to it, evangelical poverty would be a counsel appropriate to a particular vocation and not a precept obligatory for all Christians. This distinction kept evangelical poverty confined incommunicado for a long time within the narrow limits of religious life, which focuses on "the evangelical counsels." Today the distinction is only another source of misunderstandings.

Because of all these ambiguities and uncertainties we have been unable to proceed on solid ground; we have wandered along an unsure path where it is difficult to advance and easy to wander. We have also fallen into very vague terminology and a kind of sentimentalism which in the last analysis justifies the status quo. In situations like the present one in Latin America this is especially serious. We see the danger, for example, in various commentaries on the writings of Bossuet regarding "the eminent dignity of the poor in the Church"; or in symbolism like that which considers the hunger of the poor as "the image of the human soul hungering for God"; or even in the expression "the Church of the poor," which—in spite of the indisputable purity of intention of John XXIII—is susceptible to an interpretation smacking of paternalism.

Clarification is needed. In the following pages we will attempt to sketch at least the broad outlines. We will try to keep in mind that—as one spiritual writer has said—the first form of poverty is to renounce the idea we have of poverty.

BIBLICAL MEANING OF POVERTY

Poverty is a central theme both in the Old and the New Testaments. It is treated both briefly and profoundly; it describes social situations and expresses spiritual experiences communicated only with difficulty; it defines personal attitudes, a whole people's attitude before God, and the relationships of people with each other. It is possible, nevertheless, to try to unravel the knots and to clear the horizon by following the two major lines of thought which seem to stand out: poverty as a scandalous condition and poverty as spiritual childhood. The notion of evangelical poverty will be illuminated by a comparison of these two perspectives.

Poverty: A Scandalous Condition

In the Bible poverty is a scandalous condition inimical to human dignity and therefore contrary to the will of God.

This rejection of poverty is seen very clearly in the vocabulary used. In the Old Testament the term which is used least to speak of the poor is *rash,* which has a rather neutral meaning. As Gelin says, the prophets preferred terms which are "photographic" of real, living people. The poor person is, therefore, *ébyôn,* the one who desires, the beggar, the one who is lacking something and who awaits it from another. He is also *dal,* the weak one, the frail one; the expression *the poor of the land* (the rural proletariat) is found very frequently. The poor person is also *ani,* the bent over one, the one laboring under a weight, the one not in possession of his whole strength and vigor, the humiliated one. And finally he is *anaw,* from the same root as the previous term but having a more religious connotation— "humble before God." In the New Testament the Greek term *ptokós* is used to speak of the poor person. *Ptokós* means one who does not have what is necessary to subsist, the wretched one driven into begging.

Indigent, weak, bent over, wretched are terms which well express a degrading human situation. These terms already insinuate a protest. They are not limited to description; they take a stand. This stand is made explicit in the vigorous rejection of poverty. The climate in which poverty is described is one of indignation. And it is with the same indignation that the cause of the poverty is indicated: the injustice of the oppressors. The cause is well expressed in a text from Job:

> Wicked men move boundary-stones
> and carry away flocks and their shepherds.
> In the field they reap what is not theirs,
> and filch the late grapes from the rich man's vineyard.
> They drive off the orphan's ass
> and lead away the widow's ox with a rope.
> They snatch the fatherless infant from the breast
> and take the poor man's child in pledge.
> They jostle the poor out of the way;
> the destitute huddle together, hiding from them.
> The poor rise early like the wild ass,
> when it scours the wilderness for food;
> but though they work till nightfall,
> their children go hungry.
> Naked and bare they pass the night;
> in the cold they have nothing to cover them.
> They are drenched by rain-storms from the hills
> and hug the rock, their only shelter.
> Naked and bare they go about their work,
> and hungry they carry the sheaves;
> they press the oil in the shade where two walls meet,
> they tread the winepress but themselves go thirsty.
> Far from the city, they groan like dying men,
> and like wounded men they cry out; . . .
> The murderer rises before daylight
> to kill some miserable wretch (Job 24:2-12, 14).

Poverty is not caused by fate; it is caused by the actions of those whom the prophet condemns:

These are the words of the Lord:
    For crime after crime of Israel
    I will grant them no reprieve
because they sell the innocent for silver
    and the destitute for a pair of shoes.
They grind the heads of the poor into the earth
    and thrust the humble out of their way . . .
    (Amos 2:6-7).

There are poor because some people are victims of others. "Shame on you," it says in Isaiah,

you who make unjust laws
and publish burdensome decrees,
depriving the poor of justice,
robbing the weakest of my people of their rights,
despoiling the widow and plundering the orphan (10:1-2).

The prophets condemn every kind of abuse, every form of keeping the poor in poverty or of creating new poor people. They are not merely allusions to situations; the finger is pointed at those who are to blame. Fraudulent commerce and exploitation are condemned (Hos. 12:8; Amos 8:5; Mic. 6:10-11; Isa. 3:14; Jer. 5:27; 6:12), as well as the hoarding of lands (Mic. 2:1-3; Ezek. 22:29; Hab. 2:5-6), dishonest courts (Amos 5:7; Jer. 22:13-17; Mic. 3:9-11; Isa. 5:23, 10:1-2), the violence of the ruling classes (2 Kings 23:30, 35; Amos 4:1; Mic. 3:1-2; 6:12; Jer. 22:13-17), slavery (Neh. 5:1-5; Amos 2:6; 8:6), unjust taxes (Amos 4:1; 5:11-12), and unjust functionaries (Amos 5:7; Jer. 5:28). In the New Testament oppression by the rich is also condemned, especially in Luke (6:24-25; 12:13-21; 16:19-31; 18:18-26) and in the Letter of James (2:5-9; 4:13-17; 5:16).

But it is not simply a matter of denouncing poverty. The Bible speaks of positive and concrete measures to prevent poverty from becoming established among the People of God. In Leviticus and Deuteronomy there is very detailed legislation designed to prevent the accumulation of wealth and the consequent exploitation. It is said, for example, that what remains in the fields after the harvest and the gathering of olives and grapes should not be collected; it is for the alien, the orphan, and the widow (Deut. 24:19-21; Lev. 19:9-10). Even more, the fields should not be harvested to the very edge so that something remains for the poor and the aliens (Lev. 23:22). The Sabbath, the day of the Lord, has a social significance; it is a day of rest for the slave and the alien (Exod. 23:12; Deut. 5:14). The triennial tithe is not to be carried to the temple; rather it is for the alien, the orphan, and the widow (Deut. 14:28-29; 26:12). Interest on loans is forbidden (Exod. 22:25; Lev. 25:35-37; Deut. 23:20). Other important measures include the Sabbath year and the jubilee year. Every seven years the fields will be left to lie fallow "to provide food for the poor of your people" (Exod. 23:11; Lev. 25:2-7), although it is recognized that this duty is not always fulfilled (Lev. 26:34-35). After seven years the slaves were to regain their freedom (Exod. 21:2-6) and debts were to be pardoned (Deut. 15:1-18). This is also the meaning of the jubilee year of Lev. 25:10ff. "It was," writes de Vaux, "a general emancipation . . . of all the inhabitants of the land. The fields lay fallow: every man re-entered his ancestral property, *i.e.* the fields and houses which had been alienated returned to their original owners."

Behind these texts we can see three principal reasons for this vigorous repudiation of poverty. In the first place, poverty contradicts the very meaning of *the Mosaic religion*. Moses led his people out of the slavery, exploitation, and alienation of Egypt so that they might inhabit a land where they could live with human dignity. In Moses' mission of liberation there was a close relationship between the religion of Yahweh and the elimination of servitude:

> Moses and Aaron then said to all the Israelites, "In the evening you will know that it was the Lord who brought you out of Egypt, and in the morning you will see the glory of the Lord, because he has heeded your complaints against him; it is not against us that you bring your complaints; we are nothing." "You shall know this," Moses said, "when the Lord, in answer to your complaints, gives you flesh to eat in the evening, and in the morning bread in plenty. What are we? It is against the Lord that you bring your complaints, and not against us" (Exod. 16:6-8).

The worship of Yahweh and the possession of the land are both included in the same promise. The rejection of the exploitation of some people by others is found in the very roots of the people of Israel. God is the only owner of the land given to his people (Lev. 25:23, 38); he is the one Lord who saves his people from servitude and will not allow them to be subjected to it again (Deut. 5:15; 16:22; Lev. 25:42; 26:13). And thus Deuteronomy speaks of "the ideal of a brotherhood where there was no poverty." In their rejection of poverty, the prophets, who were heirs to the Mosaic ideal, referred to the past, to the origins of the people; there they sought the inspiration for the construction of a just society. To accept poverty and injustice is to fall back into the conditions of servitude which existed before the liberation from Egypt. It is to retrogress.

The second reason for the repudiation of the state of slavery and exploitation of the Jewish people in Egypt is that it goes against *the mandate of Genesis* (1:26; 2:15). Man is created in the image and likeness of God and is destined to dominate the earth. Man fulfills himself only by transforming nature and thus entering into relationships with other men. Only in this way does he come to a full consciousness of himself as the subject of creative freedom which is realized through work. The exploitation and injustice implicit in poverty make work into something servile and dehumanizing. Alienated work, instead of liberating man, enslaves him even more. And so it is that when just treatment is asked for the poor, the slaves, and the aliens, it is recalled that Israel also was alien and enslaved in Egypt (Exod. 22:21-23; 23:9; Deut. 10:19; Lev. 19:34).

And finally, man not only has been made in the image and likeness of God. He is also *the sacrament of God.* We have already recalled this profound and challenging Biblical theme. The other reasons for the Biblical rejection of poverty have their roots here: to oppress the poor is to offend God himself; to know God is to work justice among men. We meet God in our encounter with men; what is done for others is done for the Lord.

In a word, the existence of poverty represents a sundering both of solidarity among men and also of communion with God. Poverty is an expression of a sin, that is, of a negation of love. It is therefore incompatible with the coming of the Kingdom of God, a Kingdom of love and justice.

Poverty is an evil, a scandalous condition, which in our times has taken on enormous proportions. To eliminate it is to bring closer the moment of seeing God face to face, in union with other men.

Poverty: Spiritual Childhood

There is a second line of thinking concerning poverty in the Bible. The poor person is the "client" of Yahweh; poverty is "the ability to welcome God, an openness to God, a willingness to be used by God, a humility before God."

The vocabulary which is used here is the same as that used to speak of poverty as an evil. But the terms used to designate the poor person receive an ever more demanding and precise religious meaning. This is the case especially with the term *anaw,* which in the plural (*anawim*) is the privileged designation of the spiritually poor.

The repeated infidelity to the Covenant of the people of Israel led the prophets to elaborate the theme for the "tiny remnant" (Isa. 4:3; 6:13). Made up of those who remained faithful to Yahweh, the remnant would be the Israel of the future. From its midst there would emerge the Messiah and consequently the first fruits of the New Covenant (Jer. 31:31-34; Ezek. 36:26-28). From the time of Zephaniah (seventh century B.C.), those who waited the liberating work of the Messiah were called "poor": "But I will leave in you a people afflicted and poor, the survivors in Israel shall find refuge in the name of the Lord" (Zeph. 3:12-13). In this way the term acquired a spiritual meaning. From then on poverty was presented as an ideal: "Seek the Lord, all in the land who live humbly by his laws, seek righteousness, seek a humble heart" (Zeph. 2:3). Understood in this way poverty is opposed to pride, to an attitude of self-sufficiency; on the other hand, it is synonymous with faith, with abandonment and trust in the Lord. This spiritual meaning will be accentuated during the historical experiences of Israel after the time of Zephaniah. Jeremiah calls himself poor (*ébyôn*) when he sings his thanksgiving to God (20:13). Spiritual poverty is a precondition for approaching God: "All these are of my own making and all these are mine. This is the very word of the Lord. The man I look to is a man downtrodden and distressed, one who reveres my words" (Isa. 66:2).

The Psalms can help us to understand more precisely this religious attitude. To know Yahweh is to seek him (9:11; 34:11), to abandon and entrust oneself to him (10:14; 34:9, 37:40), to hope in him (25:3-5, 21; 37:9), to fear the Lord (25:12, 14; 34:8, 10), to observe his commandments (25:10); the poor are the just ones, the whole ones (34:20, 22; 37:17-18), the faithful ones (37:28; 149:1). The opposite of the poor are the proud, who are the enemy of Yahweh and the helpless (10:2; 18:28; 37:10; 86:14).

Spiritual poverty finds its highest expression in the Beatitudes of the New Testament. The version in *Matthew*—thanks to solid exegetical studies—no longer seems to present any great difficulties in interpretation. The poverty which is called "blessed" in Matt. 5:1 ("Blessed are the poor in spirit") is spiritual poverty as understood since the time of Zephaniah: to be totally at the disposition of the Lord. This is the precondition for being able to receive the Word of God. It has, therefore, the same meaning as the Gospel theme of spiritual childhood. God's communication with us is a gift of love; to receive this gift it is necessary to be poor, a spiritual child. This poverty has no direct relationship to wealth; in the first instance it is not a question of indifference to the goods of this world. It goes deeper than that; it means to have no other sustenance than the will of God. This is the attitude of Christ. Indeed, it is to him that all the Beatitudes fundamentally refer.

In *Luke's* version ("Blessed are you poor" [6:20]) we are faced with greater problems of interpretation. Attempts to resolve these difficulties follow two different lines of thinking. Luke is the evangelist who is most sensitive to social realities. In his Gospel as well as in Acts the themes of material poverty, of goods held in common, and of the condemnation of the rich are frequently treated. This has naturally led to thinking that the poor whom he blesses are the opposite of the rich whom he condemns; the poor would be those who lack what they need. In this case the poverty that he speaks of in the first Beatitude would be *material poverty*.

But this interpretation presents a twofold difficulty. It would lead to the canonization of a social class. The poor would be the privilieged of the Kingdom, even to the point of having their access to it assured, not by any choice on their part but by a socio-economic situation which had been imposed on them. Some commentators insist that this would not be evangelical and would be contrary to the intentions of Luke. On the opposite extreme within this interpretation are those who claim to avoid this difficulty and yet preserve the concrete sociological meaning of poverty in Luke. Situating themselves in the perspective of wisdom literature, they say that the first Beatitude opposes the present world to the world beyond; the sufferings of today will be compensated for in the future life. Extraterrestrial salvation is the absolute value which makes the present life insignificant. But this point of view implies purely and simply that Luke is sacralizing misery and injustice and is therefore preaching resignation to it.

Because of these impasses, an explanation is sought from another perspective: Matthew's. Like him Luke would be referring to *spiritual poverty,* or to openness to God. As a concession to the social context of Luke there is in this interpretation an emphasis on real poverty insofar as it is "a privileged path towards poverty of soul."

This second line of interpretation seems to us to minimize the sense of Luke's text. Indeed, it is impossible to avoid the concrete and "material" meaning which the term *poor* has for this evangelist. It refers first of all to those who live in a social situation characterized by a lack of the goods of this world and even by misery and indigence. Even further, it refers to a marginated social group, with connotations of oppression and lack of liberty.

All this leads us to retrace our steps and to reconsider the difficulties—which we have recalled above—in explaining the text of Luke as referring to the materially poor.

"Blessed are you poor for yours is the Kingdom of God" does not mean, it seems to us: "Accept your poverty because later this injustice will be compensated for in the Kingdom of God." If we believe that the Kingdom of God is a gift which is received in history, and if we believe, as the eschatological promises—so charged with human and historical content—indicate to us, that the Kingdom of God necessarily implies the reestablishment of justice in this world, then we must believe that Christ says that the poor are blessed *because* the Kingdom of God has begun: "The time has come; the Kingdom of God is upon you" (Mark 1:15). In other words, the elimination of the exploitation and poverty that prevent the poor from being fully human has begun; a Kingdom of justice which goes even beyond what they could have hoped for has begun. They are blessed because the coming of the Kingdom will put an end to their poverty by creating a world of brotherhood. They are blessed because the Messiah will open the eyes of the blind and will give bread to the hungry. Situated in a prophetic perspective, the text in Luke uses the term *poor* in the tradition of the first major line of thought we have studied: poverty is an evil and therefore incompatible with the Kingdom of God, which has come in its fullness into history and embraces the totality of human existence.

AN ATTEMPT AT SYNTHESIS: SOLIDARITY AND PROTEST

Material poverty is a scandalous condition. Spiritual poverty is an attitude of openness to God and spiritual childhood. Having clarified these two meanings of the term *poverty* we have cleared the path and can now move forward towards a better understanding of the Christian witness of poverty. We turn now to a third meaning of the term: poverty as a commitment of solidarity and protest.

We have laid aside the first two meanings. The first is subtly deceptive; the second partial and insufficient. In the first place, if *material poverty* is something to be rejected, as the Bible vigorously insists, then a witness of poverty cannot make of it a Christian ideal. This would be to aspire to a condition which is recognized as degrading to man. It would be, moreover, to move against the current of history. It would be to oppose any idea of the domination of nature by man and the consequent and progressive creation of better conditions of life. And finally, but not least seriously, it would be to justify, even if involuntarily, the injustice and exploitation which is the cause of poverty.

On the other hand, our analysis of the Biblical texts concerning *spiritual poverty* has helped us to see that it is not directly or in the first instance an interior detachment from the goods of this world, a spiritual attitude which becomes authentic by incarnating itself in material poverty. Spiritual poverty is something more complete and profound. It is above all total availability to the Lord. Its relationship to the use or ownership of economic goods is inescapable, but secondary and partial. Spiritual childhood—an ability to receive, not a passive acceptance—defines the total posture of human existence before God, men, and things.

How are we therefore to understand the evangelical meaning of the witness of a real, material, concrete poverty? *Lumen gentium* invites us to look for the deepest meaning of Christian poverty *in Christ:* "Just as Christ carried out the work of redemption in poverty and under oppression, so the Church is called to follow the same path in communicating to men the fruits of salvation. Christ Jesus, though He was by nature God . . . emptied himself, taking the nature of a slave (Phil. 2:6), and being rich, he became poor (2 Cor. 8:9) for our sakes. Thus, although the Church needs human resources to carry out her mission, she is not set up to seek earthly glory, but to proclaim humility and self-sacrifice, even by her own example" (no. 8). The Incarnation is an act of love. Christ became man, died, and rose from the dead to set us free so that we might enjoy freedom (Gal. 5:1). To die and to rise again with Christ is to vanquish death and to enter into a new life (cf. Rom. 6:1-11). The cross and the resurrection are the seal of our liberty.

The taking on of the servile and sinful condition of man, as foretold in Second Isaiah, is presented by Paul as an act of voluntary impoverishment: "For you know how generous our Lord Jesus Christ has been: He was rich, yet for your sake he became poor, so that through his poverty you might become rich" (2 Cor. 8:9). This is the humiliation of Christ, his *kenosis* (Phil. 2:6-11). But he does not take on man's sinful condition and its consequences to idealize it. It is rather because of love for and solidarity with men who suffer in it. It is to redeem them from their sin and to enrich them with his poverty. It is to struggle against human selfishness and everything that divides

407

men and enables them to be rich and poor, possessors and dispossessed, oppressors and oppressed.

Poverty is an act of love and liberation. It has a redemptive value. If the ultimate cause of man's exploitation and alienation is selfishness, the deepest reason for voluntary poverty is love of neighbor. Christian poverty has meaning only as a commitment of solidarity with the poor, with those who suffer misery and injustice. The commitment is to witness to the evil which has resulted from sin and is a breach of communion. It is not a question of idealizing poverty, but rather of taking it on as it is—an evil—to protest against it and to struggle to abolish it. As Ricoeur says, you cannot really be with the poor unless you are struggling against poverty. Because of this solidarity—which must manifest itself in specific action, a style of life, a break with one's social class—one can also help the poor and exploitated to become aware of their exploitation and seek liberation from it. Christian poverty, an expression of love, is solidarity *with the poor* and is a protest *against poverty*. This is the concrete, contemporary meaning of the witness of poverty. It is a poverty lived not for its own sake, but rather as an authentic imitation of Christ; it is a poverty which means taking on the sinful condition of man to liberate him from sin and all its consequences.

Luke presents the community of goods in the early Church as an ideal. "All whose faith had drawn them together held everything in common" (Acts 2:44); "not a man of them claimed any of his possessions as his own, but everything was held in common" (Acts 4:33). They did this with a profound unity, one "in heart and soul" (*ibid.*). But as J. Dupont correctly points out, this was not a question of erecting poverty as an ideal, but rather of seeing to it that there were no poor: "They had never a needy person among them, because all who had property in land or houses sold it, brought the proceeds of the sale, and laid the money at the feet of the apostles; it was then distributed to any who stood in need" (Acts 4:34-35). The meaning of the community of goods is clear: to eliminate poverty because of love of the poor person. Dupont rightly concludes, "If goods are held in common, it is not therefore in order to become poor for love of an ideal of poverty; rather it is so that there will be no poor. The ideal pursued is, once again, charity, a true love for the poor."

We must pay special attention to the words we use. The term *poor* might seem not only vague and churchy, but also somewhat sentimental and aseptic. The "poor" person today is the oppressed one, the one marginated from society, the member of the proletariat struggling for his most basic rights; he is the exploited and plundered social class, the country struggling for its liberation. In today's world the solidarity and protest of which we are speaking have an evident and inevitable "political" character insofar as they imply liberation. To be with the oppressed is to be against the oppressor. In our times and on our continent to be in solidarity with the "poor," understood in this way, means to run personal risks—even to put one's life in danger. Many Christians—and non-Christians—who are committed to the Latin American revolutionary process are running these risks. And so there are emerging new ways of living poverty which are different from the classic "renunciation of the goods of this world."

Only by rejecting poverty and by making itself poor in order to protest against it can the Church preach something that is uniquely its own: "spiritual poverty," that is, the openness of man and history to the future promised by God. Only in this way will the Church be able to fulfill authentically—and with any possibility of being listened to—its prophetic function of denouncing every injustice to man. And only in this way will it be able to preach the word which liberates, the word of genuine brotherhood.

Only authentic solidarity with the poor and a real protest against the poverty of our time can provide the concrete, vital context necessary for a theological discussion of poverty. The absence of a sufficient commitment to the poor, the marginated, and the exploited is perhaps the fundamental reason why we have no solid contemporary reflection on the witness of poverty.

For the Latin American Church especially, this witness is an inescapable and much-needed sign of the authenticity of its mission.

CONCLUSION

The theology of liberation attempts to reflect on the experience and meaning of the faith based on the commitment to abolish injustice and to build a new society; this theology must be verified by the practice of that commitment, by active, effective participation in the struggle which the exploited social classes have undertaken against their oppressors. Liberation from every form of exploitation, the possibility of a more human and more dignified life, the creation of a new man—all pass through this struggle.

But in the last instance we will have an authentic theology of liberation only when the oppressed themselves can freely raise their voice and express themselves directly and creatively in society and in the heart of the People of God, when they themselves "account for the hope," which they bear, when they are the protagonists of their own liberation. For now we must limit ourselves to efforts which ought to deepen and support that process, which has barely begun. If theological reflection does not vitalize the action of the Christian community in the world by making its commitment to charity fuller and more radical, if—more concretely—in Latin America it does not lead the Church to be on the side of the oppressed classes and dominated peoples, clearly and without qualifications, then this theological reflection will have been of little value. Worse yet, it will have served only to justify half-measures and ineffective approaches and to rationalize a departure from the Gospel.

We must be careful not to fall into an intellectual self-satisfaction, into a kind of triumphalism of erudite and advanced "new" visions of Christianity. The only thing that is really new is to accept day by day the gift of the Spirit, who makes us love—in our concrete options to build a true human brotherhood, in our historical initiatives to subvert an order of injustice—with the fullness with which Christ loved us. To paraphrase a well-known text of Pascal, we can say that all the political theologies, the theologies of hope, of revolution, and of liberation, are not worth one act of genuine solidarity with exploited social classes. They are not worth one act of faith, love, and hope, committed—in one way or another—in active participation to liberate man from everything that dehumanizes him and prevents him from living according to the will of the Father.